1979

The Capitalist Revolution

JOHN TIPPLE

The Capitalist Revolution

A History of
American Social Thought
1890–1919

PEGASUS/NEW YORK

Foreword

Within the compass of four volumes, *The Pragmatic Nation: A History of American Social Thought Since 1865,* I have attempted to give an account of the important ideas which have influenced the political, economic, and social development of modern America. In choosing the readings in these volumes I have not been greatly concerned with literary values but have tried to treat of ideas in their meaningful social context, making my selections solely on the basis of their intrinsic worth as clear and valid expressions of the dominant ideas of the time. The main divisions of the study reflect major changes in the outlook and material framework of American society. Volume I, *The Great Money Machine,* begins after the Civil War and follows the evolution of the United States from a simple agricultural and commercial society to an industrial economy created by and ideologically dependent upon the findings of nineteenth-century science. The present volume, *The Capitalist Revolution,* second in historical sequence, is concerned with the overthrow of the established system and practices of individualistic capitalism by the organized power of corporate capitalism and with the pragmatic revolt against traditionalism that followed in its wake. Volume III, *Crisis of the American Dream,* carries the account through the boom days of the twenties and the depression-ridden thirties, marking the collapse of the business order and the faltering emergence of the welfare state. Volume IV, *The Paradox of Power,* considers the contemporary conflict between the individual and the organization and the search for assurance in a technological society.

The task of measuring the historical significance of ideas is an extremely difficult one. Perhaps the most vexing question the historian must answer is: What portion of the public was moved by and won for a particular idea? Yet ideas have consequences, and this pragmatic consideration has been my chief criterion. As Justice Holmes observed, "Every idea is an incitement. It offers itself for belief and if believed it is acted upon." Important ideas are consequential ideas, whether they come from politicians or professors, businessmen or philosophers. The active American mind has never been confined to the genteel tradition of academies but has taken ideas wherever it found them, from the market place as well as the lecture hall. The historian, being a product of his time, faces the additional danger of reading into history the ideas and opinions of a later day. In this sense, there is considerable truth in Voltaire's witticism: "History is only a pack of tricks we play on the dead." The best defense against playing such tricks on the dead is to let the living speak for themselves, as I have tried to do by introducing contemporary writing within the historical context of the time.

Essentially history is concerned with the dialectical struggle between persistence and change, between the old and the new. For every accepted idea there are always a host of challengers or rival "truths" competing for acceptance at any given time in history. Therefore, to bring into this study a genuine sense of historical dynamism, I have endeavored to follow the example of history itself by presenting with every dominant idea a counteridea which, if not its direct antithesis, offers another point of view. To capture the authentic flavor of the times, the major issues are documented by excerpts from contemporary writings which follow each section and which are indicated by an asterisk at the appropriate point in the text. By giving the losing as well as the winning side and by allowing the proponents to speak for themselves, I have sought to avoid the dishonest practice of presenting the regnant American ideology as a homogeneous body of unchallengeable "truths" resting upon the nearly unanimous consent of history.

I am, of course, heavily indebted to the critical historians and the many students of American society who have enabled me to build upon their careful research. Especially am I indebted to my wife, Edith, for practical and spiritual aid.

J.T.

Santa Barbara, May, 1969

Contents

Chapter V: The New Radicalism, 236

The Revolt of Youth, 236. The Experimental Ideal, 239. The Sexual Revolution, 243. The New Morality, 248. Progressive Education, 256. The New Social Issue, 269. The New Politics, 277. The Present Belongs to the Living, 283.

READINGS

Epilogue: The Limits of Technique, 330. The Sorcerer's Apprentices, 330. Business and Civilization, 333. A More Efficient America, 338. Pragmatic Nationalism, 342. Force and Ideas, 351.

Notes, 355

Introduction

Coming up the bay in 1904, after forty years, Henry Adams found the spectacle of New York City beyond belief. Not only was it unlike anything he had ever seen, but to one brought up on eighteenth-century values, "like nothing he had ever much cared to see." In the eyes of the returning traveler, the city had become frantic in its effort to explain something that defied meaning: "Power seemed to have outgrown its servitude and to have asserted its freedom. The cylinder had exploded, and thrown great masses of stone and steam against the sky. The city had the air and movement of hysteria, and the citizens were crying, in every accent of anger and alarm, that the new forces must at any cost be brought under control." Merely to exist under such frighteningly novel circumstances seemed to Adams to suggest that the new American, "the child of incalculable coal-power, chemical power, electric power, and radiating energy, as well as of new forces yet undetermined," [1] must be a sort of God compared with his innocent ancestors.

These immense new forces, condensed into corporations and used by leaders of industry with vigorous and unscrupulous energy, seemed to have literally torn society to pieces, rending old conventions and values, "as ocean steamers must trouble a school of herring." The task of building a continental railway system, for instance, had proved "so big as to need the energies of a generation, for it required all the new machinery to be created—capital, banks, mines, furnaces, shops, power-houses, technical knowledge, mechanical population, together with a steady remodelling of social and political habits, ideas, and institutions to fit the new scale and suit the new conditions." And then, said Adams, with his generation already mortgaged to the railways, society "hurried on to its telephones, bicycles, and electric trams."[2]

Too busy to stop the activity of their twenty-million-horsepower society, the new Americans had no time for thought: "They saw, and could see, nothing beyond their day's work; their attitude to the universe outside them was that of the deep-sea fish. Above all, they naturally and intensely disliked to be told what to do, and how to do it, by men who took their ideas and their methods from the abstract theories of history, philosophy, or theology. They knew enough to know that their world was one of energies quite new."[3]

By 1890, the technical innovations of business and industry had assumed such a dominant place in American society that they had become an influential force in shaping not only men's daily lives but their habits of thought as well. The extraordinary triumphs of technology seemed to inspire a feeling of admiration for modern and a disrespect for other times, even among the educated. From the viewpoint of the new American, merely to see the visible fruits of technical prowess—the mechanical improvements, the railroads and steel mills—or to behold the thrilling sight of a machine performing nearly all the functions of a rational being was to *know* the superiority of the present over the past. Yet, more important were the invisible effects. For, as Thorstein Veblen observed, when men came more and more under the regimen of the machine, they learned to think in the terms in which the industrial processes act—in mechanical terms of standardized means and of impersonal sequence, not in human terms of personality and of preternatural agency.[4]

To minds thus predisposed, the religious beliefs and metaphysical preconceptions of the past were no longer understandable. Instead of regarding human will as subordinate to cosmic aim, the modern outlook equated human intent with cosmic purpose. Rather than depend upon the grand but often vague intentions of the Deity, busy Americans proposed to construct a world of their own along lines of proven experience, substituting for heavenly hopes workable ideas. Under the new dispensation the business of man was no longer to pursue the good, the true, the beautiful, but to solve the practical problems of existence by using to greatest advantage the opportunities which life on earth afforded.

Prologue: The Pragmatist and the Progressive

High Ideals and Catchpenny Realities

America at the beginning of the twentieth century was, as philosopher George Santayana said, a country with two mentalities: one a survival of the beliefs and ideals of the past, the other an expression of the practices and discoveries of a newer age. That half of the American mind not intensely engaged in practical affairs remained slightly becalmed, floating gently in a backwater, "while, alongside, in invention and industry and social organization, the other half of the mind was leaping down a sort of Niagara Rapids." This division Santayana found symbolized in American architecture: a neat reproduction of a colonial mansion, "with some modern comforts introduced surreptitiously," stood beside the skyscraper. The American Will inhabited the skyscraper and was all aggressive enterprise; the American Intellect inhabited the colonial mansion and was all genteel tradition. The American Will pushed energetically forward; the American Intellect fought a slow retreat before the imperious drive of industrial expansion.[1]

These two attitudes of mind divided contemporary American thought between them, running side by side but rarely mingling. In everything from politics to philosophy, this disturbing rift in values aroused antagonism and gave rise to acrid dispute. Between what he called the unhypocritical assumptions of "high ideals" on the one hand, and on the other, the simultaneous acceptance of "catchpenny realities," the young critic, Van Wyck Brooks, saw no real choice. They were incompatible and, to him, equally undesirable; but they split American life into two irreconcilable planes, "the plane of stark intellectuality and the plane of stark business." This frank acceptance of twin values which were not expected to have anything in common seemed to Brooks to explain the dilemma of modern America: "Between university ethics and business ethics, between American culture and American humour, between Good Government and Tammany, between academic pedantry and pavement slang," there was no discernible community, no genial middle ground of understanding. Between them, these two hostile attitudes of mind threatened to tear America apart.[2]

So, without undue exaggeration, the trials and triumphs of American society from 1890 to 1919 may be examined in light of the conflict between two major points of view: Pragmatism and Progressivism. Taken in the original Greek sense of "active or businesslike," Pragmatism stood for the matter-of-fact treatment of the affairs and problems of everyday life; Progressivism, its opposite, embodied the effort to solve the new and unfamiliar problems of a technological society in terms of old and familiar ideals. The Pragmatist, to whom the world was plastic and still in the making, was chiefly occupied with "know-how," the "one best way" to advance his interests. The Progressive, to whom reality was ready-made and complete from all eternity, was therefore primarily concerned with "know-why," finding the "true" path to progress. Truth to the Progressive was the authentic reality upon which the world rested; for the Pragmatist it was merely a human construction, one of many useful hypotheses which it paid to pursue. According to William James, the leading exponent of Pragmatism, truth was made, just as health, wealth and strength were made, in the course of experience.[3]

In short, power made truth; and since power came wholly from technique, control of which was in human hands, modern man put himself in the godlike position of making truth. The end result, from the traditional point of view, was an earth-bound creed of economic success and material progress in which religion and higher ideals, if allowed at all, were valued like plumbing and central heating—merely as aid and comfort in the more urgent business of this world. Such a mundane view with its perverse, heretical attempt to explain what was higher by what was lower was, of course, anathema to the Progressive. Truth, by his standards, was not made; it was timeless, unchanging, and it prevailed absolutely. Thus, while for the flexible-minded Pragmatist, the true was the expedient way of thinking, and the right was the expedient way of behaving the Progressive held inflexibly that the true was the only acceptable way of thinking, and the right, the only acceptable way of behaving.

With such divergent definitions of reality, it was inevitable that the Pragmatist and the Progressive should find themselves at odds on most important issues. Their antagonism was described by James as a philosophic combat between the "tender-minded" and the "tough-minded," and for convenience of recognition he cataloged the two types, listing their general traits:

THE TENDER-MINDED	THE TOUGH-MINDED
Rationalistic (going by 'principles'),	Empiricist (going by 'facts'),
Intellectualistic,	Sensationalistic,
Idealistic,	Materialistic,
Optimistic,	Pessimistic,
Religious,	Irreligious,
Free-willist,	Fatalistic,
Monistic,	Pluralistic,
Dogmatical,	Sceptical.[4]

Each naturally believed the other to be inferior. The tough-minded Pragmatist thought of the Progressives as "sentimentalists and softheads"; the tender-minded Progressive considered the Pragmatists to be "unrefined, callous, or brutal." Though their enmity was largely a matter of temperament, it also reflected a change in the ideals and practices of capitalism as America moved from the nineteenth into the twentieth century.

The Pragmatist

A tough-minded confident innovator, the Pragmatist was symbolized in action by the American businessman, especially the corporate leader or the great industrialist. He was, above all, the kind of man who exercised wide and authoritative control over industry and finance and ultimately, therefore, over the economic and social development of the country as a whole. His situation at the commanding heights of American economic life enabled him to view society empirically, though with a materialistic bias, and to act expediently without hindrance from dogma.

Although he was by definition a capitalist, he was not the simon-pure ideologue of Adam Smith. While accepting the capitalist rhetoric of private property and freedom of contract, his was a much more sophisticated philosophy of profit than the dog-eat-dog variety of the Gilded Age. Because the nature and the needs of the two periods were different, the principles of free competition and individual liberty were of less importance to him than cooperation and corporate restraint. Where the rising entrepreneur of the 1870's had, in the name of individual liberty, fought to free private enterprise from state control, the new capitalist, seeking to stabilize his economic position through industrial and financial consolidation, had more to lose than gain from unrestricted cutthroat competition. Hence he not only disparaged "rugged" individualism as a menace to business stability but, in the guise of reform, actively sponsored government intervention in the economy. Though seemingly liberal, his actions were dictated less by a developing social conscience than by pragmatic considerations of self-interest.

Doubtless a few business leaders at the beginning of the century had a genuine awareness of the public nature and responsibilities of the large corporation, but most seem to have been moved more by threats from what one called "radical and unthinking parts of the public" aimed at the "possible overthrow of the system of private ownership."[5] In any case, whatever his motivation, after 1890 no big businessman could afford to ignore the challenge to the emerging corporate system from insurgent reformers. More than one million Americans in 1892 had supported the Populist demand for overthrow of the "vast conspiracy" by which "the fruits of the toil of millions are boldly stolen to build up colossal fortunes for a few." Again, in 1896, Populists teamed with Democrats nearly gained the Presidency on a platform promising to protect the people from capitalist "robbery and oppression."[6] Similarly the spectre of revolution was raised by socialist agitation and the rapid spread of Marxian doctrine among all classes. By 1911, the Socialists threatened to become a political force as well, electing a Congressman, 73 mayors, and some 1,200 public officials throughout the United States.[7] A less dreaded but more substantial threat to the existing order came from the growing Progressive movement, the bulk of whose membership consisted of middle-class Americans rebelling against the domination of powerful "interests." Along with impressive victories on state and local fronts, the Progressives came very close to capturing both major parties in 1912, splitting the Republicans and electing a Democratic President pledged to far-reaching reforms.

With the various reform groups successfully contending for the loyalty of the farmer, the worker, the small businessman, and the consumer, it became necessary, as James Weinstein has shown, for big business to adopt a program of reform designed to serve as a counterpoise to the threat of social revolution.[8] George W. Perkins, former partner of J. P. Morgan and Company and a director of both United States Steel and the International Harvester Company, acknowledged in 1911 that much of "the agitation of recent years has been unfair and harmful in many instances, [but] it has set business men to thinking." Officers of great corporations, said Perkins, "should realize that such concerns are more nearly public institutions than private property." To his mind, federal regulation was not only inevitable but feasible. He told businessmen, "if we unite and work for it now we may be able to secure it; whereas if we continue to fight against it much longer, the incoming tide may sweep the question along either to Government ownership or socialism." Agreeing with Perkins that the time had come "when we need statesmanship in business and more business-like statesmanship," the more sophisticated leaders of America's largest industrial and financial institutions set out deliberately to guide and control the reform movement in their own behalf.[9]

Increasingly aware that the days of the Robber Baron were over and that the "economic man" of classical theory was in disrepute, many big businessmen adopted after 1907 a conscious policy of supporting greater federal regulation. As utilities magnate Samuel Insull said, he preferred to "help shape the right kind of regulation" before "the wrong kind [was] forced upon him."[10] Rather than fight reform blindly, they chose to meet it intelligently by underwriting such reforms as would seem, at least from the popular point

of view, to correct the abuses and conditions on which dissatisfaction fed. In general their thinking on "social justice" closely par-
alleled that of Judge Elbert H. Gary of the Steel Trust who explained that among big businessmen there was developing a new
"determination to conduct affairs in such a way that we will not
cause injury to anybody, and, on the contrary, that we will benefit
everybody affected by us; and that includes fair and decent and
honest treatment of our employees, our stockholders, our competitors in business, our customers, and the general public, because
we believe it is not only good policy from the standpoint of
pecuniary success, but better because we believe it is right." [11] As
a result of this new spirit of tactical accommodation in business, startled Americans witnessed the unlikely spectacle of Wall
Street campaigning for financial reform and of major Eastern business interests advancing new ideas for the control of corporations.

By means of associations such as the National Civic Federation
and by working with reform factions instead of against them,
business leaders were able to shape much progressive legislation.
Though primarily an organization of big businessmen, the Federation ostensibly represented business, labor, and the public, purpos-
ing to serve as a nonpartisan forum for the discussion and imple-
mentation of constructive political reforms. By taking the initiative
in sponsoring public debate over solutions to the trust problem
at Chicago in 1907, for instance, the Federation succeeded not
only in diverting political agitation against the corporations but
in winning the backing of many well-intentioned reformers for
their program. Such tactics coupled with opportunistic politics of
the kind described by Perkins as the "proper sort of cooperation
between our statesmen and our businessmen" [12] made it possible,
as Robert Wiebe has observed, for them to delay and modify reform
measures almost at will. "As the men who filled the party purses,
they set boundaries even when they could not dictate legislation.
As a result Congress did not attempt to control the insurance
companies, pulled teeth from the measures regulating food and
drugs, delayed railroad and tariff laws despite a rising public
clamor, and modified both the Clayton and Trade Commission bills
toward the wishes of the magnates." [13] Moreover, although virtually all business proposals for reform were intended as holding

operations to institutionalize the power of big business, they were almost invariably hailed by an unsuspecting public, as well as many earnest Progressives, as signal victories for liberal reform.

Although the big businessman's conduct was unmistakably Machiavellian, he did not view it that way. In seeking to keep reform on a business basis, he was merely following the common-sense assumption that in a society dedicated to material progress businessmen should lead. To him, as to railway magnate James J. Hill, the President and the governors of the states merely served as a board of directors for that "great economic corporation known as the United States of America." [14] It was expected, therefore, that any law to regulate corporations should come from business-men who were "best able to judge of its effect upon the country." [15] This egocentric outlook combined with the all-embracing absolution of "It's business" enabled the big businessman to handle his affairs with dispatch and without the troublesome indecision that afflicted less efficient Americans.

Completely absorbed in his own advancement, the big business-man had little use for abstract principles except where, as with rights of property and liberty, they worked to his advantage. As an inadvertent iconoclast occupying a position of power, he instinctively followed an activist philosophy aimed not at under-standing the world but changing it to his own advantage. So-called "higher ideals" were not only generally useless but at times actually worked to his detriment. His working ideals were developed as practical byproducts of business activity and were prized according to their cash value. Having thus stripped down his thinking proc-esses, the businessman may have increased his practical efficiency, but he also severely limited his vision. His simplistic and short-sighted approach conveniently blinded him to problems having no bearing upon his immediate economic advantage. Not that the big businessman was necessarily unscrupulous or devoid of principles. Like any other American, he had a fund of maxims about what American society was, or ought to be. But these maxims were more in the nature of what Wiebe calls "predispositions" rather than dogmatic principles. "Whenever businessmen could, in justice to more pressing interests, they applied these principles to particular situations. When their principles proved inconvenient, businessmen shelved them, and after the awkward moment had passed, brought the maxims out again." [16]

For a philosophic explanation of this useful antilogy, the *Commercial & Financial Chronicle* said American businessmen were indebted to Professor William James. "Pragmatism, his new term in philosophy, exalts the actual and effective value of forces or phenomena in the material world above all theory or matter of detail." Because the business world was "driving ahead at a tremendous pace, with perils on every side," the businessman could not stop to ponder every move. Here was where the businessman's version of Pragmatism came to his help. By offering the simple formula that *whatever works is right*, it cleared the decks for action by sweeping away "the cobwebs and windy sophistries of the politician and the doctrinaire." [17]

Except for his position near the top of the economic pyramid, it was this practical accommodation of the ideal to the real that, more than anything else, distinguished the Pragmatist from the Progressive. For not only did both share the standard views of comfortable Americans everywhere, but the business career was not in itself an absolute line of demarcation. In the business community there were moderately prosperous merchants and manufacturers who attacked large corporations in defense of nineteenth-century capitalism as well as smaller businessmen who loyally alligned themselves with big business. Many, perhaps the majority, of small businessmen were Progressives, at least in the limited sense that they sought to restore free competition through government dissolution of the trusts. The true Progressive, however, stood apart from his contemporaries by virtue of his hard and fast principles, his ethical and ideological inflexibility in face of rapid change. Lacking the easy logic of the Pragmatist, he could neither overlook nor accommodate the vexing contradictions of modern industrial society.

The Progressive

Tender-minded yet zealous, the Progressive was typically a young, middle-class reformer with a profoundly individualistic outlook. He was, as Kansas editor William Allen White remembered, one of "hundreds of thousands of young men in their twenties, thirties, and early forties" whose "quickening sense of the inequities, injustices, and fundamental wrongs" of American society led him to engage in political activity.[18] If he belonged to a party of protest, he was never militantly proletarian, being just as suspicious of Gompers and organized labor as of Rockefeller and organized capital. A man of strong conscience, he considered himself an amateur in politics who had embarked temporarily on a crusade to right a wrong, and who, after performing his duty at full tilt, expected to return to the unorganized ranks of little businessmen, professional men, well-to-do farmers and skilled laborers from which he had come. His appraisal of the existing situation was that the evils and abuses which plagued American society were due chiefly to the energy and lack of scruple with which businessmen and politicians had taken advantage of the "plain people" of the United States. The millionaire and the trust had appropriated too many of the economic opportunities formerly enjoyed by the people; the corrupt politician had usurped too much of the power that rightfully belonged to the people. Hence his aim was simply to restore to the people by political action the opportunities and power of which they had been deprived.

In looking backward rather than forward, the so-called Progressive seemed to belie his name. The explanation for this paradoxical point of view, David Noble has suggested, was his primitivistic idea of progress. Although accepting progress as an inexorable law of the universe, he believed man advanced by discarding the mistakes accumulated in the complexity and confusion of industrial evolution and by recasting his society in accordance with a few, time-tested rules.[19] To be "progressive," insisted Woodrow Wilson, the victorious leader of reform, was "to preserve the essentials of our institutions";[20] while his ostensible rival for Progressive leadership, Theodore Roosevelt, defined it as "getting back to the principles upon which this government was founded."[21] Reform might indeed bring with it the necessity of a certain amount of reorganization, but such reorganization aimed merely at improvement of the existing political and economic machinery which, in all essentials, was considered adequate to its purposes. A little tinkering here, a few revisions there, perhaps a slight reformulation

Progressivism was dealt a death blow in 1917 when President Wilson confidently, almost jauntily, led the legions of reform into a war to make the world safe for democracy.   Brown Bros.

of basic doctrine to meet modern needs, and American democracy would be restored to its pristine state. "No man that I know of and trust," avowed Wilson, "no man that I will consent to consort with, is trying to change anything fundamental in America." [22] With some minor legal changes, aided by ritual incantation of certain phrases such as "equal rights for all and special privileges for none," and by loyal conformity to the sacred principles of the founding fathers, he, like other Progressives, hoped to bring about the miraculous consummation of American democracy. Thus, it seemed, by the unquestioned following of what was aptly called "a species of higher conservatism," the Progressive proposed to back into reform.[23]

Yet, paradoxically, though the Progressive longed for and was loyal to the older world of his father and grandfathers, he knew his generation confronted a new world demanding new methods.

"Life means change," said Roosevelt, and "a period of change is upon us." [24] Wilson more reluctantly conceded that American Life had broken away from the past: "Nothing is done in this country as it was done twenty years ago. We are in the presence of a new organization of society. . . . We have changed our economic conditions, absolutely, from top to bottom; and, with our economic society, the organization of our life." [25] With the world altered radically, asserted Wilson, nothing less than a radical reconstruction would do. "We are in a temper to reconstruct economic society as we were once in a temper to reconstruct political society, and political society may itself undergo a radical modification in the process." [26] Roosevelt too acknowledged the need for radical change in economic and political practices. "We do not propose to do injustice to any man, but we do propose adequately to guarantee the people against injustice by the mighty corporations which make up the predominant and characteristic feature of modern industrial life." [27] In the interests of the general welfare, both Progressive leaders were ready to invoke the aid of government.

According to this "newer individualism," government was to take a positive, and not merely a negative role. Justice was to be achieved, said Roosevelt, "through the resolute and conscientious use of all the machinery, public and private, State and National, governmental and individual," which was at command of the people.[28] For, as Wilson apologetically explained, "I feel confident that if Jefferson were living in our day he would see what we see; that the individual is caught in a great confused nexus of all sorts of complicated circumstances, and that to let him alone is to leave him helpless . . . and that, therefore, law in our day must come to the assistance of the individual." [29] The prescription was valid but, as events were to prove, its application faulty.

Like militant crusaders of the Middle Ages, the Progressives set out with flying banners to drive the forces of Satan from the holy land of democracy. Truth was to be the reformers' weapon, and by its blazing light they hoped to educate public opinion, to stir the popular conscience, and thus to inspire the armies of democracy to political action and tangible reform. It was necessary, said Wilson, "to open the doors and let in the light on all affairs which the people have a right to know about." [30] Politics had been too secretive, too complicated; they had consisted too much of private plots and privy understandings. The operations of big business had been concealed, hidden in labyrinthine speculation and mysterious maneuverings. The secret processes of capital must be made as open as the processes of politics, so that society might again obtain command of its own economic life.

Launching a relentless campaign of exposure, the Progressives began to smoke out the devil's legions with thousands of inflammatory articles in newspapers, books, and especially in cheap popular magazines. Although denounced as "muckraking," these indignant, factual articles of exposure had a devastating effect on national attitudes, "melting down old heroes and recasting the mold in which heroes were made." [31] There was, White noted, a sudden new interest in the underdog throughout the land. "Universally the people began to understand what slums were, what sweatshops were, what exploited labor was, what absentee landlordism had become in our urban life, what railroad rates were doing to the farmer and the consumer. . . . Into the hearts of the dominant middle class of this country had come a sense that their civilization needed recasting, that their government had fallen into the hands of self-seekers, that a new relation should be established between the haves and the have-nots." [32]

Although the Progressive reformer never accomplished his dreamed-of restoration, he did provide the nation with a wholesome, beneficial catharsis. If nothing else, as the literary liberal Vernon Louis Parrington was to comment a generation later, the muckraking movement indoctrinated the American middle class in the elementary principles of political realism and led them to rediscover a social conscience lost since the days of the Civil War. By his irreverent hand, many a totem was thrown down, and many a fetish held up to ridicule. The realities of the American past had been covered with layers of patriotic myths, and the muckrakers stripped them away. It was the muckraking Progressive who, in holy war, exposed "the flabby optimism of the Gilded Age, with its object lessons in business politics"; he who "revealed the hidden hand that was pulling the strings of the political puppets"; who lay bare the tarnished "gilding that had been carefully laid on our callous exploitation," and who "brought under common suspicion the captain of industry who had risen as a national hero from the muck of individualism." [33] By his crusading attack in the name of sacred American values, the Progressive demonstrated that America was not in fact the holy land of equalitarian democracy that it professed to be.

In his endeavor to break with laissez-faire, the Progressive familiarized the American people with the idea of governmental intervention in the interests of general welfare, and prepared the way for more realistic reform in the future. The result of his efforts, timid as they were, was a new and growing awareness of the revolutionary fact that government, as the indispensable instrument of society, had the power and the right on behalf of the people to step in and create new conditions for a better life. In a valiant attempt to restore government to the people, he prevailed upon municipal, state and national government to take steps toward democracy—if not to go all the way—by adopting the secret ballot, the graduated income tax, direct primaries, direct election of senators, the initiative, referendum and recall. While business was not eliminated from politics, there was increased governmental regulation of corporations, railroads, utilities, labor, banking and finance. If he had not wholly reformed big business, the Progressive had made Americans aware of the dangers of concentrated economic power.

By 1914, practically as well as ideologically, Progressivism had nearly spent itself, but it was the coming of World War I that struck the death blow by diverting President Wilson and his supporters away from the problems of domestic reform. As White lamented: "We poor panting crusaders for a just and righteous order were left on a deserted battlefield, our drums punctured, our bugles muted, our cause forgotten." [34] Regretfully—and prophetically as it turned out—Wilson conceded, "Every reform we have won will be lost if we go into this war. . . . War means autocracy. The people we have unhorsed will inevitably come into the control of the country, for we shall be dependent upon the steel, oil and financial magnates. They will run the nation." [35] Yet, as the President may well have anticipated, all those "poor panting crusaders for a just and righteous order" quickly gained a second wind and galloped off with him, eager for a new Armageddon to "make the world safe for democracy" that had not yet been won at home.

Chapter I

The Capitalist Revolution

Subversion: American Style

Incontestably the true revolutionary of the nineteenth century had proven to be the American businessman. He, as it turned out, had been the radical to be feared, not the sentimental philosophers of Marxian socialism. It was he, not the socialist or anarchist on his soapbox, who systematically—by means of economic innovation and technical preemption—undermined the free-market system and subverted the ideology of classical American capitalism by rendering its nineteenth-century values of individual liberty, private property and equal opportunity meaningless in modern corporate society.

Naively perhaps, but willfully, the businessman had instigated revolution. While religiously chanting the liturgy of Adam Smith, he, in his iconoclastic pursuit of profit, had demonstrated irrevocably the supremacy of organization over the individual, the primacy of control over ownership, and the superiority of cooperation over competition. Corporate capitalism built upon an advanced technology was, because of its cooperative nature and immense productivity, inherently hostile to the competitive free-market system. Where earlier capitalism had been largely a local and private matter of the acquisition and disposal of wealth, the new industrial capitalism developed under his tutelage conducted operations on a nationwide scale and engaged in vast cooperative ventures, sharing both responsibility and profits. Instead of resting upon individual ownership and control of private property and depending chiefly upon the primitive technique of barter and sale, the newer, more intricate capitalism controlled limitless resources of associated capital, operated consolidated properties under a paid management—usually separate from ownership—and had not one but several sophisticated techniques at its command. Consequently, as a result of the businessman's insurgency, the American economy, which had begun the 1870's as an individualistic commercial community centered about an open market, was in less than a generation transformed into a corporate industrial complex operating under semi-monopolistic conditions.[1]

Not bombs, but business innovations in organization and marketing had set off the capitalist revolution. Probably the most revolutionary innovation in the economy between the 1880's and the turn of the century was the creation of the giant corporation in American industry—the use of corporate consolidation to create huge industrial empires. This innovation, linking new methods of production with new forms of industrial organization was, as Alfred D. Chandler has shown, a business response to the rise of a national urban market created by completion of a national railroad network in the 1870's.[2] Such organizations as the large integrated corporation carrying on the major industrial processes of production and manufacturing as well as the primary business functions of purchasing, marketing, and finance—all within the same organizational structure—had hardly existed, outside the railroads, before the 1880's. By 1900 they had become the dominant force in American industry. With few exceptions, the U. S. Commission on Industrial Relations reported, control of the great basic industries of the country was in the hands of a single large corporation or concentrated in the several largest.[3] Thus, by the beginning of the twentieth century, the oligopolistic structure of modern American industry—domination of the major industrial areas by the "Big Two" or "Big Three"—as the case might be—was already determined.

With the scope of capitalist endeavor enormously enlarged, the methods and goals and the relationship of the individual capitalist to the system also changed radically. Business activity in mid-nineteenth-century America, like warfare in the Middle Ages, had been a very personal affair. To the entrepreneur as well as the knight, personal skill and prowess had proved essential to his

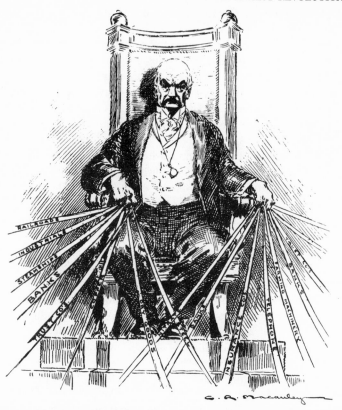

Probably the most revolutionary development in the American economy between the 1880's and the turn of the century was the use of corporate consolidation to create huge financial empires such as that of J. P. Morgan, which controlled 341 directorships in 112 corporations, having combined resources of over $22 billion.

From *Everybody's Magazine*, XXIII (Sept., 1910).

success. To get things done—to revolutionize the pattern of production by exploiting inventions or risking untried techniques—had called for individual vision and daring. Ironically, however, by his very success in rationalizing economic change, the entrepreneur undermined and eventually destroyed his own function and position.

Once business affairs had gotten beyond Adam Smith's "natural propensity to truck and barter," it was discovered that economic self-interest, for the sake of corporate profits, demanded techniques of management as efficient as those of production. The successful conduct of giant enterprises depended less on bold tactics and daring forays and more on the systematization and unification of economic endeavor. Efficient operation no longer relied upon personal force and willpower but, as a rule, required instead that the interests of the individual be subordinated to those of the corporation. Moreover, since there was a physical limit to what one man could do well, the increased size of corporate operations called for the delegation of responsibility; thus the management of big business passed from the individual entrepreneur to a hierarchy of bureaucrats who, rather than embarking on swash-buckling adventures for personal gain, engaged cooperatively in the administration of profits, finding new incentive in the hope of promotion and higher salary as a reward for efficient service. Deflected from the valorous pursuit of private profit, the entrepreneur found himself ingloriously dehorsed, no longer a dashing field commander but a staff officer behind a desk.

This momentous revolution in personal incentive—abandonment of the classic motive behind capitalism—was accompanied by an equally remarkable upset in the accepted role of the capitalist. With business discretion in the hands of salaried managers who exercised the powers of ownership without the legal right of ownership, the individual capitalist lost his formerly commanding position at the top of the economic pyramid. In relinquishing control of his property, he was reduced, for all ostensible purposes, to the inactive status of a pensioner whose fortune was largely dependent upon the initiative and effort of others. Thus, in the end, the giant, bureaucratic corporation not only devastated the free-enterprise system by driving out small and medium-sized firms and expropriating their owners, but in perfecting sophisticated management techniques, it cast out the entrepreneur and stealthily appropriated the powers and functions belonging tradi-tionally to the capitalist.

In remaking the economy, the big businessman inadvertently revolutionized the society around him. By 1919, corporations employed 86 per cent of all wage earners and produced 87.7 per cent of the total value of all products.[4] With the wealth, opportunities and energies of thousands concentrated in a single organization, there was not a person, place or institution in the land that did not in some way feel the ubiquitous presence of the corporation. Its size alone was often sufficient to challenge fundamental social and political relationships, and overshadow the society around it. As an awed commentator wrote of the newly formed United States Steel Corporation at the beginning of the century: "It receives and expends more money every year than any but the very greatest of the world's national governments; its debt is larger than that of many of the lesser nations of Europe; it absolutely controls the destinies of a population nearly as large as that of Maryland or Nebraska, and indirectly influences twice that number." [5]

In 1904 it was asserted by the financial expert John Moody that the seemingly irresistible tendency toward concentration and combination had resulted in the formation of two huge "supertrusts." Of the greater trusts, Moody estimated 37 per cent were Morgan "properties"—that is, had intimate connections with the banking house of J. P. Morgan & Company—while the other 63 per cent were said to belong to the Standard Oil or Rockefeller interests. Although the Morgan group controlled such gigantic enterprises as the steel and shipping trusts, the electrical-supply trust, the rubber trust, and a score or more of smaller aggregations, its magnificent holdings were dwarfed by the gargantuan agglomeration of the Rockefeller group. The latter were in fact recognized as "the real fathers of the Trust idea in this country," and controlled the most far-reaching and most successful of all "trusts," the Standard Oil Company. In 1900, this corporation, with a minimal par value capitalization of $97.5 million, absolutely dominated the United States oil industry, reputedly supplying 84 per cent of domestic demand and over 90 per cent of foreign. But it was not merely in oil and allied industries that the Rockefeller interests were dominant; by shrewd use of their tremendous earnings, they had gained control over the copper trust, the smelter's trust, and a host of minor industries. They were closely identified with the mammoth tobacco trust and also influenced United States

Steel and other Morgan properties. In addition, the Rockefeller empire included the entire public-service aggregation of Greater New York, representing over $725 million capital, plus the Gould–Rockefeller railroads capitalized at over $1.3 billion. The Rockefeller dominions were further supplemented and welded together by banking and financial interests headed by the National City Bank of New York in close alliance with large life-insurance companies such as Equitable and Mutual of New York. While, as Moody emphasized, it was not possible to do more than approximate the varied and extensive ramifications of the Morgan and Rockefeller holdings, there was no question that, between them, these groups dominated the commercial and financial life of the nation.[6]

Far from being in any real sense rivals or competitors for power, these two great financial empires were, Moody noted, "harmonious in nearly all particulars."[7] Instead of war between them, it was commonly recognized in Wall Street that there was a "grand close alliance," and this was borne out by the investigations of Senator Robert LaFollette, who showed in 1908 that fewer than a hundred men acting in concert controlled the great business interests of the country.[8] Five years later, in 1913, his charge of an ever-tightening circle of wealth and influence was confirmed by the Pujo Committee, which revealed that J. P. Morgan & Company, the First National and National City Banks of New York held 341 directorships in 112 corporations having combined resources of over $22 billion.[9] This inventory, though admittedly incomplete, found a single network of interests controlling more than three times the assessed value of all real and personal property in New England, or more than twice the value of all property in the thirteen southern states, or more than all the property in the twenty-two states west of the Mississippi.[10]

The Farmers' Protest

To alarmed Americans, the nation and its ideals appeared in grave danger of being swallowed up by the monolithic corporate system, a formidable leviathan whose astounding growth apparently recognized no natural bounds and whose vast power was more centralized than the political organization of the country itself. Although the nation was undergoing phenomenal economic expansion and the prospects of national prosperity seemed better than ever before, there nevertheless grew up a widespread feeling of hostility toward big corporations. This gathering antagonism, which reached a peak in 1912, was compounded of three main elements: resentment, disenchantment, and fear.

Resentment came from those whose lives, pursuits, and status had been upset by the revolutionary new forces of corporate industrialism: the small-town merchant driven out of business, the farmer squeezed of his profits, the village lawyer stripped of position and opportunity, the worker enslaved to the machine—all those hurt, frustrated, bewildered Americans who looked upon the trusts as foreign invaders bent upon the destruction of all that was good in America. Reeling under the first blows of modern technique, they felt rather than understood its shattering impact upon their hopes, habits and beliefs.

"Never in the history of the world was society in so terrific flux as it is right now," wrote Jack London in his socialist novel *The Iron Heel.* "The swift changes in our industrial system are causing equally swift changes in our religious, political, and social structures. An unseen and fearful revolution is taking place in the fibre and structure of society. One can only dimly feel these things. But they are in the air, now, to-day." [11]

The world had never seen anything comparable to the immense material progress of the United States in the last quarter of the nineteenth century. Never had any society experienced in so short a time such an expansion of all that pertained to business, and never before had any people been able to produce so much with so little sweat and so few manhours. Some of the innovations had been eminently destructive and occasioned great disturbances in the economy, entailing losses of capital, radical changes in methods of production, and undesirable shifts in occupation on the part of individuals. And yet, as the popular economist David A. Wells reminded pessimists, for the majority of Americans the movement had been upward and not downward.

In his study of recent economic changes, Wells piled statistic upon statistic to impress his countrymen with the wonder-working prodigies of the new capitalism. The existence of the present populations of Europe and the United States—indeed the continuance and progress of civilization itself—had been made possible, in his opinion, solely through the use of machines in place of man. He proudly pointed out that in the past few decades the displacement of muscular labor by machinery had run as high as 80 per cent in some American industries. Skipping over the fate of the technologically unemployed, he marveled that the labor of three men for one year produced all the flour a thousand other men ordinarily ate in a year, that one American cotton-mill worker could supply the annual wants of 1,600 fully clothed Chinese or 3,000 partially clad East Indians. Not only did the United States produce millions of paper bags per week, but "a purchaser can now also take his butter or lard in paper trays that are brine and grease proof; his vinegar in paper jars that are warranted not to soak for one hour; a bottle of wine wrapped in a corrugated case that would not break if he dropped it on the pavement, and his oysters in paper pails that will hold water overnight." [12] Obviously the lesson the stunned reader was expected to draw from this avalanche of facts and figures was that Americans had never been better off.

Not all Americans, however, were able to take such an optimistic view. While not blind to America's amazing technological progress, they questioned whether the powerful forces of industrialism and corporate capitalism would be used to promote the greatest good of the greatest number or merely to build colossal fortunes for a few. Aside from the Socialists, the most radical criticism of the business system came from the Populists, a political faction made up chiefly of farmers but having significant support from industrial workers, social reformers and intellectuals. Populist resentments stemmed in part from bad crops and hard times, and from the growing realization that American agriculture stood in the same subservient position to American industrialism that the colonies occupied toward England a century and a quarter earlier.[13] Like the patriot of 1776, the farmer was fighting for his independence from a system which threatened, as had the British imperialism of another day, to hold him in economic and political bondage.

Far from opposing technology, American farmers were most

A WALL-STREET VIEW

Disparaged by Wall Street as an unruly mob of hayseeds and crack-pots, Populism was the uprising of millions of dissatisfied farmers who charged organized capital with monopolizing the wealth created by their toil.   From *Literary Digest*, Sept. 19, 1896.

receptive to mechanization, as the early success of the McCormick reaper proved. If they resented the machine it was because, monopolized by the few, it was being used to exploit rather than to benefit society. "Instead of using it to displace men," protested the Topeka *Advocate*, "it should have been used to reduce the hours of labor." The evil lay not in technology but in its social misuse. "Has society, as a whole, derived the benefits from the use of labor-saving machinery that it might have done under a different system?" asked the Kansas newspaper. It then replied, "We think not. Under the prevailing system the capitalist has been the chief beneficiary." [14] The Populist solution was not to turn back the clock but rationally to control the new productive forces in the larger interests of society. "The people do not want to tear up the railroads nor pull down the factories," declared the *Platte County Argus*. "They want to build up and make better everything." [15]

The antagonism between the farmer and the big businessman came to a head in William Jennings Bryan's famous "cross of gold" speech in 1896. Speaking for the "producers of wealth," he accosted the "owners of wealth" with a passionate plea for recognition: "We say to you that you have made the definition of a business man too limited in its application. The man who is employed for wages is as much a business man as his employer; the attorney in a country town is as much a business man as the corporation counsel in a great metropolis; the merchant at the cross-roads store is as much a business man as the merchant of New York; the farmer who goes forth in the morning and toils all day . . . is as much a business man as the man who goes upon the board of trade and bets upon the price of grain; the miners who go down a thousand feet into the earth . . . and bring forth from their hiding places the precious metals . . . are as much business men as the few financial magnates who, in a back room, corner the money of the world. We come to speak for this broader class of business men." [16] But it proved an empty rhetorical triumph, for in the presidential battle that followed, Bryan and his Populist supporters, impeded by dubious alliance with the silver interests, lost by a half million votes to the well organized forces of big business and their personable puppet, William McKinley.

The Business Defense

Attacks on the new business system were decried by its defenders as the ancient outcry of ignorance against innovation. Conceding that some alleged disadvantages might exist, they tended for the most part to dismiss them as imaginary or theoretical, while lauding the advantages as real and substantial. "There seems to be a great readiness in the public mind to take alarm at these phenomena of growth," observed William Graham Sumner from the ivy towers of Yale; "there might rather seem to be reason for public congratulation. We want to be provided with things abundantly and cheaply; that means that we want increased economic power. All these enterprises are efforts to satisfy that want, and they promise to do it." [17] It was ridiculous, in his opinion, to attempt to reach the end while making war on the means. The trust was simply one of our big ways of doing things, said promoter Charles R. Flint, and the billion-dollar corporation doing business in the world at large was no more to be feared than the $10,000 partnership in a country village.[18]

Concentration of wealth and control, it was argued, was a necessary step in social evolution. The United States had arrived at a stage in economic development where business could not be done on the scale of fifty years earlier. As the railway magnate James J. Hill expressed it, "We have reached a period when the old-fashioned methods will prove inadequate. . . . There are too many people to be fed, housed and clothed to permit of the wasteful system which would maintain a horde of idle middle-men." [19] At the time, he had in mind a grandiose plan for consolidation of the Hill–Morgan and Harriman properties into one vast railroad empire, and his view was typical of most big businessmen who regarded the tendency toward consolidation as inevitable. To make "artificial opposition" from alleged democratic, moral, religious or other motives was, from their point of view, to kill the goose that laid the golden eggs. It was proper to propose checks and safeguards, but as S. C. T. Dodd, creator of the Standard Oil Trust, went to great pains to demonstrate, an onslaught on concentration meant the sacrifice of real benefits for the sake of false prejudices.°

Troubled Americans were reassured that the new business system was completely unlike the old competitive commercialism with its buccaneering profiteers. "Since the public-be-damned period," professed E. H. Gary of United States Steel, "there has been a change—an awakening." [20] New business methods, it was claimed, had created new business values. Certainly, after 1907, big business did seem to have grown up. Gone was the sense of conspiracy and secret scheming that had once characterized the operations of business and financial magnates, and this change was reflected in the mass media. Slashing muckraking attacks on "The Despotism of Combined Millions" gave way to fulsome articles in praise of "The 'Big Business' Man As a Social Worker." Publicists wrote of

° S. C. T. Dodd, *The Advantages of Consolidation.* See p. 5.

Inspired Millionaires, while the popular press lauded "The Awakening of the American Business Man." No doubt this changing image was due at least in part to the big businessman᾽ growing concern with public relations. To counter the widespread rebellion against the profit system, business organizations such as the National Civic Federation undertook educational campaigns to instruct public opinion in "the real meaning of socialism" and the need to combat it "if our American political system and its underlying economic institutions are to be preserved."[21]

Not only was big business becoming aware of the advantages of good public relations, but as Walter Lippmann noted, it required a different order of ability to conduct the steel trust than it did to manage a primitive blast furnace by means of a partnership.[22] A giant corporation, wrote railway executive Marshall M. Kirkman, was "methodically organized and drilled. It has its commanders, its rank and file; its officers, sub-officers and privates. The officers and employees . . . are trained to obey in all matters relating to their business. . . . Insubordination . . . is as great an offense as insubordination in an army. . . . [In fact] the United States army forms, in many respects, a good model for corporate organization."[23] This was the "real news about business," it seemed to Lippmann.[24] With administration in the hands of an army of businessmen divorced from ownership and thus freed from the necessity of petty profiteering, the new business system was producing a new kind of businessman able to devote more of his energies to the service of human progress.

Although it was demonstrably true that the changing scale of modern industry was revolutionizing the discipline, incentives, and outlook of the business world, there was no gainsaying that industry was still managed for business ends. There was, as Lippmann maintained, "obviously a great difference in outlook between the Vanderbilt policy of 'the public be damned' and the McAdoo policy of 'the public be pleased.'" The old concept of private property had also been "very much modified." Few big businessmen after the nineties would have denied that they were running quasi-public enterprises and that "something more" was demanded of them than private exploitation.[25] But, as economist Thorstein Veblen insisted, investments were still made for profit, and industrial plants and processes were operated solely on the basis of their profit-yielding capacity.[26]

While big businessmen confidently claimed that increased size in business organization always resulted in greater business efficiency, lawyer and reformer Louis D. Brandeis proved statistically that the huge profits of trusts were not in fact due to increased efficiency, but to purposely contrived monopolistic control of the market—"to the exercise by a small body of men of the sovereign taxing power." ° Where corporations had a high degree of control, profits were great; where they did not, profits were small. Indeed, Brandeis found the purpose of combination was frequently not efficiency at all but its very opposite—"the desire to capitalize failures" by bribing others not to compete, so less efficient concerns could survive and unite.[27] As cataloged by the muckraker Henry Demarest Lloyd, these malpractices included "blowing up competitors, as the oil monopoly has done; shutting up works and throwing men out of employment, as the sugar monopoly has done; selling the machinery of rivals for junk, as the nail monopoly has done; paying big bonuses to others not to run, as the steel monopoly has done; restricting production, as the coal monopoly has done; buying up and suppressing new patents, as the telephone monopoly has done." [28]

Whatever might be the gains of monopoly from a purely technical point of view, it was quite apparent the community was largely at the mercy of the giant corporations. The United States was becoming increasingly a nation of corporations and employees, and the enlarged scope of corporate operations removed them almost wholly from the realm of "petty trafficking" formerly associated with business. Corporations had become major institutions of society, and as Brandeis observed, the questions which concerned them were more nearly questions of statesmanship than of business policy. "The magnitude, difficulty and importance of the problems involved are often as great as in the matters of state. . . . The relations between rival railroad systems are like the relations between neighboring kingdoms. The relations of the great trusts to the consumers or to their employees is like that of feudal lords to commoners or dependents." [29] The omnipotence of large

---

° Louis D. Brandeis, *Trusts and Efficiency*. See p. 54.

business corporations was a fact of American life that could no longer be disputed.

Progressivism and Monopoly

All successful trusts and industrial combinations embraced at least some elements of monopoly or, as John Moody said, they could not exist.[30] From the business point of view, monopoly was a logical and necessary development of industrial progress. Technology, it was discovered, could prove a troublesome genie. Unless checked, technological "efficiency" led to what businessmen indulgently called "overproduction"—an unprofitable excess of supply over demand. To maintain "reasonable" profits, it was therefore necessary to gain industrywide control over production through business coalition or combination. Once such control was obtained, it was then possible by deliberately restricting production to hold back the cornucopia of technology and to regulate consumption, not according to the needs of the nation, but to satisfy the desire of business for profit.

Under the new business system, therefore, one of the first things to go was the traditional concept of price competition. In capitalist reality as distinguished from the textbook model, the old kind of competition no longer counted. As S. C. T. Dodd frankly admitted and his employer, the Standard Oil Company, ably demonstrated, industrial centralization led inevitably toward monopoly power. "Every combination in business, whether by partnership or corporate organization, prevents competition between the persons combined; and in proportion as the business is widely and successfully conducted, its interference with the competition of others increases. The larger the business, the greater the number of persons and the amount of capital engaged in it, the greater is the power of those who conduct it over production and prices."[31] As a director of United States Steel openly proclaimed in *World's Work*: "Competition that competes, that is real, that is earnest, under present conditions of life, has become too destructive to be tolerated."[32] The view of most big businessmen was summed up by the creator of America's largest industrial corporation,

J. P. Morgan. "I like a little competition," he told a congressional committee, "but I like combination better."[33]

Yet, despite a near epidemic of mergers and consolidations, the monopolistic position of big business was never absolute. As Gabriel Kolko has shown, the two industrial giants of the day, United States Steel and the Standard Oil Company, steadily lost their dominant control over production. The steel trust's share of the national output fell from 61.6 per cent in 1901 to 39.9 per cent in 1920; while Standard's share of refining dropped from 90 per cent in 1899 to 50 per cent in 1921.[34] But even though individual firms lost their preeminence, this did not herald a return to free competition. Instead it meant oligopoly, a potentially advantageous situation of near monopoly where a handful of top firms dominated an industry, dictating prices and regulating production by voluntary agreement. Thus the purpose of the famous "Gary Dinners" held at the Waldorf-Astoria in 1907 and 1908 was to fix prices by "gentlemen's agreements" among the leaders of the steel industry.

Progressives, however, viewed the efforts of corporate leaders to curb destructive and unprofitable competition with unbridled suspicion. To them it appeared that the trusts had begun to function less as devices for the self-government of industry than as arrangements for the imposition of conditions under which the livelihood of society should be carried on. As Henry Demarest Lloyd charged in his classic *Wealth Against Commonwealth* (1894), the *Uncle Tom's Cabin* of the Progressive Era, the business system had raised up a new breed of rulers—"corporate Caesars." "We now have Captains of Industry, with a few aids, rearranging from office-chairs this or that industry, by mere contrivances of wit compelling the fruits of the labor of tens of thousands of their fellows, who never saw them, never heard of them, to be every day deposited unwilling and unwitting to their own credit at the bank; setting, as by necromancy, hundreds of properties, large and small, in a score of communities, to flying through invisible ways into their hands; sitting calm through all the hubbub raised in courts, legislatures, and public places, and by dictating letters and whispering words remaining the master magicians of the scene; defying, though private citizens, all the forces and authorities of a whole people; by the mere mastery of compelling brain, without putting hand to anything, opening or closing the earth's treasures of oil or coal or gas or copper or what not; pulling down or putting up great buildings, factories, towns themselves; moving men and their money this way and that; inserting their will as part of the law of life of the people—American, European, and Asiatic—and, against the protest of a whole civilization, making themselves, their methods and principles, its emblematic figures." [35]

Americans began to realize that they were governed more by corporations than the state. Abrupt changes in the character of social progress suddenly revealed to them the immense public powers reposed in corporations and the dangerous extent to which corporate structure had shown itself capable of expansion beyond the activity legitimately chartered by government. The popular press pointed out that corporations had attained giant stature by evasion of natural law and defiance of statute law. Big businessmen had not only broken—or perhaps repealed—"natural laws" and enacted artificial advantages nullifying the traditional checks and balances of classical capitalism; they had taken advantage of the American system of local self-government and popular distrust of governmental intervention to organize corporate entities beyond the reach of local statutes and officials. Rather than the natural outgrowth of natural laws, as its supporters contended, the giant corporation was, as William Jennings Bryan rightly insisted, "the natural outgrowth of unnatural conditions created by man-made laws." He summarized the situation by saying, "What government creates, it can control." [36] Either these man-made monsters would destroy the system of ideas, institutions, and practices out of which they had issued, or else be subdued by them.

Despite mounting insistence that something be done to protect the people from the dangers of monopoly, Americans were divided as to the proper course for the federal government to pursue. The most widely held view, especially among farmers and small businessmen, was that trusts were unnatural and dangerous and should be smashed. "God hates monopoly, and so do we," was the rancorous attitude of those who saw corporations as "great engines of oppression" and therefore wished to invoke the power of the state to bring about their "complete and prompt annihilation." [37] Opposed to the "trustbusters" were the "trust regulators," those who recognized that consolidation had certain advantages but believed the state must regulate corporations to ensure that these

THE TRAFFIC "COP"
by O. E. CESARE
He governs everybody with the consent of everybody
and everybody gets ahead.

Once Americans began to realize that in their daily lives they were
governed more by corporations than by the state, they called upon
the federal government to police big business and to restore competition by controlling monopoly.   From *Harper's Weekly*, Mar. 7, 1914.

advantages were realized by the public. This smaller, more moderate group included many influential public and professional men
whose attitude was that "We have to learn how to secure for the
public the advantages of monopoly, administered in the anti-
monopolistic spirit." [38] This split in the electorate was reflected
by the two leading contenders for reform leadership in 1912,
Theodore Roosevelt and Woodrow Wilson. While both were
convinced that the only way to meet the threat of a billion-dollar
corporation was by invoking the protection of a hundred-
billion-dollar government, they differed over the role and objec-
tives of government intervention.

Ex-President Roosevelt, who was more of a Pragmatist than a
Progressive, considered corporations and combinations indispensable in the business world. Although as President, he had acquired
a popular reputation as a "trustbuster," he had even then serious

misgivings about the effectiveness and value of antitrust laws, preferring instead a regulated centralization of economic power. "It has been a misfortune," he told the American people in 1907, "that the national laws on this subject have hitherto been of a negative or prohibitive rather than an affirmative kind, and still more that they have in part sought to prohibit what could not be effectively prohibited, and have in part in their prohibitions confounded what should be allowed and what should not be allowed." [39] What was needed, he felt, was not sweeping prohibition of all combination, good or bad—which might itself restrain competition—but adequate supervision and regulation to prevent any restraint of competition from being detrimental to the public. To this end, Roosevelt called for the establishment of a strong federal regulatory commission which would maintain "permanent active supervision" over corporations, much as the government already did for the national banks and as the Interstate Commerce Commission did for the railroads.

While he was sharply criticized for breaking with the traditional American belief in unlimited individualism and unlimited competition, Roosevelt defended his proposed commission as "only in form an innovation. In substance it is merely a restoration; for from the earliest time such regulation of industrial activities has been recognized in the action of the lawmaking bodies; and all that I propose is to meet the changed conditions in such manner as will prevent the Commonwealth abdicating the power it has always possessed, not only in this country, but also in England before and since this country became a separate nation." [40] In short, by advocating the extension of governmental power as the controlling force in the economy, Roosevelt was simply prescribing the mercantilist remedy proposed by Alexander Hamilton more than a hundred years before and, by so doing, was realistically endorsing a policy which since the 1860's had been steadily, if furtively, supplanting laissez-faire as public policy.°

During the presidential campaign of 1912, Wilson, then governor of New Jersey, bitterly attacked Roosevelt's position. Rejecting the cure as worse than the illness, he protested, "You can't find your

---

°Theodore Roosevelt, *The New Hamiltonianism.* See p. 60.

way to social reform through the forces that have made social reform necessary."[41] To set up a regulatory commission under existing conditions was, in his opinion, only a proposal to turn over the government of the United States to the corporations: "The national administration having for sixteen years been virtually under the regulation of the trusts, it would be merely a family matter were the parts reversed and were the other members of the family to exercise the regulation."[42] Most suspicious to him was the fact that big businessmen who were themselves the objects of popular hostility—E. H. Gary of United States Steel, for instance, and George W. Perkins, partner of J. P. Morgan—were among the most avid supporters of federal regulation. What such a program would lead to, insisted Wilson, was an avowed partnership between the government and the trusts in which the president of the United States would serve simply as president of a board of directors. Nor were Wilson's suspicions unfounded. The Interstate Commerce Commission, set up to guard the public interest, had been taken over almost immediately by the very interests it was supposed to regulate, and had become instead a sort of protective barrier between the railroad corporations and the people.

Rejecting the doctrine that monopoly was inevitable, Wilson purposed to "rescue" business by government action. The average American had lost his economic freedom, he charged, because of an "un-American set of conditions" that enabled a small number of men to exclude their fellows from equal opportunity.° Therefore, said Wilson, with apologies to Jefferson, government "in our day must come to the assistance of the individual . . . to see that he gets fair play; that is all, but that is much. Without the watchful interference, the resolute interference, of the government, there can be no fair play between individuals and such powerful institutions as the trusts."[43] His proposals for the regulation of competition, however, were vague: "not one single legitimate or honest arrangement is going to be disturbed; but every impediment to business is going to be removed, every illegitimate kind of control is going to be destroyed."[44] Apparently his intent, according to Arthur Link, was to rewrite the rules of business practice so clearly

---

° Woodrow Wilson, *The New Jeffersonianism.* See p. 63.

that there could be no doubt as to their meaning and to enforce these rules by the normal processes of law.[45] Obviously, if this were so, then his "silent revolution" was no more a revolution than that of 1800. Stripped of rhetoric, this naive solution was merely a reassertion of the Jeffersonian ideal of limited government.

In taking the stand that he was against the trusts but for big business, Wilson revealed it was sentiment, not logic, that inspired his antitrust campaign. By his equivocation he expressed the confusion of a society which, to quote Thurman Arnold, "unconsciously felt the need of great organizations, and at the same time had to deny them a place in the moral and logical ideology of an [individualistic] social structure."[46] Here, said Lippmann, lay the inner contradiction of Woodrow Wilson. As an intelligent man, Wilson knew there was a new world demanding new methods, but he dreamed of an older world and was torn between the two.[47] While he implicitly rejected laissez-faire, he was reluctant to invoke the central power needed to control a centralized economic system. So Wilson temporized, hoping through the application of old-fashioned morals to steer a safe course between plutocracy and socialism.

The reason for Wilson's failure of nerve was correctly attributed by Roosevelt to his innate conservatism. His overriding belief that liberalism meant the limitation of governmental power and not the increase of it, was castigated by Roosevelt as "a bit of outworn academic doctrine which was kept in the schoolroom and the professorial study for a generation after it had been abandoned by all who had experience of actual life. It is simply the *laissez-faire* doctrine of the English political economists three-quarters of a century ago. It can be applied with profit, if anywhere at all, only in . . . a community before the days of Fulton, Morse and Edison. To apply it now in the United States at the beginning of the Twentieth century, with its highly organized industries, with its railways, telegraphs and telephones, means literally and absolutely to refuse to make a single effort to better any one of our social or industrial conditions."[48]

But rather than make a realistic attempt to deal with the antagonisms between individual freedom and organized power, Wilson and his Progressive followers chose to tilt at windmills, squandering the new formula of governmental intervention in a vain effort to recapture a bright past which, for all practical purposes, was dead and beyond recall.

The Struggle Over Organization

Not all opponents of industrial organization were in the antitrust camp. When it came to the controversial matter of labor unions, business leaders almost without exception condemned organization. For its part, organized labor did not disapprove of trusts, if they in turn would recognize that the growth of labor unions as the necessary counterpart of the growth of industrial combinations. But though the union might renounce trustbusting, the corporations heartily endorsed "labor-busting" and launched an aggressive campaign to break up labor organizations.

Power was with the corporations. Big business had a firm grip on state and local governments and used the courts, police, militia, and federal troops to protect its own property. State and federal courts were, for the most part, virulently antilabor. In the first seven years after passage of the Sherman Act in 1890, the Supreme Court handed down only one decision against a business combination (1897); yet, in the same period, federal courts upheld twelve antitrust actions against labor combinations, although the act was never intended by Congress to apply to unions. Labor leader Eugene Debs was imprisoned in 1894 for violating the antitrust act, but despite flagrant violations by corporations, and even adverse court rulings, no businessman was sent to jail under its provisions until seventy years later. Likewise, nearly every important strike from the Homestead Strike of 1892 to the Steel Strike of 1919 was won by the corporations through the use of court injunctions, troops or, as in the Pullman Strike (1894), both. While trusts and mergers were publicly defended as belonging to a new and better phase of social evolution—"a wholesome, irresistible, natural progression from lower forms of industrial life to higher ones"—labor unions were widely denounced, especially in the business-controlled press, as "criminal monopolies" at war with the principles on which society was founded.[49]

From a logical and ethical standpoint, the stubborn resistance of organized business against the attempt to organize labor into effective unions was both unreasonable and unfair. Modern business enterprise, as noted earlier, had found it necessary for the sake of profits to counter excess machine productivity with restrictive economic techniques. To maintain "reasonable prices," it resorted to monopolistic organization; to stabilize the market, it contrived artificial scarcity by restricting production and blocking technical advance; to sustain demand, it adopted a scheme of planned obsolescence, producing shoddy goods of inferior quality that had a short life and would require early replacement. While business regarded its own use of such techniques as a sign of economic "maturity," the adoption of similar tactics by labor—monopolistic organization to maintain "reasonable wages," the "closed shop" to stabilize the labor market by creating artificial scarcity, and "featherbedding" to sustain the demand for employment by resisting technical advance through retention of superfluous jobs—were denounced by businessmen as "immoral" attempts "to get something for nothing."

Twenty-one people were killed, many injured, and half a million dollars' worth of property was destroyed in 1910 when frustrated unionists dynamited the Los Angeles *Times* which for many years had been carrying on a war against organized labor.   Brown Bros.

At root of the dispute between business and labor was a conflict of values. The everyday life of the workingman differed appreciably from that of the businessman, and this difference was reflected in divergent economic goals. The revision of the economic system envisaged by the workingman was not concerned with natural liberty, private property rights and individual discretion, but with job security, a living wage and the right of cooperative action to attain those goals. It was formulated not according to business expediency, but in terms of technological potential and social necessity. Thus, while the union and the trust were both products of industry organized around the machine process, their aims were ideologically, though not inherently, antagonistic.

Union action, Veblen pointed out, was markedly hostile to the natural-rights foundation of common law. "Many pious phrases have been invented to disguise this iconoclastic trend of trade-union aims and endeavors; but the courts, standing on a secure and familiar natural rights footing, have commonly made short work of the shifty sophistications which trade-union advocates have offered for their consideration. They have struck at the root of the matter in declaring trade-union regulations inimical to the natural rights of workman and employer alike, in that they hamper individual liberty and act in restraint of trade." [50] While organized labor seldom went so far as to overtly dispute the merits of the natural-rights dogma, the logical outcome of its actions was, like those of organized business itself, to undercut the institutional heritage of capitalism.

Aware of this basic conflict but deliberately minimizing ideological differences, Samuel Gompers, president of the American Federation of Labor, directed his efforts toward improvement of the workers' material well-being. A consummate Pragmatist, Gompers did not join in the hue and cry against trusts and business associations. "We welcome their organization," he said, "but we ask them to follow the path of moderation and reason, the same that they demand of us as workingmen. When they assume a right for themselves, they cannot deny that same right to us. They are organizing; organization is the order of the day." [51] As Gompers recognized, large corporations and unions occupied somewhat analogous positions in the American political economy. Both were the products of industrial consolidation—the A.F. of L. being a complex superorganization of unions built around craft skills. Both believed in associated action for themselves and competition for their adversaries. Both demanded governmental recognition and protection but disliked the idea of government regulation.[52] But as Gompers told the U.S. Commission on Industrial Relations in 1914, while the condition of the working people had improved very materially during the past few decades, they were still not getting their share of the wealth produced because existing institutions were more favorable to the interests of the employer than to those of the workingman.° "The facts are these: When an employer has a mass of unorganized working people working for him he is master of all he surveys, and any attempt on the part of workmen to petition or request a change is looked upon by him as a rebellion."[53] Labor, therefore, in order to achieve its goals, had to conquer its share of the national product by aggressive associated action.

Although Gompers always maintained that the interests of employer and worker were opposed, he was against the socialization of industry and called for evolution, not revolution. Through strikes and boycotts, its chief weapons, the A.F. of L. sought, by threatening profits, to force employers to bargain with the union on wages, hours, and working conditions. It built up a "defense fund" to support strikers during work stoppages, and it also sent out labor organizers who were not always well received by respectable citizens, but were classed as "agitators" and frequently subjected to rough treatment by the forces of law and order. The Federation urged its members to buy only goods bearing union labels and placed the products of non-union companies on its "We Don't Patronize" list. The A.F. of L. likewise engaged in "nonpartisan" politics. Gompers was an active member of the National Civic Federation whose big business leaders nominally supported his pragmatic trade unionism as an antidote to state socialism. The labor organization also sought to influence public opinion by publishing union literature and to gain favorable legislation by lobbying. In short, its goals and methods were an endeavor to compromise between business notions of what ought to be in

°Samuel Gompers, *Goals of the American Labor Movement.* See p. 66

industrial matters and labor's opinions of what industrial conditions demanded and what the worker would tolerate.

To protect their own interests against the menace of trade unionism, businessmen, between 1885 and 1920, formed some two thousand business "unions" or employers' associations. One of the earliest was the General Managers' Association, composed of the twenty-four railroads terminating in Chicago. In 1894 this group successfully broke up the American Railway Union. After the turn of the century, however, the best known and perhaps most belligerent protective association was the National Association of Manufacturers which occupied a sort of no-man's land between the aggressive reformers and the cooperative capitalism of big business. Like most Progressives, these moderately prosperous industrialists were small capitalists fighting to protect their values and way of life against the trusts. The threat of "Socialized Industry"—big labor and big business combined—horrified them, and as Robert Wiebe has shown, they saw the National Civic Federation as a conspiracy between the magnates and unionists directed against them.[54] Unlike the Progressives, however, they were adamantly hostile to organized labor in any form.

Made up mostly of small and middle-size manufacturers, the N.A.M. was primarily a labor-busting organization. Although it supported what it called "good unionism," the Association viewed the Gompers brand as "un-American, illegal and indecent." Clearly opposed to practically everything the American Federation of Labor advocated from the closed-shop to child-labor laws, the N.A.M. took the stand that "labor trusts" were "contrary to law and the rights of men." Through lobbying, motion pictures, pamphlets and public addresses, it sought to influence legislation and to "educate" the public in "the principles of individual liberty and ownership of property." Its president, John Kirby, Jr., a strenuous foe of labor, toured the country spreading the gospel of the employer and with bitter harangues sought to turn his countrymen against strikes and unionism.°

Nor did the N.A.M. make any serious attempt to conceal its aggressive propaganda activities. Not only did it innundate schools, colleges and debating societies with thousands of pamphlets on the

°John Kirby, Jr., *The Disadvantages of Labor Unionism.* See p. 70.

"Disastrous Effects of a National Eight-Hour Law," but it urged employers to exert their influence over the press by patronizing friendly publications and withdrawing their advertising from unfriendly ones. In its fight for law enforcement against "criminal unionists," the Association maintained a "war fund" to aid congressmen and public officials known for their antilabor views, and through a well organized Washington lobby was able to muster as many as 30,000 to 40,000 protesting telegrams in one day. As a result of such techniques, the N.A.M. and its allies were able to block practically every bill backed by the American Federation of Labor from 1902 to 1912. Although an eight-hour bill became law in 1912, the provisions for enforcement, to the great dissatisfaction of labor officials, were tempered to appease the employers. Similarly, the Clayton Act (1914), prematurely greeted as the "Magna Carta of Labor," failed to give unions the promised relief from injunctions and antitrust action because of modifications attributed to a representative of the employers' associations.[55]

Industrial Warfare

To many unskilled workers, the pragmatic approach of the A.F. of L. seemed to offer no promise of relief from wage slavery. Deprived of a living wage and bullied by employers, the discontented textile workers of New England, the lumberjacks of the Pacific Northwest who toiled ten hours a day and earned twenty cents an hour, the long-struggling miners of Colorado, section hands, harvest men, bindle-stiffs and floaters joined together in 1905 in one great industrial union, the Industrial Workers of the World. A revolutionary organization, the I.W.W. took the view that between the working class and the employing class, "a struggle must go on until the workers of the world organize as a class, take possession of the earth and the machinery of production, and abolish the wage system."[56]

Nor were their grievances imaginary. The leading causes of industrial unrest, as later determined by the Commission on Industrial Relations, were four: the unjust distribution of wealth and income; unemployment; denial of justice under the law; and denial of the right to form effective organizations. It was estimated in

1909 that in the manufacturing and mining industries, 64 per cent of the families received less than $750 a year, and 31 per cent less than $500, although the living minimum was calculated at $700 per family. At the other end of the scale were forty-four families whose aggregate incomes, according to income-tax returns of 1914, totaled at least $50 million per year—the equivalent of the earnings of 100,000 workers at $500. Moreover, statistics showed that in the basic industries of the country, workingmen were unemployed for at least one-fifth of the year, and there was at all times a permanent army of unemployed numbering in hundreds of thousands. While the workers' fight for shorter hours had established the ten-hour day in most industries before 1890, some industries still worked their employees eleven to thirteen hours, seven days a week. Working conditions were generally bad and often dangerous. The accident rate in American industry was the highest in the world. In 1915 approximately 35,000 workers were killed in American industries, and at least half of those deaths were preventable. Without adequate liability laws and compensation insurance, more than a million injured or disabled workers each year were left to shift for themselves.

There was, furthermore, an enormous mass of evidence to show that workers, as individuals and as a class, were denied justice in the enactment, adjudication and administration of the law. Pro-labor laws were only passed after long and exhausting struggles, if at all. Such beneficent measures as did become law—those requiring statement of cause of discharge, prohibiting the use of "scrip" as payment for wages, or defining the liability of employers for injuries—were largely nullified by the courts. Laws on the statute books, such as the Sherman Act, were not equally enforced. Often, under the guise of protecting property, the whole machinery of government was frequently placed at the disposal of employers for the oppression of the workers. Most paradoxically, the right to collective action to redress grievances was denied 75 to 100 per cent of the workers in transportation, mining and manufacturing by giant industrial combinations whose directors were often

not only totally ignorant of the actual operations of the corporation, but upon their own admission, knew nothing and cared
nothing about the quality of the product or the condition and
treatment of the workers from whose labor they derived their
income. Under these circumstances, it was not to be wondered that
workingmen, out of sheer self-protection, sought strength in collective action. For it had become painfully apparent to them that
under modern conditions, a cooperative solution of industrial
problems was possible only when both parties to the bargain had
enough power to command respect.[57]

Instead of stopping the labor movement, the belligerent ob-
structionism of employers bred a more militant unionism. Between 1881 and 1905, there were 36,757 strikes in this country.[58] The gravity and extent of the threat to established order
was confirmed by the Secretary of War, who reported that in 1894
there were more troops on the march than at any time since the
Civil War.[59] In Colorado alone, martial law was in effect ten times
between 1894 and 1914. "Experience, long, painful and dearly
bought," the Socialist leader Eugene Debs told the organizing
convention of the I.W.W., had taught the worker what to expect.
"The capitalist presses a button and the police are called into
action. Then the capitalist presses button No. 2 and injunctions
are issued by the judges, the judicial allies and servants of the
capitalist class. Then button No. 3 is pressed and the state troops
fall into line; and if this is not sufficient button No. 4 is pressed
and the regular soldiers come marching to the scene."[60] Gompers
was branded "a foe of the working class" for fraternizing with big
businessmen, and the Civic Federation was decried as the capitalists' way of concealing their daggers while hoodwinking those
whom they would rule and exploit.[61]

Card-carrying members of the I.W.W. never numbered more
than fifty thousand, but their dauntless spirit and defiant language
carried special meaning to the downtrodden worker who by now
preferred to die fighting than starve working. From toolboxes and
stumps, "Wobbly" agitators stirred up the "slave" and the "working

plug," and fanned the flames of discontent with songs and hymns of hate:

> For the sailors that drown when your ill found ships go crashing on the shore,
> For the mangled men of your railroads, ten thousand a year or more,
> For the roasted men in your steel mills, and the starving men on your roads,
> For the miners buried by hundreds when the fire damp explodes,
> For our brothers maimed and slaughtered for your profits every day. . . .
> We hate you with hand, and heart, and head, and body, and mind, and brain.
> We hate at the forge, in the mine and mill, in the field of golden grain.
> We curse your name in the market place as the workman talks with his mate,
> And when you dine in your gay cafe the waiter spits on your plate.
> We hate you! Damn you! Hate you! We hate your rotten breed.[62]

In the bitter, bloody conflict that raged across the country, both sides made use of violence. Maintaining that nothing would be conceded except what the workers had power to take, the I.W.W. advocated militant tactics to force concessions from employers, resorting to dynamite, arson, and industrial sabotage to gain their ends. The Commission on Industrial Relations found that the workers' violence was "seldom, if ever, spontaneous," but arose from a conviction that "fundamental rights are denied and that peaceful methods of adjustment cannot be used."[63] In Colorado, for instance, the workers had secured an eight-hour statute in 1899. When it was declared unconstitutional by a biased state court, they pushed through an amendment to the state constitution in 1902 with overwhelming popular approval, only to have a powerful lobby of mine operators, smelter owners, and ranchers defeat all attempts to enact a new law. After eleven years of struggle, an eight-hour law was finally passed in 1913. But the coal companies refused to comply, and the miners went on strike. Some nine thousand strikers with their families and belongings moved from company camps down the canyons to set up tent colonies. At the first evidence of strike sentiment, the companies had imported armed men, fortified mining properties with rifle pits, machine guns and searchlights, and brought an armored automobile with a

SUCCESS
by O. E. CESARE

For our brothers maimed and slaughtered for your profits every
    day. . . .
We hate you with hand, and heart, and head, and body, and mind,

Twenty-one people were killed, including eleven children and two
women, when in 1914 troops called to protect Rockefeller mining
interests in Colorado machine-gunned and burned a tent colony of
striking miners at Ludlow. From *Harper's Weekly*, May 23, 1914.

mounted machine gun into the coal fields, making it plain that
their intention was to fight. In response, the strikers also armed,
and violence was inevitable. After several skirmishes, state troops
and mine guards surrounded a tent colony at Ludlow and opened
fire with rifles and machine guns. Twenty-one were killed, including eleven children and two women suffocated or burned to death
when their tents were set on fire. Open warfare followed, until the
U.S. Cavalry rode to the rescue of the employers. Only after the

strike was crushed and John D. Rockefeller, Jr., owner of the most powerful of the coal companies, had become the target of national indignation, were a few concessions made. After fifteen months of starvation, bloodshed, and death, the miners were granted their legal rights—and a company union.[64]

Though losing the industrial war, the Wobblies made their point. The I.W.W.'s free-speech fights, its bold tactics at Lawrence and Paterson, its courageous campaigns among farm, lumber and mine workers in the West aroused the nation and led to creation of the Commission on Industrial Relations, which was charged by Congress to discover the underlying causes of industrial strife. After five years of investigation, questioning hundreds of witnesses, and collecting about six and a half million words, the conclusion of the Commission was that all the great industrial disputes which had attracted the attention of the country over the last quarter century had been revolutions against industrial oppression. "The fundamental question for the Nation to decide," said Basil M. Manly, director of research and investigation, "is whether the workers shall have an effective means of adjusting their grievances, improving their condition, and securing their liberty . . . or whether they shall be driven by necessity and oppression to the extreme of revolt."[65]

Labor's revolution, however, was put off until the 1930's. Although the A.F. of L. pushed through some progressive labor legislation on child labor, hours and wages of women, factory and mine inspection, and workingman's compensation, enforcement of these laws was often lax. With America's entry into World War I and the consequent withdrawal of some four million men from civilian occupations into military service, organized labor gained a temporary strategic advantage. Because employers had to compete for labor, unions were allowed to organize, and other concessions formerly denied were now freely granted. Where before the war employer pressures had kept union membership down to about 5 to 8 per cent of the total labor force, in wartime the A.F. of L. increased its ranks from 2.25 million in 1916 to 4.5 million in 1920. Its victory proved illusory, however. At the war's end, the employers turned on organized labor with renewed ferocity, virtually annihilating the I.W.W. and eventually driving the A.F. of L. backward to a position well below its prewar strength.

The Coming Metropolis

The materialistic civilization which grew up in response to the capitalist revolution found its most spectacular manifestation in the city. Centralization of enterprise brought with it an equally remarkable concentration of the nation's population. Urbanization—the combining of independent towns and villages into one large city or metropolis—kept pace with the fantastic rate of business consolidation, and almost overnight America was transformed from a predominantly rural into an urban nation, a change so swift as to appear without precedent in the history of the world.

Between 1860 and 1910, cities sprouted up with miraculous rapidity all over the United States. While the rural population had barely doubled, the urban population multiplied nearly seven times. An almost epidemic farm-to-city migration of young people and a swelling influx of alien immigrants combined to more than double the population of Chicago in the single decade from 1880 to 1890. In 1907, there died a man who was the first white child born in Chicago, when it consisted of only five houses and a fort; in his lifetime of eighty-five years, it was pointed out, he had seen the city grow from less than one hundred people to a population of more than two million.

At the beginning of the twentieth century, the city of New York contained more people within its jurisdiction than the entire country under President Washington. In a hundred years' time it had become the second-largest city in the world and, in the magnitude of its undertakings, probably first. Only four states in the union equaled it in population, and even the federal government was conducted at less expense than the Empire City until the Civil War ushered in a new era of financing. The city's annual expenditures, it was proudly claimed, exceeded $108 million. London, with 40 per cent more population, spent only 70 per cent as much. The annual budget of the Japanese Empire was only $120 million, the

Turkish Empire a mere $80 million, as were those of Holland and Switzerland combined. Moreover, New York boasted an area of three hundred square miles, while London was only one hundred and eighteen, Paris thirty, and Berlin twenty-five.[66]

This rapid urbanization was not peculiar to the United States, but characterized industrial centers all over the world. Berlin and Vienna grew even more rapidly than New York and Philadelphia. Urban growth, the economist Richard T. Ely theorized, was not a matter of human choice but of industrial evolution. "Men have not, as a rule, left the country and gone to the city as an outcome of changes in their feelings and desires. Deep underlying industrial causes have driven us into centres which have become cities."[67]

If, as the social theorist Brooks Adams assumed, civilization was measurable in terms of social centralization brought about by technology, then the city was the highest development of civilization.[68] The city represented power. Chicago was described by the novelist Frank Norris as

> the Great Gray City, brooking no rival, [imposing] its dominion upon a reach of country larger than many a kingdom of the Old World. For thousands of miles beyond its confines was its influence felt. Out, far out, far away in the snow and shadow of northern Wisconsin forests, axes and saws bit the bark of century-old trees, stimulated by this city's driving energy. Just as far to the southward pick and drill leaped to the assault of veins of anthracite, moved by her central power. Her force turned the wheels of harvester and seeder a thousand miles distant in Iowa and Kansas. Her force spun the screws of . . . innumerable squadrons of lake steamers crowding the Sault Sainte Marie. For her and because of her all the Central States, all the Great Northwest, roared with traffic and industry; sawmills screamed; factories . . . clashed and flamed; cog gripped cog; beltings clasped the drums of mammoth wheels; and converters of forges belched into the clouded air their tempest breath of molten steel.[69]

The modern city had been shaped by apparently unimportant, trifling, and inconspicuous forces. Improvement of the elevator made the apartment house and the skyscraper practicable, thus contributing to a greater density of population in a given area. The trolley, the telephone and the bicycle, encouraged urban expansion by minimizing distance, thus adding five to fifteen miles to the radius of every large city. Already, it was said in 1895, the bicycle had done more toward the improvement of ordinary highways than all that had been done before since the days of Indian paths.[70] "Everything is bicycle," wrote Stephen Crane, commenting on the astonishing vogue. "All mankind is a-wheel," and "a person on nothing but legs feels like a strange animal." America, he told readers of the New York *Sun*, was about to enter an age of subways, bloomers, and bicycles.[71]

While small-town critics viewed the city with its strange new ways as a threat to fundamental American values, many city-dwellers accepted its inevitability and recognized its potential value. They realized that for economic reasons a large part of the work of the world must be done in cities, and that the people who did that work must live in cities. Though not blind to the evils of urban life, they perceived that with intelligent planning the city could become a better place in which to live. Outstanding among these optimists was the civic reformer Frederic C. Howe, who, despite current pessimism, looked to the city for a rebirth of democracy.° For while the city exhibited a hierarchical organization of industry, with class and mass distinctions, with great wealth close beside unprecedented poverty, it had also given birth to new political forces, increasingly hostile to the industrial regimen which had created it.

Certainly within the half century, American cities had vastly improved as places of human habitation. Fifty years before neither New York nor Boston had public water, very few others had either water or gas, and the horse-trolley had not yet been thought of. Since then there had been great improvements in physical comforts and sanitary matters, and for those with the means, almost everything that was best in life could be better had in the city than elsewhere. As the social snob Ward McAllister confirmed, the contrast between the two periods was striking. In the 1860's, "There were not more than one or two men in New York who spent, in living and entertaining, over sixty thousand dollars a year. There were not a half dozen *chefs* in private families in this city." [72] The city of the nineties, however, was vivacious, glittering and cosmopolitan, swarming with the expensive amenities that made life habitable for the smart set—liveried servants and famous *cordon bleu, filet de boeuf aux truffes et champignons,* champagne

---

° Frederic C. Howe, *The City—Hope of Democracy.* See p.

The contrast between the New York skyline in 1909 and the Chicago ghetto shows the spectacular possibilities and the sordid realities of life in a twentieth-century metropolis.

dinners and fabulous balls costing the man of fashion tens of thousands for a single evening's entertainment. Although the expatriate American author Henry James might dismiss the famous New York skyline as a "pin-cushion in profile" and a huge "fifty-floored conspiracy," [73] his stay-at-home compatriot Theodore Dreiser was excited by the spectacle of urban life. New York, he granted, wore a "cruel and mechanical look," but all in all it was for him the first city in the world—"first in force, unrivaled in individuality, richer and freer in its spirit than London or Paris." [74]

But along with the gains, there were also losses. The city had replaced simplicity, individual freedom and equality of fortune with complexity, dependence, poverty and misery; substituted the hotel, flat, tenement, boarding house and flop house for the home; replaced trees, gardens and open meadows with a maze of utility poles, filthy slums, grimy factories, and dark congested streets filled with the accumulated rubbish of technological progress: noise, dirt, smoke, and an all-pervasive ugliness. The "turmoil and squash" of Chicago overwhelmed the visiting British writer Rudyard Kipling, who offended its tender civic pride by refusing to recognize and the making of money" as progress.[75] But the awful price the city exacted was notoriously manifest in the fact that in the city the rich were richer, and the poor were poorer than elsewhere.

"Slum, semi-slum, and super-slum—to this has come the evolution of cities."[76] This mordant observation of Patrick Geddes seemed to apply with particular vengence to large American cities at the beginning of the twentieth century. Three-quarters of the people of New York City, it was estimated in 1890, lived in slums. On the lower East Side, the most densely populated spot in the world, housing of the poor was declared by an investigating commission to be so unclean and uncomfortable as to make home life almost impossible. "Tenement conditions in many instances have been found to be so bad as to be indescribable in print; vile privies and privy sinks; foul cellars full of rubbish, in many cases of garbage and decomposing fecal matter; dilapidated and dangerous stairs; plumbing pipes containing large holes emitting sewer gases throughout the houses; rooms so dark that one cannot see the people within them . . . the list might be added to indefinitely."[77] Here indeed was social dynamite, as Jane Addams, America's most distinguished social worker warned.[78]

To a native-born, white Anglo-Saxon Protestant caught in the clash of values between farm and city, individualism and collectivism, the past and the present, the city appeared an especial menace. In it, all the perils of civilization were concentrated and magnified. As civilization grew more complex and urbanized, and the individual more fractional and dependent, it became increasingly important that men should be dependable. A moral failure on the part of a farmer living out on a prairie made little difference to the world; but a moral failure on the part of an official of a large city bank might prostrate the business of the community and throw thousands out of employment. Increased responsibilities implied the need of firmer principles, but in the city, where relations were closest and most complicated, the two traditional sources of moral strength, the home and the church, were the weakest. Private homes were fast disappearing, and in the larger cities there were only half as many churches in proportion to the population in 1890 as there had been fifty years before.

Even more alarming, the city seemed to imperil the very quality of American life by attracting hordes of foreigners who concentrated there to a much greater degree than the native population. Unrestricted immigration—which had been supported by industrialists with no nobler motive than an abundant and cheap labor supply—now threatened to overwhelm free institutions by mere numbers. Gathered in clannish, poverty-stricken enclaves, thousands of the foreign-born fell easy prey to vice and crime. Not only was illiteracy three times as common among immigrants as among native citizens, but since most were uninstructed in American institutions, neither reading nor speaking English, they were incapable of forming individual judgments on public questions and were thus easily manipulated by saloonkeepers and political bosses. With all this in mind, the Congregational minister Josiah Strong expressed the fears of many rural people when he declared there was no greater danger to our civilization than the ignorant foreign riff-raff who fed the noxious growth of corruption in our "rabble-ruled" cities.°

Although the immigrant was made the scapegoat for the evils of the city, the ultimate source of most urban ills was the new business system which, in preempting the power of economic planning, had unwittingly and perhaps unwillingly taken over the larger function of social planning. But because business values placed the demands of profit before the needs of the community, it had been derelict in its social responsibilities: with the result that along with economic and technical benefits, the capitalist revolution also brought social evils. With the giant corporation had come monopoly power; with increased productivity, economic exploitation; with industrial efficiency, industrial warfare; with the metropolis, the super slum. It had destroyed the old civilization but had not yet proved the superiority of the new. "It will certainly be embarrassing," Miss Addams told her contemporaries, "to have our age written down triumphant in the matter of inventions . . . but defeated in that it lost its head over the achievement and forgot the men." [79]

° Josiah Strong, *The Modern City a Menace*. See p. 78.

Readings: The Capitalist Revolution

The Advantages of Consolidation

S. C. T. DODD (1836–1907) *A corporation lawyer, Dodd's reputation was founded upon his organization in 1882 of the Standard Oil Trust. Although in the 1870's he had fought the battles of the consumers and independents against the Rockefeller interests, he became general solicitor for Standard in 1881. A man of strict integrity, he refused to allow John D. Rockefeller to place to his credit for gradual payment a block of stock which eventually would have made him a multimillionaire. At his death, his estate totaled less than $300,000. He was a firm believer in federal incorporation of business companies and favored a constitutional amendment to that effect.*

To stop co-operation of individuals and aggregation of capital would be to arrest the wheels of progress—to stay the march of civilization—to decree immobility of intellect and degradation of humanity. You might as well endeavour to stay the formation of the clouds, the falling of the rains, or the flowing of the streams, as to attempt by any means or in any manner to prevent organization of industry, association of persons, and aggregation of capital to any extent that the ever-growing trade of the world may demand.

So far, you may say, I have been dealing in glittering generalities. I shall descend to particulars to show how capital through manufacture and commerce has benefited mankind. . . .

The last thirty years have witnessed a concentration of industry and a combination of capital never before dreamed of. It is the natural and inevitable result of steam, the railway and the telegraph. Distant places are brought closer together; business is not bounded by the lines of the town, the state or the nation. The world is the market, and business and capital in business must be as boundless as the trade. . . .

From "Aggregated Capital: Its History and Influence," *The Trust: Its Book*, James H. Bridge, ed. (New York: Doubleday, Page & Co., 1902), pp. 47–48, 51–53, 64–65, 68–71, 78–79.

In twenty separate branches of industry, in which concentration of business and aggregation of capital were most manifest, from 1860 to 1885, wages increased from $8.64 to $9.88 per week, while the purchasing power of wages in the products thus manufactured increased from 100 per cent to 150 per cent. In the industries in which special concentration took place the increase of purchasing power of wages has been far the greatest. In railway transportation it amounts to 142 per cent, in telegraph 283 per cent, in petroleum 900 per cent.

There is no mistaking the fact that concentration is the order of development; concentration of people in large cities, concentration of handicrafts in large factories, concentration of transportation in great railway systems. To successfully resist it we must banish steam and discharge electricity from human service. Man is made for co-operation. Savages unite only in war. Civilized people unite in work. The evolution of association is the evolution of civilization. Considering that this tendency is inevitable, is it wise to resist it? Is it not wise to consider carefully how it may more and more be made a power for good, and less and less a power for evil?

Contrast the countries where industries are concentrated, where capital is greatest, and machinery most effective, with those where larger partnerships and corporations are almost unknown, where industry is not organized and large aggregations of capital are not the rule. The condition of labor is always worst where capital is small. Business drifts in old ruts, cannot attempt new enterprises; manufacturing is done by hand or by defective machinery; products are dearer, wages lower, a greater number of laborers are idle, and their general condition much more deplorable.

The last quarter of a century has witnessed a concentration of business such as the world before never knew. What is the result? Has competition been destroyed? On the contrary, it was never so strong. Effort impels to effort—combination begets combination. New industries are built up—new markets are opened—new methods of manufacture are invented. It is the law of life. By each striving to get ahead, all make progress.

Have prices been increased? On the contrary, combination in business and low prices have ever gone hand in hand. Combination has never been so great as in the last twenty-five years and prices have never ruled so low.

Has the individual been crushed out? To some extent undoubtedly as a solitary individual. But he has found a larger sphere for his efforts through association with other individuals. No day has ever equalled today in business opportunities offered intelligent and industrious men. . . .

I know that there are persons in this audience who want to get up and "jaw back." They want to ask, why is it, if all you have said is true, that there are still thousands of poor, thousands out of employment? Why is it that the centres of commerce and of manufactures are also centres of pauperism and misery? Why is it that while the capitalist lives in his palace, workmen herd in slums and hovels? Has aggregated capital banished suffering and want? Has it given to every man a fair chance or even a hope in life?

I wish I could answer these questions satisfactorily. My object has been to show what capital has done and what it is capable of doing, not to claim that it can cure all the evils and inequalities of life. Neither do I claim that it has not left much undone. I assert that capital is a necessary factor in all the progress we have made, and that, just in proportion as capital is aggregated and business concentrated, more labour is demanded, greater wealth is produced, wages are increased and prices are diminished. . . .

The power given by aggregated capital may be abused. This no one can deny. Whatever is capable of good is capable of evil. Every force may be used for destruction as well as for production. Fire burns, water drowns, the air wrecks ships and cities, steam explodes, electricity kills. Shall we abolish these forces, or shall we control and utilize them? The powers of government, of law and of the church have been abused. Shall we therefore abolish government, law and church? . . .

Like other forces of industry, association and aggregated capital have done harm and are undoubtedly capable of abuse, but that man is blind to all that history has taught, and doubly blind to all that reason is capable of teaching, who claims that they therefore should be destroyed, or their power for good limited.

Trusts and Efficiency

LOUIS D. BRANDEIS (1856–1941) *A liberal jurist and presidential adviser, Brandeis was graduated from Harvard Law School (1878) and practiced in Boston until 1916 when he was appointed to the U.S. Supreme Court. Because of his advocacy of public causes, he was known as the "people's attorney," successfully fighting for their interests against the leading lawyers of the country who were mainly engaged in supporting the claims of corporations. An opponent of bigness in business or government, he urged upon President Wilson a policy of "regulated competition" as the middle road between corporate absolutism and totalitarianism.*

It may safely be asserted that in America there is no line of business in which all or most concerns or plants must be concentrated in order to attain the size of greatest efficiency. . . . For a unit of business may be too large to be efficient as well as too small. And in no American industry is monopoly an essential condition of the greatest efficiency.

The history of American trusts makes this clear. That history shows:

First. No conspicuous American trust owes its existence to the desire for increased efficiency. "Expected economies from combination" figure largely in promoters' prospectuses; but they have never been a compelling motive in the formation of any trust. On the contrary, the purpose of combining has often been to curb efficiency or even to preserve inefficiency, thus frustrating the natural law of survival of the fittest.

Second. No conspicuously profitable trust owes its profits largely to superior efficiency. Some trusts have been very efficient, as have some independent concerns; but conspicuous profits have been secured mainly through control of the market—through the power of monopoly to fix prices—through this exercise of the taxing power.

From *Collier's*, Sept. 14, 1912. Reprinted in *Business—A Profession* (Boston: Small, Maynard & Co., 1914), pp. 199, 200–07, 210–11, 214–17.

Third. No conspicuous trust has been efficient enough to maintain long, as against the independents, its proportion of the business of the country without continuing to buy up, from time to time, its successful competitors.

These three propositions are also true of most of the lesser trusts. If there is any exception, the explanation will doubtless be found in extraordinary ability on the part of the managers or unusual trade conditions.

And this further proposition may be added:

Fourth. Most of the trusts which did not secure monopolistic positions have failed to show marked success or efficiency, as compared with independent competing concerns.

THE MOTIVES FOR TRUST BUILDING

The first proposition is strikingly illustrated by the history of the Steel Trust. The main purpose in forming that trust was to eliminate from the steel business the most efficient manufacturer the world has ever known—Andrew Carnegie. The huge price paid for his company was merely the bribe required to induce him to refrain from exercising his extraordinary ability to make steel cheaply. Carnegie could make and sell steel several dollars a ton cheaper than any other concern. Because his competitors were unable to rise to his remarkable efficiency, his business career was killed; and the American people were deprived of his ability—his genius—to produce steel cheaply. As the Stanley Investigating Committee found, the acquisition of the Carnegie Company by the promoters of the Steel Trust was *"not the purchase of a mill, but the retirement of a man."*

That finding is amply sustained by the evidence.

The commissioner of the Steel Plate Association, Mr. Temple, testified:

> They had to buy the Carnegie Steel Company. Mr. Carnegie, with his then plant and his organization and his natural resources, was in a position where he could dominate the entire situation; and had the United States Steel Corporation not been formed about the time it

was—some ten years ago—the steel business not only of America but of the world today would be dominated by Andrew Carnegie.

George W. Perkins, himself a director of the Steel Trust, through whose firm (J. P. Morgan & Co.) the bribe to Carnegie was paid, confirms Temple's statement:

> The situation was very critical. If the Steel Corporation had not been organized, or something had not been done to correct a very serious condition at that time, in my judgment by this time Mr. Carnegie would have personally owned the major part of the steel industry of this country. . . .

And Herbert Knox Smith, Commissioner of Corporations, after elaborate investigation, declared:

> The conclusion is inevitable, therefore, that the price paid for the Carnegie Company was largely determined by fear on the part of the organizers of the Steel Corporation of the competition of that concern. Mr. Carnegie's name in the steel industry had been long synonymous with aggressive competition, and there can be little doubt that the huge price paid for the Carnegie concern was, in considerable measure, for the specific purpose of eliminating a troublesome competitor, and Mr. Carnegie in particular. This, it may be noted, was the interpretation generally placed upon the transaction in trade and financial circles at the time.

The price paid for the Carnegie Company, about April 1, 1901, was $492,006,160 in United States Steel Corporation securities —of the then market value of $447,416,640 in cash. The value of the actual assets of the Carnegie Company on December 31, 1899, as sworn to by Carnegie, had been only $75,610,104.06. The total assets of the concern on March 1, 1900, as shown by the balance sheet, were only $101,416,802.43. And Commissioner Herbert Knox Smith, making a very generous estimate of the net value of the tangible assets of the Carnegie Company on April 1, 1901, fixes it at only $197,563,000. The bribe paid to eliminate Carnegie's efficiency was thus at least $250,000,000. . . .

As Commissioner Herbert Knox Smith reported to the President:

> A steel war might have meant the sudden end of the extraordinary period of speculative activity and profit. On the other hand, an averting of this war, and the coalition of the various great consolidations, if successfully financed, would be a tremendous 'bull' argument. It would

afford its promoters an opportunity for enormous stock-market profits through the sale of securities.

So Carnegie was eliminated, and efficiency in steel making was sacrificed in the interest of Wall Street; the United States Steel Corporation was formed; and J. P. Morgan & Co. and their associates took for their services as promoters the additional sum of $62,500,000 in cash values.

THE SOURCES OF MOST PROFITS

The second proposition—that conspicuous trust profits are due mainly to monopoly control of the market—is supported by abundant evidence equally conclusive.

The Standard Oil Trust stood preëminent as an excessive profit taker.

When Commissioner Herbert Knox Smith made his report to President Roosevelt in 1907, the trust had for a generation controlled about 87 per cent of the oil business of America. It had throughout that period been managed by men of unusual ability. And yet Commissioner Smith reports:

> The conclusion is, therefore, irresistible that the real source of the Standard's power is not superior efficiency, but unfair and illegitimate practices. . . .
>
> Considering all the branches of the oil industry together, the difference in cost between the Standard and the independent concerns is not great. . . .
>
> It is true, that taken as a whole, the Standard Oil Company is a more efficient industrial machine than any one of its competitors. Nevertheless, careful estimates based upon data submitted by a number of independent concerns as to the cost of pipe-line transportation, refining, and distributing oil, as compared with the Standard's cost for these operations, indicate that the total difference in efficiency between the Standard and the independent concerns is not very great. . . .
>
> A comparison between the costs of the Standard and the costs of the present independent concerns, does not fully show the fallacy of the Standard's claim to have reduced prices by its superior efficiency. The present independent concerns are by no means so efficient as those which would have come into existence in the absence of the restraints imposed by the monopolistic and unfair methods of the Standard. Had the oil business continued to develop normally, it is practically certain

that there would have been in the United States today a limited number of large oil concerns, the efficiency of which would be considerably greater than that of the present independents.

BUYING COMPETITORS

The third proposition—that trusts are not efficient enough to hold their relative positions in the trade as compared with the independents without buying up successful competitors—is also supported by abundant evidence.

The Steel Trust furnishes a striking example of this. Corporation Commissioner Herbert Knox Smith, reporting on the operations of the Steel Trust for the ten years following its formation (1901–10), says:

> Notwithstanding the great additions made by the corporation to its properties from earnings, and the acquisition of several important competing concerns including the Tennessee Coal and Iron Company, its proportion of the business in nearly every important product, except pig iron and steel rails, is less than it was in 1901. . . .
>
> This table shows that, whereas the Steel Corporation in 1910 had fully maintained the share of the country's total production of pig iron it held in 1901, its proportion of the production of nearly all steel products had declined, and in most cases sharply declined. The only important exception was steel rails. . . .
>
> Taking the production of steel ingots and castings as a basis, it will be seen that the Steel Corporation's percentage of the total fell from 65.7 per cent in 1901 to 54.3 per cent in 1910. This figure, perhaps, is the best single criterion by which to judge the change in the corporation's position in the steel industry from a producing standpoint. . . . It should be noted that the decline in the production shown by this comparison of 1901 and 1910 percentages was practically continuous for most products throughout the entire period.

That was the condition in 1910. A year later the Steel Trust's proportion of the production of the country had fallen below fifty per cent.

It may be doubted whether steel rails would have been an "exception" to the steady decline in the Steel Corporation's proportion of the country's business had it not been for the steel–rail pool and the close community of interest between the Steel Corporation and the railroads. As the Stanley Committee finds:

Of the $18,417,132,238 invested in railways in the United States, the directors of the Steel Corporation have a voice in the directorates of or act as executive officers of railroad companies with a total capitalization and bonded indebtedness of $10,365,771,833. . . .

UNSUCCESSFUL TRUSTS

Of the truth of the fourth proposition, stated above—that most of the trusts which did not secure monopolistic positions have failed to show marked success or efficiency as compared with the independent competing concerns—every reader familiar with business must be able to supply evidence. Let him who doubts examine the stock quotations of long-established industrials and look particularly at the common stock which ordinarily represents the "expected economies" or "efficiency" of combination. . . .

Perhaps the most conspicuous industrial trust which was not able to secure control of the market is the International Mercantile Marine. That company had behind it the ability and resources of J. P. Morgan & Co., and their great influence with the railroads. It secured a working agreement with the Hamburg American, the North German Lloyd and other companies; but it could not secure control of the Atlantic trade, and in the seven years since its organization has not paid a dividend on its $100,000,000 of stock. Its common stands at $5\frac{1}{8}$, its preferred at $18\frac{7}{8}$, and they stood little better before the *Titanic* disaster. On the other hand, the $120,000,000 stock of the Pullman Company, which has like influence with the railroads but succeeded in securing a monopoly, stands at $170\frac{3}{4}$.

Efficient or inefficient, every company which controls the market is a "money-maker." No, the issue of "Competition versus Monopoly" cannot be distorted into the issue of "Small Concerns versus Large." The unit in business may, of course, be too small to be efficient, and the larger unit has been a common incident of monopoly. But a unit too small for efficiency is by no means a necessary incident of competition. And a unit *too large* to be efficient is no uncommon incident of monopoly. Man's work often outruns the capacity of the individual man; and no matter how good the organization, the capacity of an individual man usually determines the success or failure of a particular enterprise—not only financially to the owners but in service to the community. Organization can do much to make concerns more efficient. Organization can do much to make larger units possible and profitable. But the efficacy even of organization has its bounds. There is a point where the centrifugal force necessarily exceeds the centripetal.

The New Hamiltonianism

THEODORE ROOSEVELT (1858–1919)   *Theodore Roosevelt, the twenty-sixth president of the United States, was graduated from Harvard, read law briefly and engaged in historical writing. As Assistant Secretary of the Navy, he issued in advance the orders for Admiral Dewey to attack the Spanish fleet at Manila, then when war broke out he resigned and organized the "Rough Riders," becoming a popular hero for a vainglorious charge up a Cuban hill in which he lost a quarter of his men. His most notable achievements as president were the antitrust suit against the Northern Securities Co., his sponsorship of the conservation of natural resources and of food inspection, and his "taking" of the Panama Canal Zone by questionable means of Dollar Diplomacy.*

The suit against the Steel Trust by the Government has brought vividly before our people the need of reducing to order our chaotic Government policy as regards business. As President, in Messages to Congress I repeatedly called the attention of that body and of the public to the inadequacy of the Anti-Trust Law by itself to meet business conditions and secure justice to the people, and to the further fact that it might, if left unsupplemented by additional legislation, work mischief, with no compensating advantage; and I urged as strongly as I knew how that the policy followed with relation to railways in connection with the Interstate Commerce Law should be followed by the National Government as regards all great business concerns; and therefore that, as a first step, the

From "The Trusts, the People, and the Square Deal," *Outlook,* Nov. 18, 1911, pp. 649, 651–53, 655–56.

powers of the Bureau of Corporations should be greatly enlarged, or else that there should be created a Governmental board or commission, with powers somewhat similar to those of the Interstate Commerce Commission, but covering the whole field of interstate business, exclusive of transportation (which should, by law, be kept wholly separate from ordinary industrial business, all common ownership of the industry and the railway being forbidden). In the end I have always believed that it would also be necessary to give the National Government complete power over the organization and capitalization of all business concerns engaged in interstate commerce. . . .

The Anti-Trust Law cannot meet the whole situation, nor can any modification of the principle of the Anti-Trust Law avail to meet the whole situation. The fact is that many of the men who have called themselves Progressives, and who certainly believe that they are Progressives, represent in reality in this matter not progress at all but a kind of sincere rural toryism. These men believe that it is possible by strengthening the Anti-Trust Law to restore business to the competitive conditions of the middle of the last century. Any such effort is foredoomed to end in failure, and, if successful, would be mischievous to the last degree. Business cannot be successfully conducted in accordance with the practices and theories of sixty years ago unless we abolish steam, electricity, big cities, and, in short, not only all modern business and modern industrial conditions, but all the modern conditions of our civilization. The effort to restore competition as it was sixty years ago, and to trust for justice solely to this proposed restoration of competition, is just as foolish as if we should go back to the flintlocks of Washington's Continentals as a substitute for modern weapons of precision. The effort to prohibit all combinations, good or bad, is bound to fail, and ought to fail; when made, it merely means that some of the worst combinations are not checked and that honest business is checked. Our purpose should be, not to strangle business as an incident of strangling combinations, but to regulate big corporations in thoroughgoing and effective fashion, so as to help legitimate business as an incident to thoroughly and completely safeguarding the interests of the people as a whole. . . .

Nothing of importance is gained by breaking up a huge interstate and international industrial organization *which has not offended otherwise than by its size,* into a number of small concerns without any attempt to regulate the way in which those concerns as a whole shall do business. Nothing is gained by depriving the American Nation of good weapons wherewith to fight in the great field of international industrial competition. Those who would seek to restore the days of unlimited and uncontrolled competition, and who believe that a panacea for our industrial and economic ills is to be found in the mere breaking up of all big corporations, simply because they are big, are attempting not only the impossible, but what, if possible, would be undesirable. They are acting as we should act if we tried to dam the Mississippi, to stop its flow outright. The effort would be certain to result in failure and disaster; we would have attempted the impossible, and so would have achieved nothing, or worse than nothing. But by building levees along the Mississippi, not seeking to dam the stream, but to control it, we are able to achieve our object and to confer inestimable good in the course of so doing.

This Nation should definitely adopt the policy of attacking, not the mere fact of combination, but the evils and wrongdoing which so frequently accompany combination. The fact that a combination is very big is ample reason for exercising a close and jealous supervision over it, because its size renders it potent for mischief; but it should not be punished unless it actually does the mischief; it should merely be so supervised and controlled as to guarantee us, the people, against its doing mischief. We should not strive for a policy of unregulated competition and of the destruction of all big corporations, that is, of all the most efficient business industries in the land. Nor should we persevere in the hopeless experiment of trying to regulate these industries by means only of lawsuits, each lasting several years, and of uncertain result. We should enter upon a course of supervision, control, and regulation of these great corporations—a regulation which we should not fear, if necessary, to bring to the point of control of monopoly prices. . . .

But punishment should not be the only, or indeed the main, end in view. Our aim should be a policy of construction and not one of destruction. Our aim should not be to punish the men who have made a big corporation successful merely because they have made it big and successful, but to exercise such thoroughgoing supervision and control over them as to insure their business skill being exercised in the interest of the public and not against the public interest.

The New Jeffersonianism

WOODROW WILSON (1856–1924)   *Woodrow Wilson, the twenty-eighth president of the United States, graduated from Princeton and, after many years of teaching, became the first nonclerical president of that university. A scholarly, religious man with an evangelical sense of mission, he was put forward as a conservative Democrat over William Jennings Bryan and was elected president in 1912 as a result of a split in Republican ranks. Although intelligent and sincere, he was never an ardent social reformer. While his first administration was notable for tariff reform, the Federal Reserve Act, the Federal Trade Commission, and the Clayton Antitrust Act, his presidency was also distinguished by a brazen policy of Dollar Diplomacy, with the United States intervening in Latin American affairs on a scale never contemplated by Roosevelt or Taft.*

Gentlemen say, they have been saying for a long time, and, therefore, I assume that they believe, that trusts are inevitable. They don't say that big business is inevitable. They don't say merely that the elaboration of business upon a great co-operative scale is characteristic of our time and has come about by the natural operation of modern civilization. We would admit that. But they say that the particular kind of combinations that are now controlling our economic development came into existence naturally and were inevitable; and that, therefore, we have to accept them as unavoidable and administer our development through them. . . .

  I answer, nevertheless, that this attitude rests upon a confusion

From *The New Freedom* (New York: Doubleday, Page & Co., 1913), pp. 163–66, 172, 177–78, 180, 187–88. Reprinted by permission of the Estate of Edith Bohling Wilson.

of thought. Big business is no doubt to a large extent necessary and natural. The development of business upon a great scale, upon a great scale of co-operation, is inevitable, and, let me add, is probably desirable. But that is a very different matter from the development of trusts, because the trusts have not grown. They have been artificially created; they have been put together, not by natural processes, but by the will, the deliberate planning will, of men who were more powerful than their neighbors in the business world, and who wished to make their power secure against competition.

The trusts do not belong to the period of infant industries. They are not the products of the time, that old laborious time, when the great continent we live on was undeveloped, the young nation struggling to find itself and get upon its feet amidst older and more experienced competitors. They belong to a very recent and very sophisticated age, when men knew what they wanted and knew how to get it by the favor of the government.

Did you ever look into the way a trust was made? It is very natural, in one sense, in the same sense in which human greed is natural. If I haven't efficiency enough to beat my rivals, than the thing I am inclined to do is to get together with my rivals and say: "Don't let's cut each other's throats; let's combine and determine prices for ourselves; determine the output, and thereby determine the prices: and dominate and control the market. . . ."

I take my stand absolutely, where every progressive ought to take his stand, on the proposition that private monopoly is indefensible and intolerable. And there I will fight my battle. . . . What these gentlemen do not want is this: they do not want to be compelled to meet all comers on equal terms. I am perfectly willing that they should beat any competitor by fair means; but I know the foul means they have adopted, and I know that they can be stopped by law. . . .

I have been told by a great many men that the idea I have, that by restoring competition you can restore industrial freedom, is based upon a failure to observe the actual happenings of the last decades in this country; because, they say, it is just free competition that has made it possible for the big to crush the little.

I reply, it is not free competition that has done that; it is illicit competition. It is competition of the kind that the law ought to stop, and can stop—this crushing of the little man.

You know, of course, how the little man is crushed by the trusts. He gets a local market. The big concerns come in and undersell him in his local market, and that is the only market he has; if he cannot make a profit there, he is killed. They can make a profit all through the rest of the Union, while they are underselling him in his locality, and recouping themselves by what they can earn elsewhere. Thus their competitors can be put out of business, one by one, wherever they dare to show a head. Inasmuch as they rise up only one by one, these big concerns can see to it that new competitors never come into the larger field. . . .

That is the difference between a big business and a trust. A trust is an arrangement to get rid of competition, and a big business is a business that has survived competition by conquering in the field of intelligence and economy. A trust does not bring efficiency to the aid of business; it *buys efficiency out of business*. I am for big business, and I am against the trusts. . . .

The dominating danger in this land is not the existence of great individual combinations—that is dangerous enough in all conscience—but the combination of the combinations—of the railways, the manufacturing enterprises, the great mining projects, the great enterprises for the development of the natural water-powers of the country, threaded together in the personnel of a series of boards of directors into a "community of interest" more formidable than any conceivable single combination that dare appear in the open.

The organization of business has become more centralized, vastly more centralized, than the political organization of the country itself. Corporations have come to cover greater areas than states; have come to live under a greater variety of laws than the citizen himself, have excelled states in their budgets and loomed bigger than whole commonwealths in their influence over the lives and fortunes of entire communities of men. Centralized business has built up vast structures of organization and equipment which overtop all states and seem to have no match or competitor except the federal government itself.

What we have got to do—and it is a colossal task not to be

undertaken with a light head or without judgment—what we have got to do is to disentangle this colossal "community of interest." No matter how we may purpose dealing with a single combination in restraint of trade, you will agree with me in this, that no single, avowed, combination is big enough for the United States to be afraid of; but when all the combinations are combined and this final combination is not disclosed by any process of incorporation or law, but is merely an identity of personnel, or of interest, then there is something that even the government of the nation itself might come to fear—something for the law to pull apart, and gently, but firmly and persistently, dissect.

Goals of the American Labor Movement

SAMUEL GOMPERS (1850–1924)   *A well known labor leader, Gompers was born in a London tenement and from his earliest days was intimately acquainted with the problems of laboring people. Although an admirer of Marx, he never became a Socialist, but preferred to strike out on a more pragmatic course of his own. Always regarding "theorizers" and "intellectuals" as "industrially impossible," he founded the American Federation of Labor in 1886 on the practical basis of more wages, more leisure, more liberty. As its president for thirty-seven years, he pursued the less glamorous policy of industrial negotiation rather than political action, recognizing the weak position of labor and asking only for the same immunity from interference by courts and legislatures already granted to organized capital.*

The workers of the United States do not receive the full product of their labor. It is impossible for any one to say definitely what proportion the workers receive in payment for their labor, but due to the organized labor movement they have received and are

From an abstract of statements made before the United States Commission on Industrial Relations at its hearings in New York City, May 21–23, 1914, as published in the *American Federationist*, XXI (Aug., 1914), pp. 621–26, 629. Reprinted by permission of the American Federation of Labor.

receiving a larger share of the product of their labor than ever before in the history of modern industry. One of the functions of organized labor is to increase the share of the workers in the product of their labor. Organized labor makes constantly increasing demands upon society for rewards for the services which the workers give to society and without which civilized life would be impossible. The process of increasing the share is not always gradual, but it is continual. The organized labor movement has generally succeeded in forcing an increase in the proportion the workers receive of the general product.

The working people—and I prefer to say working people and to speak of them as really human beings—are prompted by the same desires, the same hopes of a better life as are all other people. They are not willing to wait for a better life until after they have shuffled off this mortal coil but they want improvements here and now. They want to make conditions better for their children so that they may be prepared to meet other and new problems of their time. The working people are pressing forward, making their demands and presenting their claims with whatever power they can exercise in a natural, normal manner to secure a larger and constantly increasing share of what they produce. They are working toward the highest and the best ideals of social justice. . . .

In improving conditions from day to day the organized labor movement has no "fixed program" for human progress. If you start out with a program everything must conform to it. With theorists, if facts do not conform to their theories, then so much the worse for the facts. Their declarations of theories and actions refuse to be hampered by facts. We do not set any particular standard, but work for the best possible conditions immediately obtainable for the workers. When they are obtained then we strive for better. . . .

The efforts of the American labor movement to secure a larger share of the income are directed against all who illegitimately stand between the workers and the attainment of a better life. This class includes all who have not made honest investment in honest enterprise. Employers, capitalists, stockholders, bondholders—the capitalist class generally—oppose the efforts of the workers in the A.F. of L. and in other organizations to obtain a larger share of the product. Very much of the opposition to the efforts of the working people to secure improved conditions has come from those who obtain what may be called an unearned share in the distribution. The beneficiaries of the present system of distribution desire to retain as much as possible of their present share or to increase that proportion. But an additional reason that leads to opposition is that there are employers who live in the twentieth century, yet who have the mental outlook of the sixteenth century in their attitude toward the working people, and who still imagine that they are "masters of all they survey." These employers think that any attempt upon the part of the working people to secure improvements in their condition is a spirit of rebellion that must be frowned down. But we organized workers have found that after we have had some contests with employers, whether we have won the battle or lost it, if we but maintain our organization there is less difficulty thereafter in reaching a joint agreement or a collective bargain involving improved conditions of the workers.

The stronger the organization of the workers the greater the likelihood of their securing concessions. These concessions are not altogether because of the strength shown by the employees, but result in part from the changed attitude of the employer. . . .

Because employers as a class are interested in maintaining or increasing their share of the general product and because workers are determined to demand a greater and ever greater share of this same general product the economic interests between these two are not harmonious. . . .

In the initial stages of the altered relations between workers and employers improvements are forced upon employers by collective bargains, strikes, and boycotts. Later there is a realization upon the part of the employers that it is more costly to enter into long strikes and lockouts than to concede conditions without interrupting the industry. As the vision and the understanding of the employer change, his attitude toward his workmen and the relation between employer and workers also change, so that the sentiments and views of employers are often in entire accord with those of the organizations of working people.

However, the gains made by the organized labor movement in this country have generally been wrung from the employing classes. What workingmen of America have obtained in improved conditions, higher wages, shorter hours of labor, was not handed to them on a silver platter. They have had to organize, they have had to show their teeth, they have had to strike, they have had to go hungry, and to make sacrifices in order to impress upon the employers their determination to be larger sharers in the products of labor. . . .

While the National Association of Manufacturers is absolutely hostile to the labor unions and everything they represent, yet it is not an association in which a labor leader is either accepted or tolerated. . . . The avowed purpose of the National Association of Manufacturers is active organization for warfare against organized labor. It has a severer purpose, which is to prevent organizations of working people from protecting themselves or their interests. . . .

The A.F. of L. has an independent policy, an independent political policy—a policy so independent politically that it is independent of the Socialist party too. It is concerned more about achievements than it is about the instrumentality for achievement. We have achieved through the American labor movement more real betterment for the working people than has been accomplished by any other labor movement in the world.

The Disadvantages of Labor Unionism

JOHN KIRBY, Jr. (1850–1925) *A wealthy manufacturer and stubborn foe of organized labor, John Kirby, Jr. insisted his midwestern factories be run on the "open shop" or non-union plan. To counter the growing power of unions, he helped organize the Citizens' Industrial Association of America in 1904 and was a member of its executive committee until its union with the National Council of Industrial Defense, of which he was chairman from 1910 until his death. Under his aggressive leadership as president of the National Association of Manufacturers 1909–13, that organization became the outstanding labor-busting force in the country.*

The disadvantages of labor unionism may be summed up as follows:

That it puts a premium on indolence.

That it encourages its members to wage an unlawful and merciless warfare against their fellow laborers who disagree with them.

That in their demands upon and dealings with employers they ignore the spirit as well as the letter of fair dealing as between man and man.

That their demands are not limited to such as would be recognized as fair and proper in ordinary business life.

That they advocate and practice a policy of limiting output to a degree entirely inconsistent with the pay demanded, always to the detriment of the public.

That labor unionism deprives our American boys of the opportunity to learn trades and thus erects a barrier to their following the occupations of their choice and adoption, creates a scarcity of skilled mechanics and thereby restrains and limits our industrial resources, besides contributing to the undesirable class of citizens known as loafers and tramps.

That it seeks to establish a class line between labor and capital

From an address made before the Young Men's Hebrew Association, New York City, Nov. 7, 1909. *N.A.M. Pamphlet No. 2*, pp. 35–37.

by adopting policies and pursuing methods which tend to destroy ambition, handicap energy and inspire men to become good union men rather than honorable, thrifty and well-to-do citizens.

That it adopts methods of intimidation, coercion and even murder as means for accomplishing its purposes.

That it persistently and incessantly urges and demands legislation which if enacted into law would remove all legal barriers to their unholy and cowardly boycotts, as well as to their brutal and property-destroying practices; legislation which would be favorable to labor unionists as a class and injurious to all other classes of citizens.

That it resorts to unfair, dishonorable and cruel methods to deprive non-unionists of their right to earn an honest living, and to thus compel them to become unionists or suffer themselves, and those dependent upon them for support, to starve.

That it constitutes a trust of the most vicious and dangerous type which, if permitted to progress to its logical culmination, would result in incalculable injury and annoyance to all citizens themselves included.

That it is an irresponsible organization with which, in many cases, contracts cannot be entered into with confidence that their provisions will be recognized as sacred obligations to be fulfilled.

That it impedes and discourages personal advancement through personal effort.

That it is an avenue for graft and illegal and wrongful "deals" between the walking delegate of the unions and unscrupulous employers.

That it is a hindrance to the upbuilding of character tending to promote the betterment of mankind and develop good citizenship.

That the attitude of the officers of the American Federation of Labor towards the courts finds its justification in the creeds of socialism and anarchy and the example of these men, whatever their pretenses may be, to the lawlessly inclined element of society is to encourage men to defy law and commit crimes.

That the aim of unionism is to control things which it has no right to control, and that such control as it has secured has been attained through fear of violence, boycott or destruction of property, and is therefore the domination of force.

The aim of this government, to protect its citizens against forcible control against their desires, is set at defiance by the action of the American Federation of Labor and its allied unions in seeking, by force and other unlawful methods, to monopolize the labor market. This is purely hostile to the government itself, and therefore a menace to governmental institutions.

That from every angle from which this question can be viewed, labor unionism of the Gompers–Mitchell type is uneconomic in principle, decidedly adverse to public policy and therefore a menace to society.

The City—Hope of Democracy

FREDERIC C. HOWE (1867–1940) *A liberal lawyer and civic reformer, Howe as a young man set his heart on becoming a journalist, but during the hard times of 1892–93, was unable to find a job and turned to the law. As a successful lawyer, he was active in public affairs and came under the influence of Cleveland's great reform mayor, Tom. L. Johnson, who pressed him into the cause of municipal reform. He made himself an expert on municipal problems by studying cities here and in Europe, conceiving of civic revival as a dynamic experiment to improve the citizen economically, culturally, and morally by intelligent planning of the environment.*

The modern city marks an epoch in our civilization. Through it, a new society has been created. Life in all its relations has been altered. A new civilization has been born, a civilization whose identity with the past is one of historical continuity only.

We but dimly appreciate the full import of this fact. And yet, it is more significant, possibly more pregnant for the future than any previous political or social change. "Revolutionary" is an expression so loosely used that it scarce impresses us. But the modern city marks a revolution—a revolution in industry, politics,

From *The City, The Hope of Democracy* (New York: Charles Scribner's Sons, 1905), pp. 9–10, 21–22, 24–31.

society, and life itself. Its coming has destroyed a rural society, whose making has occupied mankind since the fall of Rome. It has erased many of our most laborious achievements and turned to scrap many of our established ideas. Man has entered on an urban age. He has become a communal being. The increasing pressure of population is fast filling up the waste places of the globe. This, of itself, forecasts the life of the future. And in consequence, the city will no longer be an incidental problem. It has already become the problem of society and the measure of our civilization. . . .

The nineteenth century has unloosed the genii of industrialism, and we cannot go back to the simple agricultural conditions of an earlier age. They are as closed to us as is the patriarchal one of simple nomadism. The city has become the central feature in modern civilization, and to an ever increasing extent the dominant one. Never before outside of China, with the possible exceptions of ancient Rome and Babylon, has society been organized on such a basis, and the earlier type of city, it need hardly be said, offers little in common with the modern "abyss," which, like a whirlpool, draws to its vortex the good and the bad, the strong and the weak, and which, in some form or other, is the final form of organized political life. For formerly the town was an ecclesiastical, feudal guild, or commercial affair. Its trade was carried on through the agency of the fair. Politically, more democratic than feudalism, it was still a close corporation. Socially, it was aristocratic. Its gates were barred to the stranger. The octroi was a barrier to prevent intercourse.

And this rural civilization, whose making has engaged mankind since the dawn of history, is passing away. The modern city has erased the landmarks of an earlier society. Man has entered on an urban age, the final stage of his development. The past is as closed to us as are the barbed enclosures of the occupied West to the dispossessed Red Man. Nature has been harnessed, the earth has been tapped, the dormant energy of the earth's resources has been subjugated, and mankind has become bound together by millions of Lilliputian bands drawing mankind into an intimate relationship, a common dependency, from which there is no escape and no return possible to the early life of domestic industry, personal independence, and political simplicity. We have tasted the wine of many wants; our life has become one of divided powers and responsibilities, and society has developed into an organism like the human body, of which the city is the head, heart, and centre of the nervous system. . . .

This *bouleversement* of society, this change from the country to the city, from individualism to communalism, from the self-sufficient household to the self-sufficient city; this shifting of the centre of life from the individual to the many, from isolation and independence to unity and dependence, has been accompanied by gains and losses to society. The city has woven our lives into the lives of others. No longer is each household an independent one, producing for its own wants alone and supplied from within. The texture of the fabric has been altered. It is now closely woven. And this change is far more than an industrial one—a mere adjustment of mankind to his work. It is but part of man's desire for a larger life, for freer social intercourse, for amusement, as well as a response to the industrial revolution which has superseded domestic industry by the machine.

Within the city the game of life is played, and there are many capital prizes. Here, opportunity and fortune are to be found. Here business centres. Here life is full and human. The farm offers none of these things. It is barren of great possibilities, barren, even, of a living, the farmer says. The city is El Dorado, the promised land which fires the imagination. Failure may come, it is true, but there is the chance, and life, movement, and recreation even in failure. The saloon is something, while the streets, the parks, the theatre, the church, one's fellows, all make up the canvas of life even to the poorest.

And the city has given the world culture, enlightenment, and education along with industry and commercial opportunity. The advance in recent years in this regard has been tremendous. Compare our London, Paris, Berlin, or New York with these cities fifty years ago. Then, life in any large sense was limited to a few. Today, to an ever increasing mass of the population, opportunities are crowding one upon another. Not only is education generously adapted to the needs of all, but night schools, art exhibitions, popular lectures and concerts, college settlements, the parks, playgrounds, a cheap press, labor organizations, the church, all these are bringing enlightenment at a pace never before dreamed of. Day by day opportunities gain in volume. A decade almost encompasses the history of such movements for democratic opportunity.

All this is enlarging life, modifying our civilization, deepening the significance of democracy. It is rendering possible a higher standard of living. A new conception of municipal purpose has come in. It is neither conscious nor defined as yet, but in the midst of the outward manifestations of municipal activity, an unrecognized broadening of the culture and life of the city is going on, of immense significance to the future.

Much of this is being expressed through private channels. But that the private activities of today will become the public ones of tomorrow is inevitable. The crèche, kindergarten, settlement, playgrounds, public baths, lodging houses, hospitals were inspired by private philanthropy. They are slowly passing under public control. Merely to enumerate what has been done during the past few years in the matter of school administration would form a chapter in itself. The same is true of the care of juvenile offenders. It is manifest in every department of city affairs. The possibility of life is increasing more rapidly than at any other period in the history of the world. It is less than a decade since Josiah Quincy, while mayor of Boston, proposed the erection of public baths and gymnasiums and the opening of playgrounds in the poorer sections of the city. When made, the suggestion was assailed as socialistic. Today, without protest, the City of Boston expends $500,000 annually for parks and playgrounds and over $100,000 annually for baths and gymnasiums. Over $3,000,000 has been expended for these purposes in a few years' time. There are now twenty-one playgrounds in the city; while summer camps, public concerts, bathing beaches, and public lavatories have still further added to the comfort of the poor. During this interval, appropriations for these purposes have crept into the budgets of nearly all of our large cities, while kindergartens, summer schools, manual training, free lectures, and public concerts are rapidly finding a place in city administration along with the expenditures for police, fire, and health protection.

But such a schedule of items is but a small part of the gain which civilization has made through the city. They are but evidences of the fact that life has become a social, not an isolated thing. The entire groundwork of society is being relaid under a system of closer political relationship. But a few generations ago, civilization was based on individualistic lines. The city has brought us whatever sense of social responsibility we now have. In a sense all this is socialism. We do not call it that. But neither does the German nor the Englishman call the undertakings of his city socialistic.

The humanizing forces of today are almost all proceeding from the city. They are creating a new moral sense, a new conception of the obligations of political life, obligations which, in earlier conditions of society, did not and could not exist. Step by step individual rights have been merged into larger social ones. And it is this very increase in public activities that renders the city as attractive to the rich as it is to the poor. In earlier days, even the most elementary public functions were performed by the individual. He paved, cleaned, and lighted the street before his door. He was his own constable. Such health protection as he enjoyed was the result of his own vigilance. Education was conducted at home or by the church. The library was a priestly possession, as was all learning. His house was his castle, even in the midst of the city, and society offered him little save the administration of justice and protection from foreign foes.

Today the city protects his life and his property from injury. It safeguards his health in countless ways. It oversees his house construction, and protects him from fire. It cleans and lights his streets, collects his garbage, supplies him with employees through free employment bureaus. It educates his children, supplies them with books, and in many instances with food. It offers him a library, and through the opening of branches almost brings it to his door. It offers nature in the parks; supplies him with opportunities for recreation and pleasure through concerts, lectures, and the like. It maintains a public market; administers justice; supplies nurses, physicians, and hospital service, as well as a cemetery for burial. It takes the refuse from his door and brings back water, gas, and frequently heat and power at the same time. It inspects his food, protects his life, and that of his children through public oversight of the conditions of factory labor. It safeguards him from contagious diseases, facilitates communication upon the streets, and in some instances offers opportunities for higher technical and professional education.

All these intrusions into the field of private business have involved no loss of freedom to the individual. Every increase of public activity has, in fact, added to personal freedom. Whatever the motive, the real liberty of the individual has been immeasurably enlarged through the assumption of these activities by the city. . . .

Such are some of the palpable gains which the city has brought. But the real gain is far more than an enumeration of services or a schedule of activities. The real significance of it all is found in the fact that democracy has been forced into activities which have heretofore lain outside of the sphere of government. The relationships of society are changing. We are being drawn into an intimacy, a solidarity, which makes the welfare of one the welfare of all. A finer spirit is being born. The city is being socialized. It is coming to feel the cruelty of nature's laws and to alleviate their poignancy. The hospitals, parks, kindergartens, playgrounds, and reform schools were the first expression of this feeling. The movement has since changed in character. Its motives are justice, rather than philanthropy, and it is expressing itself in a demand for reform in our methods of taxation, the solution of the housing problem, in a desire for cheaper water, transportation, and light.

What the lines of future activity will be, we can only conjecture. Measured by what has been done in the past ten years, the change will be tremendous. For, once organized, modern democracy moves with increasing momentum. We may call it socialism if we will. This will scarce check its advance. And when these newer services come, their arrival will be welcomed by all classes just as were the public schools, libraries, parks, and water works, the police, fire, and health departments, whose control by the city has increased the happiness and safety of city life to all.

The Modern City a Menace

JOSIAH STRONG (1847–1916)   *A clergyman and social reformer,
Josiah Strong became a national figure with the publication in
1885 of his book* Our Country, *a powerful expression of the fears
and aspirations of white Anglo-Saxon America. After its success
he devoted all his energies to seeking practical solutions of urban
problems. As a Calvinist, he viewed world history and the rise
of the city as the progressive revelation of God's will. Not only
did he believe God's design had decreed the superiority of the
Anglo-Saxon race, but he was convinced that if America failed,
the world would fail.*

. . . Look, first, at the demand which the twentieth century city
will make on a higher intelligence. The development of mechanical
power, which created modern civilization, took place chiefly in
the city. It is not strange, therefore, that wealth has increased much
more rapidly in the city than in the country, as we have already
seen. Wealth, of course, is power, and the rapid increase and
concentration of it creates many and difficult problems, particularly
in a democracy whose institutions were framed with special refer-
ence to preventing the concentration or long retention of power.
These problems, therefore, are at the same time most urgent and
most perplexing in the city, where wealth is being massed; and
it is there that the highest order of intelligence is needed for their
solution. . . .

The problems of government increase with the increase in population. As cities become more populous, relations whose harmony
must be preserved increase in number and complexity. A mistake
is further reaching; it has a longer leverage; and as efficient government grows more essential it becomes increasingly difficult. To
administer the affairs of a village of 1,000 inhabitants is a simple
matter, requiring only ordinary intelligence; the government of
a city of 100,000 is much more complicated; while that of a city
of 1,000,000 or of 5,000,000 demands expert knowledge, ability,
and character of the very highest order.

From *The Challenge of the City* (New York: Eaton & Mains, 1907), pp. 41–55,
63–68.

Our political development in the United States has been along national and state lines rather than municipal. The principles of the state and national governments are well settled and clearly defined, but those of municipal organization and government are confused and uncertain. We are as yet in the experimental stage, and need the insight and genius of the highest statesmanship to solve the new and complex problems of the city, which are the problems of the new civilization. Among them are those created by the industrial revolution which has taken place during the nineteenth century—such as adjusting an aristocratic system of industry to a democratic system of government.

If upon these and other municipal problems we should bring to bear the wisdom of the fathers who framed the constitution, not a scrap of it would be wasted. It does not seem to me extravagant to say that higher intellectual qualities are required to solve these problems than to administer successfully the office of the nation's chief executive.

Does any one imagine that we are meeting these high demands? As our cities grow larger are we calling to office larger-minded men, capable of grappling with these profound problems? As a general rule, the larger our cities the worse and more incompetent is their government. We are permitting the most ignorant classes to control them. . . .

The character of the men who usually get control of our largest cities, such as New York, Philadelphia, and Chicago, together with the corruption which has been laid open in recent years, indicates that the moral development of the city has by no means kept pace with its material growth. . . .

The city, in a position to dictate to state and nation, and yet incapable of self-government, is like Nero on the throne. As the city, by virtue of its preponderating population, is soon to ascend the throne, it is well to glance at some of the powers which are reaching after the city's scepter.

As the saloon sustains important relations to the law, it desires to control both those who make the laws and those whose duty it is to enforce them. It has already become a political institution of power. Politicians are careful not to antagonize it. Its political support or opposition is apt to be decisive. . . . An astute politician in New York, reputed to be a total abstainer and a Church member, said he would rather have the support of the saloons than that of the churches. . . .

Again, another fact which must be faced is that our foreign population is largely concentrated in the city.

We do not forget our indebtedness to the immigrants. They have borne the brunt of the toil and hardship in subduing the continent and in developing its resources. They shared the sacrifice to save the Union. . . . But we must not be blind to the fact that in several ways the foreign population puts a great strain on our institutions. Many are naturalized without being Americanized, which means ignorant power; and that is always dangerous. . . .

When we consider that the quality of immigration is growing less desirable, it is not reassuring to reflect that Europe could send us an unceasing stream of 3,000,000 every year—as many as our entire population in twenty-eight years or 300,000,000 in a century. . . . Judging the future by the past, it is improbable that any legislation will dam this stream. Our population will continue to swell by this foreign flood, and whatever strain it puts on American institutions, that strain is more than three times as great in our large cities as in the whole country. In 1890, of the male population in our eighteen largest cities . . . those who were foreign by birth or parentage numbered . . . more than two and a half times as many as the native American stock. This proportion has been largely increased by the immigration of the last sixteen years.

These elements, as they come to us, are clay in the hands of the political potter. If they remain uninstructed as to good citizenship, and incapable of forming individual judgments concerning public questions, the boss will certainly rule the city when the city rules the nation.

Wendell Phillips once said: "The time will come when our cities will strain our institutions as slavery never did." That day is drawing near; and our probation of one generation is none too long in which to meet the peril of the materialistic city by building it up in intelligence and character.

Chapter II

The Capitalist Ethic

The American Promise

A disenchantment, profound and disturbing, struck millions of Americans whose dreams of a better future were shattered by the disruptive impact of the capitalist revolution. The promise which had loomed so large in their patriotic outlook was, as Herbert Croly phrased it, "comfort and prosperity for an ever increasing majority of good Americans." [1] Although from the beginning the national ideal had been thoroughly worldly, it had carried always the added implication that by virtue of a more abundant life Americans would arrive at a better society and become in general worthier men. But, with the coming of the turbulent nineties, it became apparent that materially and morally the American promise was failing to bear its expected fruits.

Daily disenchanted Americans read of the sins and follies of the malefactors of great wealth, of spreading class conflict, and of sullen hosts of unemployed. Popular magazines played up sensational accounts of vast, boss-ridden cities and wretched slums rampant with vice, crime and insanity. Caught in a furious flood of energy that spewed out indifferently riches and pauperism, luxury and deprivation, Americans were beginning to realize that blind material progress could become a tyrannical master. A despotic, inhuman, mechanical force seemed to have taken charge of their fate, speeding up their lives, driving them in a headlong rush toward unknown destinations, jerking them up in elevators and pouring them down into subways. Thrust into shoving elbowing crowds, imprisoned in noisy factories, shut in dark tenements, they were all the while endlessly exhorted to buy this and that. Yet, as they were ruefully aware, there was no turning back. America was already pledged to the capitalist system with its ruthless mechanical consolidation of force. The only question left, as Henry Adams said, was in whose interest so complex and so powerful a machine should be run.[2]

The accepted answer, of course, was that the nation was built on business, and if it were to run at all, it had to be run by businessmen on business principles. According to this artless persuasion, what was good for business was good for the country. Business was glorified by its partisans as "the American philosophy," and the zealous publicist Elbert Hubbard went so far as to proclaim business a "science" and the businessman "our only scientist."[3] To him from whom all blessings flowed Americans must look—and wait—for an applied science of economics that would eradicate poverty, disease, crime and all other ills that plagued society.

Without doubt the most beneficial result of business determination of the popular welfare was the marked improvement in the mechanism of production. In the substitution of machines for human labor and in the minuteness and perfection of the division of labor, American industry led the world. Its productive efficiency was affirmed by census statistics which showed that between 1850 and 1910 the value of manufactured products increased twentyfold. Steel production alone jumped 150 per cent in the first decade of the new century. The great technological innovations that accompanied the development of electricity, the internal-combustion engine, and industrial chemistry had their beginnings in these years, and after 1897 were to be employed on a grand scale by the automobile industry. In a magazine advertisement of 1906, Henry Ford was already boasting of his company's mastery of the technique of mass production:

> We are making 40,000 cylinders, 10,000 engines, 40,000 wheels, 20,000 axles, 10,000 bodies, 10,000 of every part that goes into the car—think of it! For this car we buy 40,000 spark plugs, 10,000 spark coils, 40,000 tires, all *exactly alike*.[4]

Along with "flivvers," the unremitting requirements of the machine process gave rise to a new doctrine of efficiency—scientific man-

An Assembly Line
of the
Ford Motor Company

The Ford factory in 1914 symbolized for many people the promise
of American life. Not only had Henry Ford become the popular hero
of mass production, his assembly lines flooding the highways with
a half million almost identical cars, but the automobile manufacturer
startled the nation by announcing that as "a plain act of social
justice" he would thenceforth pay his workers a minimum wage of
$5 a day.   Culver Pictures, Inc.

agement. In practical application, scientific management was
simply a technique for achieving maximum industrial productivity
through the most efficient use of both machines and men. Instead of relying on inefficient rule-of-thumb methods, it applied
scientific study and analysis to discovering the one best method.
A famous and often quoted example of its successful application
was the speed-up in handling pig iron at Bethlehem Steel in
1898. This crude work was done by men with no other implements than their hands. The pig-iron handler stooped down,
picked up a bar or "pig" weighing about 92 pounds walked a
few feet, then dropped it on a pile. As the efficiency expert
remarked, the work was so crude and elementary that "it would
be possible to train an intelligent gorilla . . . to become a more
efficient pig-iron handler than any man can be." Yet there was
sufficient "science" in the handling of pig iron to enable the
efficiency expert, by eliminating waste motion, to raise the

amount handled per man per day from 12.5 to 47 tons.[5]

Because of such sensational successes in industry, scientific management by 1912 had gained wide popular acceptance in the United States. Its matter-of-fact principles inspired fulsome praise in popular magazines, and its immediate application was enthusiastically advocated as the universal remedy for nearly every problem of society. Technology was contagious, and—as Veblen foretold—the viewpoint of the industrial assembly line with its canons of technical efficiency and mechanical standardization must eventually pervade all modern human activities.

As a social ideal, scientific management proclaimed the practical superiority of method over belief. Since man was the chief source of error in a technical system, efficiency called for the elimination of all human variability. As its expounder, Frederick Winslow Taylor, expertly put it: "In the past the man has been first; in the future the system must be first." [*] Regarding the methods of scientific management as "an evolution representing survival of the fittest," the efficiency expert asserted that everything, including man, must be subordinated to method: "One of the very first requirements for a man who is fit to handle pig iron as a regular occupation is that he shall be so stupid and phlegmatic that he more nearly resembles the ox than any other type." [6] According to Taylor, the principal profit from the standardization of parts and processes, both human and machine, went to the world at large in the form of doubled productivity of the necessities and luxuries of life. Greater prosperity followed higher wages and higher profits, and a speed-up in the civilization process brought about by shorter hours of work allowed increased opportunity for education, culture and recreation. Just where the pig-iron handler or trained gorilla was to be dropped off this conveyor-belt to utopia, Taylor never specified. Nor did this oversight disturb his zealous disciples, who never faltered in their determination to apply the truths of scientific management to all human activity.

Enthusiasts prescribed the "efficiency" methods of the factory for individuals, homes, schools and colleges, and even urged the application of business methods to politics and religion. Theodore Roosevelt was held up by William James as an excellent example

---

[*] Frederick Winslow Taylor, *Scientific Management.* See p. 108.

of the "energizer" who utilized his personal powers to the hilt,[7] and Walter Lippmann joined in with a call for "more brains, less sweat."[8] Not only were politicians severely admonished for not running the nation efficiently at "higher pressure," but the Presbyterian clergy was criticized for its shocking waste of time and energy and warned that all this must cease if the church was not to fall behind the times. Education, too, was called upon to join the march forward, for at colleges and universities the efficiency expert found much to distress a systematic mind. He was appalled to find, for instance, that Harvard was managed along lines almost a century old, that gardners refrained from work about college grounds until professors began to lecture, and that lecture rooms were never fully in use or used fully only part of the time, causing an appalling waste computed on the "student-per-foot-per-hour" standard. Professors served on too many committees; the elective system was capricious; students loitered on the way to class.[9] Measured by business standards, the institutions of higher education were not the learning factories they should be.

But, as some observers protested, what was economically efficient was not necessarily socially efficient. Sociologist E. A. Ross declared, "Those who are business men—and nothing more—slip easily into the fallacy of rating well-being by dollar-income. What this type of man most longs for is not *welfare*, but *prosperity*. The wealth he habitually considers is bankable wealth. Values that are not pecuniary values strike him as moonshine." Because of this "business fallacy," American society placed no restrictions on the activities of the businessman. "If his refinery taints the air, if his chimneys smut the sky, if his waste poisons our streams, we tolerate it."[10] It was notorious beyond dispute that there were business profits that cost a hundred times their worth in noneconomic values, in the sacrifice of beauty and quiet, the waste of life and limb, the exploitation of men, women, and children.

Despite its hold on the popular imagination and regardless of many absurd or unfounded claims made on its behalf, the new doctrine of scientific management almost always favored management over the worker. As the U.S. Commission on Industrial Relations noted, its aim was laudable, but practice fell far short of the ideal. Too often "scientific management" meant only getting more work out of the laborer.[11] Imbedded in the scheme were bonus and piece systems, together with methods of contracting and fining which had long been fought by unionists. Organized labor, Gompers told the A.F. of L. convention in 1911, did not welcome "the spectacle of steel works where, under an inspector, stop watch in hand, one man is carrying five tons of pig-iron where he formerly carried three, or of a bicycle shop where one girl does the work formerly done by three, when she is not carried out fainting, or where in a textile mill a girl is paid for the ordinary day's work after she has striven and strained and almost completed the allotted bonus task of doing two days' work in one." [12] Although scientific management claimed to be the workers' best protection, it failed generally to protect them from overexertion, exhaustion, and industrial accident. The price of our industrial supremacy, *Everybody's* reported in 1907, was a half million men, women and children killed and maimed. Said the magazine: "When a nation has more railroads, greater mines, taller buildings, than any other nation, and is running its trains faster, operating its mines more extensively, and erecting its buildings at a higher rate of speed than any other . . . dares attempt—and incidentally cares little about the lives of its toilers—that is about the slaughter record you may expect."[13]

While acknowledging the businessman as a part-time benefactor, these Progressive critics were also aware that the greatest obstacle to social efficiency was the short-sighted moneymaker who, acting collectively in a plutocracy, imposed his narrow interpretation of welfare on industry, politics and public opinion. If this nation were to approach the task of satisfying human demands with the least friction and the least waste, contended the radical democrat Walter Weyl, Americans must free themselves from the single standard of the dollar mark and substitute a "higher form of efficiency" which would place new insistence upon human life and human happiness.° "What is attainable by the majority—life, health, leisure, a share in our natural resources, a dignified existence in society—is contended for by the majority against the opposition of men who hold exorbitant claims upon the continent." The spirit of the new democracy, Weyl maintained, was not unalienable

---
° Walter E. Weyl, *Social Efficiency*. See p. 111.

rights negatively and individualistically interpreted, but those same rights, "life, liberty, and the pursuit of happiness," extended and given a social interpretation.[14]

This point of view broke radically with the individualistic democracy of Jefferson and Jackson, and was an attempt to find a middle-road between laissez-faire liberalism and Marxian socialism. Like most Progressives, Weyl was disenchanted with the old individualism that had justified the monopolist and the sweat shop and deluded Americans into seeing equality and democracy where exploitation and despotism actually ruled. Unlike most Progressives, however, Weyl pronounced the old Jeffersonian democracy "done for." At every point he saw social development blocked by ancient social ideals which still cumbered modern brains. The revered rights of the founding fathers might prevail against political despotism, but they had proven powerless against economic despotism. "The right of habeas corpus, the right to bear arms, the rights of free speech and free press could not secure a job to the gray-haired citizen, could not protect him against low wages or high prices, could not save him from a jail sentence for the crime of having no visible means of support."[15]

The only democracy possible in modern America, Weyl argued—and New Dealers twenty years later sought to prove—was a socialized democracy involving common action and a common lot. Social efficiency demanded a consolidation of American society to match its economic centralization. As apprehensive Progressives perhaps innately realized, however, the new democracy advocated by radical liberals called for a revolution comparable in force and extent to that which had given rise to the new capitalism. But the Progressives were not ready for revolution, not yet prepared to honor a new ethic emphasizing social rather than private interest, collective rather than individual responsibility.

Rich and Poor

For all their reluctance to break with cherished principles, the Progressives were forced to acknowledge that the individual in freely and energetically pursuing his own private gain had not proven to be the inevitable public benefactor Adam Smith had presumed. Concession was made in the Progressive Party Platform of 1912, which stated: "We demand that the test of true prosperity shall be the benefits conferred thereby on all the citizens, not confined to individuals or classes, and that the test of corporate efficiency shall be the ability better to serve the public; that those who profit by control of business affairs shall justify that profit and that control by sharing with the public the fruits thereof." [16]

Despite exuberant business booms, enormous industrial expansion, and a host of newly minted millionaires, the period from 1865 to 1914 was one of economic instability for the nation at large. Largely because of the businessman's selfish activities—senseless overcapitalization, wild speculation, and ruthless profit-taking—the years from 1873 to 1896 were, in fact, a "long-wave" depression. Within this short span of twenty-three years, the country underwent two major depressions, in 1873 and again in 1893, which lasted nearly ten years and inflicted widespread

The Breakers, sumptuous 76-room summer home of Cornelius Vanderbilt II, Newport, Rhode Island, conspicuously testified to the tremendous growth of wealth and luxury brought about by the capitalist revolution. In such pretentious pleasure palaces, used only six weeks or two months during the season, the very wealthy were said to "devote themselves to expense regardless of pleasure." Culver Pictures, Inc.

Along with the billionaire, the capitalist revolution produced millions of paupers whose mean lives were exhausted in a constant struggle against hunger and poverty. Huddled in squalor in one room, this family bear witness to "the slow but awful degradation of man through endless, hopeless, and joyless labor." Brown Bros.

suffering and mass unemployment. In the first décade of the twentieth century, prosperity was twice checked by financial upsets. The Panic of 1903, which put an end to the great consolidation boom, not only caused heavy losses to stockholders but dealt a severe blow to the notion that size was invariably correlated with business efficiency by overturning 85 per cent of newly formed industrial combinations. In turn, the so-called "Rich Man's" Panic of 1907 sharply revealed the inelasticity of the money monopoly. A more disastrous depression might have occured in 1914 had it not been for the sudden influx of war orders from Europe. In sum, during the entire period from the end of the Civil War in 1865 to the beginning of World War I in 1914, there were only seventeen and a half partly or wholly prosperous years out of fifty.

More dramatic evidence of the failure of the American economic system to live up to its promise of comfort and prosperity for the majority of people was the gross inequality of conditions between the rich few at one end of the social scale and the multitude of poor at the other. For along with the billionaire, the capitalist revolution had spawned ten million paupers. According to the research of Professor Willard King, the "Rich" representing 2 per cent of the population owned 60 per cent of the wealth, the "Middle-Class" making up 33 per cent of the nation owned 35 per cent, while the "Poor" comprising 65 per cent of the people owned not more than 5 per cent of the total wealth of the country.[17] Startling contrasts were drawn in popular magazines between the wretched lot of underpaid millions who suffered grinding poverty and tenement squalor while their wealthy employers lived in sybaritic luxury with liveried lackeys, sleeping between satin sheets costing $500 a pair, and entertaining with a lavish disregard for expense.[18] Charles Schwab, the steel executive, for example, lived in regal splendor in a Fifth Avenue chateau which cost about $7 million and required an estimated $50,000 a month for upkeep alone. Such huge incomes as his reportedly led J. P. Morgan to remark, "The trouble with the United States Steel Corporation is to find a president of ability who does not need all his time to spend his salary properly." [19] While Schwab recklessly threw away thousands on the tables at Monte Carlo, the majority of steelworkers, according to the Pittsburgh Survey of 1907–08, earned less than enough to support themselves in decency and comfort.[20]

Among conservative and well-to-do classes the tendency in the nineties was to regard the problem of poverty as greatly exaggerated in its extent and significance. A writer in the *North American Review* attributed the appearance of increasing misery to increasing population, but denied it was any greater than before.[21] The conservative editor of the *Nation*, E. L. Godkin, took a similar stand, blaming the discontent of the workingman with his lot on impressionistic propaganda about poverty, especially the Marxist's allegation that the laborer was being cheated out of his share of profits by the capitalist.[22] Andrew Carnegie even considered poverty a blessing.[23] Although other observers did not go so far, most of them refused to accept poverty as a social problem, and attempted to explain it away as a defect of individual character. "The bulk of the pauperism of any community," wrote Francis A. Walker, a leading conservative economist of the day, "which has not been demoralized and debauched by bad legislation of the socialistic variety is due to the misconduct of individuals, or to their weakness of will and infirmity of purpose . . . or to Ishmaelitish proclivities repugnant to civilization."[24] Even those Progressives who believed the facts of poverty were far worse than most intelligent Americans suspected, tended to think along traditional lines.

With the coming of the twentieth century, however, a new view of poverty gained acceptance among radical liberals, and opinion regarding its cause and cure underwent a significant change. A wider, though inequitable, diffusion of wealth not only gave Americans a foretaste of the good life which modern industry could create, but led many to question the old assumption that poverty was the normal condition of the masses. "In the midst of plenty," wrote Lippmann in 1914, "the imagination becomes ambitious, rebellion against misery is at last justified, and dreams have a basis in fact." His optimistic view was borne out by the findings of the Commission on Industrial Relations: "With the inexhaustible natural resources of the United States, her tremendous mechanical achievements, and the genius of her people for organization and industry, there can be no natural reason to prevent every able-bodied man of our present population from being well-fed, well housed, comfortably clothed, and from rearing a family of moderate size in comfort, health, and security."[25]

How far Americans were from realizing this ideal was made strikingly apparent by the ever growing disproportion between the social surplus and social misery. With due allowance for hyperbole, there was a disconcerting element of reality in banker Frederick Townsend Martin's charge that American business was producing two great new classes, "the Idle Rich and the Slaves of Industry." In a blasphemous exposure of the frivolous escapades of high "society" into which he had been born, Martin mercilessly exposed the extravagances of the very rich who lived on unearned profits drawn from the toil of other men.* But, as he was guiltily aware, at the same time the rich were seeking to relieve the ennui of voluntary idleness with costly games and dinners, the involuntarily idle—the millions of jobless poor—were fighting the familiar

* Frederick Townsend Martin, *The Idle Rich.* See p. 214.

pangs of hunger in a desperate struggle to keep alive. The young heir, Anson Phelps Stokes, might wire from Yale to his mother at her hundred-room "cottage" in the Berkshires, ARRIVING THIS EVENING WITH CROWD OF NINETY-SIX MEN, only to receive from Mrs. Stokes the return wire, MANY GUESTS ALREADY HERE. HAVE ONLY ROOM FOR FIFTY.[26] Yet, in the cold dark tenements of Boston, as reformer Benjamin Flower graphically related, a widowed mother and her seven children ate, cooked, lived and slept in one damp cellar room.*

This disturbing social imbalance was, withal, responsible for a more sober and searching analysis of poverty. By dramatically exposing the lives of the poor, muckrakers made thousands of thoughtful Americans aware that the causes of mass poverty were beyond control of the individual. "A salient fact about our modern social thinking," Weyl noted in 1912, "is that we no longer so light-heartedly attribute to a personal delinquency the residual, persistent poverty of great masses of the population. We no longer so often hear the *dictum* that any one who wants a job can get one; that no man need be idle; that all men can save against the rainy day, when they may be injured by industrial accident or discharged because of middle-age. We have become more temperate in our social judgments and our social admonitions."[27] The Alger idylls of fifty years before—"the charming inculcation of thrift to the desperately poor"[28] in stories about the astounding progress of the newsboy or the grocer's clerk to wealth and position through pluck, frugality, and an opportune marriage to his employer's daughter—gave way to countless investigations of the real condition of the poor in which the industrial causes of poverty were gradually recognized.

Where once the poor were described as lazy, immoral, intemperate and dirty, now they were identified simply as that portion of the population which was "inadequately fed, clad, and sheltered."[29] The lurking fear of want, glorified by old-fashioned economists as one of the highest incentives to industry and considered, as Howells said, "almost sacred, and worthy of at least as much veneration as capital punishment," was no longer acceptable as the cornerstone of modern civilization.[30] Radical liberalism

* Benjamin Flower, *Slaves of Industry*. See p. 222.

rejected the old concept of economic man. As Lippmann remarked, "man as a slot machine set in motion by inserting a coin" had fallen into disrepute because commercialism had failed to serve civilization.[31] Now, Weyl declared, society must become responsible "not only for the mere physical survival of the individual, but equally for the provision of facilities by which the highest physical, intellectual, moral, and social capacities of all citizens, born and to be born, may best be secured."[32]

For Whites Only

In spite of its concern for the underdog everywhere, when it came to the Negro—the most exploited group in the nation—Progressivism was for "whites only." Though national leaders such as Theodore Roosevelt and Woodrow Wilson displayed liberal attitudes toward the race question, their concern was largely academic. Like most Progressives, they never had any real contact with the Negro, nor were they under any political pressure on his behalf. Prior to World War I, the great mass of Negroes were concentrated in the South where, as Weyl observed, they were "too poor, weak, ignorant, and disunited to make effective protest."[33]

It was recognized that the Negro problem was the mortal spot of the new democracy but sectionalism and racial prejudice precluded direct political action on a national scale. The dogma of white supremacy was unquestioned, and few reformers, northern or southern, were ready to answer affirmatively Ray Stannard Baker's question—"Does democracy really include Negroes as well as white men?"[34] Southern "liberals" wished the Negro well but considered him, at best, an incompetent ward of white society. Northern Progressives, including Baker, adopted attitudes not unlike those of the South, holding that colored people must first prove themselves in simple lines of work before they could expect larger opportunities.

Essentially this was the strategy of accommodation enunciated by Booker T. Washington, Negro educator and former slave, whose views dominated Negro thought at the turn of the century. In his famous Atlanta Exposition Address of 1895, known both

favorably and unfavorably as the "Atlanta compromise,"
Washington publicly advocated a policy of conciliation and grad-
ualism, accepting segregation and separate-but-equal treatment in
the hope that through economic advancement, the Negro
would eventually gain recognition of his rights in the South.°
Largely blaming the Negro himself for his condition and tactfully
minimizing the depth and extent of racial prejudice—going so far
as to describe the southern white man as the Negro's "best
friend"—he opposed political agitation and favored instead a
program of economic self-help. "The trouble with the Negro,"
said the Tuskegee don, "is that he is all the time trying to get
recognition, whereas what he should do is to get something to
recognize." [35] So, in accordance with the dominant business theory
of welfare, he recommended economic accumulation and the
cultivation of Christian virtues as the best way of improving the
status of the Negro in America. By proving their usefulness to
society through the acquisition of wealth, black people would earn
the respect of the white man and thus in time would be accorded
all the political rights to which their ability, character and material
possessions entitled them.

Washington's policy of accommodation won quick approval from
white leadership, North and South, but not all southern whites saw
the racial issue in the same light. Southern Populists such as Tom
Watson contended that the South encouraged racial hatred to
prevent poorer whites and Negroes from joining forces to challenge
existing economic arrangements: "You are kept apart that you may
be separately fleeced of your earnings. You are made to hate each
other because upon that hatred is rested the keystone of the arch
of financial despotism which enslaves you both. You are deceived
and blinded that you may not see how this race antagonism per-
petuates a monetary system which beggars both." [36] Watson felt
that the poor of both races should combine against the upper
classes. "Let us draw the supposed teeth of this fabled dragon by
founding our new policy upon justice—upon the simple but profound truth that, if the voice of passion can be hushed, the self-
interest of both races will drive them to act in concert." [37] The

---

°Booker T. Washington, *Black Capitalism.* See p. 230.

Chain-gangs were the brutal modern equivalent of slavery. Mines, factories, and some of the largest farms in the South were operated on the convict lease system. To meet the demand for more convicts by white employers, black men were given excessive sentences for trivial offenses.

Brown Bros.

Negroes responded enthusiastically, thronging by thousands to his rallies to stand side by side with white farmers; the poorer whites, however, found it hard to accept the idea that their material interests cut across racial lines. Since political equality was a necessary step in the economic liberation of both groups, they feared that social equality might follow. After many failures which he blamed upon the "bugaboo of negro domination," Watson deserted his Negro allies and joined his former enemies. In a complete reversal, he now called for repression of the Negro as a national menace and openly condoned lynching. "In the South," he explained, "we have to lynch him occasionally and flog him, now and then, to keep him from blaspheming the Almighty, by his conduct, on account of his smell and his color."[38]

As the nineteenth century drew to a close, the Negro's position in American society grew steadily worse. Since 1877 there had been a steady and persistent drive to eliminate the Negro from the political and social life of the South, and the repressive forces had gained the upper hand. Politically disenfranchised, socially segregated and economically degraded, downgraded by law and terrorism, the Negro became a pariah whose sole lot in life was to serve the white man as a beast of burden. When it was suggested that the federal government intervene on the Negro's behalf, editor E. L. Godkin of the *Nation*—the leading journal of the white establishment—opposed it on grounds that it was an attempt to pervert "a political structure specially created for the benefit of valor, foresight, industry, and intelligence, to the special needs of the ignorant, the weak, the lazy and incompetent."[39]

Lynching, the *North American Review* observed in 1904, had never been so common or existed over so extended a region.[40] In the sixteen years from 1884 to 1900, the number of persons lynched in the South—including several burned at the stake—was 2,080, most of whom were Negroes. Their offenses ranged from stealing seventy-five cents and talking with white girls over the telephone, to rape and murder. While most lynchings took place in the South, the ratio was also increasing in the North, where racial antagonisms and "talk of social equality" triggered racial violence. But, as Ray Stannard Baker noted, in the northern cities the prejudice was also economic, for there the race problem overlapped the labor problem.[41] Not only had job competition led to exclusion of Negroes from unions and to discrimination in hiring, but the hostility among union labor had grown more intense because of the common use of Negroes as strikebreakers. Both the great Chicago stockyards strike in 1904 and the teamsters strike in the following year were broken by employers bringing in thousands of Negroes. Yet, not all of the Negro's difficulties in the North were racial; a good part was due to his lack of vocational training and industrial skills.

After 1900 race riots became commonplace in both the North and the South. Mob violence was set off in most instances not by Negro protest—though at the turn of the century there were black boycotts of segregated trolleycars in perhaps a dozen southern cities—but by whites who wanted to keep the Negro "in his place." In 1908 in Springfield, Illinois, Lincoln's hometown, a savage mob of several thousand whites sought to drive the Negroes from town, sacking and plundering their homes and stores, and attacking every Negro they could lay their hands on. A reporter who talked to many of them the day after three unfortunate Negroes were burned to death found no difference of opinion on the question. "Why, the niggers came to think they were as good as we are!" was the final justification offered, not once but a dozen times.[42] The same disposition was shown in Atlanta where, two years before, sensationally exaggerated newspaper reports of crimes allegedly committed by Negroes sent a white mob racing through the streets. The mob, it was reported, made no attempt to find the criminals, but "expressed its blind, unreasoning, uncontrolled race hatred by attacking every man, woman, or boy it saw who had a black face. A lame bootblack, an inoffensive, industrious Negro boy, at the moment actually at work shining a man's shoes, was dragged out and cuffed, kicked and beaten to death in the streets. Another young Negro was chased and stabbed to death with jack-knives in the most unspeakably horrible manner. The mob entered barber shops where respectable Negro men were at work shaving white customers, pulled them away from their chairs and beat them. Trolley cars were stopped and inoffensive Negroes were thrown through the windows or dragged out and beaten."[43] Of the seventy Negroes killed or maimed by the mob, not one was a criminal. Every one, as the report of a white committee showed, was industrious, respectable and law-abiding. When faced by such evidence, no thinking Negro could fail to see that his industry and material prosperity earned him the resentment of whites, not their respect.

After Booker T. Washington's program of accommodation failed to bring the hoped-for results, his leadership was challenged by dissatisfied Negroes. The most influential of the dissenters was W. E. B. DuBois, a Massachusetts-born Negro and a Harvard Ph.D., who in 1903 launched a full-scale attack against the Tuskegean, criticizing not only his policy of compromise but taking an opposite stand on nearly every important issue. Where

Washington put prosperity before politics, DuBois stressed political activity; Washington proposed to build the Negro's future on economic individualism, DuBois believed the path of progress for the black man lay not in Get and Grab—"not in private hoarding, squeezing and cheating"—but in the larger ideal of human brotherhood and cooperation.° Washington looked to the White House, to Presidents Roosevelt and Taft for political favors, and to rich philanthropists like John D. Rockefeller and Andrew Carnegie for money. DuBois declared the natural friends of the Negro were not the rich and great but the poor, the masses. Like Watson, whose failure he regarded as a calamity for black people, DuBois held that the poor of both races had been made tools of oppression against the workingman's cause. When it came to the most controversial question of all—what should the Negro do about discrimination—his answer was the exact opposite of Washington's: "Do not submit! agitate, object, fight." [44]

To carry his program into effect, DuBois joined with a small group of Negro intellectuals in 1905 to form the Niagara Movement. Its declaration of principles said: "We refuse to allow the impression to remain that the Negro–American assents to inferiority, is submissive under oppression and apologetic before insults. Through helplessness we may submit, but the voice of protest of ten million Americans must never cease to assail the ears of their fellows, so long as America is unjust." [45] Never numbering more than four hundred, the movement accomplished relatively little in its five-year life, but it led to a liason with a number of influential white liberals and Socialists and to the formation in 1909–10 of the National Association for the Advancement of Colored People, whose express aim was to fight for the Negro's constitutional rights. Though daringly radical for its time, the NAACP program was but the beginning for DuBois, whose goal was complete political, industrial and social equality. "The Negro must have power; the power of men, the right to do, to know, to feel and to express that knowledge, action and spiritual gift." But, DuBois told his race, power in modern society meant organization. If the Negro were to get anywhere, he must organize as efficiently as the giant corporation. [46]

° W. E. Burghardt DuBois, *Black Progressivism*. See p. 129.

DuBois' program may have been more appealing to the new generation of black men, but Washington's efforts were neither futile nor entirely misguided. Beginning with little, he did much for his people. At the time he took over the Negro leadership, it seemed impossible to gain the sympathy and cooperation of the South. He was able nevertheless by tact and discretion to wring some concessions from the white supremacists. He made it possible for the black man to obtain a common school education plus industrial training at public expense. If he became a thorough convert to the ideals of materialism, it was because he intuitively grasped the spirit of the age. Black capitalism was an accurate appraisal of capitalist values. It failed because Washington overestimated the good faith of the white man and underestimated the extent of racial prejudice. DuBois was undeniably correct, however, in charging that Washington's doctrine of accommodation tended to make whites shift the burden of the Negro problem to the black man and stand aside as critical and rather pessimistic spectators, when in justice the burden belonged to the nation.

The Gospel of the Machine

Sad as was the Negro's plight, it could not be directly attributed to capitalism. What business leadership promised Americans, white and black, was not equality but affluence. In fact, as the orthodox economist and capitalist defender John Bates Clark presciently informed readers of the *Independent* in 1901, America in the ensuing fifty years would present a condition of "vast and ever growing inequality." The rich would grow richer and the multimillionaires approach the billion-dollar mark. If this capitalist future were not the earthly Eden of the socialists, yet it would have its compensations. The capitalist might become too rich to sleep, while the laborer would grow so relatively rich that he could live in comfort and rest in peace. Moreover, because of an increase in comforts and refinements, he would become a morally higher type of man.[47]

This characteristically American identification of wealth with morality gained new impetus and a new interpretation after the beginning of the twentieth century. In the older Protestant ethic founded on scarcity and virtuous self-denial, the principle was that, in the long run, wealth came only to the moral man. The newer capitalist ethic turned the older belief upside down by suggesting that a man's or a nation's morality was a direct consequence of the abundance of things possessed. "Material prosperity," confirmed the right Reverend William Lawrence, Bishop of Massachusetts, "is helping to make the national character sweeter, more joyous, more unselfish, more Christlike." [48] For thousands of years, said the business publicist Gerald Stanley Lee, religion had tried to make men intimate enough to be good. But business and technology in a few generations had made modern men spiritual and, instead of the "lonely each-on-your-own-hill morals of the Old Testament," brought a new, "incredibly socialized" piety. "Christ and St. Paul," declared Lee, "converted a few thousand individuals in each generation out of millions of so-called Christians. Railroads, gas bills, and coal trusts, and telephones are going to convert us all." [49]

For reasons of prudence and pride, as Robert Wiebe has shown, big businessmen began to sell themselves along with their products. They hired public relations experts and established propaganda bureaus with the deliberate intention of winning popular approval. Public relations became an important response to the "sensationalism" and "prejudice writing" of the "muckrake men." The railroads, among the most severely criticized, maintained the most elaborate system, while other large corporations such as Standard Oil, United States Steel, and International Harvester also hired publicity agents to spread the story of industry's blessings to the nation. [50] As an aid in selling the new capitalism to the people, a Civic Federation directive reminded businessmen that "Socialism has the great sentimental advantage of being based upon a desire to benefit all human beings" and advised that "in opposing socialism this sentimental advantage must be claimed and held for the anti-socialist view." [51]

If in the economic field human conduct was narrowly restricted by capitalism, in the noneconomic field—"the greater and more significant part of life"—capitalism was said to impose no penalties on virtue or beauty. Although this capitalistic liberation of the human spirit was largely of a negative nature, it was justified as being none the less real for being indirect. On the grounds that capitalism was evolving a broader and more liberal humanity than the world had ever known, the economist Alvin S. Johnson, an outstanding student of J. B. Clark, wrote of capitalism as endowed with a "soul." ° In countering the "new social conscience" which he accused of interpreting good and evil in class terms—"Labor is its Esau, Capitalism its Jacob"—Johnson argued that capitalism guaranteed a range of personal growth not compatible with the regimentation of a socialist state. Admittedly capitalism in its present stage of development was ugly, characterized by haste and vandalism; nevertheless he found the social influence of capitalistic toleration very considerable. Racial and social prejudice, for instance, were strongest in economically backward areas, and he pointed out that in the Old South, still in a precapitalistic stage, the social gulf between races was widest.[52]

It was perhaps inevitable that once the machine process began to create a rival culture in which technical criteria dominated nontechnical considerations, the new capitalism should generate a morality and religion of its own. With scientific management being hailed as a complete moral law, a workable combination of the New Testament and evolution, the old moral and religious precepts seemed ambiguous and untrustworthy. Regardless of what the "goody-goody" books said, apostles of the new ethic proclaimed that efficiency was not to be judged by preconceived standards of honesty or morality, but honesty and morality were to be reconsidered and revised by the light of efficiency. "The modern Diogenes," it was said, "does not go about with a lantern seeking goodness; he looks for efficiency and expects goodness to be thrown in. He imposes a merit test and that test is based upon visible, countable results. He looks at the service rather than the server, and finds the cash-register worth a dozen certificates of character." [53] Goodness was, in fact, "making good."

As the cross had been the symbol of Christian renunciation, the new symbol of worldly arrogation was the machine. In its bearing on modern life, the machine was in every sense a radical and unprecedented force. Since it had no instincts, customs or loyalties, it ruthlessly undercut the traditional cultural foundations of human life. The machine, as Veblen said, was "leveller, a vulgarizer," act-

° Alvin S. Johnson, *The Soul of Capitalism.* See p. 134.

ing to disintegrate the institutional heritage of all degrees of antiquity and authenticity. "Men trained by the mechanical occupations to materialistic, industrial habits of thought are beset with a growing inability to appreciate, or even to apprehend, the meaning of religious appeals that proceed on the old-fashioned grounds of metaphysical validity."[54] Not only were modern men in danger of losing the point of view of sin, but the concept of a supernatural God was becoming alien to their habit of mind. "The machine, their master, is no respecter of persons and knows neither morality nor dignity nor prescriptive right, divine or human."[55] All that was formerly held to be respectable, noble, and dignified in human life and ideals, including, ironically, the whole metaphysical framework upon which the business system rested, now seemed irrelevant to technological mastery.

To the truly modern, the erosion of old values by the machine was not to be lamented but heralded as a sign of progress. It meant, exulted Gerald Stanley Lee, that history was losing its monopoly over men's minds. "The inertia of men, instead of being that of foundations, conventions, customs, facts, sogginess, and heaviness, is getting to be an inertia now toward the future."[56] In similar vein, Carroll D. Wright, U.S. Commissioner of Labor, proclaimed the age of machinery, the age of mind. "For brain is king, and machinery is the king's prime minister."[57] Machines, in his opinion, typified the intellectual and moral progress of man. Machinery was declared an elevating influence, and the practical results of the factory system purported to be better morals, better sanitary conditions, better health, better wages. Those in charge of factories were more than producers; they were "managers of great missionary establishments." For, said Wright, the factory system, when properly run, "outstrips the pulpit in the actual work of the gospel."[58]

The acceptance of the machine as a spiritual force posed a special challenge to the churches. With skyscrapers everywhere outsoaring steeples, men were demanding a religion to match their machines. "Unless your God is a God I can worship in a factory, He is not a God I care to worship in a church," professed the modern apostate. "The religion that lives in a machine age, and that cannot see and feel the meaning of that machine age, is a religion which is not worthy of our machines." [59] The shocking fact was that factory workers were staying away from church. Although there were many diagnoses, the fact of working-class alienation was admitted and deplored by most Protestant clergymen. One reason why preachers were less successful in getting people to want the old-fashioned kind of goodness than businessmen were selling automobiles, cameras, and phonographs, suggested Lee, was because in the modern age advertisements were more pertinent than sermons, and shop windows on Fifth Avenue displayed goodness more attractively than the churches. "If the church shop windows, for instance, were to make displays of goodness up and down the great Moral Fifth Avenue of the world. . . . there would be rows and tiers of Not-Things piled up—Things for People Not to Be, and Things for People Not To Do." [60] From the popular point of view, goodness presented in this negative way was not only unappealing but out of date. While one might not agree with Lee that more spiritual energy was expended over the counters of a great department store—where men and women "measur[ed] out their souls before God in dress goods, shoes, boas, hats, silk, and bread and butter"—than in the churches, there was no denying that in the twentieth-century scheme of things, the good American was no longer a penitent ascetic but a virtuous consumer. [61]

When the thoughtful American contemplated "the eastern sky ablaze with chewing gum, the northern with toothbrushes and underwear, the western with whiskey, and the southern with petticoats, the whole heavens brilliant with monstrously flirtatious women," and when he glanced at magazines "in which a rivulet of text trickles through meadows of automobiles, baking powders, corsets and kodaks," he began to sense with Lippmann his powerlessness before the torrential appeals of the new faith. [62] But his uneasiness was allayed by the blandishments of prosperity. Mass production, he was told, was only possible where there was mass demand, and mass demand could be created only by advertising. By increasing personal wants, advertising was said to raise the standard of living. New luxuries were invented daily and speedily became necessities through the medium of the advertisement. "How long," asked the *Independent*, "without advertising would it have taken to have developed and made known to everybody the automobile and the hand camera, the player-piano and the phonograph, the office utilities, the toilet accessories and all the thousand 'Yankee notions' that make our life so pleasant and complete?"[63] If, as the new gospel asserted, progress consisted in the creation of new wants and happiness in their satisfaction, then the advertiser was a modern saint. Hailed as "an accelerator of civilization," the advertiser was proclaimed a "public educator, more proficient in the art of teaching than the graduates of our normal schools."[64]

Although the majority of Americans accepted the rapid growth of advertising as a certain sign of moral and material progress, there were still those who were distressed by its "shameless uglifying" and repelled by its indecency and dishonesty. "In the city," complained E. A. Ross, "every accessible spot where the eye may wander frantically proclaims the merits of somebody's pickles or Scotch whiskey," or, "follow the country lane, the forest path or the trout brook, and you find fences, barns, trees and boulders shouting to you of pills, fly-screens and canned soup."[65] Even the usually tolerant William James, who was philosophically committed to change, could not accept newspaper medical advertisements with their detailed accounts of Mr. Mingo's kidneys, Mr. Hawkshaw's bronchi, or Mrs. Hecla's skin. "Like Ulysses," grumbled James, "these worthies have become a part of all that we have met; and all experience is an arch where-through their entrails gleam as it were iridescently upon us, until the world looms to our imagination in a sort of catarrhal vapor, or as if bathed in a cancerous and haemorhoidal mist."[66]

Advertising, Lippmann complained, was the effort of businessmen to take charge of consumption as well as production. Not content to supply a demand, as the textbooks say, they "educated" the demand as well. The consumer was told "what he wants, then he wants it."[67] Because of the scale on which modern business was organized, the ordinary purchaser, like the unorganized worker, was deprived of the knowledge and power to make a fair bargain. Hence the consumer was almost entirely at the mercy of the advertiser. Most notorious in this respect was the patent-medicine business, the so-called "poison trust," which was an out-and-out swindle almost from the beginning. Newspapers and

magazines carried pages and pages of advertisements for "medi-
cines" containing dangerous amounts of alcohol, cocaine or mor-
phine, and billboards screamed assurances of fantastic "cures" for
anything and everything. PERUNA, a miraculous ninety-proof
moneymaker, claimed to cure cancer, catarrh, consumption, dys-
pepsia, appendicitis, colic, mumps and rheumatism. Other "universal" remedies swore to prevent loss of hair, smallpox, old age
and sunstroke. Although Samuel Hopkins Adams' exposure of such
flagrantly false patent-medicine ads in *Collier's* in 1905 aroused
considerable indignation and led to token legislation—as did Upton
Sinclair's exposure of unsavory meat-packing practices in *The
Jungle* (1906)—these transgressions scarcely checked propagation
of the new faith.

Only a few critics viewed these unethical practices as the inevitable consequence of capitalist morality. Far from regarding the
businessman's eagerness to sell his goods as a "sacred passion," they
questioned the validity of a creed which demanded that men sell
their souls for worldly gain. If the good of business condoned lying
in ads and labels, then, they contended, it justified any evil. Preaching the "social gospel"—the application of Christian principles to
modern industrial society—a small group of Protestant clergymen
reproved the capitalist for acting as if the only dependable motive
of human action was profit.[68] The Reverend Washington Gladden,
who was one of them, created a national sensation by refusing a
missionary contribution from John D. Rockefeller as "tainted
money," charging that a man who aggrandized himself by despoil-
ing his competitors was, in the sight of God, "just as truly a robber
as the man who puts his pistol to your head in a dark alley."[69]

While the social gospelists realized the saving element in the
modern situation was that on many points the interests of great
corporations were identical with the common good, they were also
aware that the business system, as its past conduct proved, stood
ready to break down any barrier of law or religion that interfered
with the pursuit of profit. Unlike most businessmen, who seemed
interested in abstract good only as it might have a bearing on
profits, these Christian reformers did not reckon the moral well-
being of society as the sum of its technical or pecuniary efficiency.
It was not possible, in their opinion, to measure goodness or virtue

by the stopwatch or the cash register. Though the efficiency expert might believe the remedy for human error lay in systematic management and represent goodness as a matter of "fitting in," the Christian could never accept the idea that ethical perfection resided in economic utility. Thus the Baptist minister Walter

'HE STIRRETH UP THE PEOPLE'

JESUS CHRIST

THE WORKINGMAN OF NAZARETH
WILL SPEAK
AT BROTHERHOOD HALL
— SUBJECT —

- THE RIGHTS OF LABOR

If capitalism were to escape the wrath of the rising social passion, charged Christian Socialists, it must accept Christ as its Lord and actualize his teachings in a new social machinery that would organize the world for the common good of all. From *The Masses*, Dec., 1913, cover.

Rauschenbusch, a leader in the social-gospel movement, condemned the new business faith as blasphemous and immoral because it placed things above men, the exigent before the spiritual.°

In the end, the ultimate question to be decided was whether America would be able to transform the special interests of big business into the material and spiritual wellbeing of society at large. As the lady muckraker Ida Tarbell put it: "Every practice, law, system of religion, government or society must be finally sifted down to this: Is it moral—are men better or worse for it? . . . There you have the final test for kings and captains of industry, for armies and factories, for laws and social dicta." [70] Apparently the capitalist system passed the test. Despite wholesale exposures of unsocial behavior by large corporations and serious doubts about the merits of a machine-made civilization, the majority of Americans chose to believe in the new capitalism as men had once believed in the princely and priestly establishments of an earlier age—not only offering up their lives, hopes, and personal welfare in return for its blessings but, as a nation, accepting the business view as the only authoritative account of reality.

° Walter Rauschenbusch, *The Case of Christianity Against Capitalism.* See p. 137.

Scientific Management

FREDERICK WINSLOW TAYLOR (1855–1932) An efficiency
engineer, Taylor intended to prepare for law, but because of
weak eyesight abandoned his study and went to work in an
industrial shop. From observation and study of manufacturing
conditions and methods, he evolved a theory that by studying
scientifically every minute step and operation in a manufacturing process, data could be obtained as to the maximum productive capacity of both man and machine and that the application
of such data would not only bring about increased industrial
efficiency but benefit society as a whole.

Scientific management is not any efficiency device, not a device
of any kind for securing efficiency; nor is it any bunch or group
of efficiency devices. It is not a new system of figuring costs; it
is not a new scheme of paying men; it is not a piecework system;
it is not a bonus system; it is not a premium system; it is no scheme
for paying men; it is not holding a stop watch on a man and writing
things down about him; it is not time study; it is not motion study
nor an analysis of the movements of men; it is not the printing and
ruling and unloading of a ton or two of blanks on a set of men
and saying, "Here's your system; go use it." It is not divided
foremanship or functional foremanship; it is not any of the devices
which the average man calls to mind when scientific management
is spoken of. . . .

In its essence, scientific management involves a complete mental
revolution on the part of the workingman engaged in any particular
establishment or industry—a complete mental revolution on the
part of these men as to their duties toward their work, toward
their fellow men, and toward their employers. And it involves the

From the testimony of Frederick Winslow Taylor, *Hearings Before Special Committee of the House of Representatives to Investigate the Taylor and Other Systems
of Shop Management* (Washington, 1911–12), III, pp. 1377–1508.

equally complete mental revolution on the part of those on the management's side—the foreman, the superintendent, the owner of the business, the board of directors—a complete mental revolution on their part as to their duties toward their fellow workers in the management, toward their workmen, and toward all of their daily problems. And without this complete mental revolution on both sides scientific management does not exist.

That is the essence of scientific management, this great mental revolution. Now, later on, I want to show you more clearly what I mean by this great mental revolution. I know that perhaps it sounds to you like nothing but bluff—like buncombe—but I am going to try and make clear to you just what this great mental revolution involves, for it does involve an immense change in the minds and attitude of both sides, and the greater part of what I shall say today has relation to the bringing about of this great mental revolution. So that whether the details may be interesting or uninteresting, what I hope you will see is that this great change in attitude and viewpoint must produce results which are magnificent for both sides, just as fine for one as for the other. Now, perhaps I can make clear to you at once one of the very great changes in outlook which come to the workmen, on the one hand, and to those in the management on the other hand.

I think it is safe to say that in the past a great part of the thought and interest both of the men on the side of the management, and of those on the side of the workmen in manufacturing establishments has been centered upon what may be called the proper division of the surplus resulting from their joint efforts, between the management on the one hand, and the workmen on the other hand. The management have been looking for as large a profit as possible for themselves, and the workmen have been looking for as large wages as possible for themselves, and that is what I mean by the division of the surplus. Now, this question of the division of the surplus is a very plain and simple one (for I am announcing no great fact in political economy or anything of that sort). Each article produced in the establishment has its definite selling price. Into the manufacture of this article have gone certain expenses, namely, the cost of materials, the expenses connected with selling it, and certain indirect expenses, such as the rent of the building, taxes, insurance, light and power, maintenance of machinery, interest on the plant, etc. Now, if we deduct these several expenses from the selling price, what is left over may be called the surplus. And out of this surplus comes the profit to the manufacturer on the one hand, and the wages of the workmen on the other hand. And it is largely upon the division of this surplus that the attention of the workman and of the management has been centered in the past. Each side has had its eye upon this surplus, the workingman wanting as large a share in the form of wages as he could get, and the management wanting as large a share in the form of profits as it could get; I think I am safe in saying that in the past it has been in the division of this surplus that the great labor troubles have come between employers and employees.

Frequently, when the management have found the selling price going down they have turned toward a cut in the wages—toward reducing the workman's share of the surplus—as their way of getting out whole, of preserving their profits intact. While the workman (and you can hardly blame him) rarely feels willing to relinquish a dollar of his wages, even in dull times, he wants to keep all that he has had in the past, and when busy times come again very naturally he wants to get more. Thus it is over this division of the surplus that most of the troubles have arisen; in the extreme cases this has been the cause of serious disagreements and strikes. Gradually the two sides have come to look upon one another as antagonists, and at times even as enemies—pulling apart and matching the strength of the one against the strength of the other.

The great revolution that takes place in the mental attitude of the two parties under scientific management is that both sides take their eyes off of the division of the surplus as the all-important matter, and together turn their attention toward increasing the size of the surplus until this surplus becomes so large that it is unnecessary to quarrel over how it shall be divided. They come to see that when they stop pulling against one another, and instead both turn and push shoulder to shoulder in the same direction, the size of the surplus created by their joint efforts is truly astounding. They both realize that when they substitute friendly cooperation and mutual helpfulness for antagonism and strife they are together able to make this surplus so enormously greater than it was in the past that there is ample room for a large increase in wages for the workmen and an equally great increase in profits for the manufacturer. This, gentlemen, is the beginning of the great mental revolution which constitutes the first step toward scientific management. It is along this line of complete change in the mental attitude of both sides; of the substitution of peace for war; the substitution of hearty brotherly cooperation for contention and strife; of both pulling hard in the same direction instead of pulling apart; of replacing suspicious watchfulness with mutual confidence; of becoming friends instead of enemies; it is along this line, I say, that scientific management must be developed.

Social Efficiency

WALTER E. WEYL (1873–1919)   *A writer on economics and an important theorist of the new radicalism, Weyl was a founding editor of the* New Republic *from 1914 to 1916. A pupil of Simon Nelson Patten at the University of Pennsylvania, he belonged to the "new-school" economists who concerned themselves with actual economic behavior rather than abstract theory. As an editorial colleague said, "His method was to comprehend, no matter where it led him. He asked questions and he explained, and always when he honestly could, he gave the benefit of the doubt." His thoughtful analysis of American society influenced not only the first Roosevelt's New Nationalism but the second's New Deal.*

The plutocracy rests its defense upon the ground of historical necessity. It has come to be because it was the fittest to be. It survives because it meets our national needs. What though it be ugly, smoky, noisy, parsimonious, murderous, if, all things considered, the plutocracy is the most economical form of national organization, then it will live. It can cure itself of minor ills. It

From *The New Democracy* (New York: Macmillan, 1912), pp. 139–46, 149–50.

can outgrow youthful immoderations, for the plutocracy, it must be remembered, is still very young. The plutocracy believes that the American will not exchange an effective for an ineffective business organization. He will not quarrel with his bread and butter.

The plutocracy claims to be a progressive, upbuilding force. It . . . cites many pages of statistics to prove (what is already evident) that during its domination we have been growing stupendously wealthy. One cannot read our government bulletins or the files of technical journals; one cannot glance over the daily paper or walk through the streets, without realizing that in everything which pertains to material progress we are moving at a giant's pace. The trust puts an end to the waste and brutality of an unregulated business war. The trust imposes peace. It may be the peace of industrial despotism. But it is peace.

The plutocracy admits that in the conflict with competitive business the trust often won illegally. But illegality was equally the weapon of its rivals, and a too scrupulous respect for the law was never a condition of the contest. Even without such illegalities the trust would have been eventually victorious, for its being was decreed by the law of business evolution. Even trusts burdened by an excessive capitalization survived and prospered, because they gave a greater profit than their constituent companies had done. Combination, where possible, made competition impossible, and, if combination resulted in monopoly and extortion, these were, after all, goals to which each competitor of the trust had secretly aspired.

Because of its alleged efficiency, the plutocracy claims remission of past sins and indulgence for future transgressions. We forgave the pioneer his crudity, recklessness, and exaggerated individualism, because *for his time* he made the most effective use of the still unconquered continent. We then sent gentlemen to Congress whom we should now send to jail, and we then rewarded with fortunes men who might today end in almshouses. At the present time, on this argument, our toleration of the old individualist should descend to the equally typical representatives of a new economic development. The overwhelming of the citizens at the polls and in the primaries, the rise of a more subtle and ramified political corruption, the evolution of a powerful boss, were but the political expression of a contemporaneous economic evolution, the rise of the trust. And this stupendous development, the plutocracy insists, was but a step in a progress from chaos to order; a step towards a wiser, and longer-viewed exploitation of the continent.

Not only does the plutocracy assert that this end justifies the means, but it also claims that, because of its higher industrial organization, it has a broader ethical basis and a wider program of social reform than had the competitive business which preceded it. Not being so hard pressed as were its forerunners, the plutocracy can afford a little virtue. Or, rather, it cannot afford *not* to have a little virtue, for our growing business concentration has changed the incidence of certain industrial evils, so that they who cause the damage occasionally suffer from it. From considerations of policy as well as because of its acknowledged leadership of industry, the plutocracy has been obliged to accept certain industrial responsibilities, and has thus developed its own code of social morality.

Under the old *régime,* competitors did not mind any conceivable waste of natural resources or human lives. The community paid. Jekyll could not afford philanthropy in competition with Hyde. With increasing concentration of business control, however, it is becoming wiser to mitigate certain evils of unregulated employment, and make the additional cost a fixed charge to customers, rather than let things go and pay the cost of negligence in taxes. The growing popularity of company-paid pensions to employees, of welfare work, even of reductions in hours—although these have another side—is indicative of a certain rudimentary sense of responsibility on the part of big business. That this broader ethical view is largely determined by the desire for profits does not detract from its social beneficence. . . .

The plutocracy's code of reform includes a charity designed to widen the eye of the needle. It is a business charity, with organization and prevention of waste; with efficiency and byproducts. It is a charity which has evolved (following industrial changes) from the instinctive, soul-saving giving of the Middle Ages, through a competitive, shrieking, advertising charity, to a well-organized, far-seeing charity on a trust basis. The plutocracy believes in the prevention of non-economic causes of poverty in so far as such prevention does not interfere with business arrangements. It believes in special institutions for the blind, halt, insane, feeble-minded. It believes in laws against child beating, and, with reservations, in laws against child labor. It believes in welfare work for employees. It assists many forms of ameliorative social work.

Other ideals of the plutocracy are of larger import. The plutocracy believes, as does the democracy, in an increase of national productivity. It therefore recognizes the advantages of education, especially of a technical education, which makes the nation a more effective industrial group. It desires more railroads and better railroads, improved technical processes, irrigation of deserts, filling in of swamps. It usually desires peace, social security, and general wellbeing. It is opposed to an unprofitable waste of things which cost money. It desires a healthy community in which all men can work, and it essays the extirpation of contagious diseases, which social barriers cannot exclude from the homes of the rich. It desires the governmental development of such national resources as cannot be profitably exploited by individuals, and it encourages unremunerative public activities, translatable into private profits. Finally, the plutocracy is imbued with certain humanitarian, artistic, and educational ideals, in no direct way undermining the influence or lessening the welfare of the group.

This program of the plutocracy, halting though it be, is as much superior to the negative social program of the earlier individualist as is the organization of the Standard Oil Company to that of the little companies which have been superseded. If the plutocracy were attacked by individualists alone, its arguments would avail, and its social program, like its industrial labors, would justify its existence.

But the plutocracy is also assailed by men who desire, not a return to individualism, but a progress toward democratic socialization. These opponents of the plutocracy point out its wastes, inefficiencies, and injustices, and accuse it of standing in the way of a complete harmonization of our industrial organization with our political and social aspirations.

The plutocracy's argument from prosperity is turned against itself. Who gets the prosperity? Why, after the wastes of production have been so largely eliminated, do we still suffer from over-work, child labor, sweating, industrial disease, preventable accident, slums, poverty, wretchedness? Why do wages remain low after the plutocracy has established a little order in industry? Why does an increasing inequality accompany an improved utilization of the resources of the continent?

In lessening the wastes of production, the plutocracy has increased many of the wastes of consumption. By improving industrial processes it has drawn attention to heightened inequalities of distribution. Our senseless inequalities of distribution, from our new point of view, are poor economy and low efficiency, because a gross inequality means a lessened pleasure in the consumption of wealth. A masterpiece of art in a private gallery, seen by a hundred people, gives less pleasure than would the same masterpiece in a public gallery seen by a million people. A million dollars of commodities consumed by one overrich man gives less pleasure than would the same sum added to the expenditure of ten thousand people. If the plutocracy's wiser utilization of our national resources leads only to an increasing inequality of wealth and income, the net gain to the people may be dubious.

It is exactly as though the plutocracy, with its brand-new tool, the trust, had trebled our production of coal, but had distributed the fuel so badly, overstoking some boilers and understoking others, that the total production of heat was no greater than before. It is as though the plutocracy, boasting of its trebled production of coal, and exulting in its increased output of smoke and ashes, had failed to realize that a shivering people was demanding, not more coal, not more smoke, not more ashes, but more heat. What the people want is not wealth, but distributed wealth; not a statistical increase in the national income, but more economic satisfactions, more widely distributed. . . .

The new democracy accepts the plutocracy's theory of the survival of the fittest civilization. It recognizes that the efficient utilization of our national resources means the wealth, bread, life of the people, and that all political aspirations must conform to this underlying economic factor. The democracy, however, instructed by its wants, interprets the word utilization in a new sense. Where the plutocracy means the greatest wealth, the democracy means the widest range of economic satisfactions. Where the plutocracy thinks of profits, the democracy thinks of recreation, leisure, a wise expenditure, and a healthful toil. Where the plutocracy emphasizes a saving in wages, the democracy emphasizes a saving in labor.

The democracy does not believe that a nation is rich because the majority owes the minority money and labor. The democracy does not wish the nation to possess that "wealth" which is merely the capitalized value of an economic rent due from the people to monopolists, but it does desire meat, potatoes, school books, public parks, and surcease from excessive toil. The democracy interprets utilization as such a production, distribution, and consumption of wealth as will give the highest excess of economic pleasure over economic pain to the largest number of people for the longest possible time. Upon this end all the industrial, political, social, and ethical ideals of the democracy converge.

The Idle Rich

FREDERICK TOWNSEND MARTIN (1849–1914)   *Frederick Townsend Martin, a banker and philanthropist, was born into the most fashionable Newport and New York society. But unlike most of his set, he was deeply interested in the conditions of labor and of poverty. Convinced that the old social order was doomed, he wrote* The Passing of the Idle Rich *to illustrate his theory that decay always follows idleness and extravagance. The work had a tremendous vogue, running in serial form in the muckraking* Everybody's Magazine *and, being dramatized, appeared on stage at the Garden Theatre in New York in 1913.*

For thirty years, since 1880, we have been piling up wealth in the hands of men who do not work. In almost every year there has been pouring from our mills a steady grist of idlers. It has gone so far that today, in every city of the Union, the class of the idle

From *The Passing of the Idle Rich* (Garden City, N.Y.: Doubleday, Page & Co., 1911), pp. 89–92, 29–39, 41–46, 55–58.

rich has reached proportions that to the thoughtful student of events are alarming. The millionaire habit has spread until today men of millions are far more numerous in our great cities than were men of one tenth the wealth twenty years ago.

I do not desire to criticize wealth; for I am not a Socialist, and I entertain no Utopian dreams concerning the equal distribution of wealth among the people or the public control of all sources of wealth. . . .

Yet, I confess, the terrific sweep of industrialism across this land throughout the past century appalls me as I study it. . . . For the grim fact stands out beyond denial that the men who are the workers of the nation, and the women and the children dependent upon them, are not today given the opportunities that are their proper birthright in free America; and that, struggle as they will, save as they may, lift their voices in protest as they dare, they cannot obtain from our industrial hierarchy much more than a mere living wage. And, on the other hand, it is equally true that the wage of capital is high, that the class of idle rich has grown out of all proportion, and that it has taken upon itself a power and an arrogance unsurpassed in the industrial history of the world.

Somewhere there is something wrong. I speak as a rich man. I speak as a representative of the class of which I write, and to which in particular I address myself. . . .

There is a vast difference between the healthy, wholesome spending of money for amusements, pleasures, and recreations and the feverish searching for some new sensation that can be had only at a tremendous cost. The simple expenditure of money, even in startling amounts, eventually fails to produce the thrill that it ought to have, and when the man or woman of fortune, with little to think of but the constant hunt for amusement and novelty, begins to suffer from continuous *ennui*, the result is frequently amazing and sometimes sickening.

A wearied, bored group of men arranged a dinner. They had been attending dinners until such functions had lost interest for them. Similarly their friends were wearied by the conventional dinner of the time. Why not prepare a meal, the like of which had never been before? Why not amuse society and astonish the part of the community that is outside of society? They did so. The dinner was served on horseback on the upper floor of a fashionable New York resort, the name of which is known from coast to coast; the guests were attired in riding habits; the handsomely groomed horses pranced and clattered about the magnificent dining-room, each bearing, besides its rider, a miniature table. The hoofs of the animals were covered with soft rubber pads to save the waxed floor from destruction. At midnight a reporter for an active and sensational morning newspaper ran across the choice bit of news. He telephoned the information to his city editor and the reply of that moulder of opinion was brief and to the point.

"You're lying to me," said the editor.

The most sensational paper in town refused to believe its reporter, who attempted later on to reach the scene of the event, but was repulsed and driven away.

"How much did it cost?" the public inquired interestedly. The man who paid the bill knew. The public and its newspapers guessed, their estimates running from ten thousand to fifty thousand dollars.

The fond owner of a diminutive black-and-tan dog gave a banquet in honour of the animal. The dog was worth, perhaps, fifty dollars. The festivities were very gay. The man's friends came to his dinner in droves, the men in evening clothes and the women bedecked in shimmering silks and flashing jewels. In the midst of the dinner, the man formally decorated his dog with a diamond collar worth fifteen thousand dollars. It contained seven hundred small brilliants, varying in weight from one sixth to one carat. The guests shouted their approval, and the dinner was regarded as a huge success.

The leader of a wealthy clique in a Western city was struck with a unique idea. He was tired of spending money. There was nothing new for which to spend it. He gave a "poverty social." The thirty guests came to his palatial home in rags and tatters. Scraps of food were served on wooden plates. The diners sat about on broken soap boxes, buckets, and coalhods. Newspapers, dust cloths, and old skirts were used as napkins, and beer was served in a rusty tin can, instead of the conventional champagne. They played being poor for one night, and not one of them but joined in ecstatic praise of their host and his unusual ability to provide a sensation. . . .

At the conclusion of an elaborate affair in New York City, the guests leaned back in their chairs to listen to the singers. The cigarettes were passed around. Oddly enough, the banquet had not been marked until that moment, and, as the host was famous for the unusualness of his dinners, many of the diners were disappointed. Their disappointment gave way to admiration. Each cigarette was rolled, not in white paper, but in a one hundred dollar bill and the initials of the host were engraved in gold letters. This strange conceit was applauded until the voices of the singers struggled amid the uproar. . . .

A well known metropolitan spender has an annual bill of some ten thousand dollars for shoes alone. His order stands in every manufactory in America and Europe. Whenever a new style of men's shoes is designed, a sample pair is immediately shipped to him. He cannot possibly wear a tenth of the shoes sent to him, but he has the satisfying knowledge that he is never behind the style.

The wife of a Western man owns a pet monkey. The little beast lives in a private room and is constantly attended by a valet. It rides abroad behind its private trotter, has its own outfit of clothes, its dining table, and a bed made of solid ivory, tipped with gold ornaments. All told, perhaps a dozen human beings minister to the comfort of the little simian and the mistress cheerfully pays from ten to fifteen thousand dollars yearly on this one extravagance. She became dissatisfied with the dining service in the monkey-room of her home, and her pet now eats its meals off solid silver plates. . . .

A man of common name, but of uncommon wealth, decided to have a home in New York City. He purchased the palace of a friend who had died and paid for it two million dollars, which was popularly supposed to be one half the original cost of the pile. On his garden, to make space for which he tore down a building that had cost a hundred thousand, the new owner spent five hundred thousand dollars. His bedstead is of carved ivory and ebony, inlaid with gold. It cost two hundred thousand dollars. The walls are richly carved and decorated with enamel and gold; they cost sixty-five thousand dollars. On the ceiling, the happy millionaire expended twenty thousand in carvings, enamels, and gold, and ten pairs of filmy curtains, costing two thousand a pair, wave in the morning breeze. The wardrobe in this famous bedroom represents an outlay of one hundred and fifty thousand dollars and the dressing table sixty-five thousand. The wash stand cost thirty-eight thousand, and the bed hangings, fifty dollars a yard. The chimney-piece and overhanging mantel threw into general circulation eight thousand more, and the four doors consumed another ten thousand. . . .

But why enumerate any more of these instances? Our papers are full of them.

Slaves of Industry

BENJAMIN O. FLOWER (1858–1918)   *A liberal editor and social reformer, Flower had a consuming sympathy for the poor and oppressed. In his youth he embarked on a passionate journalistic agitation for betterment of human relations that continued until his death. At Boston he founded the* Arena, *a famous muckraking magazine, in 1889, and served as editor through most of its twenty-year existence. His wide interest in the great social, political and educational questions of the day led him to become president of the National League for Medical Freedom and of the Free Press Defense League.*

It is difficult to over-estimate the gravity of the problem presented by those compelled to exist in the slums of our populous cities, even when considered from a purely economic point of view. From the midst of this commonwealth of degradation there goes forth a moral contagion, scourging society in all its ramifications, coupled with an atmosphere of physical decay—an atmosphere reeking with filth, heavy with foul odors, laden with disease. In time of any contagion the social cellar becomes the hot-bed of death, sending forth myriads of fatal germs which permeate the air for miles around, causing thousands to die because society is too

From *Civilization's Inferno* (Boston: Arena Publishing Co., 1893), pp. 23–35, 37–40, 70–72.

short-sighted to understand that the interest of its humblest member is the interest of all. The slums of our cities are the reservoirs of physical and moral death, an enormous expense to th state, a constant menace to society, a reality whose shadow is at once colossal and portentous. In time of social upheavals they will prove magazines of destruction; for, while revolution will not originate in them, once let a popular uprising take form and the cellars will re-inforce it in a manner more terrible than words can portray. . . .

It is not my present purpose to dwell on the causes which have produced these conditions. I wish to bring home to the mind and heart of the reader a true conception of life in the slums, by citing typical cases, illustrating a condition prevalent in every great city of the Union and increasing in its extent every year. I shall confine myself to uninvited poverty as found in cultured Boston, because I am personally acquainted with the condition of affairs here, and because Boston has long claimed the proud distinction of being practically free from poverty.

I shall . . . briefly describe scenes which fell under my personal observation during an afternoon tour through the slums of the North End, confining myself to a few typical cases which fairly represent the actual condition of numbers of families in the slums of our prosperous city. . . .

The first building we entered faced a narrow street. The hallway was as dark as the air was foul or the walls filthy. Not a ray or shimmer of light fell through transoms or sky-light. The stairs were narrow and worn. By the aid of matches we were able to grope our way along, and also to observe more than was pleasant to behold. It was apparent that the hallways or stairs were seldom surprised by water, while pure, fresh air was evidently as much a stranger as fresh paint. After ascending several flights, we entered a room of undreamed-of wretchedness. On the floor lay a sick man. He was rather fine looking, with an intelligent face, bright eyes, and a countenance indicative of force of character. No sign of dissipation, but an expression of sadness, or rather a look of dumb resignation peered from his expressive eyes. For more than two years he had been paralyzed in his lower limbs, and also affected with dropsy. The spectacle of a strong man with the organs of locomotion dead, is always pathetic; but when the victim of such misfortune is in the depths of abject poverty, his case assumes a tragic hue. There, for two years, he had lain on a wretched pallet of rags, seeing his faithful wife tirelessly sewing, hour by hour and day by day, and knowing full well that health, life and hope were hourly slipping from her. This poor woman supports the invalid husband, her two children and herself, by making pants for leading Boston clothiers. No rest, no surcease, a perpetual grind from early dawn often till far into the night; and, what is more appalling, outraged nature has rebelled; the long months of semi-starvation and lack of sleep have brought on rheumatism, which has settled in the joints of her fingers, so that every stitch means a throb of pain. Thus with one of the most painful diseases enthroned in that part of the body which must move incessantly from dawn till midnight, with two small dependent children and a husband who is utterly powerless to help her, this poor woman struggles bravely and uncomplainingly, confronted ever by a nameless dread of pending misfortune. Eviction, sickness, starvation—such are the ever-present spectres, while every year marks the steady encroachment of disease, and the lowering of the register of vitality. Moreover, from the window of her soul falls the light of no star athwart the pathway of life.

The next place visited was in the attic of a tenement building even more wretched than the one just described. The general aspects of these houses, however, are all much the same, the chief difference being in the degrees of filth and squalor present. Here in an attic lives a poor widow with three children, a little boy and two little girls. They live by making pants at starvation wages. Since the youngest child was two and a half years old she has been daily engaged in overcasting the long seams of the garments made by her mother. When we first called she had just passed her fourth birthday, and now overcasts from three to four pairs of pants every day. There, on a little stool, she sat, her fingers moving as rapidly and in as unerring a manner as an old experienced needle-woman. These three children are fine looking, as are most of the little Portuguese I visited. Their large heads and brilliant eyes seem to indicate capacity to enjoy in an unusual degree the matchless delight springing from intellectual and spiritual development. Yet the wretched walls of their little apartment practically mark the limit of their world; the needle their inseparable companion; their moral and mental natures hopelessly dwarfed; a world of wonderful possibilities denied them by an inexorable fate over which they have no control and for which they are in no way responsible. . . .

Among the places we visited were a number of cellars or burrows. We descended several steps into dark, narrow passageways, leading to cold, damp rooms, in many of which no direct ray of sunshine ever creeps.. We entered one room containing a bed, cooking-stove, rack of dirty clothes and some broken chairs. On the bed lay a man who has been ill for three months with rheumatism. This family consists of father, mother, and a daughter in her teens, *all of whom are compelled to occupy one bed*. They eat, cook, live, and sleep in this wretched cellar and pay over fifty dollars a year rent. This is a typical illustration of life in this underground world.

In another similar cellar or burrow, we found a mother and seven boys and girls, some of them quite large, *all sleeping in two medium-sized beds in one room;* this apartment is also their kitchen. The other room is a storehouse for kindling wood the children gather and sell, a little store and living-room combined. Their rent is two dollars a week. The cellar was damp and cold; the air stifling. Nothing can be imagined more favorable to contagion both physical and moral than such dens as these. Ethical exaltation or spiritual growth is impossible with such environment. . . .

In an attic in another tenement we found a widow weeping and working by the side of a little cradle where lay a sick child, whose large, luminous eyes shone with almost phosphorescent brilliancy from great cavernous sockets, as they wandered from one to another, with a wistful, soul-querying gaze. Its forehead was large and prominent, so much so that, looking at the upper part of the head, one would little imagine how terrible the emanciation of the body, which was little more than skin and bones, speaking more eloquently than words of the ravages of slow starvation and wasting disease. The immediate cause of the poor woman's tears was explained to us in broken English, substantially as follows: She had just returned from the dispensary where she had been unsuccessful in her effort to have a physician visit her child, owing to her inability to pay the quarter of a dollar demanded for the visit. . . .

From this attic, after visiting many other quarters scarcely less terrible, and all presenting substantially the same picture of chronic wretchedness, we descended several steps, and found ourselves in a cellar apartment about half underground. The ceiling was only seven and one half feet from the floor. If these rooms ever contained any salable articles of furniture, they had disappeared; and the woman related to us, with quivering lip and tears starting from her eyes, the terrible fact that for three days they had had no fire. On one of these days the thermometer at the Blue Hill Observatory had registered two degrees below zero. The husband, who had lost his work on account of sickness, had just succeeded in securing some broken-up wood, in pay for a day's work. Neither the man nor woman had any appearance of being addicted to drink. The man said, with feeling, "All I want is work." The poor woman, in consequence of being thus exposed in this damp and freezing cellar, without a spark of fire, was in agony from rheumatism; her lungs also were affected. Seldom have I witnessed a scene so absolutely hopeless, so dreary, so well calculated to bring a feeling of overpowering heartsickness to any sensitive soul, as this. Here was a family of seven, apparently sober and reasonably intelligent, only asking for work. The rent paid is one dollar and a half a week, for a den not fit for dumb animals to live in. The atmosphere, owing to the proximity of outbuildings, was horrible beyond description.

After relieving the present needs of these sufferers we left the apartment, knowing that the cloud had, for the moment, been lifted; yet the relief was only temporary. The next month, through sickness or inability to obtain work, they were liable to be in as deplorable a condition as we had found them; and this is a single typical case taken from hundreds who are practically in the same condition. No *charity* work, however wisely carried on, can take the place of *justice;* and though charity, at the present time, is very necessary, it is radical social and economic changes that are urgently demanded. This commonwealth of misery and despair is largely the legitimate product of unjust social conditions. Its inhabitants are victims of human selfishness and greed—prisoners of poverty—driven toward starvation by the merciless lash of law, in the hands of injustice. This is a fact which cannot be too often stated.

Black Capitalism

BOOKER T. WASHINGTON (1856–1915)   *Booker T. Washington was born in slavery and worked his way through Hampton Institute in Virginia. He taught there until 1881, when he was chosen to head a new normal school for Negroes chartered by the Alabama legislature. As founder and principal of Tuskegee Institute, he set forth a program of vocational training that favored working with the hands at the expense of higher education. Tactfully seeking the economic advancement of the Negro without offending the dominant white elements of the South, he publicly accepted segregation and the separate-but-equal doctrine, but secretly he spent thousands of dollars fighting disenfranchisement and Jim Crow laws.*

One-third of the population of the South is of the Negro race. No enterprise seeking the material, civil, or moral welfare of this section can disregard this element of our population and reach the highest success. I but convey to you, Mr. President and Directors, the sentiment of the masses of my race when I say that in no way have the value and manhood of the American Negro been more fittingly and generously recognized than by the managers of this magnificent Exposition at every stage of its progress. It is a recognition that will do more to cement the friendship of the two races than any occurrence since the dawn of our freedom.

Not only this, but the opportunity here afforded will awaken among us a new era of industrial progress. Ignorant and inexperienced, it is not strange that in the first years of our new life

An address at the Cotton States & International Exposition, Atlanta, Georgia, Sept., 1895. Reprinted in *Up From Slavery* (New York: Doubleday, Page & Co., 1901), pp. 218–25.

we began at the top instead of at the bottom; that a seat in Congress or the state legislature was more sought than real estate or industrial skill; that the political convention or stump speaking had more attractions than starting a dairy farm or truck garden.

A ship lost at sea for many days suddenly sighted a friendly vessel. From the mast of the unfortunate vessel was seen a signal, "Water, water; we die of thirst!" The answer from the friendly vessel at once came back, "Cast down your bucket where you are." A second time the signal, "Water, water; send us water!" ran up from the distressed vessel, and was answered, "Cast down your bucket where you are." And a third and fourth signal for water was answered, "Cast down your bucket where you are." The captain of the distressed vessel, at last heeding the injunction, cast down his bucket, and it came up full of fresh, sparkling water from the mouth of the Amazon River. To those of my race who depend on bettering their condition in a foreign land or who underestimate the importance of cultivating friendly relations with the Southern white man, who is their next-door neighbour, I would say: "Cast down your bucket where you are"—cast it down in making friends in every manly way of the people of all races by whom we are surrounded.

Cast it down in agriculture, mechanics, in commerce, in domestic service, and in the professions. And in this connection it is well to bear in mind that whatever other sins the South may be called to bear, when it comes to business, pure and simple, it is in the South that the Negro is given a man's chance in the commercial world, and in nothing is this Exposition more eloquent than in emphasizing this chance. Our greatest danger is that in the great leap from slavery to freedom we may overlook the fact that the masses of us are to live by the productions of our hands, and fail to keep in mind that we shall prosper in proportion as we learn to dignify and glorify common labour and put brains and skill into the common occupations of life; shall prosper in proportion as we learn to draw the line between the superficial and the substantial, the ornamental gewgaws of life and the useful. No race can prosper till it learns that there is as much dignity in tilling a field as in writing a poem. It is at the bottom of life we must begin, and not at the top. Nor should we permit our grievances to overshadow our opportunities.

To those of the white race who look to the incoming of those of foreign birth and strange tongue and habits for the prosperity of the South, were I permitted I would repeat what I say to my own race, "Cast down your bucket where you are." Cast it down among the eight millions of Negroes whose habits you know, whose fidelity and love you have tested in days when to have proved treacherous meant the ruin of your firesides. Cast down your bucket among these people who have, without strikes and labour wars, tilled your fields, cleared your forests, builded your railroads and cities, and brought forth treasures from the bowels of the earth, and helped make possible this magnificent representation of the progress of the South. Casting down your bucket among my people, helping and encouraging them as you are doing on these grounds, and to education of head, hand, and heart, you will find that they will buy your surplus land, make blossom the waste places in your fields, and run your factories. While doing this, you can be sure in the future, as in the past, that you and your families will be surrounded by the most patient, faithful, law-abiding, and unresentful people that the world has seen. As we have proved our loyalty to you in the past, in nursing your children, watching by the sick-bed of your mothers and fathers, and often following them with tear-dimmed eyes to their graves, so in the future, in our humble way, we shall stand by you with a devotion that no foreigner can approach, ready to lay down our lives, if need be, in defence of yours, interlacing our industrial, commercial, civil, and religious life with yours in a way that shall make the interests of both races one. In all things that are purely social we can be as separate as the fingers, yet one as the hand in all things essential to mutual progress.

There is no defence or security for any of us except in the highest intelligence and development of all. If anywhere there are efforts tending to curtail the fullest growth of the Negro, let these efforts be turned into stimulating, encouraging, and making him the most useful and intelligent citizen. Effort or means so invested will pay a thousand per cent interest. These efforts will be twice blessed—"blessing him that gives and him that takes.". . .

Nearly sixteen millions of hands will aid you in pulling the load upward, or they will pull against you the load downward. We shall constitute one-third and more of the ignorance and crime of the

South, or one-third its intelligence and progress; we shall contribute one-third to the business and industrial prosperity of the South, or we shall prove a veritable body of death, stagnating, depressing, retarding every effort to advance the body politic.

Gentlemen of the Exposition, as we present to you our humble effort at an exhibition of our progress, you must not expect over-much. Starting thirty years ago with ownership here and there in a few quilts and pumpkins and chickens (gathered from miscellaneous sources), remember the path that has led from these to the inventions and production of agricultural implements, buggies, steam-engines, newspapers, books, statuary, carving, paintings, the management of drug-stores and banks, has not been trodden without contact with thorns and thistles. While we take pride in what we exhibit as a result of our independent efforts, we do not for a moment forget that our part in this exhibition would fall far short of your expectations but for the constant help that has come to our educational life, not only from the Southern states, but especially from Northern philanthropists, who have made their gifts a constant stream of blessing and encouragement.

The wisest among my race understand that the agitation of questions of social equality is the extremest folly, and that progress in the enjoyment of all the privileges that will come to us must be the result of severe and constant struggle rather than of artificial forcing. No race that has anything to contribute to the markets of the world is long in any degree ostracized. It is important and right that all privileges of the law be ours, but it is vastly more important that we be prepared for the exercises of these privileges. The opportunity to earn a dollar in a factory just now is worth infinitely more than the opportunity to spend a dollar in an opera-house.

In conclusion, may I repeat that nothing in thirty years has given us more hope and encouragement, and drawn us so near to you of the white race, as this opportunity offered by the Exposition; and here bending, as it were, over the altar that represents the results of the struggles of your race and mine, both starting practically empty-handed three decades ago, I pledge that in your effort to work out the great and intricate problem which God has laid at the doors of the South, you shall have at all times the patient, sympathetic help of my race; only let this be constantly in mind, that, while from representations in these buildings of the product of field, of forest, of mine, of factory, letters, and art, much good will come, yet far above and beyond material benefits will be that higher good, that, let us pray God, will come, in a blotting out of sectional differences and racial animosities and suspicions, in a determination to administer absolute justice, in a willing obedience among all classes to the mandates of law. This, this, coupled with our material prosperity, will bring into our beloved South a new heaven and a new earth.

Black Progressivism

W. E. BURGHARDT DU BOIS (1868–1963)   *A Harvard Ph.D. and an influential Negro leader of mixed ancestry, DuBois helped to found the biracial NAACP in 1909. Until 1933 he was its chief Negro leader and editor of its journal,* The Crisis. *Believing that the Negro race would be saved only by its exceptional men, "the Talented Tenth," he urged the training of a college-bred elite to lead and elevate the Negro masses. Although he became a Marxist after a visit to the Soviet Union, he did not declare himself a Communist until his ninetieth year. He died in Ghana, having become a citizen of that nation shortly before his death.*   •

Easily the most striking thing in the history of the American Negro since 1876 is the ascendancy of Mr. Booker T. Washington. It began at the time when war memories and ideals were rapidly passing; a day of astonishing commercial development was dawning; a sense of doubt and hesitation overtook the freedmen's sons—then it was that his leading began. Mr. Washington came, with a simple definite programme, at the psychological moment when the nation was a little ashamed of having bestowed so much sentiment on Negroes, and was concentrating its energies on Dollars. His programme of

From *The Souls of Black Folks* (Chicago: A. C. McClurg & Co., 1903), pp. 41–59.

industrial education, conciliation of the South, and submission and silence as to civil and political rights . . . startled and won the applause of the South, it interested and won the admiration of the North; and after a confused murmur of protest, it silenced if it did not convert the Negroes themselves. . . .

But Booker T. Washington arose as essentially the leader not of one race but of two—a compromiser between the South, the North, and the Negro. Naturally the Negroes resented, at first bitterly, signs of compromise which surrendered their civil and political rights, even though this was to be exchanged for larger chances of economic development. The rich and dominating North, however, was not only weary of the race problem, but was investing largely in Southern enterprises, and welcomed any method of peaceful coöperation. Thus, by national opinion, the Negroes began to recognize Mr. Washington's leadership; and the voice of criticism was hushed.

Mr. Washington represents in Negro thought the old attitude of adjustment and submission; but adjustment at such a peculiar time as to make his programme unique. This is an age of unusual economic development, and Mr. Washington's programme naturally takes an economic cast, becoming a gospel of Work and Money to such an extent as apparently almost completely to overshadow the higher aims of life. Moreover, this is an age when the more advanced races are coming in closer contact with the less developed races, and the race-feeling is therefore intensified; and Mr. Washington's programme practically accepts the alleged inferiority of the Negro races. Again, in our own land, the reaction from the sentiment of war time has given impetus to race-prejudice against Negroes, and Mr. Washington withdraws many of the high demands of Negroes as men and American citizens. In other periods of intensified prejudice all the Negro's tendency to self-assertion has been called forth; at this period a policy of submission is advocated. In the history of nearly all other races and peoples the doctrine preached at such crises has been that manly self-respect is worth more than lands and houses, and that a people who voluntarily surrender such respect, or cease striving for it, are not worth civilizing.

In answer to this, it has been claimed that the Negro can survive only through submission. Mr. Washington distinctly asks that black people give up, at least for the present, three things—

First, political power,

Second, insistence on civil rights,

Third, higher education of Negro youth—and concentrate all their energies on industrial education, the accumulation of wealth, and the conciliation of the South. This policy has been courageously and insistently advocated for over fifteen years, and has been triumphant for perhaps ten years. As a result of this tender of the palm-branch, what has been the return? In these years there have occurred:

1. The disfranchisement of the Negro.

2. The legal creation of a distinct status of civil inferiority for the Negro.

3. The steady withdrawal of aid from institutions for the higher training of the Negro.

These movements are not, to be sure, direct results of Mr. Washington's teachings; but his propaganda has, without a shadow of doubt, helped their speedier accomplishment. The question then comes: Is it possible, and probable, that nine millions of men can make effective progress in economic lines if they are deprived of political rights, made a servile caste, and allowed only the most meagre chance for developing their exceptional men? If history and reason give any distinct answer to these questions, it is an emphatic *No*. And Mr. Washington thus faces the triple paradox of his career:

1. He is striving nobly to make Negro artisans business men and property-owners; but it is utterly impossible, under modern competitive methods, for workingmen and property-owners to defend their rights and exist without the right of suffrage.

2. He insists on thrift and self-respect, but at the same time counsels a silent submission to civic inferiority such as is bound to sap the manhood of any race in the long run.

3. He advocates common-school and industrial training, and depreciates institutions of higher learning; but neither the Negro common-schools, nor Tuskegee itself, could remain open a day were it not for teachers trained in Negro colleges, or trained by their graduates.

This triple paradox in Mr. Washington's position is the object of criticism by two classes of colored Americans. One class is spiritually descended from Toussaint the Savior, through Gabriel, Vesey, and Turner, and they represent the attitude of revolt and revenge; they hate the white South blindly and distrust the white race generally, and so far as they agree on definite action, think that the Negro's only hope lies in emigration beyond the borders of the United States. And yet, by the irony of fate, nothing has more effectually made this programme seem hopeless than the recent course of the United States toward weaker and darker peoples in the West Indies, Hawaii, and the Philippines—for where in the world may we go and be safe from lying and brute force?

The other class of Negroes who cannot agree with Mr. Washington has hitherto said little aloud. . . . They acknowledge Mr. Washington's invaluable service in counselling patience and courtesy in such demands; they do not ask that ignorant black men vote when ignorant whites are debarred, or that any reasonable restrictions in the suffrage should not be applied; they know that the low social level of the mass of the race is responsible for much discrimination against it, but they also know, and the nation knows, that relentless color-prejudice is more often a cause than a result of the Negro's degradation; they seek the abatement of this relic of barbarism, and not its systematic encouragement and pampering by all agencies of social power from the Associated Press to the Church of Christ. . . . They do not expect that the free right to vote, to enjoy civic rights, and to be educated, will come in a moment; they do not expect to see the bias and prejudices of years disappear at the blast of a trumpet; but they are absolutely certain that the way for a people to gain their reasonable rights is not by voluntarily throwing them away and insisting that they do not want them; that the way for a people to gain respect is not by continually belittling and ridiculing themselves; that, on the contrary, Negroes must insist continually, in season and out of season, that voting is necessary to modern manhood, that color discrimination is barbarism, and that black boys need education as well as white boys.

In failing thus to state plainly and unequivocally the legitimate demands of their people, even at the cost of opposing an honored leader, the thinking classes of American Negroes would shirk a heavy responsibility—a responsibility to themselves, a responsibility to the struggling masses, a responsibility to the darker races of men whose future depends so largely on this American experiment, but especially a responsibility to this nation—this common Fatherland. It is wrong to encourage a man or a people in evildoing; it is wrong to aid and abet a national crime simply because it is unpopular not to do so. The growing spirit of kindliness and reconciliation between the North and South after the frightful differences of a generation ago ought to be a source of deep congratulation to all, and especially to those whose mistreatment caused the war; but if that reconciliation is to be marked by the industrial slavery and civic death of those same black men, with permanent legislation into a position of inferiority, then those black men, if they are really men, are called upon by every consideration of patriotism and loyalty to oppose such a course by all civilized methods, even though such opposition involves disagreement with Mr. Booker T. Washington. We have no right to sit silently by while the inevitable seeds are sown for a harvest of disaster to our children, black and white. . . .

The black men of America have a duty to perform, a duty stern and delicate—a forward movement to oppose a part of the work of their greatest leader. So far as Mr. Washington preaches Thrift, Patience, and Industrial Training for the masses, we must hold up his hands and strive with him, rejoicing in his honors and glorying in the strength of this Joshua called of God and of man to lead the headless host. But so far as Mr. Washington apologizes for injustice, North or South, does not rightly value the privilege and duty of voting, belittles the emasculating effects of caste distinctions, and opposes the higher training and ambition of our brighter minds—so far as he, the South, or the Nation, does this—we must unceasingly and firmly oppose them. By every civilized and peaceful method we must strive for the rights which the world accords to men, clinging unwaveringly to those great words which the sons of the Fathers would fain forget: "We hold these truths to be self-evident: That all men are created equal; that they are endowed by their Creator with certain unalienable rights; that among these are life, liberty, and the pursuit of happiness."

The Soul of Capitalism

ALVIN S. JOHNSON (1874–   )   *An economist and journalist, Johnson received his Ph.D. from Columbia in 1902 and taught at several universities before 1917 when he became editor of the* New Republic. *In 1923 he became director of the New School for Social Research founded in 1919 by Thorstein Veblen, James Harvey Robinson, and Charles A. Beard to study the "new social order." Though trained in the old school, he became dissatisfied with the limitations of orthodox economics and introduced numerous theoretical innovations in attempting to apply it more closely to the observed facts.*

There is no such thing as capitalism, say the conservatives. It is an empty sound, a curse in the name of a false god, directed by the revolutionaries against the world of things as they are, as they always have been and always shall be. Capitalism is a reality, say the radicals. It is the appropriate designation of the current system—a vulgar, hideous system, a brute mechanism set in motion by the energy of blind greed, a mechanism through which human values and human lives are thrust, to emerge smudged and flat and dead. The soul of capitalism? Pernicious paradox!

Capitalism is no less a reality than was feudalism. The capitalist employer is the most prominent figure in the modern state, just as the knight was the most prominent figure in the mediæval. . . . Capitalism is, to be sure, not the whole of modern life; nor was feudalism the whole of the life of the Middle Ages. . . . [But] we must yet admit . . . a general tendency to translate all current experience into capitalistic terms. Such instances are but indications of the collective conviction that capitalism is the most significant fact in modern life. Why then do our conservatives insist upon rejecting the term, upon denying the very content of the concept? Chiefly because those who have depicted capitalism have sketched it in black crayon, instead of painting it in the rosy hues of romance. . . .

Capitalism, like every other social system, implies a class that

From *The Unpopular Review,* I (April–June, 1914), pp. 227–31, 234, 237, 240.) Reprinted by permission of the author.

rules and a class that is controlled. The ruling class—*pace* those political theorists who refuse to know that a ruling class exists—is composed of the capitalist employers. And how do the capitalist employers differ from any others of the masters that the world has known? Not merely in that they possess accumulations and pay wages in money. These are incidental facts. What is essential is that the capitalist employers, in so far as they are truly such, are controlled in all their active dealings by the principle of commercialization.

And commercialization is a psychical phenomenon. It is the substitution, in economic conduct, of a process of calculation for a process of feeling and will. The antithesis between the two processes has long been recognized by practical men, under the form of the contrast between "business" and "sentiment.". . . The capitalist employer in a competitive trade is quickly taught by bitter experience that it is not his function to judge and choose. His business is to calculate; and the less noneconomic principles of action interfere with his decisions, the more certain he is of success. All elements essential to his business present themselves in the guise of exchange values. All magnitudes, thus, are commensurate: you compare one with the other and choose the greater. . . .

If I am a capitalist employer, operating under conditions of keen competition, I buy no more readily from an honest man than from a rogue, provided the rogue can give good title to the things he sells. I hire men, Teutons or Slavs or Latins, white, black or yellow, with a sole view to their effectiveness for purposes of profit. I may have private opinions on religion or politics or morals; on the use of alcohol or opium or tobacco. But unless I can relate such manifestations of virtues or vices to the point of profit, I must suppress these opinions, in my active dealings with men. It follows, then, that in all that concerns the capitalist employer, in all that concerns his essential rulership, he is a respecter of the liberties of men. . . .

Toleration and its counterpart, personal liberty, these are the first constituents of the soul of capitalism. Capitalistic toleration, it is true, originates in interest, and is limited by interest. If capitalism admonishes me to tolerate atheism in my foreman, so long as it does not interfere with his efficiency, it equally admonishes me to extirpate excessive piety in his person, if, for example, intervals of ecstatic contemplation divert his attention from my interests. Morally such toleration is vastly inferior to that which is founded upon a broad sentiment of humanity and a recognition of the presumption involved in the prescribing of rules to one's fellow man. But ethical toleration can find lodgment only in the breasts of the chosen few. "Neither do I condemn thee." Of all the miracles, is not this expression of toleration the greatest? Millions upon millions have repeated the sentiment devoutly; but to how few has it become a rule of life!

Capitalistic toleration, on the other hand, is a sentiment not too refined for the most vulgar souls. Indeed, its appeal is probably strongest to the very most vulgar; certainly, to the most selfish. A high-minded employer may seek to bring up his working-folk in the way they should go—that is, his own conception of the Way. It is the greedy materialist who says: "What do I care how my workmen eat and drink and play, what they read, how they vote, worship and marry? It's all one to me, so they deliver the goods." Ethical toleration selects for its votaries the few and the unselfish; capitalistic toleration selects the many and the selfish. And it is for this reason that the liberty based upon capitalistic toleration is the broadest and most substantial of all. "City air makes free," says the proverb. Not because the city is the abode of choice souls, but because the city is capitalistic. . . .

If capitalism had offered the working class nothing but the crumbs of middle-class liberty, the diatribes of the revolutionaries would be not without justification. For admittedly, liberty has been gained in far greater measure by the capitalist employer than by the workman. But capitalism has done vastly more for labor than this. It has given rise to that most interesting and important of all modern social phenomena, the solidarity of labor. As an active, working concept, the fraternity of labor is just as certainly a product of capitalism as is social toleration. The latter is the soul of capitalism, as it manifests itself in the class of employers, the former, as it manifests itself in the class of employees. . . .

For the working class, solidarity is producing results quite analogous to those produced in the class of capitalistic employers

by the pursuit of profit. Solidarity is unthinkable without a measure
of toleration. The American trade unionist learns to tolerate the
alien origin, the broken speech and uncouth manner, the strange
religion, and the unexpected outlook upon life, of the foreign
workman who must either become a brother unionist and faithful
ally, or a scab and an enemy. And out of this toleration is created
a sphere of personal freedom from social encroachment such as
no workman of an earlier epoch ever enjoyed. Fraternity and
liberty, these are the positive acquisitions won by labor out of the
very oppression of capitalism. Of the revolutionary trinity only
equality remains beyond the visible horizon. And even equality
may be brought nearer, if not realized, through the further perfecting of working-class liberty and fraternity.

Capitalism is material, gross, ugly. Yes, but it has a soul—toleration, liberty, fraternity. And this, like most souls, is not so much
in being as in becoming. It is only in the most highly capitalistic
centers that even business has partly freed itself from elements of
personal oppression. There is no state nor city in which the
fraternity of labor is more than an emerging fact. Under capitalism,
workingmen are brothers, but there is still a vast deal of the Cain
and Abel in their feelings toward one another. Remove the pressure
of capitalism at this instant, and the lessons of fraternity would
quickly be forgotten. Relax the profit motive, and mankind would
again stand forth in its pristine narrowness and bigotry and
cruelty.

The Case of Christianity
Against Capitalism

WALTER RAUSCHENBUSCH (1861–1918)   *A Baptist clergyman,
Rauschenbusch was profoundly disturbed by the Depression of
1893 which brought into stark relief the spiritual poverty and
economic injustice of American life. He found his religious ideas*

Reprinted with permission of The Macmillan Company from *Christianizing the
Social Order* (New York: Macmillan, 1912), pp. 235–38, 311–15.

*"didn't fit" and was compelled to seek a new relation between
religion and social problems. Influenced by Henry George and
the Fabian socialists, Sidney and Beatrice Webb, he became a
Christian Socialist which, according to him, differed from orthodox socialism in that it set positive religious faith against a
materialistic philosophy. While accepting economic determinism,
it stressed religious regeneration as a factor in the salvation of
society.*

Capitalism is the most efficient system for the creation of material
wealth which the world has ever seen. Wherever it invades an old
civilization, the ancient organization of production is doomed and
goes down before it. This technical efficiency proves that the system
must have powerful moral forces and cohesions in it. . . .

On the other hand, the defenders of capitalism often inflate its
stock. They assume that the whole spiritual and material advance
of modern civilization is due to the capitalistic system, just as the
Roman Catholic Church sets all the moral progress made by
Western humanity in fifteen hundred years to its own credit. The
increase in moral and intellectual force during the nineteenth
century was largely due to the spread of democracy and education.
The material triumphs of our era are due to the rise of science.
Applied science would have served any social order that might
have been in existence during the last century. If socialism succeeds
capitalism, it will probably make even larger use of science than
the short-sighted haste of economic individualism has been able
to do. Capitalism can claim as its virtue and achievement only
what its peculiar organization and spirit alone were adapted to
accomplish. It has served civilization best in two directions: in
developing the application of machine power to production, and
in furthering the organization of associated groups of workers on
a large scale. Profit could best be made by power machines and
by gang work; consequently capitalism developed both. At these
points it was in line with human progress and boosted it. It entered
into a working partnership with science in so far as science could
build machinery, develop the exactness of operation necessary for
machine work, analyze and combine material, and in general aid
production and the creation of profit. For all aid it gave science
in this way it deserves our gratitude. . . .

But the great powers of human goodness that lie latent in our economic life are largely kept down or misdirected through the constitutional maladjustment of social forces in capitalism. The power of association is thwarted or soured by the competitive struggle and the autocratic relation into which the leaders are placed over against the workers. The profit system lures the economic stewards of society into tricking or extorting from those whom they ought to serve. Our economic system in its fundamental structure is still nonmoral or immoral, nonchristian or unchristian. It offends the thoughtless by its excesses, and the thoughtful by its essence and spitit. The more the Christian spirit rises to clear-sighted ascendency in any individual or any social group, the more offensive and intolerable does the ethic of capitalism seem. . . .

Let us sum up the case of Christianity against capitalism.

We saw that the distinctive characteristic of the capitalistic system is that the industrial outfit of society is owned and controlled by a limited group, while the mass of the industrial workers is without ownership or power over the system within which they work. A small group of great wealth and power is set over against a large group of propertyless men. Given this line-up, the rest follows with the inevitableness of a process in physics or chemistry.

Wherever the capitalist class remains in unorganized and small units, they will struggle for the prizes held out by modern industry. . . . Wherever the competitive principle is still in operation, it intensifies natural emulation by the size of the stakes it offers, enables the greedy and cunning to set the pace for the rest, makes men immoral by fear, and puts the selfish impulses in control. The charge of Christianity against competitive capitalism is that it is unfraternal, the opposite of coöperation and teamwork.

Capitalism gives the owners and managers of industry autocratic power over the workers. The dangers always inherent in the leadership of the strong are intensified by the fact that in capitalistic industry this power is unrestrained by democratic checks and fortified by almost absolute ownership of the means of production and life. Consequently the master class in large domains of industry have exacted excessive toil, and have paid wages that were neither a just return for the work done nor sufficient to support life normally. The working class is everywhere in a state of unrest and embitterment. By great sacrifices it has tried to organize in order to strengthen its position against these odds, but the master class has hampered or suppressed the organizations of labor. This line-up of two antagonistic classes is the historical continuation of the same line-up which we see in chattel slavery and feudal serfdom. In recent years the development of corporations has added a new difficulty by depersonalizing the master. The whole situation contradicts the spirit of American institutions. It is the last entrenchment of the despotic principle. It tempts the class in power to be satisfied with a semimorality in their treatment of the working class. It is not Christian.

The capitalist class serves society in the capacity of the middleman, and modern conditions make this function more important than ever before. But under the capitalistic organization this wholesome function is not under public control, and the relations created call out the selfish motives and leave the higher motives of human nature dormant. Under competition business readily drifts into the use of tricky methods, sells harmful or adulterated goods, and breaks down the moral self-restraint of the buyer. Under monopoly the middleman is able to practice extortion on the consumer. The kindly and friendly relations that abound in actual business life between the dealer and the consumer are due to the personal character of the parties and the ineradicable social nature of man, and are not created by the nature of business itself.

In all the operations of capitalistic industry and commerce the aim that controls and directs is not the purpose to supply human needs, but to make a profit for those who direct industry. This in itself is an irrational and unchristian adjustment of the social order, for it sets money up as the prime aim, and human life as something secondary, or as a means to secure money. The supremacy of profit in capitalism stamps it as a mammonistic organization with which Christianity can never be content. "Profit" commonly contains considerable elements of just reward for able work; it may contain nothing but that; but where it is large and dissociated from hard work, it is traceable to some kind of monopoly privilege and power—either the power to withhold part of the earnings of the workers by the control of the means of production, or the ability to throw part of the expenses of business on the community, or the power to overcharge the public. In so far as profit is derived from these sources, it is tribute collected by power from the helpless, a form of legalized graft, and a contradiction of Christian relations. . . .

Devotion to the common good is one of the holy and divine forces in human society. Capitalism teaches us to set private interest before the common good. It follows profit, and not patriotism and public spirit. If war is necessary to create or protect profit, it will involve nations in war, but it plays a selfish part amid the sacrifices imposed by war. It organizes many of the ablest men into powerful interests which are at some points antagonistic to the interest of the community. It has corrupted our legislatures, our executive officers, and our courts, tampered with the organs of public opinion and instruction, spread a spirit of timidity among the citizens, and vindictively opposed the men who stood for the common good against the private interests.

When men of vigorous character and intellectual ability obey the laws of capitalism, and strive for the prizes it holds out to them, they win power and great wealth, but they are placed in an essentially false relation to their fellow-men, the Christian virtues of their family stock are undermined, their natural powers of leadership are crippled, and the greater their success in amassing wealth under capitalistic methods, the greater is the tragedy of their lives from a Christian point of view.

These are the points in the Christian indictment of capitalism. All these are summed up in this single challenge, that capitalism has generated a spirit of its own which is antagonistic to the spirit of Christianity; a spirit of hardness and cruelty that neutralizes the Christian spirit of love; a spirit that sets material goods above spiritual possessions. To set things above men is the really dangerous practical materialism. To set Mammon before God is the only idolatry against which Jesus warned us.

Chapter III

The Modern Leviathan

Wealth Against Commonwealth

There was at the turn of the century a mounting fear that the forces of capital and industry had not only outgrown those of the republic but threatened to take over the sovereign powers of government itself. Seemingly the giant corporation with untold millions of wealth, as Thomas Hobbes said of the great LEVIATHAN, had "the use of so much Power and Strength conferred on him, that by terror thereof, he is enabled to forme the wills of them all, to Peace at home, and mutuall ayd against their enemies abroad. . . . ", to prescribe "the Rules, whereby every man may know, what Goods he may enjoy, and what Actions he may doe" and to choose "all Counsellors, Ministers, Magistrates, and Officers, both in Peace, and War." [1]

This fear found its most extreme expression in the writings of the Populists who, to a man, were convinced the plutocracy reigned supreme in the United States. Mary E. Lease spoke the convictions of many an American when she announced, "Wall Street owns the country. It is no longer a government of the people, by the people, and for the people, but a government of Wall Street, by Wall Street and for Wall Street." [2] "Day by day," Tom Watson fretted, "the power of the individual sinks. Day by day the power of the wealthy classes, of the corporations, rises." [3] And in his futuristic novel, *Caesar's Column*, Ignatius Donnelly predicted that, unless existing trends were checked, America of the late twentieth century would fall into the hands of a military-industrial elite holding absolute power and defended by fleets of airships armed with superbombs and poison gas.[4]

While not all Americans envisaged a future so black, there were vast numbers who believed business control of government to be a political actuality. They differed, however, in their appraisals of its power and extent, and in their explanations of how it had come about. Some, agreeing with Veblen, saw it as not so much the rule of the moneyed class as the political embodiment of the moneymaking ideal.[5] Because of the settled habit of seeing all events from the business point of view, the management of political affairs, like everything else, had fallen by common consent into the hands of businessmen to be guided by business considerations. Hence, even part from what was invidiously called "corrupt" politics, modern politics was business politics. To the Socialists Jack London and William Dean Howells, the plutocracy was the inexorable consequence of historical determinism, the final cumulative stage of capitalism before the great proletarian revolution.[6] Others, notably Henry Adams and Henry Demarest Lloyd, explained it as merely a commercial despotism more powerful than the political despotisms of the past because of its nearly absolute control over the forces of modern science and technology.[7] But perhaps the most widespread view, and probably the one shared by nearly all Progressives, was that government was merely a lackey of big business.

"Twenty-five years ago," the Progressive–Republican editor, William Allen White stated in 1910, "an extra-constitutional government began to take charge of this country. This superficial government did not cover the entire country until the late nineties. But from 1897 to 1903 it was dominant, and probably in many matters it was superior to the constitutional government. There was the constitutional government and the business government in the city, in the county . . . in the state and in the nation." But once the two governments amalgamated—as White believed had happened—the charge could no longer be made that "business runs the government" because now, in all important respects, business *was* the government.[8]

Democratic distrust of the state had greatly facilitated the accumulation of political power by corporations. The constitutions of the various states had almost all been constructed on the principle that government was a necessary evil, and the less responsibility imposed on legislatures and other governmental agencies, the better it was for the citizen. The attitude of Americans toward their political institutions led early in the nineteenth century to a prodigal concession of public powers to "private" corporations. In order to meet demands for canals, railways and banks, it was deemed necessary to confer upon groups of citizens the powers of organization that society denied to the state on the grounds that this was safer for society than if the state assumed them itself. As organizations midway between the state and the individual, corporations in their earlier stages excited few apprehensions because they were, in theory at least, democratically organized and were based substantially on individual contract. In fact, because of their collective economic power, they were regarded as far more effective defenders of personal liberty than the individual man himself.

By confusing corporations with themselves as individuals, however, Americans allowed capitalism to develop an incongruous new social structure at odds with their traditional political structure. Since the individual's interest was considered identical with that of society, so it was assumed when the corporation was created that, since it was composed of a group of individuals, its interests also coincided with those of society. The corporation therefore was legally represented as an individual having rights and duties in itself. Such fictions and analogies were innocent and convenient enough so long as corporations were comparatively small and insignificant. But, as Woodrow Wilson protested, it was another matter to treat huge industrial organizations as legal persons when in them were concentrated the energies and power of thousands. In his opinion this "fatuous, antiquated and quite unnecessary fiction" masked the fact that society was "building up bodies economic outside its bodies politic" which threatened to dominate the bodies political themselves.[9] The irony was that after 1890 the average American found that under the cloak of laissez-faire, increased governmental activity had actually been provided, not by the legally constituted state, but by corporations. He discovered, in fine, that citizenship in his country had been "largely metamorphosed into membership in corporations and patriotism and fidelity to them."[10]

So, despite their nebulous position in the American political mythology, their putative nonexistence in the accepted order of things, the corporations exercised real and substantial power. Popular reaction to this unorthodox development was shock and dismay. The corruption of American politics was laid on the threshold of business, as Parrington said, "like a bastard on the doorsteps of the father." [11] Typical was the angry uproar that followed publication in 1902 of Lincoln Steffens' appalling account of civic turpitude in *McClure's Magazine*. Indicting almost every major city in the United States, Steffens wrote, "Wherever and whenever I have shadowed a corrupt politician to the end of his crooked trail, I have been brought to the back door of some corrupting business man." [12] What was true of the cities was also purportedly true of the states. Behind the "bad" politician lurked the "good" businessman. "No lackey was ever more subservient to its master," it was charged, "than Pennsylvania to its railroads, or than the State of California to the Southern Pacific." [13] On the national level, the chief business of the Senate at Washington seemed to be to serve the financial oligarchy of Wall Street. New York, not Washington, appeared to be the capital of the United States. The upper house of the national government was so packed with the affluent representatives of corporate wealth that it was dubbed the "House of Dollars" and the "Millionaires' Club." Senators were commonly referred to by their corporate affiliation— the Steel Senator, the Standard Oil Senator, the Railroad Senators, and so on. The open, flagrant dereliction of its constitutional responsibilities was branded by David Graham Phillips "The Treason of the Senate," and publication of his tremendously popular exposé in *Cosmopolitan* in 1906 made plain to thoughtful Americans everywhere that "the interests" dominated the political as well as the industrial machinery of the nation. [14]

Of the various explanations of how this had come about—commercial Machiavellianism, Marxian determinism, technological usurpation—the most convincing, albeit the least dramatic, was simple political opportunism. Wealth had always meant power, and the increased concentration of economic power which was the nineteenth century's legacy to the twentieth had inevitably to find political expression. But because American institutions with their individualistic bias did not recognize organized wealth as a legitimate form of political activity—providing neither constitutional sanctions nor checks on collective action—large corporations were put in the position of exerting an enormous amalgamated power by secret, illicit and often corrupt means. To obtain favorable laws or defend itself against hostile legislation, giant corporations had to resort to extralegal means: bribery, threats, lobbying and all kinds of political jobbery.

There is no doubt that these indirect methods proved hugely successful. *Banker's Magazine* frankly admitted as much in 1901: "As the business of the country has learned the secret of combination, it is gradually subverting the power of the politician and rendering him subservient to its purposes."[15] Whenever it came to a conflict between the national business organization and the national political organization, business usually won. And perhaps logically, for as Professor William Graham Sumner of Yale pointed out, there was no form of political power so ill-fitted to cope with plutocracy as democracy:

> Democracy has a whole set of institutions which are extra-legal, but are the most powerful elements in it; they are the party organization, the primary, the convention, etc. All this apparatus is well-adapted to the purposes of plutocracy: it has to do with the formative stage of political activity; it is very largely operated in secret; it has a large but undefined field of legitimate, or quasi-legitimate, expenditure, for which there is no audit. As the operations of this apparatus are extra-legal they are irresponsible, yet they reach out to, and control, the public and civil functions. Even on the field of constitutional institutions, plutocracy always comes into the contest with a small body, a strong organization, a powerful motive, a definite purpose, and a strict discipline, while on the other side is a large unorganized body, without discipline, with its ideas undefined, its interests illy understood, with an indefinite good intention.[16]

By knowing what they wanted and how to get it, business leaders were able to sidetrack Progressive reform and to divert federal regulation *of* business into federal regulation *for* business. Although Wilson savagely attacked "special privilege" during the campaign, once in the White House, as Arthur Link has shown, he abandoned his plan for business control and adopted the Rooseveltian policy for the regulation of business by federal commission.[17] Uncertain as how to carry out his legislative program and reluctant to invoke full federal power, the new President was prevailed upon by spokesmen of the business community to accept the idea of the "self regulation" of business. So, instead of carrying out his plan to put teeth in the antitrust laws, Wilson placed his faith in a Federal Trade Commission designed along lines already laid down by the National Civic Federation and the United States Chamber of Commerce. Rather than wielding a club over big business, the new Commission was expected to be helpful to the corporations by prohibiting unfair trade practices and acting as a "friendly adviser" to businessmen. The rest of his "reform" measures suffered a similar fate. The Clayton Antitrust Act, as he himself conceded, was as weak as water, and the newly created Federal Reserve Board, originally intended to break the stranglehold of the big bankers over credit, was in effect turned over to their representatives. By 1914, it was apparent to puzzled Progressives, as the President said, that "the antagonism between business and Government is over." [18]

Rather than a "triumph of conservatism," however, the capture of government by big business was a victory for corporate radicalism. In staving off a counterrevolution by the conservative forces of reform, big businessmen were not concerned with the preservation of the political and social relations traditionally associated with either capitalism or democracy, but were seeking to legitimatize a revolutionary new power structure. By obtaining a political rationalization of the capitalist revolution, they intended not merely to stabilize their economic position but to inaugurate a radically new kind of cooperation between government and business. Since the Gilded Age, American businessmen had been aware and acted on the premise that while politics did not determine prosperity, it could determine the distribution of prosperity. Only in the first decade of the twentieth century, however, did the big businessman discover, as the editors of the *International Socialist Review* put it, "that he can carry on certain portions of the productive process more efficiently through *his* government than through private corporations." "Some muddleheads," the *Review* went on, "think that will be Socialism, but the capitalist knows better." [19] The significant phenomenon of the Progressive era, as he was well aware, was not business control over politics but the emergence of state capitalism, the incipient consolidation of government and business.

Corporate Feudalism

In their initial disillusionment, Progressive Americans had questioned the entire political system. As the ark of the republic, the federal Constitution came under especially hard scrutiny. To their consternation they discovered—or rather rediscovered—after nearly one hundred years of Constitution worship, the essentially undemocratic nature of that governing instrument.

Democratic government by the people, they learned, was not the object which the founding fathers had in mind, but the very thing they wished to avoid. This was the conclusion of Professor Woodrow Wilson of Princeton: "The Federal government, was not by intention a democratic government. In plan and structure it had been meant to check the sweep and power of popular majorities." [20] Oddly enough, his view that the government originated and was organized upon the initiative and primarily in the interest of the mercantile and wealthy classes was very similar to that first formulated by Federalist opponents of Jeffersonian democracy during the War of 1812. But while the original propounders had regarded that action favorably, modern critics such as Croly, Lippmann, and Charles A. Beard seized upon it as a betrayal of democracy. [21] No one, however, did more to make this the standard interpretation of Progressives than a controversial professor at the University of Washington, J. Allen Smith, an economist turned political theorist.

In his hard-hitting *The Spirit of American Government* (1907), Smith pulled no punches. "It is the general belief . . . that the Constitution of the United States is the very embodiment of democratic philosophy. The people take it for granted that the framers of that document were imbued with the spirit of political equality and sought to establish a government by the people themselves. Widely as this view is entertained, it is, however, at variance with the facts. . . . It may be said without exaggeration that the American scheme of government was planned and set up to perpetuate the ascendency of the property-holding class in a society leavened with democratic ideas. . . . The men who framed and set up our Federal government were shrewd enough to see that if the interests of the property-holding classes were to be given effective protection, it was necessary that political power should rest ultimately upon a class basis. This they expected to accomplish largely through the judicial veto and the power and influence of the Supreme Court."[22]

Most of the political problems of democracy, Smith believed, could be traced to the economic bias of the Constitution and its distrust of majority rule. Lawyers and constitutional writers had been too much preoccupied with the thought of defending and glorifying the work of the fathers and not enough interested in disclosing its true relation to modern thought and tendencies. As a consequence, twentieth-century Americans in attempting to make an eighteenth-century undemocratic Constitution the vehicle of democratic rule were bound to fail because it was framed for one purpose while they were trying to use it for another.

While accepting Smith's interpretation of the Constitution, the radical journalist Herbert Croly went even further in seeking the cause of this irreconcilable contradiction between the body and the spirit of American government. From the beginning of American national history, he found two different and, in some respects, antagonistic principles at work in our political life: the nationalistic libertarianism of Alexander Hamilton and the democratic individualism of Thomas Jefferson. As he conceived it, the difference between them was less a difference of purpose than of the means whereby a purpose should be accomplished: "The Federalists [Hamilton], representing as they did chiefly the people of wealth and education, demanded a government adequate to protect existing propertied rights; but they were not seeking any exceptional privileges—except those traditionally associated with the ownership of private property. The anti-Federalists [Jefferson], on the other hand, having less to protect and more to acquire, insisted rather upon being let alone than in being protected."[23] Inasmuch as the anti-Federalists were at times unruly democrats and suspicious of strong government, the Federalists came, justly or unjustly, to identify both anti-Federalism and democracy with political disorder and social instability. This prejudice was very influential in determining the character of the federal Constitution which, as Croly said, was the expression "not only of a political faith, but also of political fears."[24] Hence, instead of entrusting the welfare of the new government to the good will of the whole people, Hamilton as Secretary of the Treasury sought through various fiscal and financial measures to base the perpetuation of the Union upon the interested motives of a minority of well-to-do citizens by making them the special beneficiaries of the federal government. The result was the people at large came more than ever to distrust the national government, and in the political reaction that followed, President Jefferson pursued an equalitarian policy of "hands off" on the grounds that government interference implied favoritism and a distrust of the people. As a consequence of the triumph of Jefferson and the defeat of Hamilton, the nation for the next hundred years adopted "a system of unrestricted individual aggrandizement and collective irresponsibility" which, according to Croly, had ended in a plutocratic rule that denied both genuine liberty and meaningful equality.[25]

Although convinced that Hamilton perverted the "American national ideal" almost as much as Jefferson perverted the "American democratic ideal," Croly considered Jefferson's "fatal policy of drift" to have been much more injurious than Hamilton's narrow conception of nationality because it sacrificed "a desirable liberty to an undesirable equality."[26] Under modern conditions, he contended, liberty could be protected only by an energetic national government, and equality could be realized only by the efficient national organization of democracy. In short, the pursuit of Jeffersonian ends by Hamiltonian means became Croly's pragmatic formula for a new nationalism.

In his provocative book, *The Promise of American Life* (1909), Croly argued democracy could be revitalized by nationalizing it.° Americans could safely run the risk of increasing the powers of the central government, he believed, because of their intrinsic faith in democracy. Not only did he advocate greater centralization of government to match the growing centralization of American social and economic activity, but he insisted that "national efficiency" demanded a radical change in government attitudes toward business and labor. Huge corporations and labor unions contributed to American efficiency. Deliberately to undo this work of economic consolidation in the name of equal rights would be,

° Herbert Croly, *The New Nationalism.* See p. 177.

in his opinion, a step backward. So Croly advised that the process of industrial organization should be allowed to work itself out, with the idea that under federal supervision the semi-monopolistic corporations and organized labor could be converted into efficient agents of democratic nationalism.

A democratic nationalism seemingly based upon the radical forces reformers were fighting, upon "that concentration of wealth, and of the power exercised by wealth"[27] was rejected by Progressives and Socialists alike. "It is bad enough to have the overgrown corporations to restrain and control," said Governor Wilson. "It would be infinitely worse if they were combined with government itself."[28] Moreover, instead of nationalism and democracy working together in tandem as Croly's radicalism prescribed, indications were that business conservatives would support the former and eschew the latter. The National Association of Manufacturers, for instance, came out vehemently against such democratic reforms as the graduated income tax, direct election of senators, the initiative, referendum and recall, as "contrary to the spirit of our government;" on the other hand, it vigorously endorsed a strong militia and a large army and navy, not only for national defense but "to squelch the rebellion that springs into existence with every strike."[29]

There was also the paradoxical question of how effectively an autocratic organization such as the giant industrial corporation could be pressed into the service of democracy. Though outwardly nothing appeared more democratic than the corporation with its officers and board elected by universal suffrage, in practice most stockholders did not vote, they signed proxies held by management. Thus it was neither difficult nor unusual for a small group of insiders to dominate properties belonging to thousands of investors and worth billions of dollars. Equally damaging to democratic hopes was the fact that behind the corporations were the lawyers who, as a class, held a professional monopoly of governmental functions. As William Howard Taft, who was later named Chief Justice of the Supreme Court, made clear, the legal profession on the whole was less than lukewarm in its support of democracy: "We are not in favor of the rule of all the people as an end desirable in itself. We love democracy, not because of the name but because of what

Drawn by Arthur Young   From *The Masses*, Apr., 1913, cover.
SERENE ON-LOOKER; (To The Striker) "VERY UNFORTUNATE SITUATION,
BUT WHATEVER YOU DO, DON'T USE FORCE."

it accomplishes. We are in favor of a rule by as many of the people
in a democracy as will secure a good government and no more." [30]

In light of these tendencies, the reformer William J. Ghent took
the view that an alliance between business and government would
lead, not to "a higher form of democracy," but to a benevolent
feudalism.° Though a Fabian Socialist, he threw out the Marxian

°William J. Ghent, *Our Benevolent Feudalism.* See p. 182.

dream of a cooperative commonwealth as too sanguine, and likewise rejected Wilson's neo-Jeffersonian vision of a middle-class democracy founded upon a slightly modified individualism as totally unrealistic. Instead he predicted the coming society would be a true feudalism in the sense that it would be built around a social and economic hierarchy; but unlike the old feudalism, it would be restrained by the spectre of democracy. It would therefore temper its exactions to an endurable limit and distribute its benefits to a degree that would make for an apathetic, if not a satisfied, people.[31]

Certainly something resembling feudalism was already visible in America. Nearly a century before, the French social theorist Fourier had predicted that the organization of the business classes into affiliated monopolies would lead to a commercial feudalism; according to an editor of the *Wall Street Journal,* his prediction was on its way to fullfillment in 1905.[32] Its benevolent aspect found expression in the paternalism of a few large corporations whose welfare programs included technical education for workers, kindergartens for their children, low cost housing, cafeterias, gymnasiums, clinics, sickness and accident insurance, bible training, and even landscaping of factory grounds. Generally welfare work was undertaken not out of purely philanthropic motives but to forestall recognition of unions. Typical was the approach of United States Steel. There Elbert Gary and George Perkins, whom *Survey* called "broad gauge business men," evolved a program of open shop paternalism acclaimed by the business press as the showcase of the new capitalism.[33] First the company ruthlessly drove the unions from its properties, then with elaborate publicity launched a series of welfare projects. Gary gave the rationale of the corporation's policy. Labor organizations existed, he said, either because employers foolishly recognized them or because the employees felt abused. Therefore, he instructed the presidents of the subsidiaries, "make it certain all the time that the men in your employ are treated as well, if not a little better, than other men who are working for people who deal and contract with unions . . . and, so far as you can, cultivate a feeling of friendship, and influence your men to the conclusion that it is for their interests in every respect to be in your employ."[34]

The less benevolent side of the new feudalism was apparent enough in Ghent's analogue of a business and industrial hierarchy with its overlords and vassals, its social gradations and outward trappings. Perhaps less evident were the ramifications of its power over the rest of society. "Yet we all know," Lincoln Steffens wrote in *Everybody's*, "that capitalists and business men who belong to the business system own an influential part of the press, and advertise in the rest; they retain the leaders of the bar, and awe the whole profession; they are the greatest employers of labor, and they set the pace for others; they are the chief patrons of art, churches, charities, and colleges. They dominate the institutions of American society in a broad sense, and, in a narrow sense, they and their families are "society." [35] It was equally notorious that the American feudality "has had clergymen silenced, editors discharged, professors dismissed, judges appointed, United States Senators defeated, and presidents elected"—thus embodying, in Lloyd's words, "not only the form but the fact of arbitrary power, of control without consent, of rule without representation." [36]

Doubtless the most extreme form of modern feudalism was to be found in "company towns"—mining and lumber camps, textile and steel centers—where the people were dependent upon a single industry for their livelihood. There the U.S. Commission on Industrial Relations discovered "industrial feudalism is the rule rather than the exception." [37] In such isolated communities, corporations exerted virtually absolute control over the social and economic life of the inhabitants, either by usurpation of local political powers or by domination of local authorities, and in many cases acted in complete defiance of the fundamental rights of citizens.

Typical of such corporate feudalities were the mining camps of the Colorado Fuel & Iron Company. By discouraging home ownership and refusing to sell building lots, the Rockefeller firm forced the miners to rent at excessive rates company houses which were described as "hovels, shacks, and dugouts unfit for the habitation of human beings." [38] If a miner protested these conditions, he risked the simultaneous loss of his job, his home, and even the right to remain in the community. Furthermore, until the practice was forbidden by law, the company paid wages, not in U.S. currency, but in scrip redeemable only at company-owned "pluck-me" stores whose high prices extracted an annual return of 20 per cent. This nonbenevolent feudalism extended even to educational, religious and intellectual matters. As the Commission discovered, in the words of Graham Adams, "Mine superintendents and company officers dictated the selection of school teachers and dismissed those to whom they objected. No one could erect a church building without CFI permission. J. F. Welborn, president of the company, considered it management's prerogative to fire ministers who opposed the firm or who exhibited 'socialistic tendencies.' A Commission investigator discovered that the firm censored movies, books, and magazines. It proscribed not only anti-capitalist literature but such works as Darwin's *Origin of the Species* and *The Rubaiyat of Omar Khayyam*." [39] A company spokesman explained, "We wish to protect our people from erroneous ideas." [40] In the opinion of the Commission, however, such arrant disregard of the rights of citizens presented "every aspect of a state of feudalism except the recognition of specific duties on the part of the employer." [41]

Plainly, as *Outlook* observed in a 1910 editorial, America was at the parting of the ways. The two tendencies in American politics were represented by Wilson's new freedom and Croly's new nationalism, the one emphasizing individualism, the other organization. Both recognized the danger of special interests, but what one proposed as a remedy the other regarded as an aggravation: "One sees peril in a strong National Government, the other accounts it the public safeguard; one regards the individual as the end, the organization as a means, the other regards the organization as an end and would subordinate the individual interests to the interests of the social order." [42] Ironically, in the great national debate that followed, Croly's candidate, Roosevelt, lost both the election and his program to his victorious opponent; while Wilson won the Presidency only to taste the bitter truth of his own contention that Hamiltonian means lead to Hamiltonian ends.

Economic Imperialism

Capitalism was supreme in America, and though at home it seemed content to use the political machinery of representative government, its methods of expansion overseas were the negation of democracy. Just as modern politics was essentially business politics, so modern diplomacy was becoming Dollar Diplomacy, tending to be guided more and more by business considerations. During the first two decades of the twentieth century, powerful United States corporations penetrated relatively weak Latin American countries where they established virtual economic protectorates over the people and resources of those less-advanced areas. With the tacit approval and, on occasion, the overt support of the United States government, Navy and Marines, this expanding empire of American business often went far beyond purely economic means to gain its ends and was able, in many instances, to superimpose its will over that of supposedly sovereign states.

For those who looked with concern upon the new expansionism of American capitalism, the year 1898 was the great historical turning point. In that fateful year, the United States went to war with Spain and emerged with conquered territory. Although the United States had always pursued a course of territorial expansion, this was the first time the nation had seized lands beyond the continental limits. The acquisition of distant islands—Hawaii, Puerto Rico, the Philippines—it was alleged, threatened not only to burden the country with new diplomatic, strategic and military responsibilities, but to transform a democratic republic into an imperial state. This glamorous and seductive role, anti-imperialists insisted, negated American traditions: politically it denied the ideal of self-government by imposing American rule over backward and illiterate natives considered incapable of governing themselves; economically it violated the principles of free enterprise by assuming control over the livelihood of people who were to be subjects, not citizens; socially it contradicted the theory of equal rights by decreeing that millions of non-Europeans were to be treated as inferiors by their white conquerors; and intellectually it repudiated the claim that America was a nation founded on reason by supposing that a democracy could at no risk to itself take dominion over another people without their consent.

In spite of their righteous protestations, however, history suggests that war and colonialism were as American as apple pie. Only those blind to the true character of the American people, declared sociologist Franklin H. Giddings, could suppose that a people wholly unapt for war and altogether loath to enter upon military adventures was suddenly transformed into a military nation by the chance sinking of a battleship in Havana harbor and by the outcry of yellow journals demanding vengence; or that a people content with its existing territorial and commercial opportunities was, by mere accident of an inglorious naval victory, converted overnight into a nation bent upon world empire. The fact was, said Giddings, that, "The warlike spirit existed long before the destruction of the *Maine;* and the demand for new outlets for both commercial enterprise and political ingenuity was already insistent many years before the battle of Manila Bay." [43]

Four times in four generations Americans had gone to war—in the case of the Mexican War, solely for territorial conquest—and more than once during the last quarter of the nineteenth century they had been in a state of mind verging on a declaration of war. Besides fighting on land or sea in Europe, Africa, and Central America, they had at home—even when engaged in the bloodbath of civil war—carried on for more than two hundred years a ruthless and relentless war of extermination and expropriation against the American Indian. If the essential definition of colonialism is the control of territory, resources and people, then, as historian William Appleman Williams recently remarked, "American policy toward the Indian, and toward the Negro from 1650 to 1863, certainly satisfies those criteria and therefore belies the assertion that the United States has never been a colonial power. It is customary and accurate to talk about the Negro during those years as a slave, but slavery is only the most extreme form of colonial exploitation." [44] There was also a significant degree of colonialism involved in the economic and political controls exercised by the Eastern states over the Western territories during the nineteenth century. Moreover, as the diplomatic historian Thomas A. Bailey points out, "The United States was a Far Eastern power . . . fifty years or so before our ill-informed expansionists clamored for the Philippines so as to make America an active force in the Eastern Hemisphere. It was Commodore Perry who, with seven warships and the velvet glove, forced open the bamboo portals of Japan in 1854. It was 'Blood-is-thicker-than-water' Tattnall who went to the rescue of the British off the Chinese forts in 1859. It was an American warship, in the midst of our own Civil War, that helped punish the Japanese feudal lord at Shimonoseki in 1864. It was a fleet of five American warships that demolished five Korean forts and killed some two hundred Koreans in 1871. And it was Commodore Shufeldt who initiated our diplomatic relations with Korea in 1882." [45] In short, the flash of Dewey's guns marked not a sudden turn of events but "merely spotlighted a maturation that had long since taken place." [46]

Far from apologizing for their transgressions, Americans regarded them as evidence of their racial superiority and as the fulfilment of their manifest destiny. As the Congregational minister Josiah Strong boasted in 1885, the time was coming when "this race of unequalled energy, with all the majesty of numbers and the might of wealth behind it—the representative, let us hope, of the largest liberty, the purest Christianity, the highest civilization— having developed peculiarly aggressive traits calculated to impress its institutions upon mankind, will spread itself over the earth." [47]

If the policy and principles were old, what was new about American imperialism in the twentieth century was its economic rationalization. By 1900 the United States had become a serious contender in world markets. Already Europeans complained that Americans were fashioning the world in their image, and patriotic Englishmen spoke out against the American commercial invasion of their islands. As one irate Briton grumbled,

> In the domestic life we have got to this: The average man rises in the morning from his New England sheets, he shaves with "Williams' " soap and a Yankee safety razor, pulls on his Boston boots over his socks from North Carolina, fastens his Connecticut braces, slips his Waltham or Waterbury watch in his pocket, and sits down to breakfast. There he congratulates his wife on the way her Illinois straight-front corset sets off her Massachusetts blouse, and he tackles his breakfast, where he eats bread made from prairie flour (possibly doctored at the special establishments on the lakes), tinned oysters from Baltimore and a little Kansas City bacon, while his wife plays with a slice of Chicago ox-tongue. The children are given "Quaker" oats. At the same time he reads his morning paper printed by American machines, on American paper, with American ink, and, possibly, edited by a smart journalist from New York city.
>
> He rushes out, catches the electric tram (New York) to Shepherd's

Bush, where he gets in a Yankee elevator to take him on to the American-fitted electric railway to the City.

At his office, of course, everything is American. He sits on a Nebraskan swivel chair, before a Michigan roll-top desk, writes his letters on a Syracuse typewriter, signing them with a New York fountain pen, and drying them with a blotting-sheet from New England. The letter copies are put away in files manufactured in Grand Rapids. . . .

At lunch-time he hastily swallows some cold roast beef that comes from the Mid-West cow . . . and then soothes his mind with a couple of Virginia cigarettes. To follow his course all day would be wearisome. But when evening comes . . . he finishes up with a couple of "little liver pills" "made in America." [48]

American businessmen were invading world markets because, as Adam Smith had prophesied, the seeming tendency of industrial productivity was to outrun the effective demand. Every improvement in methods of production and control, every consolidation of ownership and control appeared to accentuate the trend. Early in 1897, the New York *Journal of Commerce* pointed out that the nation's industrial plant had been developed far beyond the needs of domestic consumption. The wire-nail industry was said to have machinery to make four times as many nails as the American market could consume; rail mills, locomotive shops and glass factories were reportedly in a similar situation. "Dependent solely upon local business," commented John D. Rockefeller in 1899, "we should have failed years ago. We were forced to extend our markets and to seek for export trade." [49]

Not only did it appear that more goods could be produced than could be sold at a profit, but the business system was also producing a surplus of profits for which there seemed to be no remunerative investment at home. Consequently, the majority of the nation's businessmen who, before the war, had been antiwar and anti-imperialist—became at news of Dewey's victory suddenly and enthusiastically expansionist, insisting the Philippines be retained as an outlet for surplus American goods and capital, and as a gateway to the markets of eastern Asia.

Economic imperialism was now argued as the logical extension of capitalism to internationalism. That argument, summed up by the English economist J. A. Hobson, was to the effect that "whereas various real and powerful motives of pride, prestige and pugnacity, together with the more altruistic professions of a civilising mission, figured as causes of imperial expansion, the dominant directive motive was the demand for markets and for profitable investment by the exporting and financial classes within each imperialist regime."[50] In the United States the argument for economic imperialism was advanced by the financial writer Charles A. Conant.° The civilized nations of the world were now entering upon a contest for financial and commercial supremacy on a grander scale than any in the past, and the quest that was forcing itself upon the American people, said Conant, was where to find openings for the future productive investment of their saved capital. In his opinion that demand was so urgent that either new outlets for capital must be found or, to ward off economic collapse, state socialism must supercede capitalism.[51]

The majority of Americans, including many Progressives, ignored the contradictions between American ideals and American behavior and supported the imperialistic surge with few qualms. As humanitarians they had upheld the war to free the poor Cubans and Filipinos from Spanish misrule; as traditionalists they were infected with chauvinistic dreams of American destiny and were ready to concede with Woodrow Wilson that "the great pressure of a people moving always to new frontiers, in search of new lands, new power, the full freedom of a virgin world, has ruled our course and formed our policies like a Fate."[52] Dedicated to what was called an "imperialism of righteousness," both Protestant and Catholic clergymen in the United States urged retention of the Philippines as a "higher obligation," with the suggestion, of course, that "The conquest by force of arms must be followed up by conquest for Christ."[53] Many earnest Progressives were thus not only convinced it was the white man's duty, his *burden*, to carry the material and political blessings of American civilization everywhere, but those of a more pragmatic cast of mind, such as Croly, felt that "In spite of 'old-fashioned democratic' scruples and prejudices, the will to play that part for all it was worth would constitute a beneficial and necessary stimulus to the better realization of the Promise of our domestic life."[54]

° Charles A. Conant, *The Economic Basis of Imperialism.* See p. 186.

Only a distinguished minority of dissenters was unable to accept this modern American concept of knight-errantry at face value. Among them were men of great distinction, including some of the most eminent figures of the literary and intellectual world—William Dean Howells, Mark Twain, William Vaughn Moody, Hamlin Garland, William James, E. L. Godkin, President Charles W. Eliot of Harvard and David Starr Jordan of Stanford—but the anti-imperialists were politically disorganized and did not have control of a major party as did the expansionists. Most of them, moreover, were in the unfortunate position of opposing the results of a war they had either favored or failed to oppose. While they had supported the war to free the Philippines from Spain, they were not prepared to endorse the ruthless postwar suppression of the Filipino independence movement by United States forces.

Theirs was an unpopular cause; yet they openly and courageously stated their objections in the platform of the American Anti-Imperialist League (1899):

> We hold that the policy known as imperialism is hostile to liberty and tends toward militarism, an evil from which it has been our glory to be free. We regret that it has become necessary in the land of Washington and Lincoln to reaffirm that all men, of whatever race or color, are entitled to life, liberty, and the pursuit of happiness. . . . We insist that the subjugation of any people is "criminal aggression" and open disloyalty to the distinctive principles of our Government.
>
> We earnestly condemn the policy of the present National Administration in the Philippines. It seeks to extinguish the spirit of 1776 in those islands. We deplore the sacrifice of our soldiers and sailors . . . in an unjust war. We denounce the slaughter of the Filipinos as a needless horror. We protest against the extension of American sovereignty by Spanish methods.
>
> We demand the immediate cessation of the war against liberty, begun by Spain and continued by us. . . .
>
> We deny that the obligation of all citizens to support their Government in times of grave National peril applies to the present situation. If an Administration may with impunity ignore the issues upon which it was chosen, deliberately create a condition of war anywhere on the face of the globe, debauch the civil service for spoils to promote the adventure, organize a truth-suppressing censorship and demand of all citizens a suspension of judgment and their unanimous support while it chooses to continue the fighting, representative government itself is imperiled.[55]

Imperialism, its opponents contended, found its inspiration in dollars, not duty. Although its vaunted pretexts were "piety, profits, and patriotism," the consequences, they averred, were more likely to be depravity, debts, and despotism. The White Man's Burden, said William Jennings Bryan, was more aptly the Poor Man's Load,[56] and with apologies to Rudyard Kipling the anti-imperialist poet Ernest Crosby wrote derisively:

> Take up the White Man's burden,
>   Send forth your sturdy kin
> And load them down with Bibles
>   And cannon-balls and gin.
> Throw in a few diseases
>   To spread in tropic climes,
> For there the healthy niggers
>   Are quite behind the times.[57]

The most withering blast of all came from Mark Twain, who scored the pious hypocrisy of the missionaries and derided the American imperialism of righteousness as being no better than the European variety of Joseph Chamberlain and William II.°

When the economic consequences of Far Eastern imperialism were reckoned, the anti-imperialists were proven right. Aside from the price of twenty million dollars paid to Spain for the Philippine Islands, the United States bought an insurrection which cost almost as many lives as the Spanish War and which led both sides to engage in barbaric violations of civilized conduct. As for business, profits from the Philippine trade turned out to be infinitesimal, and the gigantic market for goods and capital in the Far East never materialized. An economic study made in 1929 showed that what investors gained was at the expense of American consumers, producers or taxpayers, and concluded that over the years the cost to the United States far exceeded any commercial benefit derived from the islands.[58] Beyond that, as World War II confirmed, the military value of the Philippines was not only dubious but disastrous, for in 1941 they proved to be the Achilles' heel of our strategic position.

Subsequent economic developments—the Crash of 1929 and the Depression of the 1930's—suggested, moreover, that the problem confronting American capitalism in 1900 perhaps had not been

° Mark Twain, *To the Person Sitting in Darkness.* See p. 190.

These Filipinos fighting for independence ungratefully declined the "blessings of civilization" as offered by the United States Army.

From *Harper's Weekly,* Apr. 8, 1899.

overproduction but underconsumption. To a considerable extent, America's productive powers had been held in leash by inequalities of distribution. The excessive share that went to profits, capital and other surpluses rather than to wages, salaries or social services, led to oversaving and increased productive power without a corresponding increase in the purchase of consumer goods. Rather than using the state to gain external markets by political pressure and military force, probably all that was needed at the time to keep capitalism on a profitable and expansive domestic basis was such wage concessions to labor and such extensions of social service as would have righted the disequilibrium between production and consumption.

War and the State

Whether they liked it or not, Americans at the turn of the century were increasingly preoccupied with the problems of world power. Recent military adventures had deeply involved the nation in Far Eastern and Latin American affairs, and its rising economic power served more and more to entangle its interests with those of other great powers. According to the pragmatic historian Brooks Adams, the Spanish War had upset the equilibrium of the world. For upward of a thousand years the economic center of the world had been moving westward, and the war with Spain was the shock that marked the passage of the seat of empire from Europe to America. The phase of civilization which mankind was now entering was to be a period of greater stress and competition, and he warned his countrymen, "Economic competition in its intensest form is war."[59] From the beginning of history, rival systems had fought with and destroyed each other, and now, said Adams, fate had cast the United States into the vortex of the fiercest struggle the world had ever known. "She has become the heart of the economic system of the age, and she must maintain her supremacy by wit and by force, or share the fate of the discarded."[60]

Despite his dire prognostications, Adams saw auspicious opportunity for the United States to become a greater seat of wealth and power than ever were England, Rome and Constantinople. But to maintain such an empire presupposed a national organization equal to the great burden it must bear. Since in this country there was, in his opinion, no administration in the modern sense of the word, the task of America for the next fifty years must be the perfection of organization, both civil and military. For Adams was convinced that national survival depended upon the cheap and efficient administration of large units. "From the retail store to the empire," he wrote, "success in modern life lies in concentration. The active and economical organizations survive: the slow and costly perish."[61] The best example of the success of the modern method of centralization was Germany—the nation which, along with Russia, Adams viewed as our most "deadly and determined" adversary in the coming struggle for power. After victory over France in 1870, the German empire had been organized around a corporate administration powerful enough to subordinate individual to general interests. In America, on the other hand, the national government had been created to meet the wants of a scanty agricultural population at a time when movement was slow; consequently it was clumsy and inefficient, unable to deal with rapidly accelerating masses of men and machines, and had no more necessary relation to the conduct of affairs in the twentieth century than Franklin's methods in electricity would have had to the manipulation of a modern dynamo.[62] Hence the United States, if it were to survive as a nation, must abandon worn-out political traditions and move toward collectivism. "Such a concentration," said Adams, "might, conceivably, be effected by the growth and amalgamation of great trusts until they absorbed the Government, or it might be brought about by the central corporation, called the Government, absorbing the trusts. In either event, the result would be approximately the same. The Eastern and Western continents would be competing for the most perfect system of State Socialism."[63]

By suggesting that the nation was an organism subject to nature's law of the survival of the fittest, Adams, in effect, invested the state with a being of its own, above and beyond the people. This modern tendency to apotheosize the state as a force completely independent of any other earthly power ran directly counter to American political tradition. Traditionally American political theorists had disavowed a mystique of the state. The Declaration of Independence held that government was the instrument and creature of society and, as a contrivance of human reason, could never be set irretrievably above its creators. But significantly, where Tom Paine spoke of "the rights of man," the twentieth-century sociologist Franklin H. Giddings wrote of "the rights of the state."[64]

The importation into the United States of the exotic neo-Hegelian idea of the state as a power unto itself was largely due to numerous American intellectuals and scholars who, like Brooks Adams, had found it intellectually fashionable to take their post-graduate training at German universities. There, along with their beer, they imbibed the Teutonic notion of the state as a moral entity and of war as a moral necessity to advance the aims of the state.

"If we grasp the conception of the State from this higher aspect," expounded the German ultranationalist General Friedrich von Bernhardi, we shall see "it is political idealism which calls for war, while materialism—in theory at least—repudiates it. . . . All petty and private interests shrink into insignificance before the grave decision which a war involves. The common danger unites all in a common effort, and the man who shirks this duty to the community is deservedly spurned. . . . The brutal incidents inseparable from every war vanish completely before the idealism of the main result." [65] To this effect he quoted from Frederick the Great: "War opens the most fruitful field to all virtues, for at every moment constancy, pity, magnanimity, heroism, and mercy shine forth in it." And again, in the same passage, from the German nationalist Heinrich von Treitschke: "War is elevating because the individual disappears before the great conception of the State. The devotion of the members of a community to each other is nowhere so splendidly conspicuous as in war. . . . What a perversion of morality to wish to abolish heroism among men!" [66]

Nor was this extravagant idealization of war and the state confined to German writers. Perhaps the closest American approximation of Treitschke was Professor John W. Burgess of Columbia who, like Adams, had done a large part of his graduate work in Germany. To Burgess, as to his Prussian counterpart, the sovereignty of the state was permanent and unlimited. "It is begging the question to appeal to the consciousness of the world or of humanity against the consciousness of the state," because, he reasoned, the state has "original, absolute, unlimited, universal power" over the individual and all associations of individuals. Under certain circumstances, Burgess thought the use of war to secure the ends of the state was not only justifiable, but commendable, "not only commendable, but morally obligatory," for in principle "the state can do no wrong." [67]

This idea of the state as power was transmitted to his student, Theodore Roosevelt, who often expressed the view that the state existed primarily in order to assert itself against other equally independent powers. "Warlike power" was for Roosevelt "the prerequisite for the preservation of social values." Sounding very much like Bernhardi, he worried lest we become "a nation of mere hucksters, putting gain above national honor." Constantly invoking "hairy-chested Darwinian virtues," the ex-president berated Americans for their "flabby cosmopolitanism" and "flabby pacifism," calling for a manly foreign policy which would spare us the indignity of "national emasculation."[68] Similarly the influential evangel of New Nationalism, Herbert Croly, argued for preparedness, agreeing with the navalist Captain Alfred Thayer Mahan and Hudson Maxim, the inventor of smokeless powder, that it would be fatal for America to seek peace at the expense of military efficiency. National politics, said Croly, aimed primarily at efficiency, "that is, at the successful use of the force resident in the state to accomplish the purposes desired by the Sovereign authority." With Teutonic stress, he emphasized that the state was based upon force, and in internal as well as external relations, its success depended at bottom upon the efficient use of force. "The democrats who disparage efficient national organization," he wrote scornfully, are "merely seeking to exorcise the power of physical force in human affairs by the use of pious incantations and heavenly words."[69]

In all these sentiments many Americans joined and, with the martial theorist General Homer Lea, sang enthusiastically the glory of war, deprecating the shameful condition of a nonmilitant people. Those who glorified war usually upheld two sets of ideals: first the state as the supreme ideal, and second the various human virtues which war was believed to create or restore. Their ideal of the state, as with Burgess, was something more than government. The state was a mystical conception, above religion, industry and politics. As the church had served as the medium for the spiritual salvation of man, so the state was the medium for his political salvation. War, said General Lea, created the state. "War is but a composite exemplification of the struggle of man upward: the multiplication of his individual efforts into one, and the aspirations of his diurnal strife turned toward a greater and nobler end, not of himself but of his race."[70] War was the life of the state, and scorn of war, like the denial of death, was self-deception. War was inevitable, and therefore, Lea contended, the first task of American statesmanship was the preservation of the "national or militant instinct" in the virtues of the people.°

According to these pragmatic idealists, the virtues war brought

---

° Homer Lea, *The Idealism of War*. See p. 194.

forth were three: courage, self-sacrifice, and patriotism. Compared with these, the ideals of peace were selfish, sordid and degenerate; their unfortunate tendency, grumbled Roosevelt, was "to make good men weak and to make virtue a matter of derision to strong men."[71] War alone invited the brave man to rise above the petty affairs of daily life and to risk death for an ideal. The idealism of war, it was argued, automatically set in motion that collective feeling of loyalty in which each individual somehow shared the virtue of the whole, and was strengthened by that identification. War not only erased the distinction between the individual and the state, but enhanced the individual by putting behind him all the power and righteousness of the state.

Peace and Preparedness

Those who supported war and preparedness were especially hard on the pacifists because peace prospects were never so promising, nor the peace sentiment never so insistent and universally popular as in the first dozen years of the new century. Before 1914, there were sixty-three societies devoted to the cause of peace, including the American Peace Society, the American Society for the Judicial Settlement of International Disputes, and the ten-million-dollar Carnegie Endowment for International Peace whose earnings, ironically, shot skyward when war boosted the value of its holdings in United States Steel. No peace convention ever held in this country or any other country surpassed the National Peace Congress of 1907; its sessions in New York were attended by 10 mayors, 19 members of Congress, 4 Supreme Court justices, 2 presidential candidates, 30 labor leaders, 40 bishops, 60 newspaper editors, and 27 millionaires. Encouraging reinforcements also came from the churches and labor unions. The A.F. of L., consistently favoring reduction of armaments, was chiefly instrumental in persuading the House of Representatives to adopt a resolution in favor of the naval holiday proposed by Winston Churchill, and the United Mine Workers in 1912 proposed a strike to tie up industry in event of war. President Wilson's appointment of William Jennings Bryan as Secretary of State in 1913 renewed the hopes of the peace movement. Bryan, a Christian pacifist, pushed through treaties with twenty-seven nations providing for submission of all disputes to permanent commissions. These unprecedented victories aroused considerable optimism among advocates of peace. It did seem, as *The Peace Forum* announced in 1913, that "the age is ready for peace." [72]

The phenomenal growth of the peace movement was probably due above all else to the popular reaction against imperialism and navalism. As the anti-imperialists had anticipated, along with the acquisition of colonies came demands for a bigger army and navy, and those who had opposed overseas expansion found themselves several years later in the forefront of the fight against military expansion. Reformers who, with Jane Addams, had enlisted in the Anti-Imperialist League now issued manifestoes for the Anti-"Preparedness" Committee:

> We are a committee of American citizens formed to protest against the attempt to stampede this nation into a dangerous program of military and naval expansion. We believe that *no danger of invasion* threatens this country and that there is no excuse for hasty, ill-considered action. We protest against the effort being made to divert the public mind from those *preparations for world peace* based on international agreement which it might be our country's privilege to initiate at the close of this War. And we protest no less against the effort being made to *divert public funds*, sorely needed in constructive programs for national health and well-being, into the manufacture of engines of death. . . .[73]

Rejecting the doctrine that military efficiency was the best guarantee against war, peace advocates pointed out that in Europe in 1914 German "preparedness" had not guaranteed peace, but on the contrary had precipitated brutal and thoughtless aggression.

But those who supported arms expansion were also organized, and in their ranks were some of the best-known names in business, politics and the armed services. In 1902 the Navy League had been founded to build up the navy and to "educate" those Americans who had fallen prey to pacifist arguments for disarmament. Taking up Roosevelt's cry that "the navy is our most efficient peacemaker," [74] the League set out to indoctrinate the public with the view that battleships were cheaper than battles. But as its official organ, the *Seven Seas* magazine, suggested, the Navy League stood not merely for defense but for aggression and conquest as well. The issue of September 1915 boldly declared, "The true militarist believes that pacifism is the masculine, and humanitarianism is the feminine manifestation of national degeneracy. . . . World empire is the only logical and natural aim of a nation." [75] Again, two months later, it glowingly endorsed

Drawn by Boardman Robinson

From *The Masses*, Sept., 1916.

LOGIC

Preparedness Advocate: "If we don't prepare
as they did, it'll happen to us."

militarism as a national policy: "It is the absolute right of a nation to live to its full intensity, to expand, found colonies, to get richer and richer by any proper means such as armed conquest, commerce, diplomacy."[76] After 1909, League techniques, as Armin Rappaport has shown, proved highly effectual in marshaling propreparedness sentiment and by supplying congressmen and senators with ready-made arguments for a large navy.[77] During debate on the Naval Bill of 1914, it was said, "words, phrases, whole arguments that the League had used in its propaganda were echoed by politicians and the press" to bring about its passage. With the coming of war in Europe, peace groups were unable to stem the preparedness hysteria sweeping the country. Aided by such new organizations as the Army League (1912), the National Defense League (1913), and the National Security League (1914), the preparedness propagandists were able to play skillfully and successfully upon the fears of the American people. The defeat of peace was marked in 1916 by the melodramatic spectacle of President Wilson leading a preparedness parade of sixty thousand marchers through the main streets of Washington.

Behind Washington's preparedness parade and similar demonstrations in other cities, peace advocates claimed to detect motives other than love of country. The nation, they alleged, was being scared into "an heroic mood" not entirely for patriotic reasons, but because it was profitable to promote militarism. It may have been sheer coincidence that E. H. Gary, chairman of United States Steel, called for the expenditure of one billion dollars or more per year on armaments when his firm would have been one of the chief beneficiaries of such spending. Similarly, it may also have been patriotism that led Hudson Maxim to write a book, *Defenseless America*, painting an appalling picture of what would happen to the United States if attacked by a foreign nation. The book inspired a movie called "The Battle Cry of Peace" (an intriguing title that invited such sardonic variants as "The War Cry of Friendship," "The Death Rattle of Life," and "The Love Song of Hate"), in which the author himself appeared, holding up an instrument of warfare he had developed.[78] Shortly afterward the chain of patriotic coincidence was completed by the following announcement from a New York investment house: "The stock of the Maxim Munitions Corporation is the latest candidate for favor among the Curb war stocks. It made its appearance this week. . . . The company has arranged to take over the important inventions of Hudson Maxim for the manufacture of aerial torpedoes, bomb-throwing devices, aeroplanes, guns, etc. *Mr. Maxim himself will be president of the company.*" [79]

Similarly, the leadership of the Navy League and the National Security League, it was charged, included those who stood to profit most from increased armament. Of the nineteen persons listed as founders of the Navy League, the majority were connected to establishments which directly and through interlocking directorates monopolized the manufacture of munitions in the United States. [80] What was true of the "dollar-scarred heroes" who organized the Navy League, as Senator Robert LaFollette scathingly described them, was also reputedly true of the National Security League. Calling the roll of officers, directors, founders, and contributors, Representative Clyde H. Tavenner of Illinois found that some were steel magnates, others munitions makers, and nearly all financiers or industrialists of some kind. This unmasking of an alleged "military-industrial complex" was spread far and wide through the generosity of Henry Ford, who paid for full-page advertisements in many of the leading newspapers of the country. [81]

A Moral Equivalent for War

If the business interests that built battleships and manufactured ammunition and kept the nation armed to the teeth in times of peace were ready to push the country to the verge of war when it suited their purposes, then, contended the pacifists, it was time for Americans to reexamine their ideals. "Of all the kinds of preparedness in relation to war that should interest mankind," said *The Independent,* "none is so basic and none so obligatory as preparation to prevent war." [82] Repudiating the pagan philosophy that might makes right, the pacifist rejected militarism as a reversion to barbarism; the accompanying concept of the state as unlimited power was from his point of view "an ideal absolutely without content or meaning; a pseudo ideal, a spurious ideal, a great roaring humbug."[83] War for its own sake was a dangerous delusion that led the worker, the clerk, the teacher, the student to kill men whom they had never seen and with whom personally they had no quarrel, or to be killed by them. While never denying that manly qualities were genuine and noble virtues, the pacifist claimed them also as ideals of peace. Admittedly war brought forth these qualities, but so did everyday life. "There never has been a time that did not demand these virtues, nor will the time ever come when human beings will not be called upon, in the midst of the profoundest political peace, to endure suffering, to be brave amid dangers, to be loyal to great causes, to take risk of loss against desperate odds for the sake of ideals."[84] Courage and suffering in defense of human values were applauded by the pacifists as enthusiastically as by their opponents. But the pacifist went on to point out that there were other qualities besides courage and endurance which war aroused: murder, pillage, lust, unimaginable cruelty. What was so glorious, asked James Bissett Pratt, about broken hearts and empty homes, brimming graveyards and hospitals filled with agonizing human flesh? "War brings out human kindness: so does the earthquake and the pestilence. Has anyone ever praised the famine because it gave an opportunity for devotion? Has anyone sung the glories of the bubonic plague or cholera or leprosy? War is considered romantic and glorious; the pestilence is merely loathsome. But strip off the uniform and the gilt trappings, and war and leprosy are very much alike."[85] Why, the *New Republic* asked, did peace seem dull and war romantic? "Every sane person knows that it is a greater thing to build a city than to bombard it, to plow a field than to trample it, to serve mankind than to conquer it. And yet once the armies get loose, the terrific noise and shock of war make all that was valuable seem pale and dull and sentimental."[86] Many thoughtful Americans realized that if they were to overcome the lure of war, they must offer some kind of action more stirring and more creative. It was not enough to prove that war was irrational, illogical, horrible and costly; the important thing was to make peace interesting. As Albert J. Nock wrote in the *Atlantic*, the function of the true peace advocate was not to deplore war but to create "a peace that shall meet war on its own terms and outbid it; a peace that shall answer the normal and proper demands of the human spirit as well as war now answers them." [87] What irony it was, in his opinion, that to those whom peace disinherited, war offered equality; to those whom peace compelled to live aimlessly, war offered a clear and moving purpose; and to those condemned by peace to the futile monotony of the job, war offered escape and responsibility. If peace were to outbid war for the common man's interest, said Nock, it must gratify his very real and very human desire for equal opportunity, common purpose, and collective responsibility.

To help meet these crucial needs of the human spirit, the psychologist William James proposed what he called "the moral equivalent of war." ° In brief, his proposal was to conscript for national service a productive army of youth and to set them warring against nature, not against man. By building dams and roads, digging in fields and mines, working on railroads and ships, according to their choice, he hoped young Americans would find in peaceful duty and toil and danger the values that war and preparation for war had given in the past. Young Randolph Bourne went even further, picturing a host of eager young missionaries, both boys and girls, swarming over the land doing the things which needed to be done, but which were not then being done—food inspection, factory inspection, organized relief, care of dependents, playground service, nursing in hospitals—in general, learning how to live rather than to die.[88]

On American entrance into the war, however, the hopes and ideals of peace were speedily forgotten. The leviathan state came into its own. There was conscription of youth, but only for compulsory military service. The American people—with the exception of a few resolute men and women of principle—allowed themselves to be regimented, coerced in mind and spirit, and in the name of the state turned into a thoughtless, soulless engine of destruction. The war machine demanded unanimity, not criticism; dissent was like sand in the bearings. Driven by the instinct of the herd, men forgot the value of human life, and they no longer remembered that "states exist for men, that politics exist for human happiness." [89] As Reinhold Niebuhr protested at the time, the very

---

° William James, *The Moral Equivalent of War.* See p. 198.

With the coming of the war the hopes and ideals of peace were speedily forgotten. These Americans playing soldier yearned for a chance to "Kill the Hun!"   Brown Bros.

qualities that made their lives worthwhile in peacetime and endowed their personalities with unique distinction were those least needed in wartime.[90] The moment war was declared, the normal individual and personal goals of "life, liberty, and the pursuit of happiness" were reduced by patriotism to a concerted malevolence whose urgent and highest appeal was for the death and extermination of the enemies of the state.

War brought about, in the name of the state, the consolidation of national power with industrial power. So unobtrusively and so unconsciously did the warfare state of 1917–18 come into being that not until after the armistice did the American people begin to understand something of the nature of the military-industrial dictatorship that had been directing their lives. The end of the war found the whole industrial and economic life of the nation transformed into "as complete a military machine . . . as the world had ever seen."[91] This greatest exercise of national authority was never legislated by Congress but simply grew by executive fiat. The War Industries Board, the most powerful executive agency ever created, was a government sponsored committee of big businessmen entrusted with the complete management of American industry. It directed both production and distribution; it decided what should be produced and where, and who should have the product. Individualistic American businessmen were aghast when they realized that the economy had been nationalized.[92] As the director of the Council of National Defense later commented, "What none had foreseen had come to pass. Had any man said in 1916 that the whole productive and distributive machinery of America could be directed successfully from Washington, he would have been called a lunatic. Yet in 1918 that was being done. [Furthermore,] business willed its own domination, forged its bonds, and policed its own subjection." [93] The relation of the government to the once anarchic steel industry was praised as "the best example the war afforded of the masterly conception of industrial mobilization and functioning by the simple process of establishing effectual contact between a pooled and compactly united industry manned by its own captains and a governmental organism . . ." [94]

From an economic point of view, big businessmen discovered there was very little difference between the machinery required for commercial efficiency and that required for military purposes. Wartime industrial control effectively did away with the hit-and-miss confusion of peacetime industry with its perpetual cycle of boom and bust, and corporate leaders began to dream of an ordered economic world where executives, relieved from the nightmare of menacing losses, would be free to give their attention to maximizing profits. Moreover, having experienced the domestic advantages of state capitalism, they talked now of its possible international application. The time had come, it was said, when government and business should cooperate to secure by industrial strategy what in other days was obtained by military strategy.

Readings: The Modern Leviathan

The New Nationalism

HERBERT CROLY (1869–1930) *A liberal journalist and editor,*
Croly attended Harvard where, like many other young men of
his generation, he came under the influence of William James.
Pragmatism became the guiding philosophy of his career, and
as editor of the New Republic *from 1914 to 1928, he was "radical*
without being socialistic, pragmatic rather than doctrinaire."
Like Theodore Roosevelt, whose New Nationalism he was popu-
larly but erroneously thought to have inspired, he was an ardent
nationalist; yet unlike the blood-and-thunder hero of the Spanish
War, he emphasized the democratic and cultural aspects of
nationalism, not the military. Ironically, he died just before his
"democratic nationalism" was to find its fullest realization in
the New Deal.

The Federal political organization has always tended to confuse
to the American mind the relation between democracy and
nationality. The nation as a legal body was, of course, created by
the Constitution, which granted to the central government certain
specific powers and responsibilities, and which almost to the same
extent diminished the powers and the responsibilities of the separate states. Consequently, to the great majority of Americans, the
process of increasing nationalization has a tendency to mean
merely an increase in the functions of the central government. For
the same reason the affirmation of a constructive relation between
the national and the democratic principles is likely to be interpreted merely as an attempt on the grounds of an abstract theory
to limit state government and to disparage states rights. Such an
interpretation, however, would be essentially erroneous. It would
be based upon the very idea against which I have been continually
protesting—the idea that the American nation, instead of embodying a living formative political principle, is merely the political
system created by the Federal Constitution; and it would end in

From *The Promise of American Life* (New York: Macmillan, 1909), pp. 272–9.

the absurd conclusion that the only way in which the Promise of American democracy can be fulfilled would be by the abolition of American local political institutions.

The nationalizing of American political, economic, and social life means something more than Federal centralization and something very different therefrom. To nationalize a people has never meant merely to centralize their government. . . . The process of centralization is not, like the process of nationalization, an essentially formative and enlightening political transformation. When a people are being nationalized, their political, economic, and social organization or policy is being coördinated with their actual needs and their moral and political ideals. Governmental centralization is to be regarded as one of the many means which may or may not be taken in order to effect this purpose. Like every other special aspect of the national organization, it must be justified by its fruits. There is no presumption in its favor. Neither is there any general presumption against it. Whether a given function should or should not be exercised by the central government in a Federal system is from the point of view of political logic a matter of expediency—with the burden of proof resting on those who propose to alter any existing Constitutional arrangement. . . .

Be it added, however, in the same breath, that under existing conditions and simply as a matter of expediency, the national advance of the American democracy does demand an increasing amount of centralized action and responsibility. . . . In this connection it is sufficient to insist that a more scrupulous attention to existing Federal responsibilities, and the increase of their number and scope, is the natural consequence of the increasing concentration of American industrial, political, and social life. American government demands more rather than less centralization merely and precisely because of the growing centralization of American activity. The state governments, either individually or by any practicable methods of coöperation, are not competent to deal effectively in the national interest and spirit with the grave problems created by the aggrandizement of corporate and individual wealth and the increasing classification of the American people. They have, no doubt, an essential part to play in the attempted solution of these problems; and there are certain aspects of the whole situation which the American nation, because of its Federal organization, can deal with much more effectually than can a rigidly centralized democracy like France. But the amount of responsibility in respect to fundamental national problems, which, in law almost as much as in practice, is left to the states, exceeds the responsibility which the state governments are capable of efficiently redeeming. They are attempting (or neglecting) a task which they cannot be expected to perform with any efficiency. . . .

Proposals to increase the powers of the central government are, however, rarely treated on their merits. They are opposed by the majority of American politicians and newspapers as an unqualified evil. Any attempt to prove that the existing distribution of responsibility is necessarily fruitful of economic and political abuses, and that an increase of centralized power offers the only chance of eradicating these abuses is treated as irrelevant. It is not a question of the expediency of a specific proposal, because from the traditional point of view any change in the direction of increased centralization would be a violation of American democracy. Centralization is merely a necessary evil which has been carried as far as it should, and which cannot be carried any farther without undermining the foundations of the American system. Thus the familiar theory of many excellent American democrats is rather that of a contradictory than a constructive relation between the democratic and the national ideals. . . .

To be sure, any increase in centralized power and responsibility, expedient or inexpedient, is injurious to certain aspects of traditional American democracy. But the fault in that case lies with the democratic tradition; and the erroneous and misleading tradition must yield before the march of a constructive national democracy. . . .

Under the influence of certain practical demands, an increase has already taken place in the activity of the Federal government. The increase has not gone as far as governmental efficiency demands, but it has gone far enough to provoke outbursts of protest and anguish from the "old-fashioned Democrats." They profess to see the approaching extinction of the American democracy in what they call the drift towards centralization. Such calamitous predictions are natural, but they are none the less absurd. The drift of American politics—its instinctive and unguided movement—is almost wholly along the habitual road; and any effective increase of Federal centralization can be imposed only by most strenuous efforts, by one of the biggest sticks which has ever been flourished in American politics. The advance made in this direction is small compared to the actual needs of an efficient national organization, and considering the mass of interest and prejudice which it must continue to overcome, it can hardly continue to progress at more than a snail's pace. The great obstacle to American national fulfillment must always be the danger that the American people will merely succumb to the demands of their local and private interests and will permit their political craft to drift into a compromising situation—from which the penalties of rescue may be almost as distressing as the penalties of submission.

The tradition of an individualist and provincial democracy, which is the mainstay of an anti-national policy, does not include ideals which have to be realized by aggressive action. Their ideals are the ones embodied in our existing system, and their continued vitality demands merely a policy of inaction enveloped in a cloud of sacred phrases. The advocates and the beneficiaries of the prevailing ideas and conditions are little by little being forced into the inevitable attitude of the traditional Bourbon—the attitude of maintaining customary or legal rights merely because they are customary or legal, and predicting the most awful consequences from any attempt to impair them. Men, or associations of men, who possess legal or customary rights inimical to the public welfare, always defend those rights as the essential part of a political system, which, if it is overthrown, will prove destructive to public prosperity and security. . . . In the same way the partial legislative control of nationalized corporations now exercised by the state governments, is defended, not on the ground that it has been well exercised, not even plausibly on the ground that it can be well exercised. It is defended almost exclusively on the ground that any increase in the authority of the Federal government is dangerous to the American people. But the Federal government belongs to the American people even more completely than do the state governments, because a general current of public opinion can act much more effectively on the single Federal authority than it can upon the many separate state authorities. Popular interests have nothing to fear from a measure of Federal centralization, which bestows on the Federal government powers necessary to the fulfillment of its legitimate responsibilities; and the American people cannot in the long run be deceived by pleas which bear the evidence of such a selfish origin and have such dubious historical associations. The rights and the powers both of states and individuals must be competent to serve their purposes efficiently in an economical and coherent national organization, or else they must be superseded. A prejudice against centralization is as pernicious, provided centralization is necessary, as a prejudice in its favor. All rights under the law are functions in a democratic political organism and must be justified by their actual or presumable functional adequacy.

The ideal of a constructive relation between American nationality and American democracy is in truth equivalent to a new Declaration of Independence. It affirms that the American people are free to organize their political, economic, and social life in the service of a comprehensive, a lofty, and far-reaching democratic purpose. . . . It declares that the democracy has a machinery in a nationalized organization, and a practical guide in the national interest, which are adequate to the realization of the democratic ideal; and it declares also that in the long run just in so far as Americans timidly or superstitiously refuse to accept their national opportunity and responsibility, they will not deserve the names either of freemen or of loyal democrats. There comes a time in the history of every nation, when its independence of spirit vanishes, unless it emancipates itself in some measure from its traditional illusions; and that time is fast approaching for the American people. They must either seize the chance of a better future, or else become a nation which is satisfied in spirit merely to repeat indefinitely the monotonous measures of its own past.

Our Benevolent Feudalism

WILLIAM J. GHENT (1866–1942)   *An American-born socialist
writer and critic, Ghent was editor of the* American Fabian
*1897–98, leaving to aid "Golden Rule" Jones, the crusading
mayor of Toledo, in his campaign for governor. From 1906 to
1911, he was connected with the Rand School of Social Science,
which was a target for abuse from the conservative press, but
which became under his leadership the outstanding center for
developing socialist sentiments among the middle class. Although socialist conviction spread during these years, he judged
it a "lukewarm conviction," for the social reformers' engaging
picture of things as they were to be seemed to him as far away
as ever.*

The new Feudalism will be but an orderly outgrowth of present
tendencies and conditions. All societies evolve naturally out of their
predecessors. In sociology, as in biology, there is no cell without
a parent cell. The society of each generation develops a multitude
of spontaneous and acquired variations, and out of these, by a
blending process of natural and conscious selection, the succeeding
society is evolved. The new order will differ in no important
respects from the present, except in the completer development
of its more salient features. The visitor from another planet who
had known the old and should see the new would note but few
changes. *Alter et idem*—another yet the same—he would say. From
magnate to baron, from workman to villein, from publicist to court
agent and retainer, will be changes of state and function so slight
as to elude all but the keenest eyes.

   An increased power, a more concentrated control, will be seen.
But these have their limitations, which must not be disregarded.
A sense of the latent strength of democracy will restrain the full
exercise of baronial powers, and a growing sense of ethics will guide
baronial activities somewhat toward the channels of social betterment. . . . Our nobility will thus temper their exactions to an
endurable limit; and they will distribute benefits to a degree that
makes a tolerant, if not a satisfied, people. They may even make

From *Our Benevolent Feudalism* (New York: Macmillan, 1902), pp. 181–85,
188–98.

a working principle of Bentham's maxim, and after, of course, appropriating the first and choicest fruits of industry to themselves, may seek to promote the "greatest happiness of the greatest number." For therein will lie their greater security. . . .

Bondage to the land was the basis of villeinage in the old régime; bondage to the job will be the basis of villeinage in the new. The new régime, absolving itself from all general responsibility to its workers, extends a measure of protection, solely as an act of grace, only to those who are faithful and obedient; and it holds the entire mass of its employed underlings to the terms of day-by-day service. . . . The wage-system will endure, for it is a simpler and more effective means of determining the baron's volume of profits than were the "boon-works," the "week-works," and the *corvées* of old. But with increasing concentration on the one hand, and the fiercer competition for employment on the other, the secured job will become the laborer's fortress, which he will hardly dare to evacuate. The hope of bettering his condition by surrendering one place in the expectation of getting another will be qualified by a restraining prudence. He will no longer trust his individual strength, but when he protests against ill conditions, or, in the last resort, strikes, it will be only in company with a formidable host of his fellows. . . . Wages and dividends will be nicely balanced with a watchful regard for the fostering of content; workshops and villages of yet more approved models than any of the present will be built, and a thousand Pelzers and Pullmans will arise. Old-age pensions, or at least the promise of them, will be extended to new groups, and by all possible means the lesson that protection and security are due only to faithfulness and obedience will be made plain to the entire villein class.

Gradually a change will take place in the aspirations and conduct of the younger generations. Heretofore there has been at least some degree of freedom of choice in determining one's occupation, however much that freedom has been curtailed by actual economic conditions. But with the settling of industrial processes comes more and more constraint. The dream of the children of the farms to escape from their drudgery by migrating to the city, and from the stepping-stone of a clerkly place at three dollars a week to rise to affluence, will be given over, and they will follow the footsteps of their fathers. A like fixity of condition will be observed in the cities, and the sons of clerks and of mechanics and of day laborers will tend to accept their environment of birth and training and abide by it. It is a phenomenon observable in all countries where the economic pressure is severe, and it is yet more certain to obtain in feudal America.

The outlines of the present State loom but feebly through the intricate network of the new system. The nobles will have attained to complete power, and the motive and operation of government will have become simply the registering and administering of their collective will. And yet the State will continue very much as now, just as the form and name of the Roman Republic continued under Augustus. The present State machinery is admirably adapted for the subtle and extra-legal exertion of power by an autocracy; and while improvements to that end might unquestionably be made, the barons will hesitate to take action which will needlessly arouse popular suspicions. From petty constable to Supreme Court Justice the officials will understand, or be made to understand, the golden mean of their duties; and except for an occasional rascally Jacobin, whom it may for a time be difficult to suppress, they will be faithful and obey. . . .

Armed force will, of course, be employed to overawe the discontented and to quiet unnecessary turbulence. Unlike the armed forces of the old Feudalism, the nominal control will be that of the State; the soldiery will be regular, and not irregular. Not again will the barons risk the general indignation arising from the employment of Pinkertons and other private armies. The worker has unmistakably shown his preference, when he is to be subdued, for the militia and the Federal army. It is not an unreasonable attitude, and it is hardly to be doubted that it will be respected. The militia of our Benevolent Feudalism will be recruited, as now, mostly from the clerkly class; and it will be officered largely by the sons and nephews of the barons. But its actions will be tempered by a saner policy. Governed by those who have most to fear from popular exasperation, it will show a finer restraint.

A happy blending of generosity and firmness will characterize all dealings with open discontent; but the prevention of discontent will be the prior study, to which the intellect and the energies of the nobles and their legates will be ever bent. To that end the teachings of the schools and colleges, the sermons, the editorials, the stump orations, and even the plays at the theatres will be skilfully moulded; and the questioning heart of the poor, which perpetually seeks some answer to the painful riddle of the earth, will meet with a multitude of mollifying responses. These will be: from the churches, that discontent is the fruit of atheism, and that religion alone is a solace for earthly woe; from the colleges, that discontent is ignorant and irrational, since conditions have certainly bettered in the last one hundred years; from the newspapers, that discontent is anarchy; and from the stump orators that it is unpatriotic, since this nation is the greatest and most glorious that ever the sun shone upon. As of old, these reasons will for the time suffice; and against the possibility of recurrent questionings new apologetics will be skilfully formulated, to be put forth as occasion requires. . . .

Peace and stability it will maintain at all hazards; and the mass, remembering the chaos, the turmoil, the insecurity of the past, will bless its reign. Peace and stability will be its arguments of defence against all criticism, domestic or foreign. An observant visitor from some foreign State may pick a defect here and there; but the eloquent defender of the régime will answer: Look upon the tranquillity that everywhere prevails, and reflect upon the inquietude and anarchy of the past. The disturbances of labor have ceased, and sedition, though occasionally encountered, is easily thwarted and put down. The crudities and barbarities of other days have given way to ordered regularities. Efficiency—the faculty of getting things—is at last rewarded as it should be, for the efficient have inherited the earth and its fulness. The lowly, "whose happiness is greater and whose welfare is more thoroughly conserved when governed than when governing," as a twentieth-century philosopher said of them, are settled and happy in the state which reason and experience teach is their God-appointed lot. They are comfortable, too; and if the patriarchal ideal of a vine and fig tree for each is not yet attained, at least each has his rented patch in the country or his rented cell in a city building. Bread and the circus are freely given to the deserving, and as for the undeserving, they are merely reaping the rightful rewards of their contumacy and pride. Order reigns, each has his justly appointed share, and the State rests in security, "lapt in universal law."

The Economic Basis of Imperialism

CHARLES A. CONANT (1861–1915)   *An eminent banking authority, Conant was financial reporter for the Boston* Post *and the
New York* Journal of Commerce *until 1901, when President
McKinley appointed him to make a study of the monetary
system of the Philippines. An all-out defender of the modern
business system, he was an economic determinist whose views
were influenced, not by Marx, but by the unorthodox British
economist John A. Hobson, whom he quoted with approval.
Like Hobson he preferred capitalism to socialism, but was
convinced that capitalism had reached a crucial point in its
development and that imperialism was justified by the intense
competition of modern industrialism.*

The instinctive tendency of a race or civilization often outruns
the wisdom of its leaders. Whether for good or ill, the inborn
tendencies of race—whether for the highest achievement in art,
like the Ionian; the military conquest of the world, like the Roman;
the penetration of distant and barbarous countries for the purposes
of trade, like the Tyrian or the Venetian; the command of the
empire of the sea, like the English—these tendencies prevail by
a sort of instinct. Other races in seeking to pursue the same paths
by imitation have stumbled and gone astray. But when the current
of race or national tendencies runs strongly in a given channel it
is apt to override alike the misgivings of its sympathizers and the
protests and resistance of those who would obstruct it. The United
States today seem about to enter upon a path marked out for them
as the children of the Anglo–Saxon race, not yet traversed because
there has been so much to do at home. Almost as if by magic,
the importance of naval power as the advance agent of commercial
supremacy has flashed upon the mind of the country. The irresistible tendency to expansion, which leads the growing tree to burst
every barrier, which drove the Goths, the Vandals, and finally our
Saxon ancestors in successive and irresistible waves over the
decadent provinces of Rome, seems again in operation, demanding
new outlets for American capital and new opportunities for
American enterprise.

From the *North American Review,* CLXVII (1898), pp. 326–28, 330, 337–39.

This new movement is not a matter of sentiment. It is the result of a natural law of economic and race development. The great civilized peoples have today at their command the means of developing the decadent nations of the world. This means, in its material aspects, is the great excess of saved capital which is the result of machine production. It is proposed to point out in this article . . . how necessary to the salvation of these countries is an outlet for their surplus savings, if the entire fabric of the present economic order is not to be shaken by a social revolution. The law of self-preservation, as well as that of the survival of the fittest, is urging our people on in a path which is undoubtedly a departure from the policy of the past, but which is inevitably marked out by the new conditions and requirements of the present.

The dominant note of modern economic life, since the beginning of the epoch of machinery and of negotiable securities, has been saving for investment. Saving against the risks of loss and the weakness of old age has existed from the beginning of civilization and has been accompanied by a limited amount of saving for increasing the means of production. But saving for the sake of an income without the impairment of the principal is, in its present extension, a modern phenomenon. . . . The creation of corporations and the issue of their shares in negotiable securities afforded an outlet, toward the close of the last century and early in the present century, for savings which were becoming congested, because they could not be put to ready use. The change in the form of the investment was only an evolution from the great demands for capital which arose with the application of machinery to production upon a large scale and the discovery of methods of communication on land and sea by the use of steam. The necessity for carrying on such large enterprises as cotton mills, iron foundries, and canal, railway and steamship building by great aggregate sums of capital led to the division of the cost of the enterprise into divisible parts, which might absorb the capital of great numbers of men. For many years there was an outlet at a high rate of return for all the savings of all the frugal persons in the great civilized countries. . . .

The conditions of the early part of the century have changed. Capital is no longer needed in excess of the supply, but it is

becoming congested. The benefits of saving have been inculcated
with such effect for many decades that savings accumulate beyond
the development of new demands for capital which are legitimate,
and are becoming a menace to the economic future of the great
industrial countries. . . . The duplication of needless plant, the
multiplication of unprofitable enterprises, has flooded the market
with products which could hardly be consumed if all the means
of the community were applied to consumption, and which have
resulted, under the existing system of abstinence from consumption
for the sake of saving, in a glut of goods which has destroyed profits,
bankrupted great corporations, and ruined investors. . . .

There are three important solutions of this enormous congestion
of capital in excess of legitimate demand. One of these is the
socialistic solution of the abandonment of saving, the application
of the whole earnings of the laborer to current consumption, and
the support of old age out of taxes levied upon the production
of the community. It will be long before this solution will be
accepted in a comprehensive form in any modern civilized state.
The second solution is the creation of new demands at home for
the absorption of capital. This has occurred at several previous
stages of the world's history and is likely to continue as long as
human desires continue expansible. But there has never been a time
before when the proportion of capital to be absorbed was so great
in proportion to possible new demands. Means for building more
bicycle factories than are needed, and for laying more electric
railways than are able to pay dividends, have been taken out of
current savings within the last few years, without producing any
marked effect upon their amount and without doing more, at the
most, than to stay the downward course of the rate of interest.
Aside from the waste of capital in war, which is only a form of
consumption, there remains, therefore, as the final resource, the
equipment of new countries with the means of production and
exchange. . . .

For the means of finding new productive employments for
capital, therefore, it is necessary that the great industrial countries
should turn to countries which have not felt the pulse of modern
progress. Such countries have yet to be equipped with the mechanism of production and of luxury, which has been created in the

progressive countries by the savings of recent generations. They have not only to obtain buildings and machinery—the necessary elements in producing machine-made goods—but they have to build their roads, drain their marshes, dam their rivers, build aqueducts for their water supplies and sewers for their towns and cities. . . .

The United States cannot afford to adhere to policy of isolation while other nations are reaching out for the command of these new markets. . . . ·

Whether the United States shall actually acquire territorial possessions, shall set up captain generalships and garrisons, whether they shall adopt the middle ground of protecting sovereignties nominally independent, or whether they shall content themselves with naval stations and diplomatic representations as the basis for asserting their rights to the free commerce of the East, is a matter of detail. The discussion of the details may be of high importance to our political morality and our historical traditions, but it bears upon the economic side of the question only so far as a given political policy is necessary to safeguard and extend commercial interests. The writer is not an advocate of "imperialism" from sentiment, but does not fear the name if it means only that the United States shall assert their right to free markets in all the old countries which are being opened to the surplus resources of the capitalistic countries and thereby given the benefits of modern civilization. Whether this policy carries with it the direct government of groups of half-savage islands may be a subject for argument, but upon the economic side of the question there is but one choice—either to enter by some means upon the competition for the employment of American capital and enterprise in these countries, or to continue the needless duplication of existing means of production and communication, with the glut of unconsumed products, the convulsions followed by trade stagnation, and the steadily declining return upon investments which this policy will invoke.

The entry of the United States upon the competition for the world's markets means some radical changes in their existing policy, but it means an enlarged share in the world's earnings and in the respect of other civilized states.

To the Person Sitting in Darkness

MARK TWAIN (1835–1910)   *Born Samuel Clemens, the famous novelist and humorist began life in a small Missouri town, and his most popular books,* Tom Sawyer *and* Huckleberry Finn, *reflected his boyhood experiences during the early boom days of the Southwest. As he grew older, he turned from humor to satire, launching savage shafts at such sacred things as evangelical religion, the business system, the Republican party, the government at Washington, the "damned human race" itself. The professional funmaker of the seventies became the bitter satirist of the nineties because he was a thoroughly honest man and an independent thinker who hated all sham and humbug and who had a passionate hatred of cruelty and injustice. The sensitive and idealistic nature of the man was revealed in a comment he wrote to Howells in 1899: "I have been reading the morning paper," he said. "I do it every morning—well knowing that I shall find in it the usual depravities and basenesses and hypocrisies and cruelties that make up civilization, and cause me to put in the rest of the day pleading for the damnation of the human race."*

Shall we? That is, shall we go on conferring our Civilization upon the peoples that sit in darkness, or shall we give those poor things a rest? Shall we bang right ahead in our old-time, loud, pious way, and commit the new century to the game; or shall we sober up and sit down and think it over first? Would it not be prudent to get our Civilization-tools together, and see how much stock is left on hand in the way of Glass Beads and Theology, and Maxim Guns and Hymn Books, and Trade-Gin and Torches of Progress and Enlightenment (patent adjustable ones, good to fire villages with, upon occasion), and balance the books, and arrive at the profit and loss, so that we may intelligently decide whether to continue the business or sell out the property and start a new Civilization Scheme on the proceeds?

Extending the Blessings of Civilization to our Brother who Sits in Darkness has been a good trade and has paid well, on the whole; and there is money in it yet, if carefully worked—but not enough,

From *North American Review*, CLXXII (1901), pp. 164–66, 169–76.

in my judgment, to make any considerable risk advisable. The People that Sit in Darkness are getting to be too scarce—too scarce and too shy. And such darkness as is now left is really of but an indifferent quality, and not dark enough for the game. The most of those People that Sit in Darkness have been furnished with more light than was good for them or profitable for us. We have been injudicious.

The Blessings-of-Civilization Trust, wisely and cautiously administered, is a Daisy. There is more money in it, more territory, more sovereignty, and other kinds of emolument, than there is in any other game that is played. But Christendom has been playing it badly of late years, and must certainly suffer by it, in my opinion. She has been so eager to get every stake that appeared on the green cloth, that the People who Sit in Darkness have noticed it—they have noticed it, and have begun to show alarm. They have become suspicious of the Blessings of Civilization. More—they have begun to examine them. This is not well. The Blessings of Civilization are all right, and a good commercial property; there could not be a better, in a dim light. In the right kind of a light, and at a proper distance, with the goods a little out of focus, they furnish this desirable exhibit to the Gentlemen who Sit in Darkness:

LOVE,	LAW AND ORDER,
JUSTICE,	LIBERTY,
GENTLENESS,	EQUALITY,
CHRISTIANITY,	HONORABLE DEALING,
PROTECTION TO THE	MERCY,
WEAK,	EDUCATION,
TEMPERANCE,	
—and so on.	

There. Is it good? Sir, it is pie. It will bring into camp any idiot that sits in darkness anywhere. But not if we adulterate it. It is proper to be emphatic upon that point. This brand is strictly for Export—apparently. *Apparently.* Privately and confidentially, it is nothing of the kind. Privately and confidentially, it is merely an outside cover, gay and pretty and attractive, displaying the special patterns of our Civilization which we reserve for Home

Consumption, while *inside* the bale is the Actual Thing that the Customer Sitting in Darkness buys with his blood and tears and land and liberty. That Actual Thing is, indeed, Civilization, but it is only for Export. Is there a difference between the two brands? In some of the details, yes.

We all know that the Business is being ruined. The reason is not far to seek. It is because our Mr. McKinley, and Mr. Chamberlain, and the Kaiser, and the Czar and the French have been exporting the Actual Thing *with the outside cover left off*. This is bad for the Game. It shows that these new players of it are not sufficiently acquainted with it. . . .

Our Master of the Game plays it badly—plays it as Mr. Chamberlain was playing it in South Africa. It was a mistake to do that; also, it was one which was quite unlooked for in a Master who was playing it so well in Cuba. In Cuba, he was playing the usual and regular *American* game, and it was winning, for there is no way to beat it. The Master, contemplating Cuba, said: "Here is an oppressed and friendless little nation which is willing to fight to be free; we go partners, and put up the strength of seventy million sympathizers and the resources of the United States: play!" Nothing but Europe combined could call that hand: and Europe cannot combine on anything. There, in Cuba, he was following our great traditions in a way which made us very proud of him, and proud of the deep dissatisfaction which his play was provoking in Continental Europe. Moved by a high inspiration, he threw out those stirring words which proclaimed that forcible annexation would be "criminal aggression"; and in that utterance fired another "shot heard round the world." The memory of that fine saying will be outlived by the remembrance of no act of his but one—that he forgot it within the twelvemonth, and its honorable gospel along with it.

For, presently, came the Philippine temptation. It was strong; it was too strong, and he made that bad mistake: he played the European game, the Chamberlain game. It was a pity; it was a great pity, that error; that one grievous error, that irrevocable error. For it was the very place and time to play the American game again. And at no cost. Rich winnings to be gathered in, too; rich and permanent; indestructible; a fortune transmissible forever to the children of the flag. Not land, not money, not dominion—no, something worth many times more than that dross: our share, the spectacle of a nation of long harassed and persecuted slaves set free through our influence; our posterity's share, the golden memory of that fair deed. The game was in our hands. If it had been played according to the American rules, Dewey would have sailed away from Manila as soon as he had destroyed the Spanish fleet—after putting up a sign on shore guaranteeing foreign property and life against damage by the Filipinos, and warning the Powers that interference with the emancipated patriots would be regarded as an act unfriendly to the United States. The Powers cannot combine, in even a bad cause, and the sign would not have been molested. . . .

But we played the Chamberlain game, and lost the chance to add another Cuba and another honorable deed to our good record.

The more we examine the mistake, the more clearly we perceive that it is going to be bad for the Business. The Person Sitting in Darkness is almost sure to say: "There is something curious about this—curious and unaccountable. There must be two Americas: one that sets the captive free, and one that takes a once-captive's new freedom away from him, and picks a quarrel with him with nothing to found it on; then kills him to get his land."

The truth is, the Person Sitting in Darkness *is* saying things like that; and for the sake of the Business we must persuade him to look at the Philippine matter in another and healthier way. We must arrange his opinions for him. . . .

We must . . . coax him and coddle him, and assure him that the ways of Providence are best, and that it would not become us to find fault with them; and then, to show him that we are only imitators, not originators, we must read the following passage from the letter of an American soldier-lad in the Philippines to his mother, published in *Public Opinion*, of Decorah, Iowa, describing the finish of a victorious battle:

"WE NEVER LEFT ONE ALIVE. IF ONE WAS WOUNDED, WE WOULD RUN OUR BAYONETS THROUGH HIM."

Having now laid all the historical facts before the Person Sitting in Darkness, we should bring him to again, and explain them to him. We should say to him:

"They look doubtful, but in reality they are not. There have been lies; yes, but they were told in a good cause. We have been treacherous; but that was only in order that real good might come out of apparent evil. True, we have crushed a deceived and confiding people; we have turned against the weak and the friendless who trusted us; we have stamped out a just and intelligent and well-ordered republic; we have stabbed an ally in the back and slapped the face of a guest; we have bought a Shadow from an enemy that hadn't it to sell; we have robbed a trusting friend of his land and his liberty; we have invited our clean young men to shoulder a discredited musket and do bandit's work under a flag which bandits have been accustomed to fear, not to follow; we have debauched America's honor and blackened her face before the world; but each detail was for the best. We know this. The Head of every State and Sovereignty in Christendom and ninety per cent of every legislative body in Christendom, including our Congress and our fifty State Legislatures, are members not only of the church, but also of the Blessings-of-Civilization Trust. This world-girdling accumulation of trained morals, high principles, and justice, cannot do an unright thing, an unfair thing, an ungenerous thing, an unclean thing. It knows what it is about. Give yourself no uneasiness; it is all right."

Now then, that will convince the Person. You will see. It will restore the Business. Also, it will elect the Master of the Game to the vacant place in the Trinity of our national gods; and there on their high thrones the Three will sit, age after age, in the people's sight, each bearing the Emblem of his service: Washington, the Sword of the Liberator; Lincoln, the Slave's Broken Chains; the Master, the Chains Repaired.

It will give the Business a splendid new start. You will see.

The Idealism of War

HOMER LEA (1876–1912)   *A little hunchback with dreams of military glory, Lea dropped out of Stanford, as he told classmates,*

From *The Valor of Ignorance* (New York: Harper & Brothers, 1909), pp. 10–12, 20–27, 65–67, 70–71.

"to topple the Manchu throne." After unsuccessfully leading a raggle-taggle revolutionary army against the dowager Empress, the young "general" became military adviser to Sun Yat-sen and assisted at the birth of the new Chinese Republic. As a consulting strategist, he gained worldwide reputation, advising both the British and German general staffs. His book, The Valor of Ignorance, *chiding the United States for unpreparedness, went through twenty-four editions in Japan in one month and was made required reading for all Japanese officers. In it he not only predicted the war between the United States and Japan but described accurately and in minute detail the exact strategy used thirty-five years later by the Japanese in World War II.*

Wars—Victory—a nation. Wars—Destruction—dissolution. Such is the melancholy epitome of national existence, and such has it been from the beginning of human association until to-day. From the time, six thousand years past, when the wild highlander rolled down from the mountains of Elam and moulded with sword and brawn the Turanian shepherds into the Chaldean Empire, until within the last decade, when the Samurai of Nippon rose out of their islands in the Eastern Sea and carved for themselves a new empire on the Continent of Asia, there has been no cessation nor deviation from this inexorable law governing the formation and extinction of national entities.

All kingdoms, empires, and nations that have existed on this earth have been born out of the womb of war and the delivery of them has occurred in the pain and labor of battle. So, too, have these same nations, with the same inevitable certainty, perished on like fields amid the wreckage and cinders of their defenceless possessions.

As physical vigor represents the strength of man in his struggle for existence, in the same sense military vigor constitutes the strength of nations: Ideals, laws and constitutions are but temporary effulgences, and are existent only so long as this strength remains vital. As manhood marks the height of physical vigor among mankind, so the militant successes of a nation mark the zenith of its physical greatness. The decline of physical strength in the individual is significant of disease or old age, culminating in death. In the same manner deterioration of military strength or militant capacity in a nation marks its decline; and, if there comes not a national renascence of it, decay will set in and the consummation shall not be other than that sombre end which has overtaken the innumerable nations now no more, but who, in the vanity of their greatness, could conjecture the end of time yet not the downfall of their fragile edifices.

An analysis of the history of mankind shows that from the fifteenth century before Christ until the present time, a cycle of thirty-four hundred years, there have been less than two hundred and thirty-four years of peace. Nations succeeded one another with monotonous similarity in their rise, decline and fall. One and all of them were builded by architects who were generals, masons who were soldiers, trowels that were swords and out of stones that were the ruins of decadent states. Their periods of greatness were entirely coincident with their military prowess and with the expansion consequent upon it. . . .

The American commonwealth stands in no different relation to time and the forces of time than any other nation that has ever existed. The same elements brought about its birth and the same causes will prolong or shorten its existence as prolonged or shortened theirs. Up to the present time the life history of this Republic has varied only in the slightest degree from the elemental forces that brought all other nations into existence and governed the growth of their youth and manhood.

It is unnecessary to recall the battlefields upon which this republic was born or the subsequent wars that have marked its growth and expansion, other than to recall the invariability of that universal law governing the beginnings and rise of nations. This country, as others that have gone before, has been built up from the spoils of combat and conquest of defenceless tribes. Its expansion has been no more merciful nor merciless than the expansion of any other nation. The same inexorable law of physical strength has governed it as all others. But its conquests have been over nations and aborigines so disproportionately weak and incapable of waging war on a basis of equality that its wars have been destructive rather than inculcative of equitable military conceptions. The very ease with which this commonwealth has expanded is responsible for the erroneous beliefs now prevalent concerning the true basis of its future greatness. . . .

In considering the future of this Republic one must do so, not from the closets of its politicians, not from its alleyways with their frenzied crowds, not from theorists nor feminists, for these are but the feverish phantasms and sickly disorders of national life. It must be regarded from the heights of universal history and empirical knowledge which appertains to national existence. . . .

If this Republic is to achieve the greatness and duration its founders hoped to secure for it; if it is to continue to spread abroad over the earth the principles of its constitutions or the equity of its laws and the hope it extends to the betterment of the human race, then it must realize that this can only be done by possessing an ability and potentiality to be supreme over those nations whose ambitions and expansion are convergent. Preparations for wars consequent upon the growing compactness of the world and increasing convergence of all the world powers must go on cease-lessly and in proportion to the increase of expansion and fulness of years. . . . Excessive national wealth is . . . even in itself . . . productive of utter incapacity to execute warlike measures or even to prevent the collapse of a nation in war—the enervation through luxury, feminism, theorism, or the decay of martial inclina-tion and military capacity. This sooner or later begins to show itself in every phase of life, from National Assemblies to Debating Societies, Communism, Idealism, Universalism, and innumerable other bright, fantastic tapestries that the ingenuity of man weaves through woof and warp of human hopes and their follies.

Wealth is a factor in the naval and military strength of a nation only so long as it is regarded in its true and subordinate capacity: to build battleships, but not to fight them; to buy arms, not valor; to manufacture powder, not patriotism. But when wealth becomes so paramount in a nation's life that it forms the chief ambition of individual efforts, then the factors that constitute military strength fall away. . . .

In a nation ruled by opulence, men and the souls of men are not only the valets of wealth, but the nation itself is obsequious to it. The government pursues its course through a labyrinthine way: The interests of countless individuals are paramount to those of the state, and national ambition ceases to exist. The common-wealth in protecting individual interests resorts to expedients that are as temporary as the lives of those who make them. Yet to these transitory acts the integrity of national greatness is sacrificed. When war falls upon such a nation it becomes disunited. In the same myriad-minded manner that it carried on the mercantile projects of peace it attempts the conduct of a war; then disintegration, disaster and destruction ensue.

On the other hand, in a military power where individuals are considered only as instruments of its greatness, the dreadful intentness of its aims knows no discouragement, the straightforwardness of its progress no hesitation, the terribleness of its energy no fatigue. Neither property nor mankind disturb its calculations. It is systematic, simple in design, relentless in prosecution. Theories of finance carry with them no awe; revenues and commerce it takes as it finds them; millionaires and economists strike no terror to its heart, for the excise and stamp duties it levies are not on material resources, but on the souls and passions and ambitions of men. These resources are exhaustless, and so long as nations conceal these facts from themselves, so long must they suffer and be vanquished and die.

The Moral Equivalent of War

WILLIAM JAMES (1842–1910)   *A Harvard psychologist and philosopher, James evolved the method of pragmatism. As a reformer, the political issue which stirred him most deeply was imperialism, and he was at one time vice president of the Anti-Imperialist League. His strong views led him to exclaim in characteristic pragmatist fashion, "Damn all Empires! including that of the Absolute." Philosophically he confessed he was "against all big organizations as such, national ones first and foremost" and "in favor of the eternal forces of truth" which always operated in the individual. Good, he felt, was not something to be contemplated, but something to be brought to pass. It was this practical idealism that inspired his vigorous reaction*

From *McClure's Magazine*, August, 1910, pp. 463–65, 467–68.

to the "barnyard crowing" of Theodore Roosevelt and led him to seek a moral equivalent of war by sublimating the martial virtues to the cause of peace.

The war against war is going to be no holiday excursion or camping party. The military feelings are too deeply grounded to abdicate their place among our ideals until better substitutes are offered than the glory and shame that come to nations, as well as to individuals, from the ups and downs of politics and the vicissitudes of trade. . . .

At the present day civilized opinion is a curious mental mixture. The military instincts and ideals are as strong as ever, but they are confronted by reflective criticisms which sorely curb their ancient freedom. Innumerable writers are showing up the bestial side of military service. Pure loot and mastery seem no longer morally avowable motives, and pretexts must be found for attributing them solely to the enemy. England and we—our army and navy authorities repeat without ceasing—arm solely for "peace"; Germany and Japan it is who are bent on loot and glory. "Peace" in military mouths today is a synonym for "war expected." The word has become a pure provocative, and no government sincerely wishing peace should allow it ever to be printed in a newspaper. Every up-to-date dictionary should say that "peace" and "war" mean the same thing, now *in posse,* now *in actu.* It may even reasonably be said that the intensely sharp competitive *preparation* for war by the nations is the *real war,* permanent, unceasing; and that the battles are only a sort of public verification of the military mastery gained during the "peace" interval. . . .

All reflective apologists for war at the present day take it religiously. It is to them a sort of sacrament; its profits are to the vanquished as well as to the victor; and, quite apart from any question of profit, it is an absolute good, we are told, for it is human nature at its highest dynamic. Its "horrors" are a cheap price to pay for rescue from the only alternative supposed, of a world of clerks and teachers, of coeducation and zoöphily, of "consumers' leagues" and "associated charities," of industrialism unlimited, and feminism unabashed. No scorn, no hardness, no valor any more! Fie upon such a cattle-yard of a planet! . . .

Having said this much in preparation, and by way of conciliating the side I don't belong to, I will now confess my own Utopia. I devoutly believe in the ultimate reign of peace and in the gradual advent of some sort of a socialistic equilibrium. The fatalistic view of the war function is to me nonsense, for I know that warmaking is due to definite motives and subject to prudential checks and reasonable criticisms, just like any other form of enterprise. And when whole nations are the armies, and the science of destruction vies in intellectual refinement with the sciences of production, I see that war becomes absurd and impossible from its own monstrosity. Extravagant ambitions will have to be replaced by reasonable claims, and nations must make common cause against them. I see no reason why all this should not apply to yellow as well as to white nations, and I look forward to a future when acts of war shall be formally outlawed among civilized peoples.

All these beliefs of mine put me squarely into the anti-militarist party. But I do not believe that peace either ought to be or will be permanent on this globe, unless the states pacifically organized preserve some of the old elements of army-discipline. A permanently successful peace-economy cannot be a simple pleasure-economy. In the more or less socialistic future toward which mankind seems to be drifting, we must still subject ourselves collectively to those severities that answer to our real position upon this only partly hospitable globe. We must make new energies and hardihoods continue the manliness to which the military mind so faithfully clings. Martial virtues must be the enduring cement; intrepidity, contempt of softness, surrender of private interest, obedience to command, must still remain the rock upon which states are built—unless, indeed, we wish for dangerous reactions against commonwealths fit only for contempt, and liable to invite attack whenever a center of crystallization for military-minded enterprise is formed anywhere in their neighborhood.

The war-party is assuredly right in affirming and reaffirming that the martial virtues, although originally gained by the race through war, are absolute and permanent human goods. Patriotic pride and ambition in their military form are, after all, only specifications of a more universal and enduring competitive passion. They are its first form, but that is no reason for supposing them to be its last form. Men now are proud of belonging to a conquering nation, and without a murmur they lay down their persons and their wealth, if by so doing they may fend off subjection. But who can be sure that *other aspects of one's country* may not with time and education and suggestion enough, come to be regarded with similarly effective feelings of pride and shame? Why should men not some day feel that it is worth a blood-tax to belong to a collectivity superior in *any* ideal respect? Why should they not blush with indignant shame if the community that owns them is vile in any way whatsoever? Individuals, daily more numerous, now feel this civic passion. It is only a question of blowing on the spark till the whole population gets incandescent, and on the ruins of the old morals of military honor a stable system of morals of civic honor builds itself up. What the whole community comes to believe in grasps the individual as in a vise. The war function has grasped us, so far; but constructive interests may some day seem no less imperative, and impose on the individual a hardly lighter burden.

Let me illustrate my idea more concretely. There is nothing to make one indignant in the mere fact that life is hard, that men should toil and suffer pain. The planetary conditions once for all are such, and we can stand it. But that so many men, by mere accidents of birth and opportunity, should have a life of *nothing else* but toil and pain and hardness and inferiority imposed upon them, should have *no* vacation, while others natively no more deserving get no taste of this campaigning life at all—*this* is capable of arousing indignation in reflective minds. It may end by seeming shameful to all of us that some of us have nothing but campaigning, and others have nothing but unmanly ease. If now— and this is my idea—there were, instead of military conscription, a conscription of the whole youthful population to form for a certain number of years a part of the army enlisted against *nature*, the injustice would tend to be evened out, and numerous other benefits to the commonwealth would follow. The military ideals of hardihood and discipline would be wrought into the growing fiber of the people; no one would remain blind, as the luxurious classes now are blind, to man's real relations to the globe he lives on, and to the permanently solid and hard foundations of his higher life. To coal and iron mines, to freight trains, to fishing fleets in

December, to dishwashing, clothes-washing, and window-washing, to roadbuilding and tunnelmaking, to foundries and stoke-holes, and to the frames of skyscrapers, would our gilded youths be drafted off, according to their choice, to get the childishness knocked out of them, and to come back into society with healthier sympathies and soberer ideas. They would have paid their blood-tax, done their part in the immemorial human warfare against nature; they would tread the earth more proudly; the women would value them more highly; they would be better fathers and teachers of the following generation.

Such a conscription, with the state of public opinion that would have required it, and the moral fruits it would bear, would preserve in the midst of a pacific civilization the manly virtues which the military party is so afraid of seeing disappear in peace. We should get toughness without callousness, authority with as little criminal cruelty as possible, and painful work done cheerily because the duty is temporary, and threatens not, as now, to degrade the whole remainder of one's life. I spoke of the "moral equivalent" of war. So far, war has been the only force that can discipline a whole community, and, until an equivalent discipline is organized, I believe that war must have its way. But I have no serious doubt that the ordinary prides and shames of social man, once developed to a certain intensity, are capable of organizing such a moral equivalent as I have sketched, or some other just as effective for preserving manliness of type. Though an infinitely remote Utopia just now, in the end it is but a question of time, of skilful propagandism, and of opinion-making men seizing historic opportunities.
. . .

[After all,] the amount of alteration in public opinion that my Utopia postulates is vastly less than the difference between the mentality of those black warriors who pursued Stanley's party on the Congo with their cannibal war cry of "Meat! Meat!" and that of the "general staff" of any civilized nation. History has seen the latter interval bridged over; the former one can be bridged over much more easily.

Chapter IV

The Breakdown of Absolutes

The New Instrument of Learning

"Since monkeys first began to chatter in trees," wrote Henry Adams, "neither man nor beast had ever denied or doubted Multiplicity, Diversity, Complexity, Anarchy, Chaos." Always and everywhere, chaos was a primary fact, even in the Garden of Eden. But since Moses, every thinking being "had exhausted thought in the effort to prove Unity, Continuity, Purpose, Order, Law, Truth, the Universe, God." [1] The direction of mind had been constant since history began. Out of its own unity, its own hopes, mind had created a universal order, the essence of which was absolute truth.

After having confidently begun his life by embarking on a factitious eighteenth-century vessel—where "God was a father and nature a mother, and all for the best in a scientific universe"— Adams found himself in his old age aground on the reef of doubt. He fixed the date of his intellectual shipwreck at 1898, when Madame Curie revealed "the metaphysical bomb she called radium." Her discovery of ultimate energy that defied the orderly world of sense impressions left him with no choice but to cut loose from the wreckage of the past; for her revelation told him, in plain words, "Chaos was the law of nature; Order was the dream of man." With the trim cosmos of Isaac Newton sunk by rays, Adams declared himself "adrift on a sensual raft in the midst of a supersensual chaos." [2]

Although intensely personal, Adams' experience summed up the intellectual crisis of his generation. Unlike him, however, most of his contemporaries lacked the courage or will to break with the past, but instead fell back blindly on belief in an unproved unity and order they had themselves disproved. They retained the cherished, unreasoned faith of their fathers and grandfathers that the governing principles of order, whether of God, nature or both, prevailed over these United States. In politics, such uniform rules ordained the rights of man, determined the just course of government, and with the force of irresistible right, punished unscrupulous politicians who would subvert democratic institutions to their own ends. The same immutable precepts ruled the market, fairly regulating wages and prices, prescribing prosperity or depression, and by their impartial but equitable workings, protected the buyer from the seller and the producer from the monopolist. With equal confidence these hard and fast laws were applied to human behavior. They mysteriously governed the moral relations between man and man (and of man to woman), distinguished with infallible justice between the strong and able and the weak and sinful, raising the rich man above the pauper, and in like manner disposed the rise and fall of nations. Without exception, the most significant ideas of nineteenth-century America—capitalism, democracy, utopian socialism, unitarianism, transcendentalism, evolution and social progress—rested upon the eighteenth-century postulate of a benevolent world order.

After midcentury, however, when Darwinism initiated the attack against absolutism, the concept of an orderly universe hung upon a cast-iron framework of fixed and final law steadily lost credence. Although Spencerian evolutionism was a makeshift attempt by nineteenth-century absolutists to deny the existence of chance and to reaffirm absolute law, universal progress, and the inherent rationality of the universe, its specious scientific claims had been completely exploded by persistent and detailed inquiry in special fields of biology and physics. By the turn of the century, findings in experimental science, especially those of Marie and Pierre Curie, Max Planck, and Albert Einstein in physics, seemed to confirm the rival conception of a universe of chance and multiplicity, a wide-open universe without bounds in time and space, without final limits of origin or purpose. The effect of these discoveries was to sanction a transfer of interest from the permanent to the changing, to subordinate abstract principles to concrete realities.

Just as the once verdant American landscape had been ravaged by the invading machine, so the humane moral environment inherited from the eighteenth century was methodically vandalized by the new forces of science. Essentially innovating and radical, science had become the criterion of modernity and by its insistence on knowledge as a process—an efficient way of thinking rather than an accepted way of believing—had decreed the triumph of Baconian method. Indeed, Francis Bacon was proclaimed prophet of the "new enlightenment" and hailed by John Dewey as "the real founder of modern thought."[3]

What made the seventeenth-century philosopher especially significant to moderns was his idea of the aim and test of genuine knowledge. Like his twentieth-century counterparts, Bacon began with a repudiation of absolutism. Judging by the pragmatic criterion that knowledge is power, he condemned the great body of learning in his time as false and pretentious because it did not give power. He proposed therefore that the entire work of human understanding be commenced afresh, and "the business be done as if by machinery." He rejected the speculative pursuit of first causes as a quest for knowledge that did not exist; man could not presume

Drawn by Arthur Young   From *The Masses,* VI (July, 1915).

EFFICIENCY

According to the new philosophy of Pragmatism, men—like tools and machines —were means to be utilized. Human activity, instead of being squandered in a sporadic and futile search for higher truths, was to be redirected to concrete goals and proceed systematically to their actualization.

to attain to the mysteries of God. Since it was humanly impossible to establish a permanent, systematized, ultimate reality, Bacon discarded all teleological explanation of phenomena, maintaining that everything should be explained as following necessarily from concrete natural causes. By so doing he anticipated the modern position that recognizes only positive facts and observable phenomena, and thus abandons, as a matter of doctrine, all speculation about origins, ends, purposes and meanings as pointless. Experience, Bacon contended—some three hundred years before Dewey—was the only reliable source of knowledge; men could know nothing but their own past and present experiences.[4]

The new instrument of learning advocated by Bacon was the experimental path to truth. Supposition was to be tested by application; it was confirmed to the extent that it worked. Beliefs were rules for action, and to Bacon, as later to William James, the crucial question to be asked was "What difference would it practically make to anyone if this notion rather than that notion were true? If no practical difference whatever can be traced, then the alternatives mean practically the same thing, and all dispute is idle."[5] Truth was to be judged only by its practical performance. In a modern scientific world, as Bacon foresaw, there were no absolute truths, only progressive stages of certainty responsive to change, growth and development.

In no way did Bacon more accurately foretell the twentieth-century viewpoint than in his insistence that the purpose of knowledge was mastery over nature. Rebelling against the old view that the nature of things was fixed once and for all, he took the radical position that nature was not simply to be venerated, but exploited, shaped "as on an anvil."[6] The great obstacle to the Empire of Man over Nature, he discovered, was the failure of men to recognize utility as the proper goal of knowledge. The philosophical systems of the Greeks and Romans had been contrived merely for ornament and reputation, to please the mind and to soothe human vanity, not for the benefit and use of men. Had men in the past insisted upon a useful end for learning, had they joined human knowledge with human power, they would have long since mastered heaven and earth for the relief of man's estate. For Bacon was convinced that, once the belief that knowledge was active and operative took hold of men, the realm of ideas would no longer be something aloof and separate, but rather a collection of imagined possibilities that would stimulate men to new efforts and realizations.

This transformation of the ideal into the real Bacon called "magic," by which he meant, not hocus-pocus, but "the science which applies the knowledge of hidden forms to the production of wonderful operations." [7] His meaning was made clear in a famous illustration by John Dewey. Distance, Dewey pointed out, is an obstacle: "It separates friends and prevents intercourse. It isolates, and makes contact and mutual understanding difficult. This state of affairs provokes discontent and restlessness; it excites the imagination to construct pictures of a state of things where human intercourse is not injuriously affected by space." There were, said Dewey, two ways out. One way was "to pass from a mere dream of some heavenly realm in which distance is abolished and by some magic all friends are in perpetual, transparent communication" to philosophic reflection which would dismiss space and distance as merely subjective and hence of no real account. The other way— the one obviously preferred by both Bacon and Dewey—was to treat the fancy "as a possibility capable of realization in the concrete natural world." Observed from this point of view, said Dewey, things exhibited hitherto undetected properties; the idea of speech at a distance took on a more matter-of-fact form. Experiment proceeded, and at last a wished-for possibility became an actual fact with the invention of the telegraph and telephone. So, concluded Dewey, "The concrete environment is transformed in the desired direction; it is idealized in fact and not merely in fancy." [8]

Modern magic was, in other words, applied science or technique. For Bacon, as later with modern Americans, the supreme article of faith was belief in technique. This audacious, profane, and possibly fatuous idea that man can himself wield the thunderbolts and drive the chariot of the sun was acclaimed in twentieth-century America as "the greatest of all modern ideas, in its originality, in its widespread adoption, and in its far-reaching importance." [9] As the American scientist Jacques Loeb made plain, the question whether humanity wished to be guided by mechanistic science or by metaphysical romance was no longer a matter of academic speculation, for the Baconian dream was actually in the process of coming true.[10] The rate of scientific advancement was so rapid that in the short span of a single human life, as Adams protested, the whole aspect of life had been revolutionized. Marvel succeeded marvel so rapidly that nothing was any longer thought impossible. Through the magic of technique, the human race was bringing the struggle against nature to successful issue. "Such an issue, it may be," wrote Bacon in 1620, "as in the present condition of things and men's minds cannot easily be conceived or imagined." [11] The American living in 1900 had only to compare his own situation with that of the seventeenth-century settlers to discern that man had in a few centuries done for himself what, in all the thousands of years of human history, no supernatural agency or philosophical system had been able to do for him.

Triumph of the Will

The outlook which came to dominate American thought in the early twentieth century was, like its Baconian original, a science of applied intelligence, a mode of controlling man's active relations with the world of experienced things. In origin it was part of the current trend of thought that viewed science as "specialized common sense" and human behavior, in the words of the psychologist John B. Watson, as "a purely objective, experimental branch of natural science which needs introspection as little as do the sciences of chemistry and physics." [12] According to this utilitarian metaphysics, the universe was a self-existent, self-acting phenomenon in which neither scientific truth, religious truth, nor even moral rules were finalities. Although manifestly repudiating the absolutes and universals of an earlier day, it nevertheless contrived a modernized set of universal criteria that placed science above philosophy, utility above religion, and valued means over ends.

Where the Renaissance had achieved spiritual universalism through an ecumenical humanism, the modern view promoted practical universalism through the material comforts of applied

U.S.S. *Alabama*, 1908.

"Knowledge is power," Francis Bacon said three centuries ago, and sight of one of America's mightiest dreadnoughts proved modern man had learned the lesson well.

Culver Pictures, Inc.

science. Its claim was that the culture offered in the name of science was superior on the whole to any and all other systems of civilized life. In fact, however, it was not an all-around superiority but, as Veblen remarked, "a superiority within a closely limited range of intellectual activities," which gave it a decisive practical advantage over all other cultural schemes that had gone before or that had come into competition with it.[13] Inextricably bound up with material results, the program of science implied, as far as it went, that the being or essence of things was material rather than spiritual and found its highest expression in technique. Instead of worrying about a mythical spiritual macrocosm, it insisted man's proper concern was only with making the knowable microcosm in which he lived perform to his best advantage. The modern cosmos was the temporal world, its truths all truths of experience, its laws regularities of experience. Since the values of civilization did not fall from heaven but were presumed to grow out of man's technical mastery over nature, there could be no ultimate standards of value, no separate body of moral rules. Truth simply melted into an experienced relation among the things of experience. Thus, in retrospect, the entire course of history became merely an utilitarian process of the adjustment of capacities and conditions within specific situations.

Christened "Pragmatism," this modern outlook was formulated as a philosophy by William James, and after its promulgation in 1907 it became an almost instantaneous success. People flocked to hear the genial Harvard philosopher expound what he called "the philosophy of the future," while popular magazines ran articles on the voguish "newest philosophy," purporting to explain in simple terms what the furor was all about.[14] Its popular success was due in part to James's style of writing, which made philosophy read like literature, and in part to his exceptional ability as a lecturer, but perhaps most of all to its historic timeliness. It was, acknowledged James, "like one of those secular changes that come upon public opinion overnight, as it were, borne upon tides 'too deep for sound or foam'."[15]

The great popular appeal of Pragmatism was that it offered the common man, in language he could understand, a view of the universe that promised to satisfy both his practical and spiritual needs. Contemptuous of intellectualism, William James had set out to revolutionize the very substance of American philosophy by bringing it down from the cold heights of abstraction to the red-blooded level of everyday life. Beginning with the premise that "all our scientific and philosophic ideals are altars to unknown Gods," he pointed out that truth and falsity were not intrinsic properties of the universe but merely cravings of the human mind for assurance. "God," "Matter," "Reason," "the Absolute," "Energy," were only so many names, and like Bacon he scorned speculation about them as a futile waste of time. To free man's mind from bondage to such preconceptions, he proposed a revolutionary new way of thinking in which "Truth happens to an idea."[16]

An adventurous philosophy of change, Pragmatism rested upon the belief that reality was not ready made from all eternity but was still in the making. Instead of speculating about the true nature of reality and explaining away evil and pain, James simply said, "Reality is what men experience." The common world in which men existed as both things and thinkers, he conceived as "a world of pure experience," which was, at the same time, no one's experience exclusively. The use of philosophy, therefore, was to bring about a kind of practical adjustment to what men experience. Ideas were made true by events and were merely instruments to be used by man to meet and master his environment. The truth of an idea was in its consequences; it became true in proportion to its success in action. This mobile conception of truth was largely the philosophic incarnation of the common-sense maxim proved by the practical experience of countless generations of Americans, "Nothing succeeds like success." Action brought success; success made truth; and truth paid off—in money, power, or performance. In practice Americans had always been pragmatists, and the entire American experience seemed to validate and justify Pragmatism as the national philosophy.*

Despite his iconoclasm, his sweeping rejection of absolutism, James offered genial accommodation to religious belief. Although the omnipotent God of Heaven and Earth was philosophically unacceptable to him, he held out consolation to believers on the pragmatic grounds that if a belief in God afforded comfort to an individual and brought him into satisfactory relation with other parts of his experience, then it had a practical value and was "true." Pragmatism was willing to take any beliefs—even mystical experiences—if they had practical consequences. The only restriction James laid down was that the belief must not clash with other, greater vital benefits. He himself never felt the need for any church or creed, and was "willing to take the universe to be really dangerous and adventurous" without calling for supernatural assurances or guarantees.[17]

The overwhelming success of Pragmatism was attested to not only by the number of enthusiastic converts but also by the passionate opposition it provoked. Among the orthodox in religion and philosophy, it aroused a controversy like that of evolution thirty years before. One church paper spoke of the "pragmatic microbe"; another pitied those "innoculated with its virus." It was sternly denounced as "subversive of morality" and scornfully rebuked as a "delicate attempt of the spirit of license to get himself a respectable foothold." As a critique of certain authoritative and traditional tendencies in philosophy, it fell like a bombshell into the philosophic world where it was both praised for its vigor and originality and damned for its relativism and skepticism. Some more resentful critics refused even its claim to being a philosophy,

---

* William James, *What Pragmatism Means*. See p. 383.

dismissing it as a nonentity and as the antithesis of all that was metaphysically respectable.[18]

A frequent criticism of Pragmatism was that it tended to deal in ambiguities, to mean one thing and to say another. Because James was primarily a romantic individualist, he—like his intellectual godfather, Emerson—never relied on logic where intuition would serve as well. Rather than an academic mason patiently building his arguments brick by brick, James was, as Santayana said, "a Red Indian shooting the rapids with spasmodic skill and elemental emotions." [19] His excursions into philosophy were in the nature of raids, and while to James, "the *sense* of bounding over the waves, the *sense* of being on an adventurous voyage, was the living fact," [20] to more sedate critics his concepts gathered on the run appeared "chaotic," "slovenly," and "ambiguous." [21] From the standpoint of strict logic, they found not one but two, three, or as many as thirteen different Pragmatisms.[22] As the classicist Paul Shorey pointed out, a professed Pragmatist might logically range from a disguised positivist to a wistful poet consulting the "Oracle of the Gold-fishes." °

Although the Pragmatists were always indignant at the accusation that they taught people to believe whatever they liked, James himself admitted that there was considerable excuse for this interpretation of his doctrine. In a letter to a friend, he acknowledged his Emersonian disregard for logic, saying, "Yes, I am too unsystematic and loose!" but explained that he was so deliberately, "on account of the strong aversion with which I am filled for the humbugging pretense of exactitude." [23] For James believed, as Santayana phrased it, that "one moment should respect the insight of another, without trying to establish too regimental a uniformity." [24] Yet, in his way, James was consistent, even as Emerson was. His vitality and fresh imagination led him to break through conventions and to see, said Santayana, "that experience, as we endure it, is not a mosaic of distinct sensations, nor the expression of separate hostile faculties, such as reason and the passions . . . it is rather a flow of mental discourse, like a dream, in which all divisions and units are vague and shifting, and the whole is continually merging together and drifting apart. It fades gradually in

° Paul Shorey, *The Equivocations of Pragmatism.* See p. 224.

the rear, like the wake of a ship, and bites into the future, like the bow cutting the water."[25] For James, embarking bodily on his voyage of discovery, everything was simply what it was experienced as being.

After all, the main purpose of pragmatist metaphysics was to emphasize the primacy of the will. James might begin with a datum of fact, but it was used by him, as Philip Wiener has observed, "to show the limits of science in order to make room for faith."[26] James had a fine feeling for life and would not allow his own logical presuppositions to permanently obscure the real living world. Like a true Pragmatist, he tried to be intellectually tough-minded, but if, as some critics insisted, there were roughly two schools of Pragmatism—the tough-minded and the tender-minded—then James most assuredly belonged to the latter. Tender-hearted rather than tough-minded, he treated philosophical questions in a large, generous, practical way, hated "logic-chopping," and did not even take his own principles too seriously. And, as James Bissett Pratt remarked, it was perhaps fortunate for his conclusions that this was so, for they were reached not because of pragmatic principles so much as in spite of them.[27]

Science and Human Experience

If William James was the prophet of modern America, John Dewey was unquestionably its national philosopher. Both were Pragmatists and thoroughly opposed to absolutism, but they were temperamentally different and, in certain respects, doctrinally independent. James was contemplative and religious in outlook, having more interest in the quality than the conduct of life, while his younger colleague at the University of Chicago was essentially an activist, a modern moralist whose chief concern was with the world of visible human conduct. Although both agreed that the meaning of any truth was to be found in its consequences, James tended to relate those consequences to man's ultimate fate and wellbeing, while Dewey stressed their relationship to immediate social betterment.

Preeminently a philosopher of the tough-minded school, Dewey took modern science as his starting point. Science was to him the exemplar of knowledge, and scientific method the only authentic means of getting at the significance of everyday experience. If ever men were to be governed by intelligence, insisted Dewey, "science must have something to say about *what* we do, and not merely about *how* we may do it most easily and economically." [28] Only by turning laboratory technique to intellectual account, by transferring guess and opinion into belief authorized by inquiry, would men ever get a knowledge of the method of knowing. So Dewey proposed a general application of the methods of science to every primary concern of life. By applying experimental methods to the reconstruction of our traditional values, Dewey hoped to liberate modern man from bondage to the past and enable him to project a better future.

As he confessed, Dewey arrived at his concept of philosophic method only after yielding to many diverse and even incompatible influences. In tracing what he called his "unstable, chameleonlike" course from absolutism to experimentalism, he found that the most vital influence had been William James, whose *Principles of Psychology* (1890) had been the turning point in his thinking. What had impressed him most about James as a psychologist was his "remarkable union of the physiological and laboratory attitude with the introspective method." [29] The objective biological approach of Jamesian psychology, linking philosophy to the significant issues of actual experience, led Dewey initially to think of life in terms of life-in-action, and eventually to seek a practical synthesis or working arrangement between the conclusions of modern science and the beliefs and values that directed human activity.

In his opinion, a working union between science and experience had not been possible in the past because of the injection of an irrelevant metaphysics into scientific interpretation. Before the rise of experimental method in the seventeenth century, "a spectator theory of knowledge" prevailed, which proclaimed the superiority of contemplative over practical knowledge. Pure knowing was pure beholding. The duty of science was to disclose the universal properties of nature, while the business of philosophy was to demonstrate the being of a higher realm beyond nature. Instead of dealing with the world in which men lived, the world which was experienced, both science and philosophy snubbed practical needs and human desires in an artificial quest for the ultimate supreme reality. If men would only drop the antiquated Greek notion that knowledge was knowledge only when it disclosed absolute principles, and instead interpret the aim of knowing as the search for efficient rather than final causes, then, said Dewey, thinking would become "the art by which knowledge is practiced."[30]

The transfer of experimental method from the technical field of physical experience to the wider field of human life was to Dewey the central problem of philosophy. Science, he pointed out, was the most powerful instrument for good or evil the world had ever known; yet, so far, the social effects of its application had been accidental. This to him was the heart of the social problem and the great contradiction of modern civilization. Science had hardly been used to modify men's fundamental acts and attitudes in social matters, but it had been used to extend enormously the scope and power of interests and values which anteceded its rise. Instead of being used deliberately, systematically, for the promotion of social well-being, it had been employed primarily for private and national aggrandizement. The potentiality of science as the most powerful instrument of control which ever existed had been put to the service of the atavistic goals of commercialism and imperialism, and its larger social results left to chance and the inertia of tradition and old institutions.

Where, asked Dewey, was the moral progress to match our economic progress? In physical and commercial matters men had long since grown accustomed to identifying the true with the verified, but to put morals on an experimental basis meant to most persons surrender of all fixed standards and regulative authority. But, Dewey persisted, experimental method did not signify random and aimless action; it implied direction by ideas and knowledge. Rather than entailing complete confusion and unrestrained licentiousness, the experimental method transferred the weight and burden of morality to intelligence. It did not destroy responsibility; it only located it.

> In the end, men do what they can do. They refrain from doing what they cannot do. They do what their own specific powers in conjunction with the limitations and resources of the environment permit. The

effective control of their powers is not through precepts, but through the regulation of their conditions. If this regulation is to be not merely physical or coercive, but moral, it must consist of the intelligent selection and determination of the environments in which we act; and in an intelligent exaction of responsibility for the use of men's powers.[31]

He was convinced that a sentimental attachment to fixed ideals not only diverted attention from a critical examination of consequences and the intelligent creation of purpose, but as an aim not framed upon scrutiny of existing conditions, it simply threw men back upon past habits. As a consequence, though meaning well, men did not do what they intended to do but what they had got used to doing.

By abandoning the idea that morals were "fixed ends in themselves" toward which human endeavor was to be directed, the Pragmatist professedly was enabled to employ intelligence in framing ends and in selecting and arranging means. Since there was no final and unquestionable knowledge upon which men could automatically fall back upon in order to settle every moral problem, Dewey's experimental morality demanded observation of particular situations rather than fixed adherence to a priori principles.° Every ideal was a plan of action, and every situation had its own good. Although aware that man was thus deprived of the comfort of a transcendent, supervisory "Good," Dewey felt that he was more than compensated by a new freedom and greater responsibility in the management of his own affairs. After all, he reasoned, to idealize and to rationalize the universe at large was simply a confession of inability to master the course of things that specifically concerned us, a shifting of the burden of responsibility to the more competent shoulders of the transcendent cause. Better by far, contended Dewey, to renounce some distant vision of good for an improved world of man's own making here and now.[32]

The Morality of Means

This pragmatic view of morality did not go unchallenged. Few modern critics were ready to deny the practical value of morals

° John Dewey, *Intelligence and Morals*. See p. 228.

in guiding the reaction of the individual to his environment. But when it was maintained that this was the only value of morals—that all values were ultimately plans of action and that moral truth was always a means and never an end in itself—then, it seemed to more traditional thinkers, it was time to call a halt and reassert the old and trite thesis that man was more than the creature of a day.

If man was indeed what the Pragmatists considered him—a creature of the environment, a successful animal, whose one aim was practical reaction on his surroundings—then perhaps Dewey's was a true enough account of reality. But to the idealists, man was a twofold being. He was what the Pragmatists described and, in addition, said James Bissett Pratt, "also what Plato thought him—a citizen of the realm of eternal reason, the *outgrown* ape, who *means* more than he *is*, whose reach should and does exceed his grasp, who 'partly is and wholly hopes to be'." [33] Although not denying the great value of Pragmatism in bringing knowledge down from the skies, critics protested against its excessive practical or biological emphasis. Not only did the new morality declare that man's chief end was forwarding the life of the individual and the race, but it suggested also that to be genuinely understood, conduct had to be approached from the psycho-physiological point of view. Especially outrageous to the idealist was the behaviorist definition of the moral imperative as "the psychic correlate of a reflective, cerebro-spinal, ideo-motor process, the efferent end of which is organized into motor tracts coordinated for a specific action." [34] But if such pseudo-scientific jargon wounded both his philosophic and literary sensibilities, the Platonist was laid low by the further implication that if there seemed to be other aims than action, they were pathological or abortive.

The most serious defect of the pragmatic method, according to its critics, was that by making utility the test of truth, it tended to confuse fact and opinion and to reduce truth to expediency. Utility, it was argued, was by itself no criterion of objective truth, for it was notorious that opinion might be practically and morally efficacious, and yet false. If the truth of a belief consisted in general in its giving satisfaction, then—the realist and the empiricist objected—thinking became wholly a subjective process, a matter of wayward affections, and anything could become a pragmatic truth if applied by a Pragmatist. If the Infinite, the Eternal, Reason and Justice were merely empty names, useless fancies, then— complained the idealist and the rationalist—men were left with a merely fragmentary reality, with experience that was ever chang- ing, with thought that could never hope to achieve final truth. To so limit reality was, from their viewpoint, to deny the spiritual and rational nature of man and the validity of his ideals.

Even to such a friendly critic as Ralph Barton Perry, professor of philosophy at Yale, Pragmatism seemed to press its useful and illuminating formula too far. As a realist inclined to view things as they actually are, he felt it oversimplified, and was consequently somewhat narrow, blind, unempirical.[35] To reduce all moral judg- ments to plans of action, to add that plans of action were "moral" if they worked, and to conclude that therefore the morality of a judgment consisted in its working did not strike him as a cogent syllogism. Taken as a stand, it seemed to imply that nothing was right or wrong but thinking made it so. Beyond good and evil in the old-fashioned sense, Pragmatism suggested right and wrong were merely relative to the opinions and experience of an age, society, or even an individual. The effect of this reduction of morals to maxims of expedient conduct, argued Perry, was to make Pragmatism nothing but a creed of action for action's sake.°

In defense, Dewey denied that experimentalism ignored the question of the morality of means. Common sense, he protested, revolted against the maxim that the end justifies the means. While never retreating from his stand that nothing could justify or con- demn means except ends, he parried the realist indictment by pointing out that it was willful folly to fasten upon some single end or consequence and permit the desire for that to blot out all other undesired and undesirable consequences. Not *the* end—in the singular—justified the means; for in his view there was no such thing as a single, all-important end. An act was justified, not by picking out that one consequence which would enable us to do what we wished to do and for which we felt the need of justifica- tion, but by reckoning the plural consequences that flowed from that particular act. In general, maintained Dewey, the identifica-

° Ralph Barton Perry, *The Gospel of Action.* See p. 232.

tion of a consciously desired end with *the* end was simply a way of avoiding a consideration of consequences and of putting a pseudo-moral stamp upon success at any price.

Dewey contended that the experimental logic applied to morals avoided this pitfall. Because inquiry and discovery took the same place in the moral sphere that they occupied in the scientific, validation and demonstration became experimental, a matter of consequences. Actions were validated according to the degree by which they ameliorated existing ills; consequently, means and ends were both submitted to moral judgment. In so doing, asserted Dewey, experimentalism closed the gap between ends and means, ideals and events, putting a stop to the impossible attempt to live in two unrelated worlds, the ideal and the real. Rather than life being thought of as a dreary compromise with the best, the world was accepted "as it was," and each situation treated scientifically according to what advantage might be extracted from it. With morality based upon a study of the human condition instead of a disregard for it, Dewey was convinced science and morals would at last become allies.[36]

What Pragmatism Means

WILLIAM JAMES (1842–1910)   *William James originally studied medicine in order to be a physiologist, but drifted into psychology and philosophy. As he said, "I never had any philosophic instruction, the first lecture on psychology I ever heard being the first I ever gave." Struck by the contrast between the richness of life and the poverty of all possible formulas, he rejected the limited, orderly world of his New England forebears and chose instead to live in an adventurous world of chance. He conscientiously tried to evade doctrinal limitations, calling himself variously empiricist, pluralist, pragmatist and individualist. His character, like his thought, was unconventional and escaped simple formulation. Confident, tolerant, vital—he had, as a friend observed, the reality of his own pluralistic universe—abounding and unbounded.*

The pragmatic method is primarily a method of settling metaphysical disputes that otherwise might be interminable. Is the world one or many?—fated or free?—material or spiritual?—here are notions either of which may or may not hold good of the world; and disputes over such notions are unending. The pragmatic method in such cases is to try to interpret each notion by tracing its respective practical consequences. What difference would it practically make to any one if this notion rather than that notion were true? If no practical difference whatever can be traced, then the alternatives mean practically the same thing, and all dispute is idle. . . .

A glance at the history of the idea will show you still better what pragmatism means. The term is derived from the same Greek word πράγμα, meaning action, from which our words "practice" and "practical" come. It was first introduced into philosophy by Mr. Charles Peirce in 1878. In an article entitled "How to Make

From *Pragmatism, A New Name for Old Ways of Thinking* (New York: Longmans, Green & Co., 1907), pp. 45–58, 72–73, 79–80.

Our Ideas Clear," in the *Popular Science Monthly* for January of that year, Mr. Peirce, after pointing out that our beliefs are really rules for action, said that, to develop a thought's meaning, we need only determine what conduct it is fitted to produce: that conduct is for us its sole significance. . . .

It is astonishing to see how many philosophical disputes collapse into insignificance the moment you subject them to this simple test of tracing a concrete consequence. There can *be* no difference anywhere that doesn't *make* a difference elsewhere—no difference in abstract truth that doesn't express itself in a difference in concrete fact and in conduct consequent upon that fact, imposed on somebody, somehow, somewhere, and somewhen. The whole function of philosophy ought to be to find out what definite difference it will make to you and me, at definite instants of our life, if this world-formula or that world-formula be the true one.

There is absolutely nothing new in the pragmatic method. Socrates was an adept at it. Aristotle used it methodically. Locke, Berkeley, and Hume made momentous contributions to truth by its means. . . . But these forerunners of pragmatism used it in fragments; they were preluders only. Not until in our time has it generalized itself, become conscious of a universal mission, pretended to a conquering destiny. I believe in that destiny, and I hope I may end by inspiring you with my belief.

Pragmatism represents a perfectly familiar attitude in philosophy, the empiricist attitude, but it represents it, as it seems to me, both in a more radical and in a less objectionable form than it has ever yet assumed. A pragmatist turns his back resolutely and once for all upon a lot of inveterate habits dear to professional philosophers. He turns away from abstraction and insufficiency, from verbal solutions, from bad *a priori* reasons, from fixed principles, closed systems, and pretended absolutes and origins. He turns towards concreteness and adequacy, towards facts, towards action and towards power. That means the empiricist temper regnant and the rationalist temper sincerely given up. It means the open air and possibilities of nature, as against dogma, artificiality, and the pretence of finality in truth.

At the same time it does not stand for any special results. It is a method only. But the general triumph of that method would mean an enormous change in . . . the "temperament" of philosophy. . . . Metaphysics has usually followed a very primitive kind of quest. You know how men have always hankered after unlawful magic, and you know what a great part in magic *words* have always played. If you have his name, or the formula of incantation that binds him, you can control the spirit, genie, afrite, or whatever the power may be. Solomon knew the names of all the spirits, and having their names, he held them subject to his will. So the universe has always appeared to the natural mind as a kind of enigma, of which the key must be sought in the shape of some illuminating or power-bringing word or name. That word names the universe's *principle*, and to possess it is after a fashion to possess the universe itself. "God," "Matter," "Reason," "the Absolute," "Energy," are so many solving names. You can rest when you have them. You are at the end of your metaphysical quest.

But if you follow the pragmatic method, you cannot look on any such word as closing your quest. You must bring out of each word its practical cash-value, set it at work within the stream of your experience. It appears less as a solution, then, than as a program for more work, and more particularly as an indication of the ways in which existing realities may be *changed*.

Theories thus become instruments, not answers to enigmas, in which we can rest. We don't lie back upon them, we move forward, and, on occasion, make nature over again by their aid. Pragmatism unstiffens all our theories, limbers them up and sets each one at work. Being nothing essentially new, it harmonizes with many ancient philosophic tendencies. It agrees with nominalism for instance, in always appealing to particulars; with utilitarianism in emphasizing practical aspects; with positivism in its disdain for verbal solutions, useless questions and metaphysical abstractions. . . .

No particular results then, so far, but only an attitude of orientation, is what the pragmatic method means. *The attitude of looking away from first things, principles, "categories," supposed necessities; and of looking towards last things, fruits, consequences, facts.*

So much for the pragmatic method! You may say that I have been praising it rather than explaining it to you, but I shall presently explain it abundantly enough by showing how it works on some familiar problems. Meanwhile the word pragmatism has come to be used in a still wider sense, as meaning also a certain *theory of truth*. . . .

When the first mathematical, logical, and natural uniformities, the first *laws*, were discovered, men were so carried away by the clearness, beauty and simplification that resulted, that they believed themselves to have deciphered authentically the eternal thoughts of the Almighty. His mind also thundered and reverberated in syllogisms. He also thought in conic sections, squares and roots and ratios, and geometrized like Euclid. He made Kepler's laws for the planets to follow; he made velocity increase proportionally to the time in falling bodies; he made the law of the sines for light to obey when refracted; he established the classes, orders, families and genera of plants and animals, and fixed the distances between them. He thought the archetypes of all things, and devised their variations; and when we rediscover any one of these his wondrous institutions, we seize his mind in its very literal intention.

But as the sciences have developed farther, the notion has gained ground that most, perhaps all, of our laws are only approximations. The laws themselves, moreover, have grown so numerous that there is no counting them; and so many rival formulations are proposed in all the branches of science that investigators have become accustomed to the notion that no theory is absolutely a transcript of reality, but that any one of them may from some point of view be useful. Their great use is to summarize old facts and to lead to new ones. They are only a man-made language, a conceptual shorthand, as someone calls them, in which we write our reports of nature; and languages, as is well known, tolerate much choice of expression and many dialects. . . . Everywhere . . . [today] "truth" in our ideas and beliefs means the same thing that it means in science. It means . . . nothing but this, *that ideas (which themselves are but parts of our experience) become true just in so far as they help us to get into satisfactory relation with other parts of our experience*, to summarize them and get about among them by conceptual short-cuts instead of following the interminable succession of particular phenomena. Any idea upon which we can ride, so to speak; any idea that will carry us prosperously from any one part of our experience to any other part, linking things satisfactorily, working securely, simplifying, saving labor; is true for just so much, true in so far forth, true *instrumentally*. This is the "instrumental" view of truth taught so successfully at Chicago, the view that truth in our ideas means their power to "work". . . .

Now pragmatism has no objection whatever to the realizing of abstractions, so long as you get about among particulars with their aid and they actually carry you somewhere. Interested in no conclusions but those which our minds and our experiences work out together, she has no *a priori* prejudices against theology. *If theological ideas prove to have a value for concrete life, they will be true, for pragmatism, in the sense of being good for so much. For how much more they are true, will depend entirely on their relations to the other truths that also have to be acknowledged*. . . .

In short, [Pragmatism] widens the field of search for God. Rationalism sticks to logic and the empyrean. Empiricism sticks to the external senses. Pragmatism is willing to take anything, to follow either logic or the senses and to count the humblest and most personal experiences. She will count mystical experiences if they have practical consequences. She will take a God who lives in the very dirt of private fact—if that should seem a likely place to find him.

Her only test of probable truth is what works best in the way of leading us, what fits every part of life best and combines with the collectivity of experience's demands, nothing being omitted. If theological ideas should do this, if the notion of God, in particular, should prove to do it, how could pragmatism possibly deny God's existence? She could see no meaning in treating as "not true" a notion that was pragmatically so successful. What other kind of truth could there be, for her, than all this agreement with concrete reality?

The Equivocations of Pragmatism

PAUL SHOREY (1857–1934)   *A highly respected classicist, Shorey was one of the group of scholars whom President William Rainey Harper called to the University of Chicago at its founding in*

Reprinted from *The Dial*, November 1, 1907, pp. 273–75.

1892. His greatest contribution to scholarship was in the field of Platonic studies where he received many honors. Greatly distressed by popular exploitation of the false analogy between experiments in the laboratory and experience in man, he felt it was a fatal mistake to abandon the humanities for the thin pretensions of pseudo-science. His answer to militant moderns was that men were no nearer a final metaphysical solution than in Plato's day.

Philosophy, we are told, is an affair of temperament. And as we all have temperaments, but are not quite sure that we have philosophies, we are flattered. But, unfortunately, in addition to the genial pragmatist temperament that willingly accepts a "loose world," and could be content in the tub of Diogenes if open to the sun and air, there exists as an irreducible fact the thin, rigid, logical temperament—whether to be classified as tough or tender I hardly know. And the first reaction of this temperament to a new all-embracing philosophy that can "satisfy both kinds of demand," and at the same time agreeably tickle our sense of subtlety and ingenuity, is a lot of uncomfortable distinctions and reserves. All philosophies outside of Bedlam admit the appeal to experience. But a philosophy that peremptorily demands the "cash value" of every proposition in experiential terms may sometimes be in too great a hurry to "cash in." Some propositions, as Cicero knew, can be cashed only by a clever orator at the bank of opinion. All philosophies today accept in some sense the test by results. But a philosophy that makes special profession of so doing runs the risk, despite the *caveat* "unless the belief incidentally clashes with other vital benefits," of contemplating only immediate, obvious, emotional consequences, to the neglect of the remoter effects which must be traced by close observation and prolonged consecutive thought. The immediate results of pragmatism are readable lectures, and a pleasant stir and hum, as of "something doing" in the philosophic world. But if the remote consequences of this contribution to the gayety of nations included a weakening of the sense of logical coherence and relevancy in all who take the game seriously, a painful utilitarian calculus would be required to determine the inclination of the balance of profit and loss, and the consequent truth or falsity of the doctrine.

The comprehensiveness claimed for the new philosophy seems to rest on a series of equivocations. The Platonist's, the School-man's, the Berkeleian insistence on unequivocal definition of all ambiguous terms is triumphantly annexed as a part of the prag-matic method. But in his own practice there is nothing of which the pragmatist is so shy as the explicit acknowledgment of the double meanings of his words. "Rationalist," for example, is habit-ually taken in the sense of *a priori* absolutist, though a recognition of the meanings given to the term in Lecky's, or rather in Benn's, "History of Rationalism" would force pragmatism to choose be-tween identification with its own left wing of positivism and its right wing, "The Will to Believe." The test of theory as "working hypothesis" by its results in the scientific order of verifiable external fact is continually confounded with the test by alleged or predicted consequences in the moral, social, and emotional order. True ideas are defined as those which we can "assimilate, corroborate, vali-date, verify"—as if the indefinite subjective term "assimilate" were synonymous with the precise objectivity of "verify."

In style as well as in logic, the pragmatist manifests a great-souled superiority to consistency. He protests in the name of nominalistic devotion to the concrete richness of particular fact against such innocent abstract personifications as "The Law," "The Latin Language," but habitually speaks of his own philosophy as "she" and dwells complacently on "her" geniality, "her" compre-hensiveness, "her" democratic manners.

And it must be admitted that "she" is attractive. She jumbles unrelated things in so fascinating an Emersonian fashion that the toughest mind has a glimmering of their final reconciliation in God. She says undisputed things in such a lively way that one must be not only hard-headed but hard-hearted not to accept the disputable into the bargain. *Femme est souvent variée:* She wins our assent to the statement that abstract propositions must be verified in particular experiences, and asks us to admit that speculative opin-ions are "validated" if they warm the cockles of our heart and help us to live. She is convulsed with laughter at the old-fashioned seventeenth-century garb of the encyclopædic Leibnitz, but is willing to bury Herbert Spencer in Westminster Abbey because, in spite of his bad literary manners, his heart was in the right place and he was fond of little—facts. She affirms that absolute truth is a chimera, and infers not that probability is the guide of life and our chief study should be its degrees, but that one thing is as probable as another—and more so, if it is interesting or consoling. She begins with reason as the faculty or method by which we inquire what is, or must be, or probably will be, and ends by celebrating it as the triumphant affirmation of what we wish to be. She alternately takes "rational" in the sense of intelligible, in terms of efficient causation, and intelligible in terms of conformity to the heart's desire. She denounces metaphysics as a cobweb of verbal illusion spun by schoolmen, and instead of dropping it and devoting herself to philology, mathematics, or history, spins a new web of her own with glittering threads of metaphor and epigram.

Such is Pragmatism in its most brilliant representative, Professor James. It is not a logically coherent doctrine or method, but the picturesque expression of a temperament, and of certain lively likes and dislikes—of the genial instinct for the illuminating, the vivid, the human touch that makes his writings such good reading, of a Baconian delight in the rhetorical exaltation of scientific method and exact verification, combined with a vivacious impatience of the thing, of a distaste for the tender, solemn, periodic, and pantheistic fluency of his friend and colleague Professor Royce, and a natural preference for his own breezy, staccato, eruptive, electrifying, Emersonian manner; above all, of the wish to believe, or retain the right to believe, in certain manifestations the probability of which in the present state of our knowledge is negligible, and a consequent aversion to those close estimates of the degrees of reasoned probability which tend to circumscribe and hamper the flights of popular philosophy. . . .

But why this fierce denunciation of the harmless necessary shibboleth of the most up-to-date philosophy? Why, because it is neither necessary nor harmless, but superfluous so far as true, confusing so far as equivocal, and emasculating so far as false. A professed pragmatist may be, as we have seen, a positivist unwilling to wear his label, a half-emancipated Hegelian, a psychologist systematically exaggerating the subordination of the intellect to the will, a Kantian postulating what he cannot prove "as if" it were so, a Newmanite undermining reason in the interests of dogma; a wistful poet consulting the "Oracle of the Gold-fishes"; a Napoleonic scorner of "ideologists"; an adept in psychical research asking us to accept the indefinitely improbable because in the infinity of our ignorance we cannot prove it *a priori* impossible; a writer of genius confounding and exploiting all these tendencies in an entertaining book. . . .

There remains the supposition that Pragmatism is merely the will or the right to believe, masquerading in the garb of scientific positivism and unmetaphysical common sense. This the pragmatist pronounces "an impudent slander." But a door must be either open or shut; and if Pragmatism is not essentially the will to believe, the embarrassing question which its ingenious expositor received one morning on a post-card recurs: "Is a pragmatist necessarily a complete materialist and agnostic?"

Intelligence and Morals

JOHN DEWEY (1859–1952)   *Dewey was brought up in New England in a conventionally evangelical atmosphere of the more "liberal" sort. After a trying personal crisis, he lost interest in religion as a philosophic problem, turning to social problems for intellectual sustenance. In 1884, he went to Johns Hopkins to enter upon that new thing, "graduate work." There he was temporarily converted to the Hegelian view, but later rejected its artificial schemata to develop his own philosophy of experimentalism through which he hoped to bring about a synthesis between science and morals.*

Since the Renaissance, moral philosophy has repeatedly reverted to the Greek ideal of natural excellence realized in social life, under the fostering care of intelligence in action. The return, however, has taken place under the influence of democratic polity, commercial expansion, and scientific reorganization. It has been a liberation more than a reversion. This combined return and eman-

From *The Influence of Darwin on Philosophy and Other Essays in Contemporary Thought* (New York: Henry Holt & Co., 1910), pp. 54–60, 67–71.

cipation, having transformed our practice of life in the last four centuries, will not be content till it has written itself clear in our theory of that practice.

Whether the consequent revolution in moral philosophy be termed pragmatism or be given the happier title of the applied and experimental habit of mind is of little account. What is of moment is that intelligence has descended from its lonely isolation at the remote edge of things, whence it operated as unmoved mover and ultimate good, to take its seat in the moving affairs of men. Theory may therefore become responsible to the practices that have generated it; the good be connected with nature, but with nature naturally, not metaphysically, conceived, and social life be cherished in behalf of its own immediate possibilities, not on the ground of its remote connections with a cosmic reason and an absolute end. . . .

If we do not join with many in lamenting the stripping from nature of those idealistic properties in which animism survived, if we do not mourn the secession of the sciences from ethics, it is because the abandonment by intelligence of a fixed and static moral end was the necessary precondition of a free and progressive science of both things and morals; because the emancipation of the sciences from ready-made, remote, and abstract values was necessary to make the sciences available for creating and maintaining more and specific values here and now. The divine comedy of modern medicine and hygiene is one of the human epics yet to be written; but when composed it may prove no unworthy companion of the medieval epic of other worldly beatific visions. The great ideas of the eighteenth century, that expansive epoch of moral perception which ranks in illumination and fervor along with classic Greek thought, the great ideas of the indefinitely continuous progress of humanity and of the power and significance of freed intelligence, were borne by a single mother—experimental inquiry.

The growth of industry and commerce is at once cause and effect of the growth in science. Democritus and other ancients conceived the mechanical theory of the universe. The notion was not only blank and repellent, because it ignored the rich social material which Plato and Aristotle had organized into their rival idealistic views; but it was scientifically sterile, a piece of dialectics. Contempt for machines as the accouterments of despised mechanics kept the mechanical conception aloof from these specific and controllable experiences which alone could fructify it. This conception, then, like the idealistic, was translated into a speculative cosmology and thrown like a vast net around the universe at large, as if to keep it from coming to pieces. It is from respect for the lever, the pulley, and the screw that modern experimental and mathematical mechanics derives itself. Motion, traced through the workings of a machine, was followed out into natural events and studied just as motion, not as a poor yet necessary device for realizing final causes. So studied, it was found to be available for new machines and new applications, which in creating new ends also promoted new wants, and thereby stimulated new activities, new discoveries, and new inventions. The recognition that natural energy can be systematically applied, through experimental observation, to the satisfaction and multiplication of concrete wants is doubtless the greatest single discovery ever imported into the life of man—save perhaps the discovery of language. Science, borrowing from industry, repaid the debt with interest, and has made the control of natural forces for the aims of life so inevitable that for the first time man is relieved from overhanging fear, with its wolflike scramble to possess and accumulate, and is freed to consider the more gracious question of securing to all an ample and liberal life. The industrial life had been condemned by Greek exaltation of abstract thought and by Greek contempt for labor, as representing the brute struggle of carnal appetite for its own satiety. The industrial movement, offspring of science, restored it to its central position in morals. When Adam Smith made economic activity the moving spring of man's unremitting effort, from the cradle to the grave, to better his own lot, he recorded this change. And when he made sympathy the central spring in man's conscious moral endeavor, he reported the effect which the increasing intercourse of men, due primarily to commerce, had in breaking down suspicion and jealousy and in liberating man's kindlier impulses.

Democracy, the crucial expression of modern life, is not so much an addition to the scientific and industrial tendencies as it is the perception of their social or spiritual meaning. Democracy is an absurdity where faith in the individual as individual is impossible; and this faith is impossible when intelligence is regarded as a cosmic power, not an adjustment and application of individual tendencies. It is also impossible when appetites and desires are conceived to be the dominant factor in the constitution of most men's characters, and when appetite and desire are conceived to be manifestations of the disorderly and unruly principle of nature. To put the intellectual center of gravity in the objective cosmos, outside of men's own experiments and tests, and then to invite the application of individual intelligence to the determination of society, is to invite chaos. . . .

Democracy is estimable only through the changed conception of intelligence, that forms modern science, and of want, that forms modern industry. It is essentially a changed psychology. The substitution, for *a priori* truth and deduction, of fluent doubt and inquiry meant trust in human nature in the concrete; in individual honesty, curiosity, and sympathy. The substitution of moving commerce for fixed custom meant a view of wants as the dynamics of social progress, not as the pathology of private greed. The nineteenth century indeed turned sour on that somewhat complacent optimism in which the eighteenth century rested: the ideas that the intelligent self-love of individuals would conduce to social cohesion, and competition among individuals usher in the kingdom of social welfare. But the conception of a social harmony of interests in which the achievement by each individual of his own freedom should contribute to a like perfecting of the powers of all, through a fraternally organized society, is the permanent contribution of the industrial movement to morals—even though so far it be but the contribution of a problem. . . .

The transformation in attitude [toward moral theory] is the growing belief that the proper business of intelligence is discrimination of multiple and present goods and of the varied immediate means of their realization; not search for the one remote aim. The progress of biology has accustomed our minds to the notion that intelligence is not an outside power presiding supremely but statically over the desires and efforts of man, but is a method of adjustment of capacities and conditions within specific situations. History . . . has discovered itself in the idea of process. The genetic standpoint makes us aware that the systems of the past are neither fraudulent impostures nor absolute revelations, but are the products of political, economic, and scientific conditions whose change carries with it change of theoretical formulations. The recognition that intelligence is properly an organ of adjustment in difficult situations makes us aware that past theories were of value so far as they helped carry to an issue the social perplexities from which they emerged. But the chief impact of the evolutionary method is upon the present. Theory having learned what it cannot do, is made responsible for the better performance of what needs to be done, and what only a broadly equipped intelligence can undertake: study of the conditions out of which come the obstacles and the resources of adequate life, and developing and testing the ideas that, as working hypotheses, may be used to diminish the causes of evil and to buttress and expand the sources of good. . . .

From this point of view there is no separate body of moral rules; no separate system of motive powers; no separate subject-matter of moral knowledge, and hence no such thing as an isolated ethical science. If the business of morals is not to speculate upon man's final end and upon an ultimate standard of right, it is to utilize physiology, anthropology, and psychology to discover all that can be discovered of man, his organic powers and propensities. If its business is not to search for the one separate moral motive, it is to converge all the instrumentalities of the social arts, of law, education, economics, and political science upon the construction of intelligent methods of improving the common lot.

The Gospel of Action

RALPH BARTON PERRY (1876–1957) *A Harvard professor of philosophy, Perry was in his youth inclined toward the Christian ministry. Migrating from Princeton to Harvard in the middle nineties, he entered upon what he later described as a "perilous spiritual adventure." There, under the influence of William*

From *The Present Conflict of Ideals* (New York: Longmans, Green & Co., 1918), pp. 340–41, 343–47. Reprinted by permission David McKay Company, Inc.

James, he experienced an abrupt transition from faith to criticism and eventually abandoned the vocation of the ministry for that of the teacher and scholar. Creeds and dogmas having become impossible, he sought through realism to find a way in which he might think freely and still "do good."

The obvious objection to the gospel of action for action's sake is that it affords life no ultimate justification. It appears to make a virtue of that very purposelessness and waywardness that we ordinarily think needs to be corrected by ethics and religion. Let us ask, then, what ultimate ideals this gospel has to propose.

1. *Heroism.* The ideal that is most closely connected with this gospel, which requires least in the way of metaphysical construction and support, is the ideal of heroism. The supreme value in life, according to this view, is just to live greatly. According to Jean-Christophe, all that is necessary is that a man should be healthy. He will then be quite content to play the man's part, and let eventualities take care of themselves: "Go on to Death, you who must die! Go and suffer, you who must suffer! You do not live to be happy. You live to fulfil my Law. Suffer; die. But be what you must be—a Man."

In another passage the author says of his hero:

He was too fundamentally religious to think much about God. He lived in God; he had no need to believe in Him. That is well enough for the weak and worn, for those whose lives are anæmic. They aspire to God as a plant does to the sun. The dying cling to life. But he who bears in his soul the sun and life, what need has he to seek them outside himself?

This is also Carlyle's idea, when he says, "The chief end of life is not thought but action. Up! Up! Whatsoever thy hand findeth to do, do it with thy might." It is also Nietzsche's meaning, when he teaches men not to avoid suffering, but rather to create it, both for themselves and for others, as a condition of "the highest life, that of the conqueror. . . . "

2. *The Universal Life.* The philosophy which we are here examining is as a rule pluralistic. It either encourages a defiant assertion of self or of one's own class or party against all comers, or it recognizes the specific and irreducible value of each unit of

life, the other life no less than one's own. But there are traces here and there of a monistic trend. For after all, life is life. If there is no single all-embracing unit of life, there is at any rate the common quality of life, which begets a sense of kinship in all living creatures. . . .

In the writings of Rolland, to whom I have already . . . alluded, this sense of the common life reaches the level of religious rapture. He says of his hero [Jean-Christophe],

> The stoic principles of life, to which he had hitherto delighted to bend his will, morality, duty, now seemed to him to have no truth nor reason. Their jealous despotism was smashed against Nature. Human nature, healthy, strong, free, that alone was virtue; to hell with all the rest! It provoked pitying laughter to see the little peddling rules of prudence and policy which the world adorns with the name of morality, while it pretends to inclose all life within them. A preposterous molehill, an ant-like people! Life sees to it that they are brought to reason. Life does but pass, and all is swept away. . . .

3. *Forward Movement.* But the ultimate hope that is most characteristically associated with this gospel of action is the hope of progress. It is characteristic of life that it should *go on* and *mount higher.* To the sense of life is thus added the sense of a great onward march that is gathering volume and momentum as it goes. . . .

Unquestionably this faith in progress is open to serious objection. There is no guarantee whatever that a perpetual movement, even if it be a continuous movement, and even a forward movement in the sense of prolonging a line already marked, shall be a movement from good to better. . . .

In a recent volume representing the instrumentalist school of Dewey, and significantly entitled *Creative Intelligence,* we are told that it is the function of intelligence not to measure and compose policies in terms of present human interests, but to construct new ideals to which life may perpetually redirect its energies. Life is not so much an advance toward a goal already set as it is an achievement of new goals. Thus Professor Tufts tells us that:

> Moral progress involves both the formation of better ideals and the adoption of such ideals as actual standards and guides of life. If our view is correct we can construct better ideals neither by logical deduction nor solely by insight into the nature of things—if by this we mean things as they are. We must rather take as our starting-

point the conviction that moral life is a process involving physical life, social intercourse, measuring and constructive intelligence. We shall endeavor to further each of these factors with the conviction that thus we are most likely to reconstruct our standards and find a fuller good.

But just what it means that one ideal should be "better," or one good "fuller" than another, we are not told. There appears to be no sense in which ideals or goods are commensurable, save in the sense that some come later than others in time. There appears to be abundant justification even in the relatively sober and experimental view of these writers, for Mr. Bertrand Russell's general indictment of the new evolutionism:

> An ideal to which the world continuously approaches is, to these minds, too dead and static to be inspiring. Not only the aspirations, but the ideal too, must change and develop with the course of evolution; there must be no fixed goal, but a continual fashioning of fresh needs by the impulse which is life and which alone gives unity to the process. . . . Somehow, without explicit statement, the assurance is slipped in that the future, though we cannot foresee it, will be better than the past or the present; the reader is like the child who expects a sweet because it has been told to open its mouth and shut its eyes.

In short the gospel of action for action's sake, with its characteristic emphasis on novelty, change and creativeness, tends to view life as without destination, and without any fixed standards or orientation by which comparative attainment may be estimated. The instrumentalists, like many radical theorists, are protected against themselves by their adherence to the traditional ideal of collective human happiness, but in principle they are open to the same charge as that which may be brought against the more revolutionary exponents of irrationalism. They encourage the view that it does not make so much difference where man goes provided he is on his way.

Chapter **V**

The New Radicalism

The Revolt of Youth

To young Americans, Pragmatism meant the beginning of an hopeful new era when every generation promised to be a revolution. In this twentieth-century world of becoming, the transient was more important than the permanent. The belief, form or institution that remained unchanged was regarded not as eternally true, but as an obstacle to truth, a wall, an obstruction to be torn down. "We were for the present," said Floyd Dell, "and against the past."[1]

The world as it presented itself was accepted only as material for change. The tragedy of life, complained Randolph Bourne—who was pushing twenty-seven—was that the world was run by antiquated ideals. Ideas were always a generation behind actual social conditions. "Press, pulpit, and bar teem with the radicalisms of thirty years ago. The dead hand of opinions formed in their college days clutches our leaders and directs their activities in this new and strangely altered physical and spiritual environment. Hence grievous friction, maladjustment, social war. And the faster society moves, the more terrific is the divergence between what is actually going on and what public opinion thinks is actually going on."[2] Only the young were contemporaneous. They interpreted what they saw freshly and without prejudice. Their vision was always the truest, their interpretation always the most just.

Among young people there was an acute consciousness of the inadequacy of the old catchwords and a sincere search for issues that really were new, not just some old phrase or slogan warmed-over by tacking the word "new" before it. The recognized issues, divisions of opinion, and causes were all pronounced extinct. The typical young American, wrote Van Wyck Brooks, speaking for the new generation, had grown up "in a sort of orgy of lofty examples, moralized poems, national anthems and baccalaureate sermons" and was "charged with all manner of ideal purities, ideal honorabilities, ideal femininities, flag-wavings and skyscrapings"[3] out of which all meaning had evaporated. "In the time when we were growing up," Dell explained, "the human imagination was a chaos, filled with the wreckage of a century-long conflict . . . between Utopian ideals and machine-made facts. . . . We were living in the debris of an age that had gone spiritually to smash."[4]

The civilization characteristic of an earlier America had not entirely disappeared, but another civilization had begun to take its place. To the older generation, standing amidst the wreckage and unable to see beyond the ruins, the whole drift of things presented an appalling spectacle. To the middle-aged banker Frederick Townsend Martin, American civilization appeared to be headed full career toward disintegration:

From *The Masses*, Dec., 1915, cover.

The "flapper" typified the prewar revolt of youth. Like eager young radicals of the opposite sex, she too proposed to live the experimental ideal, and by the trial-and-error process to find out what life was all about.

Forty years ago, as a boy, I lived in a true American home. The atmosphere of that home was still under the vitalizing influence of the nation's great struggle for emancipation. Lincoln was a saint. The writings of Longfellow and Emerson, Hawthorne and Washington Irving, were constantly read. The traditions of European Society had not struck their roots deep into the social soil of the United States. We were provincial, to be sure, but there was bliss in simplicity and innocence. Morally and intellectually the life of the family and the life of the State were settled. We knew there was a God. We were positive as to just what was right and what was wrong. The Bible, the Declaration of Independence, the Constitution of the United States, the fact of the assured greatness of our country, the power of our religious, political, and social ideals to save the world—our faith in these was our Rock of Ages; and to these must be added the absolute belief in the theory that it was the sacred duty of every human being to serve his kind.

Just how far these fundamentals were now broken and scattered he would not attempt to say.

... But it is simply true that the Bible is no longer read, that religion has lost its hold, that the Constitution and laws are trampled upon by the rich and powerful, and are no longer held sacred by the poor and weak. Instead of Hawthorne, we read Zola and Gorky; instead of Longfellow and Bryant, Ibsen and Shaw. Among how many perfectly respectable, ay, even religious, people is the name of Nietzsche not more familiar than that of Cardinal Newman! I do not know whither we are going, but I do know that we are going.[5]

If the older generation did not recognize its offspring, it was because, said young Brooks, the old culture had failed utterly to meet the exigencies of modern life. "It is amazing how that fabric of ideas and assumptions, of sentiments and memories and attitudes which made up the civilization of our fathers has melted away like snow uncovering the sordid facts of a society that seems to us now so little advanced on the path of spiritual evolution." It had "disintegrated like a mummy at a touch of sunlight" because it was never a living, active culture. The younger generation found themselves born into a race that had drained away all its spiritual resources in the struggle to survive and that "continues to struggle in the midst of plenty because life itself no longer possesses any other meaning."[6]

No longer able to make the sort of "go" of life their fathers had made, the rising generation revolted against the values their elders took for granted. They felt no undue reverence for established habits of thought and scrutinized suspiciously not only existing moral, social and political institutions, but the very ideas and standards underlying them. "Why *should* we respect the conclusions of past centuries?" asked James Harvey Robinson in the *New Republic*, questioning the serviceability of accepted notions of "sound doctrine, consistency, fidelity to principle, the teachings of the ages, God's will, the dictates of conscience, eternal verities, immutable human nature, the imprescriptible rights of man." [7] Though prompted to model themselves after older men who were themselves victims of the very influences youth rejected, and though pressured by family, business, church, society and state to conform as the easiest and safest way, these young rebels refused to be tractable or docile, put remorseless questions to everything that was old and established.

The ruling generation might try to hide away the unpleasant things or pretend they did not exist, but youth, with its hatred of sophisms and glosses, dragged skeletons from closets and insisted they be explained. Gifted with a terrible propensity to see through things and impelled by an unconquerable urge to tell things as they were, youth soon discovered—as every generation must—that "the world was a very different sort of place from what our carefully deodorized and idealized education would have us believe." [8]

The Experimental Ideal

In the past the good had always been represented as that which harmonized with some end. The individual's task in life had been to choose his end, select carefully the means to that end, and by strength of will, push through to success. But youth seriously doubted both the practicability and worth of this rational ideal. One did not have to live very long, said the rebel spokesman Bourne, to discover that life was not a methodical campaign but a series of surprises not susceptible to orderly mapping. The enemy rarely came from the side expected, and the battle of life was usually fought out on vastly different lines from those so carefully foreseen and so bravely prepared for. The mistake of the older generation, as enlightened youth saw it, was that their methods had been too rigid. They started with moral dogmas, and when life obstinately refused to ratify them, their spirit was crushed, and their morality became mere lip service to fallen ideals.[9]

In place of the old rigid morality with its "textbook rules of life," radical youth substituted the experimental ideal. Life was no longer to be regarded as a battle campaign but as a laboratory where possibilities for happiness and the realization of ideals were to be tested and observed. As Bourne proclaimed: "We are not to start life with a code of its laws in our pocket, with its principles of activity already learned by heart, but we are to discover those principles as we go, by conscientious experiment. Even those laws that seem incontrovertible we are to test for ourselves, to see whether they are thoroughly vital to our own experience and our own genius."[10] These young experimenters approached life with the minds of scientists, selecting hypotheses which most nearly fit their own experience and testing them to find principles that explained their own workings to themselves.

"We had been living in a fixed world," said Dell, "And suddenly there came into our minds the magnificent and well-nigh incredible conception of Change—not petty little pseudo-Darwinian changes, trivial and orderly—but gigantic, miraculous change, an overwhelming of the old in ruin and an emergence of the new. Into our eternal and changeless world came H. G. Wells prophesying its ending, and the Kingdom of Heaven come upon earth." And with that idea of change, the younger generation looked at the world with new and fascinated eyes. "It had suddenly become real to us, because suddenly it meant something. It was going somewhere! The present was significant because it was the link of time between the future and the past. Now, we realized, was the crux of all eternity. Upon this moment hung something of the destiny of all mankind. And upon us, inhabiting this present, depended something. The future was not going to be the same as the present. It was going to be better or worse. And whether better or worse wa   ter upon which we could have our say."[11]

In r   ach of the ruling generation, these young radicals dedicated their lives to the future. There was so much to be done in the world, so much could be done if men would only dare! Throwing off the "nerveless negations" of their elders, the rising generation no longer thought of themselves as creatures of the past or victims of the present, but as creators of the future. Theirs was the youthful radicalism of Jesus—a radicalism of means, not ends. It was to know "that change is necessary and inevitable and good, that tomorrow is constantly dawning with demands for new institutions and new morals and laws." [12] Their imperative duty, as they conceived it, was to reemphasize the life of qualities and ideals, to turn again to that aspect of the world from which men had always drawn the spiritual strength that gave life real worth and meaning. As Brooks phrased it, they wanted "to live creatively, to live completely, to live in behalf of some great corporate purpose." [13]

This positive aspect was particularly noticeable in the religion of the new radicalism. Religion was to occupy the same place in their thoughts that its essential spirit had always held in the spiritual life of men. But unlike the "destructive and uncertain" religious thinking of the preceding generation, that of the new was heralded as positive and definite because it shifted the center of faith from the individual to society. Not personal but social salvation was its interest and concern. "We feel social injustice as our fathers felt personal sin," asserted Bourne.[14] The religion that would mean anything to the rising generation, he told readers of the *Atlantic Monthly*, would have to be based upon social ideals.°

The worst crime of the churches, charged *The Masses*, a shrill new voice of rebellion, was that they had suppressed Christ's essential role as a social reformer. The church had taken the name of Jesus, but had failed to follow his teachings, telling "people living in shanties Jesus is going to fix it up all right with them by giving them mansions in the sky after they're dead and the worms have eaten 'em." [15] The young editors of *The Masses*—Max Eastman, John Reed, and Dell—charged the churches with opposing attempts by the workingmen to better their lot here and now, and pointed to the fate of Frank Tanenbaum, a seventeen-year-old radical, who in the terribly cold winter of 1914 had led a mob of hungry and homeless men into a Fifth Avenue church to seek food and shelter, and for whose courage and idealism Christian

---

° Randolph S. Bourne, *For Radicals*. See p. 285.

charity gave him two and a half years in jail.[16] The real truth, affirmed by poetess Sarah N. Cleghorn, was that "Comrade Jesus" had lived and died for the poor, not the rich:

> Thanks to Saint Matthew, who had been
> At mass-meetings in Palestine,
> We know whose side was spoken for
> When Comrade Jesus had the floor.
>
> "Where sore they toil and hard they lie,
> Among the great unwashed, dwell I.
> The tramp, the convict, I am he;
> Cold-shoulder him, cold-shoulder me."
>
> By Dives' door, with thoughtful eye,
> He did to-morrow prophesy:——
> "The Kingdom's gate is low and small;
> The rich can scarce wedge through at all. . . ."
>
> Ah, let no Local him refuse;
> Comrade Jesus has paid his dues.
> Whatever other he debarred,
> Comrade Jesus hath his red card.[17]

In place of pious hypocrisies in support of the established order, the young men and women of the rising generation demanded and got a real working religious platform. When the Federal Council of the Churches of Christ in America met in Chicago in 1912, social justice became official church doctrine. In a platform almost universally adopted by the Protestent denominations, the churches declared for equal rights, uniform divorce laws, abolition of child labor, prevention of poverty, industrial compensation, old age and unemployment insurance, labor's right to organize, a minimum wage and maximum hours. And the Council concluded: "The final message is redemption, the redemption of the individual in the world, and through him of the world itself, and there is no redemption of either without the redemption of the other." [18]

Looking back a decade later on those days of faith, Floyd Dell, no longer radical but still liberal, saw them in different perspective. "As the sum-total of our efforts," he wrote disillusionedly, "we furnished needy politicians with a new kind of political capital—which they proceeded to over-capitalize and boom until the whole reform-business burst in the grand debacle of Rooseveltian 'Progressivism'." Ironically, yet tenderly, he related how the glory of that ultimate vision kindled by H. G. Wells had gradually faded away and left his generation very much in the light of common day.° Traveling back in memory to the days "when, gloriously confident, we did settlement work or dabbled in 'Charity,'" he told how they had viewed the class struggle as the very essence of contemporary life. With high hopes of a free and happy commonwealth, they had cast in their lot emotionally with the working class only to discover that their chosen protagonists of the future had their own vision of their goal. "They did not want to overthrow capitalism; they wanted lace curtains and a piano in their homes." [19]

Yet, in spite of broken and shattered ideals, the younger generation had not rebelled in vain. If nothing else, they had exposed the fallacy of a philosophy of ends which assumed a changeless, static world. By courageously facing life, growth and change, they discovered—at great spiritual cost to themselves—that tomorrow was not yesterday relived. Nor had they simply repeated the errors and delusions of the past, as older people in their cynicism like to think. Much of what these young radicals thought so wildly then became orthodox liberalism a generation later.

The Sexual Revolution

If adultery was in fact "the application of democracy to love," as H. L. Mencken sardonically noted, then these young radicals were all democrats.[20] For the younger generation was religiously, if not quite wholeheartedly, dedicated to equality of the sexes. In its concern with questions outside the realm of conventional politics and economics, the new radicalism went beyond the crabbed dogmas of Marxism. As with the bold free spirits of an earlier day, the youthful America of the 1830's and 1840's, political allegiance alone no longer distinguished the radical from the conservative. What characterized a person of advanced opinions in the first two decades of the twentieth century was his stand on such issues as youth, education and sex.[21] Sex, above

° Floyd Dell, *Servants of the Future*. See p. 290.

all, engrossed radical energies, and discussion of this once taboo subject spread through respectable society with epidemic frenzy. As one magazine commented in 1913, not without anxiety, "A wave of sex hysteria and sex discussion seems to have invaded this country. Our former reticence on matters of sex is giving way to a frankness that would startle even Paris. Prostitution, as *Life* remarks, is the chief topic of polite conversation. It has struck 'sex o'clock' in America."[22]

It soon became apparent society had not only drawn its head out of the sand of prudery where it had hidden it, ostrich-like, but now seemed about to lose it in a wild commotion over sex. If this nation had once been "prudery drunk," as William Lee Howard, M.D., charged in *Pearson's* magazine, it had since taken his advice and "shove[d] false prudery into the garbage cans."[23] Under the guise of truth, freedom and education, there arose an indelicate, indiscriminate clamor over sex. There was, as some remarked, "an absurd disproportion in the insistence on the importance of the sexual emotion."[24] Even so staunch a feminist as Charlotte Gilman felt there was too much attention to this one subject: "In order that our daughters may not be abducted . . . must [they] be publicly, graphically, and continuously reminded of the reasons why their abduction is sought?"[25]

Puritanism had been routed and succeeded by "a blatant screaming" which many found "tiresome, past telling."[26] Preachers sought to rouse dozing congregations with sermons about "white slavery"—the Victorian euphemism for prostitution—and aging moralists such as Theodore Roosevelt thundered against the "Flesh Trust," calling for flogging of male offenders.[27] On stage, a theatergoer grumbled, there was "nothing but white-slave plays and poison-needle dramas."[28] George Bernard Shaw titillated American audiences with his satire on Mrs. Warren's profession; the play *Damaged Goods*, in which the action sprang from venereal disease, marked a new epoch of candor in the theater. Depravity apparently was a valuable asset when presented for the consideration of the undepraved. Motion-picture producers were coining money by sending shows with suggestive titles about "White Slaves" and "Traffic in Souls" all over the country. Freely using the words "Original," "Authentic," "Authorized," they claimed to be dramatizations of Mr. Rockefeller's vice commission reports or of official government investigations. For purposes of profit and to revive flagging circulation, the prostitute—always the innocent victim—was idealized by *The Masses* in humorless fiction; the *Smart Set* taunted bourgeois morality by making her the subject of a novelette, and lurid vice reports packed popular magazines and crowded other news off the front page. "Is this overemphasis of sex a symptom of a new moral awakening," *Current Opinion* gasped breathlessly in 1913, "or is it a sign that the morbidity of the Old World is overtaking the New?" [29]

Certainly if the New Woman was any indicator, the old Victorian moral code had gone smash. Though dear old Dr. Eliot in urging a single moral standard for men and women had never intended that sex freedom should be interpreted into meaning sexual license,

In pressing for equality of the sexes, the suffragette became the symbol of woman in revolt. By her aggressive actions she not only obtained the ballot but precipitated a sexual revolution that undermined longstanding relations between men and women.

From *Collier's*, Feb. 21, 1914.

it logically followed, as a writer in the St. Louis *Mirror* concluded, that "we must grant today to woman the same promiscuity that society tacitly grants to the male." [30] Notoriously society smiled on the acts of the young man, called them "sport," "sowing his wild oats," and so on. Without curbs, he was free to express his animal impulses in brothels and in dissipation, while his bride-to-be was compelled to live in a rarefied atmosphere of imaginary purity. But plainly the New Woman was no longer able to accept this pinched ideal of the "lady." Like Nora in Ibsen's immensely popular play, *A Doll's House*—which became the symbol of woman in revolt—she had put up with all the masculine authoritarianism she could stand. She was tired of being treated like a doll and fed up with the male's preposterous airs of superiority, so she walked out. And said Dell, speaking for those who were at the time young male idealists, "When Nora went out, slamming the door behind her, we all applauded." [31]

For this new kind of young woman, H. L. Mencken invented a new name, the "flapper." With her skirts having "just reached her very trim and pretty ankles" and her newly coiled hair just exposing "the ravishing whiteness of her neck," he found her a charming creature. Youth was hers, and hope, and romance, and—

Well, well, let us be exact: let us not say innocence. This Flapper, to tell the truth, is far, far, far from a simpleton. . . .

Life, indeed, is almost empty of surprises, mysteries, horrors to this Flapper of 1915. . . . She knows exactly what the Wassermann reaction is, and has made up her mind that she will never marry a man who can't show an unmistakable negative. . . . She has read Christabel Pankhurst and Ellen Key, and is inclined to think there must be something in this new doctrine of free motherhood. She is opposed to the double standard of morality, and favors a law prohibiting it.
. . .

This Flapper has forgotten how to simper; she seldom blushes; it is impossible to shock her. She saw "Damaged Goods" without batting an eye, and went away wondering what the row over it was all about. The police of her city having prohibited "Mrs. Warren's Profession," she read it one rainy Sunday afternoon, and found it a mass of platitudes. . . . She plans to read Havelock Ellis during the coming summer. . . . [32]

Because the New Woman was still very much in the minority,

her American habitat was largely limited to such Bohemian centers as Greenwich Village. There, in the generous anonymity of the big city, where rents were cheap and where struggling artists and writers lived, she was free to be herself. "A moral-health resort" was how Dell, himself a youthful refugee from Victorian hypocrisy, described the Village. "For young people of talent it was a paradise; youths could have love affairs without having to 'marry the girl,' and without finding themselves fathers of families long before they were grown up themselves; and girls of talent did not have to wonder, as back in the home town, whether it was true that losing their virginities would help in the development of their artistic abilities—nor engage, as back in the home town, in intrigues of the most elaborate furtiveness and most desperate secrecy, backed up with frightful hypocrisies maintained even in the face of their 'best friends.' It was a refuge from Mother's morality."[33] There the flapper could read Edward Carpenter's *Love's Coming-of-Age* and experiment with a new code of manners founded not on covert history but "the friendly exchange of equal services" in which there should be "no sense of Mine or Thine, in property or possession."[34] In the Village, "marriages without benefit of clergy," "divorces without benefit of lawyers," and "idyls and heartbreaks without benefit of newspaper notoriety,"[35] were not considered scandalous but eminently natural. For the New Woman rejected not only Victorianism but the conventions of romantic love. With considerable dismay, young male idealists discovered the flapper didn't take their love too seriously. She, too, proposed to live the experimental life, and by the trial-and-error process, to find out what love was all about.

Shocking as were the moral irregularities of the Villagers, the guardians of national morality were even more upset by the dance craze that swept the country during the second decade of the century. American youth, the Vice President of the United States implied, was going to hell by way of the tango and the turkey-trot. A Chicago Baptist weekly found the situation "disquieting, if not alarming." Despite Havelock Ellis' disclaimer that dancing was "not merely the supreme manifestation of physical life, but also the supreme symbol of spiritual life," the University of Wisconsin threatened to expel any student guilty of turkey-trotting.[36]

While the *Atlantic* attributed the youthful revolt against restraint
to the "sophomoric glory of being wicked," [37] and the conservative
editor of the *Nation* lashed out at the "childishly flaunted paradoxes
of the naughty decade," [38] the *Dial* was not so easily put off and
called for a rally to the defense of "tried old moralities." [39]

To charges of "moral anarchism" youth's reply was, "We are
not immoral—we are 'getting on'." Changing attitudes toward sex,
dancing and the length of skirts were all simply the earmarks of
progress. "Why should a girl be required to conceal the fact forever
after that she was born a biped, and strive to create the impression
that she moves about from place to place on rollers?" [40] Prudish-
ness, not propriety, they insisted, was the issue. Admittedly their
generation had a wider unchaperoned world to play together in,
but after all, the young casuist argued, the difference was not so
much in substance as in attitude. No matter how cynical their
words or how apparently frivolous their actions, their manner of
living was perhaps not so different from the actualities of Victorian
life as from the chaste pictures of that life presented in Victorian
fiction.

The New Morality

What had happened to turn perfect models of Victorian domestic
femininity into "raging and irresponsible monsters of modernism?" [41] While psychoanalysis was blamed for fomenting the controversy over sex, Freudianism came too late to add much to the
already vigorous feminine revolt.[42] Nor was it because Ibsen wrote
A Doll's House, said Lippmann, "or because Bernard Shaw writes
prefaces." [43] Nothing she read in books had resolved the New
Woman's secret discontent into open rebellion. At first, Dell's
young male idealists had flattered themselves with the thought that
they were the Frankensteins who had turned her old grudges into
new ambitions. Only later, when the New Woman had come to
the second stage of her revolt, when she realized by experience
what was in books, did they begin to suspect the truth. "The thing
which was sending girls by the hundreds of thousands out of the
home into the shops and factories was not idealism, but necessity
. . . . capitalism was breaking up the old-fashioned home, and using

its feminine inmates for purposes of its own." [44] Whether necessity or opportunity, one thing was clear. The path of freedom for modern woman led away from home.

The "sexual question," as it was called, was a radical manifestation and the moral culmination of the struggle for women's rights. Since the beginning of the nation, women had pleaded for and been denied equal rights with men. In 1776, Abigail, wife of John Adams, wrote her husband begging him to remember that women too had a stake in the revolutionary new order:

> . . . in the new code of laws which I suppose it will be necessary for you to make, I desire you would remember the ladies, and be more generous to them than your ancestors. Do not put such unlimited power in the hands of husbands. Remember, all men would be tyrants if they could. If particular care and attention are not paid to the ladies, we are determined to foment a rebellion, and will not hold ourselves bound to obey the laws in which we have no voice or representation.[45]

The pleas of her sex, however, failed to pierce the masculine ego, and women were consigned a station in American society similar to that of the Negro. As late as 1850, wife-beating "with a reasonable instrument" was legal in nearly every state, and almost everywhere for long afterwards women were legally considered perpetual minors. If unmarried, they were wards of male relatives; if married, they became part of their husband's chattels along with house, horse and barn.

After freeing of the slaves in 1865, American women launched a new abolitionist crusade for the emancipation of their sex. From street corners and on the platform they steadily pushed their campaign for the vote, all the while bombarding Congress with petitions. By 1910, the rebellion prophesied by Abigail Adams was in full swing. Battle lines were drawn, and the intensity of the war between the sexes was dramatically revealed by the titles of articles in popular journals. To woman's plaintive question, "Are Women Human Beings?" [46] the male retort was "Women Should Mind Their Own Business"; [47] her plea for "Democraticization of Women" [48] was damned as "Petticoat Government"; [49] when accused of "Making a Man of Herself," [50] she countered with a scathing denunciation of "Man—the Timid Sex." [51] Though declaiming less about the natural inferiority of women and making fewer gibes about Adam's rib, American men in general held undauntedly to the idea that woman's place was in the home and piously, if somewhat hypocritically, sermonized about the sanctity of the home and the purity of womanhood. But the women stuck doggedly to their guns and finally gained victory in 1920 with ratification of the Nineteenth Amendment.

As it turned out, however, this marked only the beginning of the revolt of women against "sex servitude." What began as a political movement of "votes for women" and spread to an economic demand of "equal pay for equal work," inexorably swelled into a full-scale rebellion against what was on the whole, most unfairly and offensively, a "man-made world." Right of suffrage, regulation of working hours, equal property rights—none of these gains, the feminist came to realize, affected directly the most vital factors of her existence as a woman. The suffrage movement was largely a parlor affair, while it was the bedroom that chained her spirit and enslaved her body. What her soul demanded was not equal suffrage but a change in the feminine ideal.

"The lives of too many American women are still smothered with domesticity, and the outgrown ideals of home and motherhood," fretted Susanne Wilcox, distressed by the limited and superficial sense of public morality that bound her sex.[52] Almost from infancy the average girl was told that marriage was her ultimate goal, and "like the mute beast fattened for slaughter," she was kept penned up for that eventful day.[53] "Can there be anything more outrageous," asked Emma Goldman, "than the idea that a healthy, grown woman, full of life and passion, must deny nature's demand, must subdue her most intense craving, undermine her health and break her spirit, must stunt her vision, abstain from the depth and glory of sex experience until a 'good' man comes along to take her unto himself as a wife?"[54] As an already infamous radical, the views of Mrs. Goldman were doubtless less startling than those of the respected Swedish feminist, Ellen Key who, in her widely read book on love and marriage, struck at the foundations of the feminine ideal by denying that chastity in itself was a virture, challenging fidelity as the last word in marriage ethics, and disputing the worth of morality, wedded or single, at expense of the passions. Now that woman was coming into her own, even the sacred institution of marriage and the family was called into question.[55]

The point of conspicuous difference and tremendous social significance between the woman of yesterday and the woman of today, Margaret Deland told readers of the *Atlantic* in 1910, was that "We have come to appreciate the fact that our mothers were unconscientious concerning the right of children *not* to be born." Quantity, not quality, said Miss Deland, marked the mother of fifty or sixty years ago. Accepting her role as the "weaker and gentler half," she was bound to her lot as a "brood animal for the masculine civilizations of the world." Without choice, a slave to her husband's passion, she perpetuated the tyrannies of the earth by breeding hordes of human beings—"human beings so plentiful as to be cheap" and so cheap that ignorance, famine, and plague was their natural lot.[56]

American women were rising in fundamental revolt against sexual slavery, affirming their right to voluntary motherhood. The New Woman, asserted Emma Goldman, "no longer wants to be a party to the production of a race of sickly, feeble, decrepit, wretched human beings, who have neither the strength nor moral courage to throw off the yoke of poverty and slavery. Instead she desires fewer and better children, begotten and reared in love and through free choice; not by compulsion."[57] Speaking out courageously for thousands of married women who suffered silently in modesty, ignorance or fear, Margaret Sanger declared modern women "are determined to decide for themselves whether they shall become mothers, under what conditions and when." The key to liberty, she was persuaded, was "birth control"—a euphemism she coined to describe the use of contraceptives.[58] Unfortunately there were many obstacles in the way. Most women—especially those of the lower classes who were in greatest need—were completely ignorant of the possibilities of contraception and required thorough education and instruction. Between them and liberty stood a baffling barrier of law and prejudice that denied woman knowledge of her own sexual nature. Birth-control information was classed as pornography, and its dissemination forbidden by law. To attempt to get around these "Dark-Age laws" and Victorian inhibitions invited attack from the forces of reaction.[59]

Even if it meant warfare in every phase of her life, young Mrs.

Sanger was determined that woman must emerge from her ignorance and assume her responsibilities. An ardent reformer who took her radicalism seriously, she plunged into direct action by writing in 1913 a series of articles for the New York *Call* under the general title *What Every Girl Should Know*. These articles ran for three or four weeks until they were spied by the aged vice crusader Anthony Comstock and suppressed. The next issue of the *Call* appeared with an ironic epitaph in their accustomed place:

What Every Girl Should Know

NOTHING!

By Order of the Post Office Department.

Undaunted, Margaret Sanger began publication of a new magazine, the *Woman Rebel,* whose bannerhead carried the slogan, "No Gods, No Masters." She defined woman's duty, "To look the world in the face with a go-to-hell look in the eyes; to have an idea; to speak and act in defiance of convention." [60] Dutifully she followed her own advice and was forced to flee the country under threat of imprisonment.

After a deluge of letters protesting the indictment, the government dropped the case, and the controversial Mrs. Sanger returned to embark upon a stormy lecture tour which brought hisses and hurrahs, jail and much publicity. In spite of a New York state law forbidding even doctors to give contraceptual advice, she opened in the Brooklyn slums in 1916 the first American birth-control clinic. She was promptly arrested and sentenced to thirty days in the workhouse. Each arrest, however, brought added publicity and struck another blow at the weakening forces of Puritanism. During the second decade of the twentieth century, birth control gained general popular approval, and the same people who, a few years before, had fought so righteously against Mrs. Sanger were by the twenties engaged in flooding the country with millions of pamphlets discussing sex matters and venereal disease. Indicative of the radical switch in public opinion was the enlistment of Edward Bok, the strongly antifeminist editor of the *Ladies' Home Journal*, who joined in the new crusade by helping to organize the American Society of Sanitary and Moral Prophylaxis for the dissemination of sex knowledge.

The triumph of birth control and the rapid spread of contraceptual knowledge, good and bad, put a terrible strain on conventional morality. Only vaguely aware of the totally subversive effect of her program, Mrs. Sanger proposed a "new morality" to be created by womankind.° Much influenced by the English sexologist Havelock Ellis, who during her exile had befriended her and guided her reading, she advocated a healthier attitude toward sex. In her determination to free sex from the smuttiness connected with it since the days of St. Paul, she took the position that sex, far from being "dirty," was the highest expression of the feminine spirit. Once the human mind was purged of its unclean conception of sex and the sexual desires allowed free expression, she was convinced virtue would actually crowd out vice.

If nothing else it was at least a tribute to the valor of the feminist evangelists that sex in the twentieth century was no longer regarded as an unclean subject about which society should maintain a conspiracy of silence. As President Eliot of Harvard told the annual conference of the American School Hygiene Association in New York in 1911, the sex processes "if properly taught with collecting box, scalpel, microscope and paper and pencil are just as pure and innocent for children under thirteen as chemistry or physics are." [61] For youth, a writer continued in the *Call*, the modern social system was a terrific endurance test. "We surround that young, passionate, bursting blossom with every temptation to break down its resistance power, lure it into sentient, pulsating desire and eroticism by lurid literature, moving pictures, tango dances, suggestive songs, cabarets, noise, music, light, life, rhythm, everywhere, until the senses are throbbing with leashed-in physical passion—everything done to lure, but nothing to instruct. So one day the leash snaps, and another boy or girl is outside the pale." [62] Though some adults still protested youth was better off without an intimate acquaintance with "the seamy side of life," sex education was generally

° Margaret Sanger, *The New Morality*. See p. 294.

Drawn by K. R. Chamberlain   From *The Masses*, May, 1915.

FAMILY LIMITATION—OLD STYLE

Persuaded that the key to liberty for modern women was birth control,
Margaret Sanger advocated the use of contraceptives and for her
efforts was forced to leave the country under threat of imprisonment.

urged as the only thing that could save young people in "the big battle that lies beyond the home." [63]

To youth no doubt it was the thrilling dawn of a new era, but to the older generation there was nothing new about the Seven Deadly Sins which, naked and unsolicited, were daily urged upon the weary attention of adults. It was not so much the nature of the advice showered upon them to which they reasonably objected, but the fact that a great deal of it was given in the wrong way, at the wrong time, by the wrong people. The error of their self-appointed instructors, as was pointed out, was to assume that because their elders did not chatter about sex, they had never heard of it. This crude detailing of matters offensive to modesty, the breaching of Victorian standards of taste, was traced by a writer in the *Atlantic* to 1898 when the Lexow Vice Commission's activities were openly reported in New York newspapers. From then on, the general assumption was that women and youth were supposed to read whatever men read. Thus, not only had that young girl's witticism, "There are books I would not let my mother read," already been perpetrated in the nineties, but by a curious irony the once commanding word "Victorian" had come to mean "flabby and futile, prudish and trite, grandmotherly and sentimental." [64]

Yet, as the urbane essayist Agnes Repplier gently reminded the ardent but ingenuous missionaries who had lightly undertaken to remake the world, Victorian morality was not altogether the hypocritical thing it seemed to youth of the day. The well-ordered mind knew the value, no less than the charm, of reticence. In her opinion the sex enthusiasts had gone far beyond the bounds of good taste and morality.° To treat such a theme as birth control, for instance, grossly and vulgarly before the general public, stripping it of the nobility of love and the tender instinct of motherhood, leaving only the matter-of-fact functions of biology, was to her an uncondonable offense—the deeper because it claimed to be beneficial. Along with a deplorable lack of reserve went a lamentable absence of humor. What, she asked, could be thought of a woman who went to a household of strangers and volunteered to instruct its members—two discreet, retiring spinsters of eighty and sixty—in sex hygiene? She found equally absurd the sentimental

---

° Agnes Repplier, *The Repeal of Reticence*. See p. 298.

treatment of the prostitute which invariably assumed the girl played no part in her undoing, that she was "as passive as the animal bought for vivisection, as mute and helpless in the tormentors' hands." For her part, Miss Repplier was convinced that the sensationalism and sentimentality of the reformers not only stood in the way of reform, but resulted in "an extraordinary confusion of outlook," a perilous nullification of good judgment and common sense.[65]

Not only had the reaction against Victorian "hypocrisy" gone so far that reticence had ceased to be a virtue, but the throwing off of old inhibitions threatened to bring down an entire civilization. Morality, the Victorians were well aware, had always consisted in the exercise of certain inhibitions, and every civilization at bottom rested upon a morality of one sort or another, enforced by law and custom. In America more than elsewhere, the care and preservation of moral values had been entrusted mainly to women. Under the anarchic conditions of the frontier and during the chaos of industrialization when men were absorbed in more practical pursuits, women had served as the moral custodians of society. They represented cohesion, decency, and self-restraint; and the cult of the home, over which they presided, was, as Christopher Lasch has said, a sort of "national religion."[66] In these circumstances, anything that disrupted woman's role as the guardian of tradition necessarily endangered the existing social structure. Woman's rebellion against her "place" had, in Lippmann's words, "blasted the rock of ages where woman's life was centered," and, as the older generation feared, the whole cultural edifice erected upon her was bound to come tumbling down.[67]

Progressive Education

Almost universally, the new radicals looked to education for new ways of living and, by application of scientific method, hoped to reconstruct American society along moral and democratic lines. "Never before was education so necessary," maintained Walter Weyl. "Our new science prevents us from falling back upon routine, as our new ethics forbid us to depend upon traditions."[68] Modern man, Lippmann pointed out, was not yet settled in his world. "All of us are immigrants spiritually. We are all . . . immigrants in the industrial world, and we have no authority to lean upon. We are an uprooted people, newly arrived, and *nouveau riche.* . . . We are blown hither and thither like litter before the wind." [69] He too looked to education for direction. Custom and authority might work in a simple and unchanging civilization, but "in our world only those will conquer who can understand." [70]

Americans had always had a kind of superstitious faith in education's power for social uplift, but the emphasis had been upon individual rather than collective education. As Herbert Croly observed, the credulity of the Socialists in expecting to alter human nature by changing economic conditions was matched by the credulity of the good American who proposed to evangelize the individual by the expenditure of money and words. "Do we lack culture? We will 'make it hum' by founding a new university in Chicago. Is American art neglected and impoverished? We will enrich it by organizing art departments in our colleges, and popularize it by lectures with lantern slides and associations for the study of its history. Is New York City ugly? Perhaps, but if we could only get the authorities to appropriate a few hundred millions for its beautification, we could make it look like a combination of Athens, Florence, and Paris." [71] He and other new radicals found the American faith in education "credulous and superstitious" because it attached excessive importance to subsidized good intentions. "They want to be 'uplifted,' and they want to 'uplift' other people; but they will not use their social and political institutions for the purpose, because those institutions are assumed to be essentially satisfactory. The 'uplifting' must be a matter of individual, or of unofficial associated effort; and the only available means are words and subsidies." [72]

The prevailing view in the nineties and afterwards was that the primary function of education was indoctrination. While believing in individuality and self-help, William T. Harris, superintendent of St. Louis schools, expressed the prevailing view among many educators—that education's primary purpose was to train the child to respect authority: "Ninety-nine out of a hundred people in every civilized nation are automata, careful to walk in the prescribed paths, careful to follow prescribed custom. This is the result of substantial education which, scientifically defined, is the subsumption of the individual under his species." [73] Similarly the distinguished historian John Bach McMaster prescribed that history should be so taught as to convince students that there was no land "where the people are so prosperous, so happy, so intelligent, so bent on doing what is just and right as the people of the United States." [74] Educators, Merle Curti has pointed out, generally accepted the businessman's outlook and consciously or unconsciously molded the school system to accord with the canons of the profit system. Most aptly, the public schools were pointed to with pride by the influential educator, Ellwood P. Cubberley as "a manufactory, doing a half-billion dollar business each year in trying to prepare future citizens for usefulness and efficiency in life." [75] As in business, the tendency in education was toward consolidation and bigness, and as in all large corporations, the first rule of efficient service on the part of the employee or teacher was "unquestioned obedience." Not only was educational administration said to be "entirely analogous" to that of the army, navy, and great business enterprise, but the President of the National Education Association asserted in 1900 that "the real educational leaders of the age . . . are those who have a business capacity to appreciate and comprehend the business problems which are always part of the educational problem." [76]

For these and other reasons, the radicals found education in America a travesty. Schools, said Bourne, were remote and antiseptic, resembling factories, penitentiaries, orphan asylums, and in morale the "nearest thing we have to compulsory military service." [77] Instead of regarding children as living, growing social beings, they were treated as so many separate empty vessels to be filled with knowledge. Although Los Angeles, Indianapolis, and Gary, Indiana, had modern public-school systems which sought to benefit the pupil "by stimulating his own brain," most cities, it was charged, followed the assembly-line method, manufacturing a standardized product which was merely "an echo of the thought of others." [78]

While the radicals believed in free education for all from kindergarten to university, they advocated a differentiated, modernized education. Future education "must exalt social obligations above mere competitive egoisms" but must, at the same time, nurture "all socially valuable individualities."[79] The new education, announced Weyl, must expand beyond the school grounds. "The future education of the masses . . . should not be the traditional, Procrustean, unrelated, and undifferentiated education of yesterday, but an education which fully equips the child for his industrial, political, and social life. For too long the school has been half asylum, half penitentiary. For too long it has stood alone in irrelevant isolation, knowing neither factory nor farm, neither kitchen nor voting booth. For much too long it has been a place where individuality has been weeded and crushed out."[80] This did not mean that the schools should try to make intellectuals out of the multitude—sociological reality made it plain that some were fitted to be scholars, others manual workers, artists, scientists. Indeed, believing, as did most businessmen, in the benefits of an increase in national production, the new radicals recognized the advantage of technical education and supported vocational training. Their intent, however, was not to make the schools an adjunct to manufacture and commerce but to use industrial training to make school life more active, meaningful and relevant to out-of-school experience.

Since, according to John Dewey, modern America had as yet no culture, one had to be created. Moreover, since Americans could neither beg nor borrow a culture without betraying both it and themselves, it was essential in his view that American culture be consonant with American conditions instead of a refuge from them. "To set up as protector of a shrinking classicism requires only the accident of a learned education, the possession of leisure and a reasonably apt memory for some phrases, and a facile pen for others. To transmute a society built on an industry which is not yet humanized into a society which wields its knowledge and its industrial power in behalf of a democratic culture requires the courage of an inspired imagination."[81] Accordingly Dewey attached considerable importance to the introduction of standardized methods of teaching and administration as "a seeping into education" of the efficient concepts and methods which modern industrial life was making inevitable.

Through the experimental and scientific method in education,

Dewey hoped to overcome the split between learning and doing, between theory and practice. His chief criticisms of the prevailing "Schoolmaster" theory of education was that it overemployed mere symbols of knowledge—the acquisition of facts—and did not make sufficient use of positive and first-hand contact with experience, trying to fit the child to a pattern of accepted social attitudes instead of giving him methods for the continuing criticism and reconstruction of social life. His criterion of the value of school education was the extent to which it created a desire for continued growth and supplied the means for making the desire effective in fact. Although Dewey was opposed to routine which arrested growth, he neither disparaged nor disregarded the important function of habits. He believed education. to be the "constant reorganizing or reconstructing of experience," and was concerned with "not [men's] conscious beliefs nor their professed ideals but those mental sets which limit and control all conscious thinking and desire." [82] Once the experimental attitude toward life became a habit, the individual could effortlessly handle the mechanics of life, thus freeing his intelligence to meet and adapt to new circumstances.

Holding that there cannot be two sets of ethical principles, one for school and another for life outside the school, Dewey emphasized the social nature of education.° In his mind the terms "democracy" and "education" were practically synonyms, and the blatant failure of the existing system was its inability to conceive and construct the school as a social institution reflecting the fundamental principles and problems of democratic life. Part of the difficulty he traced to the "outworn philosophy of individualism," which set the individual apart from the social context in which he lived, and part to the idealist conception of mind as a purely isolated phenomenon of self whose cultivation was best served by formal instruction in schools insulated from everyday experience.[83] Dewey did not underestimate the role of the individual; rather, he inverted the order of priorities in education, charging the school with the remaking of society in order to permit the realization of the individual. "Society is a society of individuals and the individual is always a social individual. He has no existence by

---

° John Dewey, *Democracy and Education.* See p. 301.

himself. He lives in, for, and by society, just as society has no existence excepting in and through the individuals who constitute it." [84] A progressive society, as he was well aware, counted individual variations as precious, since it found in them the means of

THE FURIES!

By 1914 the former reticence concerning sex had given way to a frankness that made one magazine declare it had struck "sex o'clock" in America. Under the guise of truth and education, there was an indiscriminate clamor over sex that was viewed by many as a perilous threat to the idealism of youth.   From *Survey*, Oct. 4, 1913.

its own growth. Hence it was the office of the school in a democracy "to see to it that each individual gets an opportunity to escape from the limitations of the social group in which he was born, and to come into living contact with a broader environment."[85] Democratic education, in consistency with its ideal, must not only train its young to get along in the present world, but must promote "the best possible realization of humanity as humanity."[86]

Despite Dewey's high aims, there was considerable apprehension, if not alarm, among the older generation at the growth and spread of radical ideas in education. Issue after issue of the *Atlantic Monthly*, a traditional bastion of the old culture, carried indignant articles expressing, as one title plainly put it, "Old-Fashioned Doubts About New-Fashioned Education." The general complaint was that "The education of the past is everywhere on the defensive; old ideals are being undermined; methods that have served for generations are scorned as unworthy"; and finally, to complete the destruction, "Even the multiplication table is threatened with banishment."[87] Specifically, however, the new education was indicted chiefly upon two counts: its pseudo-scientific approach and its frankly materialistic and utilitarian bent.

In the name of science, it was charged, the new methods were withholding the simple essentials of education. The progressive theory that schoolwork must appeal to a child's fluctuating tastes and attract his involuntary attention was denounced as an overly sentimental view of education which did grievous wrong to the rising generation. As an instance of the working out of the new "painless methods" a middle-aged critic pointed to what she derisively called "intuitive English," saying, "The rising generation cannot spell, because it learned to read by the word-method; it is hampered in the use of dictionaries, because it never learned the alphabet; its English is slipshod and commonplace, because it does not know the sources and resources of its own language. Power over words cannot be had without some knowledge of the classics or much knowledge of the English Bible—but both are now quite out of fashion."[88] Another frequent criticism of the new science of pedagogy was that it was too scientific. Not only did it offer the child the "doubtful privilege of freedom from restraint" and the "doubtful boon of shelter from obligation," but educators spoke of "child-material" as if it were wood-pulp to be processed. In this era of "symbolic education" and "symbolic play" when the Santa Claus myth was rejected as a distortion of reality, and when supposedly scientific deductions were drawn from jackstones and baseball, one must sympathize, as did Agnes Repplier, with the little girl who said she wished she had lived in the time of Charles II, because then "education was much neglected." [89]

Eventually the debate narrowed down to the question of whether education should press onward in the direction of social efficiency or favor the old Platonic rule, "Education is learning to like the right things." The latter course appealed to traditionalists, who believed the proper study of the human spirit was neither the psychology of the laboratory, nor science, nor pedagogy, but humanism—a "sincere appreciation of the best things in our spiritual heritage from Homer to Tennyson." [90] The vagaries of the elective system, the advocacy of manual training as an equivalent for books, the unbounded enthusiasm for nature study, the encroachment of science on the humanities, the general substitution of persuasion for authority, were all attributed by Paul Elmer More, a conservative editor of the *Nation*, to a revival of the "daemonic" pedagogics of Rousseau. "To make instinct instead of experienced judgment the basis of education" was to More "so monstrous a perversion of the truth" as to horrify any thinking person. Yet, so appealing was Rousseau's "education of nature" to the modern mind that it had deeply modified, if not entirely transformed the practice of primary and secondary schools. Now, said More, "like a poison in the blood of society," it was spreading to colleges and universities, the last strongholds of classicism. [91]

A pessimistic view of college education was shared alike by the faculty, by thoughtful parents, and even by some of the students themselves. Intelligent critics, and a few not so intelligent, were awakening to the fact that higher educational institutions in America were not fulfilling the hopes of their founders and supporters, and were not meeting the needs of the nation. Speaking for the faculty, Woodrow Wilson, who was trying against alumni opposition to make an educational institution out of Princeton, attracted national headlines by his candid declaration that he did not wish to be the president of a Country Club and by his glum prophecy that "the colleges of this country must be reconstructed from top to bottom." [92] Even less optimistic was a Harvard professor, who speculated publicly on the futility of all higher education.[93]

Similar expressions came from less distinguished laymen who saw student life in American colleges as a series of "diverting side-shows" in which the true object of education was forgotten. One keen observer wrote, "A College is a factory for turning raw material into case-hardened athletes, kid-finished society leaders. . . . Its work is marvelous. It can take an eighteen year old youth with premature trousers, hay-stack hair, . . . and in four years can work him over into a calm-eyed football champion." [94] Another enumerated the subjects offered in the modern curriculum as follows: "How to keep a dance programme straight; Eating in all its branches; How to live on credit; Frat. House construction; The Science of making the hair stand up straight; etc." [95] Colleges, grumbled a Yale alumnus, had become "nurseries of drunkeness and vice"; and though President Taft put the weight of authority behind his alma mater, he cheerily confessed that he, too, like the fabled Dink Stover, had gambled and consumed "a sufficient quantity of sickening beer." [96] Another mature critic, after reading the letters of five hundred college seniors for a popular magazine, found little knowledge of good writing, spelling or grammar, implying that the colleges were not making good.[97] Slightly more hopeful was the article Lincoln Steffens wrote for *Harper's Weekly* entitled "How To Get An Education Even in College." [98]

The trouble with higher education, conservatives and radicals agreed, was a lack of intellectual ideals. College, for the majority of students, was a "sheltered world where one dreamed away four years of ideal life with men of one's own class and one's own prejudices"; college life, for the most part, centered around the "frats," the clubhouses, teas, drinking bouts, football games, "Proms," and other events exterior to the real spirit of college.[99] Though Bourne found these externalities played a less vital part at Columbia, he nevertheless conceded that college spirit had come to mean enthusiasm for the winning of a game, and a college that had no football team was supposed to have no college spirit. Along with "shameless conditions of actual and semi-professionalism in college teams"—much of it supported and encouraged by wealthy alumni in an attempt to win glory and renown for alma mater—the really harmful effect of football on college life, in his opinion, was that it diverted undergraduate attention from cultural interests to "a small picked body of gladiators" and squandered student energies in an "exaggerated patriotism and provincial jingoism" miscalled college spirit.[100] Yet, while there was too much interest in athletics and fraternities and too little in intellectual pursuits, the fault was not entirely the students'. Many were sent to college by newly prosperous, doting parents who, having missed a college education themselves, desired it for their sons as a badge of social prestige and encouraged them to have a good time before the serious duties of life began. Also, as Harvard man John Reed pointed out, certain professors, "the academic coaches of the faculty," instead of fostering intellectual attainments, were prone to wink at idleness, neglect of duty, social and athletic distractions.[101]

A good measure of blame fell upon the governing boards which generally were not composed of men of high intellectual ideals. Colleges and universities were run on the plan of a business corporation by a board of "amateur notables"—invariably businessmen or lawyers—who knew little or nothing of education and its purposes. This peculiar situation had come about, as Veblen wryly observed, because "business success is by common consent, and quite uncritically, taken to be conclusive evidence of wisdom even in matters that have no relation to business affairs"; so as a matter of course, "the final discretion in the affairs of seats of learning is entrusted to men who have proved their capacity for work that has nothing in common with the higher learning." [102] The paradoxical state of educational affairs was further confounded by the dogged conviction among the common run of businessmen that not only was learning of no use in business, but what was of no use in business was not worthwhile. The result was that in matters of academic policy, business values usually dominated intellectual values. There was increased emphasis on professional and technical schools and, classicists complained, a tendency to favor those "practical" subjects that had much in common with modern industry and its technological discipline.

In a competitive age of university building, with rival educational directorates vying with one another for funds, the business mania for bigness gave enrollment such importance that educational standards were readily sacrificed for mere numerical greatness. Professors were expected to be loyal organization men, and, noted Charles A. Beard of Columbia, "As long as they keep silent on living issues, their salaries will be secure. It will not be important that they should arouse and inspire students in the class room. They need not be teachers. They are asked to be only purveyors of the safe and insignificant." [103] Their tenure was uncertain, and average salaries were low; two-thirds of the full professors in bigger colleges and universities made one thousand dollars a year. There were no unions among college teachers and no collective bargaining; for, said Veblen, there appeared to be a feeling prevalent among them "that their salaries are not of the nature of wages, and that there would be a species of moral obliquity implied in overtly so dealing with the matter." [104] Nor was it uncommon for professors and scholars to be subordinated to the boyish Americanisms of regents and trustees who looked upon the educational enterprise as a quasi-athletic establishment and devoted their major endeavors to winning athletic seasons. As testimony to the anti-intellectualism of governing boards, it was a notorious fact that in the big colleges and universities the football coach was the highest-paid man on the faculty.

Faculty and system alike came under censure for "medieval" methods and ideals. Academic ritual and the mummery of caps and gowns, it was declared, had no bearing on higher learning. Their only cultural significance, suggested Veblen, was "as occasions of rehearsal in all matters of polite conformity and as a stimulus to greater refinement and proficiency in expenditure on seemly dress and equipage." [105] The lecture system was assailed as an atavistic hangover from the Middle Ages. "For the college course to be organized on a basis of lectures," said the *New Republic*, "suggests that nothing has happened since Abelard spoke in Paris to twelfth-century bookless men." [106] Now that the magic word no longer had to be communicated by word of mouth, young radicals like Bourne, Reed and Lippmann advocated a more direct approach to education. In place of the lecture, which encouraged passivity on the part of the student, they asked for free discussion and an adjustment of intellectual activity to modern social demands. They demanded a new type of professor, "a man with a free-handed, open-hearted hospitality to ideas and a sympathetic imagination for all the facts of life and the thoughts of men, rather than a hoarder of an indiscriminate mass of intellectual wealth." [107] They wanted direct answers to practical problems and eschewed the personal equation for the "dry light of science." Modern learning was revered for its "matter-of-fact, mechanical complexion" and for leaning on "statistically dispassionate tests and formulations." [108] The "new sociological course" was hailed as proving more than a substitute for the classics in the success with which it eliminated all bias of personality from the technique and study of the problems of modern life. "Those who bemoan the fate of the classics," wrote Bourne, "forget that a host of interesting courses have been introduced into the colleges of late years which provide much the discipline that the old curricula did, but which are vital and timely and of real significance to the life about the college man—courses in modern literatures, economics and politics, history and sociology." [109]

As befitted a prophet of the new radicalism, William James joined with the younger generation in criticism of higher education. He, too, opposed the lecture system on grounds that it did not consider the needs of the individual student; but the main target of his criticism was what he called "The Ph.D. Octopus." Writing in the *Harvard Monthly* for 1903, James castigated the "decidedly grotesque tendency" of colleges and universities to effect a "Doctor-Monopoly" in teaching, and he decried the academic snobbery that was bringing about a situation "in which no man of science or letters will be accounted respectable unless some kind of badge or diploma is stamped upon him, and in which bare personality will be a mark of outcast estate." Undue reverence for the doctoral degree, said James, not only interfered with the free development of talent, transferring value from the essential qualities of the teacher to an outward badge, but diverted the attention of aspiring youth from direct dealings with truth to the passing of examinations. It was his opinion that because of their snobbery and cultural exclusiveness, the institutions of higher learning were losing influence over public opinion in the United States. Unless the colleges achieved a "robuster tone," he feared they would lose their social function to popular media, especially to the dynamic new magazines which with extraordinary skill and success had become a new educational power.[110]

Yet if James was a radical in philosophy, he was only mildly progressive or even conservative in educational matters. Although he more than anyone else brought modern psychology into the classroom—nine-tenths of the teachers who studied any psychology at all in the years between 1890 and 1910 probably read James—he did not agree with Dewey about the social or democratic goals of education. While not blind to the social purposes of education, James had little patience with modern pedagogical methods, viewing education as an affair that worked itself out between the individual and his opportunities. A defender of the "Schoolmaster" theory of education, he likened the schoolroom to a battlefield on which the teacher by divination or perception, "not psychological pedagogics or theoretic strategy," won the mind of his enemy, the pupil. Like Dewey, he recognized the value of habits, but for conservative rather than practical reasons. "Habit is . . . the enormous fly-wheel of society, its most precious conservative agent. It alone is what keeps us all within the bounds of ordinance, and saves the children of fortune from the envious uprisings of the poor." [111]

Along with psychologist G. Stanley Hall, founder of the child-study movement, James believed social problems would be solved by raising better individuals. An aristocrat by birth and temperament, he took an elitist view of democracy: "The notion that a people can run itself and its affairs anonymously is now well known to be the silliest of absurdities. Mankind does nothing save through initiatives on the part of inventors, great or small, and imitation by the rest of us. Individuals of genius show the way, and set the patterns, which common people then adopt and follow." [112] Accordingly, in line with his belief that democracy demanded the best leadership, James contended that the social function of higher education was to cultivate an intellectual aristocracy conversant with the great inheritance of the past.°

Although unfashionable, the views of James and his generation

° William James, *The Social Value of the College-Bred.* See p. 305.

were not without justification. Once it was thought that a cultivated mind, a free imagination, an acquaintance with the past,
its triumphs and failures, were somehow great and good things of
themselves, making for a full and noble life. Such a life was open
to only a privileged few; but, as Ralph Barton Perry observed, the
important thing was that it was regarded as a privilege. Now that
it was so much more easily attained, higher education not only
seemed to be losing its meaning, but there was danger, said Perry,
that the very same forces of opinion that made it possible for
everybody to be usefully educated might prevent anybody from
being liberally educated.[113] The "excessive contemporaneity,"
which in More's words dragged the student "through the slums
of sociology, instead of making him at home with the noble dead,"
threatened to isolate American youth from his accumulated inheritance and leave him, narrow and unbalanced, a prey to the
passion of the hour.[114]

The unique and indispensable value of a liberal education, its
supporters agreed, was that it brought youth abreast of progress.
By taking a long look backward, each succeeding generation was
enabled to see the direction taken and the place reached. Or, as
Perry put it, it was like a relay race between those who are coming
of age today, those who came of age yesterday, and those who
will come of age tomorrow: "When one's turn comes, one has to
touch the last runner in order to take up the race in his stead,
inheriting at the start the advantage that he and others before him
have earned." [115] The value of liberal studies was not, as Santayana
said, "to recover a dead past in its trivial detail," or "to make us
grow sentimental over its remoteness, its beauty, and its ruins,"
but to want to be as wonderful as the Greeks were without copying
their way of being wonderful.[116]

The New Social Issue

In remaking American society, the new radicalism proposed to
outdo the Greeks, to create, in fact, a new civilization unlike any
that had ever existed before. Contending that history repeats itself
only when economic conditions remain static, radical theorists
pointed out that the industrial changes of the last half century in

the United States had utterly transformed the economic environment of civilization, thus nullifying the traditional assumption that universal "laws" would invariably produce like social results. In fact, it was argued, the present was so different from the past that a new social philosophy was needed to explain it.

A higher civilization was regarded as a possibility to be realized by people living in the twentieth century, but its emergence depended upon a change of opinions, ideals and institutions—in short, an ideological shift from the past to the present. As Simon Patten, most radical of the new economists emphasized, the peculiar inaptitude of traditional economic principles to the modern situation was due to the fact that they had been acquired in a primitive economy where a lack of productive power, the ability to satisfy basic needs, made avoidance of pain, of hunger and cold, the requisite for survival. Since the days of Adam Smith and David Ricardo, however, the relation of man to his physical and material environment had been drastically altered. Because of its tremendous productive power, the American economy had already emerged from the pain-deficit to the pleasure-surplus stage of human progress. Ideologically, however, Americans still clung to the perverse morality of a pain economy under the stubborn delusion that the dismal world of Ricardo and the nineteenth-century economists was their world. Accordingly, their social and economic outlook was essentially negative: they tended to be concerned more with the imaginary consequences of bad acts than the good results of praiseworthy acts and to worry more about future evils than present welfare.

"Our children's children may learn with amazement," wrote Patten in 1907, "how we thought it a natural social phenomenon that men should die in their prime, leaving wives and children in terror of want; that accidents should make an army of maimed dependents; that there should not be enough houses for workers; and that epidemics should sweep away multitudes as autumn frost sweeps away summer insects. They will wonder that the universal sadness of such a world should have appealed to our transient sympathies but did not absorb our widest interests. They will ask why there was some hope of succor for those whose miseries passed for a moment before the eyes of the tender-hearted, but none for the dwellers beyond the narrow horizon within which pity moves. And they will be unable to put themselves in our places, because the new social philosophy which we are this moment framing will have so moulded their minds that they cannot return to the philosophy that moulds ours." [117]

Taking the pragmatic view that economics rested not on absolute principles but was a reflection in thought of the environments in which men have lived, the new economists found the classical model of economic reality obsolete and irrelevant. Society, they insisted, was not a branch of physics, and the laws governing the social universe were not the same as those ruling the planets. They showed the accepted rules of economic behavior to be not natural laws but social laws imposed by outmoded views. Because the classical economists had lived in an age when the discovery of physical laws had dominated thought, they had modeled economics on physical science, beginning their economic investigations from the point of view of nature, not man. Their so-called "science", as a result, was not a study of man's activities but of the conditions that supposedly limited the actions of men. Of the many errors springing from this one-sided view, none was greater than the ignoring of man's subjective motives—his hopes, desires and intelligence. Except for his all-motivating selfishness, man, like the planets, was believed to be ruled by inflexible "natural" laws which were actually reflections in theory of current social and economic prejudices. In a theoretic world based chiefly upon physical standards in which hedonistic impulses of pleasure and pain were brought in only as modifying conditions, man subjectively was not considered a prime mover. Held in theoretic subjugation to nature, said Veblen, he was portrayed as "a lightning calculator of pleasures and pains" oscillating "like a homogeneous globule of desire" under the impulse of external stimuli. Once the impact was spent, he came to rest, "a self-contained globule of desire" as before. Treated as "an isolated, definitive human datum," man spun helplessly about his own spiritual axis, a victim of purported "laws" which he himself conceived. [118]

In place of this dismal picture, Patten offered a new approach in which man, instead of victim, would be the central point and moving factor in economic affairs. Since the progress of civilization

Freedom in twentieth-century industrial society, said new radicals, consisted not merely of political rights but was also dependent on certain economic and social rights, among which were the right to a comfortable home and wholesome surroundings, which the conventional wisdom denied to the majority of Americans.   Culver Pictures, Inc.

had made obvious the growing supremacy of man over nature, he was convinced there was no natural limitation on progress. Because the older economists had traditionally thought in terms of an objective environment, they had believed nature so niggard and its surplus so small that no radical improvement in social relations was possible. But they had been proven entirely wrong by American industry, which had demonstrated that productive power was subject to the law of increasing rather than decreasing returns and that productive power depended more on human ingenuity— capital, machinery, and inventions—than upon the material environment. Increased industrial efficiency, moreover, was being used to supply new wants of greater intensity instead of supplying old wants more completely, an unexpected state of affairs which led Patten to the unorthodox conclusion that improvements in consumption may contribute as much to economic progress as improvements in production.

Patten's unconventional attitudes led to excited commentary in the popular press. In a much discussed address in 1913, he was accused of subverting the basic article of capitalist faith by saying that in a consumption-oriented economy such as the United States, the nonsaver was a higher type than the saver. "It is foolish for persons to scrimp and save. It is argued that they are endeavoring to put something aside for a rainy day, for old age. But it is not the individual's place to do this. It is the community's." Under modern conditions, he told his shocked audience, extravagance was not a vice but a virtue. "It is no evidence of loose morality when a stenographer, earning eight or ten dollars a week, appears dressed in clothing that takes nearly all of her earnings to buy. It is a sign of her growing moral development"—and, he implied, her innate appreciation of her new role as consumer. Outraged by what they regarded as academic absurdities, true believers not only sprang to defense of thrift and the virtuous working-girl, but—innocent before the approaching millenium of installment buying and credit cards—they scoffed at the notion that any right-thinking American could be induced to buy now and pay later.

Where earlier theorists had been concerned with a nearly static economy in which man and his wants were assumed to be fixed, Patten conceived of a dynamic economy based upon progressive changes in the objective and subjective environments. Reasoning that the laws of consumption, unlike the physical laws of production, were expressions of human nature and as such were not only capable of modification but were continually being altered, he came to the conclusion that in an advanced technological society, differences in men—their use of natural forces, their purposes and outlook—were more important in explaining economic phenomena than differences in nature. Since the industrial activities and consumption of men were directed by their wants and not by obstacles set by nature, the economic environment must accordingly change progressively with changes in men. Each change in economic environment, moreover, reacted upon men through their consumption, forming new standards of life which acted upon men's social outlook and, in turn, created new motives in production. This pragmatic process, the continuous interaction between subjective and objective environments, was for Patten the key to social change and the means by which men might progress or regress.

Though believing progress must come through a social reconstruction of ideals in accordance with the economic environment, Patten did not advocate a dogmatic solution. Marxism was to him a reversion to primitive class antagonisms, and, as with classical economics, its economic determinism stood in the way of constructive efforts to reorganize society in harmony with new conditions. The problem, as he saw it, was not what were the facts or arguments valid in 1848, but what were the conclusions warranted by facts in 1912. What existed here and now in a thousand observable forms was what he called "voluntary socialism." "Every industry has changed from an antagonistic or individualistic form to one of voluntary cooperation. Social movements are on a voluntary basis from which observations may be made revealing the methods and results of social cooperation. Progress has not forced social groups into distinct classes, each with a bundle of interests to defend, but each interest has been made effective by the formation of a special group to promote it. We are all in many groups in each of which there are new faces. Our foes are not groups of antagonistic men, but incompetence, mismanagement and maladjustment." [119] His first axiom of social advance was: "Never take the chance of conflict when compromise is open." To avoid coercive state socialism, Patten urged that this principle be applied to social problems. The way of freedom was to socialize contending forces by ensuring and encouraging a diffusion of interest, so that there were large groups and strong groups but no dominating group. Freedom in twentieth-century industrial society, he argued, consisted not merely of political rights but was also dependent on social rights freely recognized and universally granted by each man to his fellow citizens. But while the rights upon which political freedom depended had been already worked out, there was no modern social or economic equivalent. Just as it had been necessary for national stability in 1789 to buttress individual liberty by adding a bill of political rights to the Constitution, so in 1912, Patten contended, an economic bill of rights was needed to prevent suppression of weak groups by the strong.°

Taking issue with this "sentimental philosophy" of reform, William Graham Sumner, representative of the older generation of economists, challenged all attempts to adjust classical theory

° Simon N. Patten, *A Social Bill of Rights*. See p. 309.

to social progress. The effect of such speculations, asserted the Yale professor, was to spread an easy optimism by suggesting that men could plan great steps in progress in academies and universities, and then realize them by resolution. He was especially perturbed by the pervasive influence of socialism. After 1900, nearly all American reformers, Progressives as well as doctrinaire Marxists, exhibited some socialistic elements in their thinking and ideals. Plainly as an arouser of emotions, if not as a practical political platform, socialism had proved a success in America. Its sentimental aspects were propagated by literary socialists such as William Dean Howells and Upton Sinclair, while its infectious economic doctrines were woven into the social criticism of Henry Demarest Lloyd and Richard T. Ely. Collegiate socialism was in vogue at all the better colleges and universities and colored the thinking of many young radicals, including Lippmann and Bourne. Socialism supplied the critique, if not the technique, for much Progressive reform; and though not always recognized, its effect was felt in all social sciences. Ten years before, Auguste Comte had been the hero of American sociologists; now Marx was hailed by Professor Albion Small as the Galileo of social science.

In Sumner's opinion, it was an intellectual affectation to consider "thought" a force and to suppose that sentiment and feeling might control society. Ideas might determine the direction in which force was to be exerted, but they were not forces able to produce results. The idea of socialism, for example, was no new thing. In one form or another it was to be found throughout all history: "It arises from an observation of certain harsh facts in the lot of man on earth, the concrete expression of which is poverty and misery." And yet, despite generations of sentimental philosophers, there had never been a period in history when there was not a "social problem." "The truth is that the social order is fixed by laws of nature precisely analogous to those of the physical order." The most man could do was by ignorance and self-conceit to mar the operation of social laws. In fact, the evils of society were to a great extent the result of the self-interest and sentimentalism of statesmen and philosophers who in the past had done just what the radicals and Socialists wanted to do now. Instead of realizing that men were bound by social laws as by physical laws, they assumed they could organize society as they chose, with the result that society was burdened with foolish theories and mischievous institutions it would take centuries of scientific study to eliminate.

"Let us not delude ourselves with any impossible hopes," Sumner advised Americans. "The social enterprise of reorganizing society in order to change what is harsh and sad in it is as impossible as a plan for changing the physical order." ° Man, he insisted, was born under the necessity of struggling for survival. "Let it be understood that we cannot go outside of this alternative: liberty, inequality, survival of the fittest; not-liberty, equality, survival of the unfittest. The former carries society forward and favors all its best members; the latter carries society downwards and favors all its worst members." Though captivating, the notion that man had economic rights was absurd because it led logically to the senseless conclusion that "a man has a natural right to whatever he needs and that the measure of his claims is the wishes he wants fulfilled." [120]

The case made by Sumner against the social reformer was convincing—if one shared his prejudices. On more objective grounds, however, it was apparent that if Patten was overly optimistic and "sentimental," then Sumner was, in his own pessimistic way, unrealistic and blinded by dogma. For he had only to look about him to see that men were changing the physical and social order radically. Right before his eyes the new capitalists were "organizing society as they chose" but, as the new radicals rightfully reproached them, without really making up their minds about what kind of society they wanted to make. Likewise, the realism of Sumner's view that the social burden imposed by the demand for economic rights would subtract from the product of society and crush the producer was challenged by the existence of a tangible and ever expanding surplus created by technological acceleration. But perhaps the most unrealistic aspect of Sumner's dogmatism was his narrow interpretation of "the facts of human life." Virtually denying any motivation except the bleak struggle for survival, he overlooked the fact that in modern industrial America the struggle was no longer a struggle against nature— technology had already won that battle—but the struggle of man

° William Graham Sumner, *The New Social Issue.* See p. 315.

against man for an equitable share of the growing social surplus. Since there was more than enough to establish a minimum standard of life below which no human being need fall, the real battle, as Patten insisted, was no longer against the natural factors of poverty and misery but against the social chaos that unnecessarily perpetuated poverty and misery. If young Americans were to face the issues of their generation squarely, they could not trust to the irresponsible policy of drift recommended by Sumner, but must follow Patten's advice. They must learn to use the new economic power and direct it toward fruitful ends.

The New Politics

Almost anyone brought up on Aristotle, Locke, and the classic thinkers of the eighteenth and nineteenth centuries would have found the political speculations of the early twentieth century unintelligible. Not only had natural rights been abandoned as a sham and an arbitrary fiction, but most of the old problems, well defined distinctions, and cumulative wisdom of the past seemed to have been discarded in favor of a new dispensation under which the primacy of the individual and his rights gave way to that of the group and its demand for social justice. With the old principles and faiths gone, one was plunged into a sea of new problems, as Herbert Schneider remarked, "without chart, compass or anchor and with naught but new waves for an horizon." [121]

Whether one regarded these new developments with fear or hope, the fact remained that political thought had cut loose from old moorings and launched out into unexplored depths. Under the influence of Pragmatism, American radicals formulated, in Schneider's words, "a theory of democracy not merely as a form of government but also as a mode of associated living, based on the ideas that individuality and freedom are themselves social products and that a democratic society is one which subordinates its institutions to the basic aim of permitting its members to grow intellectually and emotionally by widening their 'areas of shared concern,' by promoting means of communication and public expression, and by giving all a responsible participation in the processes of social and physical control." [122] According to this radical concept, society was merely a collective term for all sorts of associations into which people entered for all kinds of purposes, and the state was merely one more form of association. In fact, there was a tendency to identify the common good with non-political rather than political types of association. The state, to use Dewey's analogies, was supreme or sovereign only in the sense that the conductor of an orchestra or the umpire of a ball game or the traffic policeman are sovereign—that is, merely instrumental but subordinate to the music, the game, the traffic, the demos. The state had therefore no ends of its own and existed solely to serve the multifarious ends of various social groups.

As radical theorists saw it, the major problem in a pluralistic society such as the United States was no longer the relation between the individual and the group, but the relations of groups to each other. Though the continuity of society depended upon the preservation of a flexible balance among its parts ennabling the various interests to be carried on with the least amount of friction between them, the increasing ability of parts of the community to gratify important but selfish needs through technical progress was seen as a threat to the integrity and balance of both individual and social life. Under the traditional political and economic systems, the surplus values created by new techniques, which should have added much to the heritage of society as a whole, had been used chiefly and sometimes exclusively to satisfy the special needs of a comparatively few people. "The result," wrote Croly, "has been a forced growth of moral and social particularism. Those who reaped the benefit of technical progress were reluctant to consider its fruits as anything but their own property. Those who believed themselves dispossessed could see no way of socializing the surplus save by anti-social agitation and even violence." [123] Since this country was undergoing a process of quick and radical transformation which most of its official leaders were insufficiently prepared to understand and control, it was imperative, if society were not to be torn to pieces by irreconcilable class enmities, to harness the forces generated by the capitalist revolution for the purposes of society as a whole.

What was needed was a new and improved technique of social progress. To a man, the new radicals—Bourne, Brooks, Croly,

Dewey, Lippmann, Patten, Veblen, Weyl—believed humanity could attain mastery over the social processes. Before conscious social purpose could prevail, however, they felt it necessary to study particular social processes and problems as concretely and as practically as physical and biological processes had already been studied. Through the invention and use of its own experimental methods, social science was to seek an increasing understanding of social processes for the sake of exercising an increasing control over their subsequent behavior. Only in this way could mankind acquire the technique of social progress which it needed to make headway against the increasingly formidable organization of social particularism and reaction.

Although there was nothing very startling about the idea of social control—Comte had suggested as much early in the nineteenth century—its radicalism was implicit in its modernism. For where Comte had posited social control within the mechanistic framework of a beneficent natural order, modern exponents acknowledged no governance except conscious social impulse. Instead of seeking social truth by contemplating the order of things, their intent was to create by practical experimentation the experience upon which contemplation feeds. As the sociological pioneer Albion Small observed, men used to try to better themselves within the condition in which their lot was cast, but they now tried to better the condition itself. "They are not content with getting better wages. They want to overthrow the wage system. They do not stop with plans to provide for a rainy day. They want to abolish the rainy day. They are not content with conjugal fidelity. They want to reconstruct the family. They are not satisfied with improvements in the working of governments. They want to eliminate governments. They look with contempt upon adjustment of relations between social classes. They want to obliterate social classes." [124] With achievement now measured in terms of human happiness, no natural or supernatural power drew invisible but impassable lines beyond which they must not pursue their desires.

Radical emphasis on change of conditions rather than upon adjustment to conditions required a new moral outlook. Having rejected belief in a fixed moral order, men were urged to manufacture their own morality to suit their needs and desires. The moral problem ceased to be that of conforming to one's lot, and became one of being rational, of modifying individual conduct through intelligent action. This change in outlook, said Bourne, destroyed the old antithesis between good and evil. "We see life now rather as an incalculable and importunate stream of desire, which rises in the adult to a will-to-power. The problem of the soul becomes the direction of this desire and energy into creative channels. . . . In such a world, personality becomes more desirable than character, creative expressiveness than self-control, cooperation than justice, social freedom than rights." [125] The older moralists had believed the desires themselves were inherently evil; the new radicals, under the impetus of Freud, saw them as "energies of the soul," neither good nor bad in themselves. Much the same energies, they alleged, produced crime and civilization, lust and love, insanity and religion. Evil was merely one form of desire, not the nature of it. Desires, like dynamite, were capable of all sorts of uses, and it was the business of society to transmute these energies into fine values.

Accordingly, under the new outlook, the burden of evil fell not on the individual but society. Modern social scientists no longer thought that human beings were born with a set of commandments etched upon the soul. As evidence accumulated on the startling contrasts in the moral ideas of different times and peoples, it became clear, as Professor Edward A. Ross pointed out, that "sin evolves along with society," [126] or as young Lippmann put it, "Our conscience is not the vessel of eternal verities. It grows with our social life, and a new social condition means a radical change in conscience." [127] Since man's inherited equipment for good conduct was not dependable, the new radicals proposed to do away with evil by "sublimating" men's desires, taming their passions by supplying them with civilized outlets.

Instead of answering sin with a prohibition, Lippmann suggested a "moral equivalent" of evil as a guidepost to modern statemanship. "Social systems like ours," he wrote, "which do not even feed and house men and women, which deny pleasure, cramp play, ban adventure, propose celibacy and grind out monotony, are a clear confession of sterility in statesmanship." He considered it paradoxical that the people who were the first to decry every radical proposal as "against human nature," were the same who were in the absurd predicament of trying to still human wants with petty taboos. To find for evil its moral equivalent was, on the other hand, "to turn to the establishment of positively good things instead of trying simply to check bad ones, to emphasize the additions to life, instead of the restrictions upon it, to substitute, if you like, the love of heaven for the fear of hell." Such a program meant to him the dignified utilization of the whole nature of man because it recognized as the first test of all political systems and moral codes whether or not they were "against human nature." Politics, however pretentiously rhetorical about ideals, he regarded as irrelevant, "if the only method it knows is to ostracize the desires it cannot manage."

In sum, modern times demanded a new order of political values. From the radical viewpoint, the deepest error of American political thinking had been to consider political institutions as mechanically constructed contrivances above and beyond the men who made and lived under them. The government of the United States, as Woodrow Wilson pointed out, was a striking example of this machine conception of politics. Its checks and balances were a sort of unconscious copy of Newton's self-regulating mechanism of the heavens. But the object of democracy, Lippmann indignantly protested, was not to imitate the rhythm of the stars but to harness political power to human needs. Democratic politics must always make man the measure of all things. Every abstraction, every rule of conduct, every constitution, every law and social arrangement, was merely an instrument, deriving its value solely from its usefulness to human feelings and wants. To consider politics on any other terms than the pragmatic was, in Lippmann's opinion, to give in to idol worship.* American politics—reform or conservative—was enslaved to its own idols, bowing down to fixed ideas and exalted abstractions. If American politicians were to become creative statesmen, they must recognize that the business of politics was to provide opportunities, not to announce ultimate values; to remove oppressive evil and to invent new resources for living.[128]

Though Lippmann and his youthful cohorts might think they had blasted the rock of ages, there were many Americans—on the

* Walter Lippmann, *The New Politics*. See p. 319.

whole exemplary and fairly intelligent citizens—to whom the sacredness of property, the divinity of the constitution, Victorian sentiment, individual conscience, the Republican party, and John D. Rockefeller were still the dominant forces in their not altogether benighted world. Whether standpatters or Progressives, they were not yet willing to risk all for a newly declared "freedom" which, as the *Nation* said, seemed to place the will on the throne of the universe, "wholly autonomous, wholly creative, wholly loosed from the trammels of a past which concerns it not, and wholly lord of a future which lies at its feet." [129] They found this creed a "sociological nightmare," unsafe in all practical senses and infused with that "curious credulity" which to them was so distinguishing a feature of modern "advanced" thought.[130]

Though purporting to wish youth well in its commendable if thankless task of regenerating the human race, the older generation was more than skeptical of a doctrine that proposed to convert ethics into a science and politics into a highway to paradise. Sometimes the proponents of change seemed to them a frantic mob of "men and women who call themselves 'Progressives' without being able to read a pedometer; anarchists who, with less sense than bulls, mistake a red flag for a new Gospel; propagandists of peace who have no respect for rest; advocates of nostrums who actually resent being called quacks; women who rejoice in being 'hikers'; philanthropists who are doing their foolish best to make the underdog a mad one; lecturers who convert their lungs into cash; fashionable women who open their drawing-rooms to cranks, and their heads to whims." [131] Tired of being censured for their backward ways and beliefs, bored with the railings of "amateur sociologists," and fatigued with lectures, civic forums and suffrage teas, many would-be Progressives began to backslide.

An outspoken critic of the new politics was Paul Elmer More, a conservative editor of the *Nation* and after 1914 a professor at Princeton. Though not a Progressive, he shared their conservative bias. His view of human nature, like Freud's, was that it was at bottom a very primitive thing—but there the resemblance ended. Instead of bewailing the fact that traditional political institutions stood above human feelings and appetites, he believed that was as it should be. For he was convinced that, if society were not to be torn apart by the restless passions of the day, artificial restraints were necessary to curb the impulsive and self-seeking nature of man. Order required not only a controlling power from above but also, in accordance with the wise precedents of nature, a just subordination of inferior to superior. Justice, accordingly, did not consist primarily in the struggle for equality, but in an equitable distribution of power and benefits conforming to individual character and intelligence. In opposition to the "current cant of humanitarianism," which insisted the main purpose of government was to raise the material welfare of the masses, More held stubbornly to the Platonic view that the true aim of society was to create advantages for the upward striving of the exceptional.° The cure for democracy, to his thinking, was not *more* democracy, but *better* democracy.[132]

As the ablest spokesman for classic social philosophy, More came under vituperative attack by the new radicals. He and a Princeton colleague, Irving Babbitt, were, Lewis Mumford recalled, "effigies that we dragged mercilessly through the streets, attacked with the daggers of revolt, and on occasion made a bonfire of. . . . If we wanted to swear hard we said 'Babbitt!' 'More!'" Yet, as his critics were among the first to concede, if society had become too timid in the face of "a growling Demos" to express itself so uncompromisingly, at least it continued to act just as if it endorsed the political and moral philosophy which More courageously expounded.[133]

The Present Belongs to the Living

If the rising generation rejected the old values of America as "shabby and bloodless and worn out," it was in the hope that this country might in the future be able to give something to the world that was better than what was too generally meant by Americanism—"the worship of size, mass, quantity, and numbers." To young radicals the great failing of America was its lack of a genuine social ideal. Because Americans had been too wrapped up in the acquisitive life, their social creativity was stifled and their moral sense dulled. The American will, as a result, had succumbed to

Paul Elmer More, *The Rock of Ages*. See p. 325.

the creeping paralysis of technology, accepting machinery and more machinery and still more machinery as a *fait accompli* and had seemingly, as young Brooks lamented, given up all hope of determining the rational place of machinery in life.[134]

In vigorous revolt against the deadening mechanistic theories of the past, the radicals strove to free the American will from the inhibitions of tradition and through sublimation to convert the acquisitive instinct into a splendid new social instrument. Perhaps they had, as it seemed to some, "swallowed whole and not digested too many of the 'visions' of Mr. H. G. Wells." [135] But rather than engaging in wholesale dogmatism, they had merely advocated retail experiment. Recognizing that they lived in a new age of surplus value, economic and spiritual, they sought only to reassert Jefferson's dictum: "The present belongs to the living." They were not always practical. It was probably true, as alleged, that Lippmann would have made an "abominable alderman." [136] Yet the perspicuous Lippmann, like Croly and Weyl, veered from Marxian verbalism to the actualities of American political life. While American youth "beat the gong of revolt," they were for the most part realistically aware, as Bourne said, that "all we can ever do in the way of good to people is to encourage them to do good to themselves." [137]

Yet if, in the unsettled world of modernity, youth could no longer invoke monumental creeds, their new world of chance was also a world of new possibilities. If there was no lamp post to embrace in a giddy and reeling universe, neither must man stand pat at the mercy of brutal forces beyond his control. With the intellectual center of gravity on earth and not somewhere out in the cosmos far removed from human experience, there was increased control—and increased responsibility. Rather than robbing life of its guarantees, it was far truer to agree with Lippmann that those who attacked absolutism had only robbed absolutism of its excuse.[138] Theory located within life instead of reigning statically supreme over it, meant, as Dewey asserted, human practice was to be made responsible to human intelligence. Men no longer could shift the blame onto eternal principles; men from now on must find within themselves the certainty the external world had lost.[139]

Readings: The New Radicalism

For Radicals

RANDOLPH S. BOURNE (1886–1918)   *A cripple with a bent back
and twisted face, Bourne was the intellectual hero of the new
radicalism. At Columbia, where he was a brilliant if contentious
student, he engaged in a lone, bitter war on behalf of the
university's underpaid and overworked scrubwomen. His savage
intensity later was to win him an ardent following among the
young. Not one to wait until others were ready, he leaped into
the center of controversy, attacking the existing systems of
education, capitalism, militarism and government, but neither
repeating "the stale dogmas of Marxism" nor self-consciously
seeking martyrdom. His radicalism was a restless, controversial
criticism of current ideas and a hammering out of some clear-
sighted philosophy.*

The great social movement of yesterday and today and tomorrow
has hit us of the younger generation hard. Many of us were early
converted to a belief in the possibilities of a regenerated social
order, and to a passionate desire to do something in aid of that
regeneration. The appeal is not only to our sympathy for the weak
and exploited, but also to our delight in a healthy, free, social life,
to an artistic longing for a society where the treasures of civilization may be open to all, and to our desire for an environment where
we ourselves will be able to exercise our capacities, and exert the
untrammeled influences which we believe might be ours and our
fellows'. All these good things the social movement seems to
demand and seems to offer, and its appeal is irresistible. Before
the age of machinery was developed, or before the structure of
our social system and the relations between classes and individuals
were revealed, the appeal might have been merely sentimental.
But it is no longer so. The aims of the social movement today seem
to have all the tremendous power of a practicable ideal. To the

From *Youth and Life* (Boston: Houghton Mifflin Co., 1913), pp. 291–93, 295–96,
302–10. Reprinted by courtesy of the publishers.

satisfactions which its separate ideals give to all the finer instincts of men is added the overwhelming conviction that those satisfactions are most of them realizable here and now by concerted methods which are already partly in operation and partially successful. It is this union of the idealistic and the efficient that gives the movement its hold on the disinterested and serious youth of today.

With that conversion has necessarily come the transvaluation of many of our social values. No longer can we pay the conventional respect to success or join in the common opinions of men and causes. The mighty have been pulled down from their seats, and those of low degree exalted. We feel only contempt for college presidents, editors, and statesmen who stultify their talents and pervert their logical and historical knowledge in defending outworn political philosophies and economic codes. We can no longer wholly believe in the usefulness or significance of those teachers and writers who show themselves serenely oblivious to the social problems. We become keen analysts of the society around us; we put uncomfortable questions to our sleek and successful elders. We criticize the activities in which they engage, the hitherto sacred professions and businesses, and learn to distinguish carefully between actually productive work for society, work which makes for the material and spiritual well-being of the people for whom it is done, and parasitic or wasteful work, which simply extends the friction of competition, or lives on the labor or profits of others. We distinguish, too, between the instruction and writing that consists in handing down unexamined and uncriticized moral and political ideas, and ideas that let in the fresh air and sunlight to the thick prejudices of men. We come to test the papers we read, the teachers we learn from, the professional men we come into contact with, by these new standards. . . .

The young radical, then, in such a situation and in possession of these new social values, stands on the verge of his career in a mood of great perplexity. Two questions he must answer: "What is to be done?" and "What must I do?" If he has had an education and is given a real opportunity for the choice of a vocation, his position is crucial. For his education, if it has been in one of the advanced universities, will have only tended to confirm his radical-

ism and render more vivid the contrast between the new philosophy which is being crystallized there out of modern science and
philosophy and the new interpretations of history and ethics, and
the obscurantist attitude of so many of our intellectual guardians.

The youth, ambitious and aggressive, desires an effective and
serviceable career, yet every career open to him seems a compromise with the old order. If he has come to see the law as an
attempt to fit immutable principles of social action on a dynamic
and evergrowing society; if he has come to see the church as an
organization working along the lines of greatest spiritual resistance,
preaching a personal where the world is crying for a social gospel;
if he has come to see higher education as an esoteric institution
of savants, only casually reaching down to touch the mass of people
with their knowledge and ideas; if he has come to see business
as a clever way of distributing unearned wealth, and the levying
of a refined tribute on the propertyless workers; if he has come
to see the press as devoted to bolstering up all these institutions
in their inefficiency and inertia;—if he has caught this radical vision
of the social institutions about him, he will find it hard to fit neatly
into any of them and let it set its brand upon him. It would seem
to be a treason not only to society but to his own best self. He
would seem to have become one of the vast conspiracy to keep
things as they are. He has spent his youth, perhaps, in studying
things as they are in order to help in changing them into things
as they ought to be, but he is now confronted with the question
how the change can be accomplished, and how he can help in
that accomplishment. . . .

The first concrete duty of every youth to whom social idealism
is more than a phrase is to see that he is giving back to society
as much as or more than he receives, and, moreover, that he is
a nourisher of the common life and not a drain upon its resources.
This was Tolstoy's problem, and his solution to the question—
"What is to be done?"—was—"Get off the other fellow's back!"
His duty, he found, was to arrange his life so that the satisfaction
of his needs did not involve the servitude or the servility of any
of his fellow men; to do away with personal servants, and with
the articles of useless luxury whose production meant the labor
of thousands who might otherwise have been engaged in some

productive and life-bringing work; to make his own living either directly from the soil, or by the coöperative exchange of services, in professional, intellectual, artistic, or handicraft labor. Splendidly sound as this solution is, both ethically and economically, the tragic fact remains that so inextricably are we woven into the social web that we cannot live except in some degree at the expense of somebody else, and that somebody is too often a man, woman, or even little child who gives grudgingly, painfully, a stint of labor that we may enjoy. We do not see the labor and the pain, and with easy hearts and quiet consciences we enjoy what we can of the good things of life; or, if we see the truth, as Tolstoy saw it, we still fancy, like him, that we have it in our power to escape the curse by simple living and our own labor. But the very food we eat, the clothes we wear, the simplest necessities of life with which we provide ourselves, have their roots somewhere, somehow, in exploitation and injustice. It is a cardinal necessity of the social system under which we live that this should be so, where the bulk of the work of the world is done, not for human use and happiness, but primarily and directly for the profits of masters and owners. We are all tainted with the original sin; we cannot escape our guilt. And we can be saved out of it only by the skill and enthusiasm which we show in our efforts to change things. . . .

The solution of these dilemmas of radical youth will, therefore, not come from a renunciation of the personality or a refusal to participate actively in life. Granted the indignation at our world as it is, and the vision of the world as it might and ought to be, both the heightening of all the powers of the personality and a firm grappling with some definite work-activity of life are necessary to make that indignation powerful and purging, and to transmute that vision into actual satisfaction for our own souls and those of our fellows. It is a fallacy of radical youth to demand all or nothing, and to view every partial activity as compromise. Either engage in something that will bring revolution and transformation all at one blow, or do nothing, it seems to say. But compromise is really only a desperate attempt to reconcile the irreconcilable. It is not compromise to study to understand the world in which one lives, to seek expression for one's inner life, to work to harmonize it and make it an integer, nor is it compromise to work in some small sphere for the harmonization of social life and the relations between men who work together, a harmonization that will bring democracy into every sphere of life, industrial and social. . . .

The shock of the crassnesses and crudities of the modern social world thrown against the conventionally satisfying picture which that world has formed of itself makes any young life of purpose and sincerity a real peril and adventure. There are all sorts of spiritual disasters lying in wait for the youth who embarks on the perilous ocean of radicalism. The disapproval of those around him is likely to be the least of his dangers. It should rather fortify his soul than discourage him. Far more dangerous is it that he lose his way on the uncharted seas before him, or follow false guides to shipwreck. But the solution is not to stay at home, fearful and depressed. It is rather to cultivate deliberately the widest knowledge, the broadest sympathy, the keenest insight, the most superb skill, and then set sail, exulting in one's resources, and crowding on every inch of sail.

For if the radical life has its perils, it also has its great rewards. The strength and beauty of the radical's position is that he already to a large extent lives in that sort of world which he desires. Many people there are who would like to live in a world arranged in some sort of harmony with socialistic ideals, but who, believing they are impossible, dismiss the whole movement as an idle if delightful dream. They thus throw away all the opportunity to have a share in the extending of those ideals. They do not see that the gradual infiltration of those ideals into our world as it is does brighten and sweeten it enormously. They do not know the power and advantage of even their "little faith" which their inclinations might give them. But the faith of the radical has already transformed the world in which he lives. He sees the "muddle" around him, but what he actually feels and lives are the germs of the future. His mind selects out the living, growing ideas and activities of the socially fruitful that exist here and now, and it is with these that his soul keeps company; it is to their growth and cultivation that he is responsive. . . .

To live this life of his vision practically here in the present is thus the exceeding great reward of radical youth. And this life, so potent and glowing amongst the crude malignity of modern life, fortifies and stimulates him, and gives him the surety, which is ' sturdier than any dream or hope, of the coming time when this life will permeate and pervade all society instead of only a part.

Servants of the Future

FLOYD DELL (1887–   )   *A romantic idealist, sentimental and sensitive, Dell gravitated naturally to Greenwich Village where from 1914 to 1917 he was an associate editor of* The Masses. *Although one of the best-known literary figures in the Village, he was never a playboy nor much of a Bohemian, being rather shy and reserved by nature. A Socialist since boyhood, he was in complete sympathy with the new radicalism, yet was able a few years later to look back with objectivity upon those years of revolt.*

To the older generation, no doubt, the appearance of H. G. Wells upon the literary horizon was no very startling phenomenon.- He was to them a curious and ingenious inventor of "scientific fantasies," a kind of successor to Jules Verne. He wrote interestingly of airplaines, and Martians, and exploring the Moon. . . . But to us, in our decaying and autumnal world, his voice was the wild west wind, from whose presence the dead leaves of old esthetic creeds and pessimistic philosophies scattered "like ghosts from an enchanter fleeing"; a wind bearing winged seeds. . . . a Shelleyan wind, prophetic of the Spring. . . .

It was true; the old world was dying. Year by year it was drawing nearer to the agony of its catastrophe. We who were early readers of H. G. Wells were not among those who were surprised by the World War; we had read about it too often, and in too intimate detail, in his pages. We had faced in imagination not only its horror,

From *Intellectual Vagabondage* (New York: George H. Doran Co., 1926), pp. 222, 224–34. Reprinted by permission of the author.

but the famine, the economic ruin, and the political debacle which followed in its train. . . . It was true, too, that something new was coming to birth; and we could at least dimly glimpse that something through the smoke of ruin. . . .

The hugeness of that catastrophe, against the imagined flames of which we acted out our individual lives, did not make us small. Those flames lit our lives with their own beautiful and terrible light.

It was *our* future. We, accepting it, made it our own. Its secret was locked in our hearts, and our hands were dedicated to its service. We lived for it, and were thereby ennobled.

It may seem a little ridiculous, this dedication of our lives to the Future. It *was* a little ridiculous. But it gave us self-respect. We understood ourselves in relation to something besides our individual ambitions and our individual miseries. We were the happier in being able, under the H. G. Wells influence, to face with dignity, and with neither fear nor cynicism, the world in which we lived. We were able to expand the narrow boundaries of pessimistic estheticism, and to find nothing that is human alien to us. We developed that divinest because least selfish of man's passions, the passion of curiosity, to a pitch that gave promise of a new intellectual renascence. . . . But we were a little silly for all that.

We need not blame H. G. Wells for the fact, but it so happened that his heroes reproduced and held up to our esteem a quality which we all possessed, a quality which was an inheritance of our nineteenth-century training, and which peculiarly unfitted them, as it unfitted us, for service on behalf of the future. They were of the breed of Ibsen's tragic characters and Bernard Shaw's comic characters—the true nineteenth-century type which includes both industrial exploiters and artists. They were individualists par excellence—queer, lonely, self-opinionated, impulsive, erratic and ego-worshiping creatures, utterly undisciplined and incapable of getting along with other people except upon their own egregious terms. Regarded closely, every one of Mr. Wells' heroes is seen to be a crank, a curious and pathetic mixture of egotist and fool. If we were unable to perceive this, it was doubtless because we were so much of both ourselves. We did what we wanted to do, and thought about it afterward. And, as it happened, nothing in the world was so calculated to throw the glamour of righteousness over our impulsive follies as the notion that we were the servitors of the Future. . . .

The fact was, nobody in Mr. Wells' novels could ever have actually built or rebuilt anything; and no more could we. But we, like Mr. Wells' heroes, were admirably constituted to assist rapidly in the disintegration of existing society. Querulous and ignorant, in spite of our gospel of "love and fine thinking," we represented a generation which had endured a misbuilt civilization so long that we were destructive in all our instincts. We talked of order, but it was only as a justification for throwing more monkey-wrenches into the machinery of the existing system. Our monkey-wrenches were merely verbal, it is true, but they were not without their effect. For the intelligentsia of a given age both follows and leads the rest of society. We summed up and expressed the blind rage of the worker and the artist against a hideous civilization; and we gave a new power and definition to that rage by the words in which we uttered it. We had been dispossessed, we had nothing at stake; and suddenly we realized our power, and used it. . . . When a decaying order is about to collapse, it can still be held together for a time by the magic of words; but when the users of words are seeking to destroy rather than to conserve that order, its doom is dated. . . .

Yet if the ruin which we foretold had come suddenly, and out of its ruins there had commenced to emerge, crudely enough, a new kind of order, how would we who held these ideas have viewed that desperate attempt? With suspicion, for it would have been initiated by others than ourselves, and we would have been incapable of believing that salvation for the world could have come from other hands than our own. We would have continued to talk of "order," amidst that chaos, and from the point of view of our own ideal of perfection have sneered at the grimy labors of the real rebuilders of the world. We would have held aloof, and said, "This is not what we want."

It is a magnificent thing to be able to face the Future: but nothing in the influences which we were able to receive from the invigorating gospel of H. G. Wells was of a nature to enable us to face the Present.

Bernard Shaw seemed at first equally a friend of all our follies and an encourager of all our weaknesses. His profound vagabond antipathy to "romance," though taking the form of an apparently paradoxical Puritanism, won our hearts at the outset. And in the whole field of the sexual relationship, throughout his literary career, Shaw did not fail to reassure us in our erotic cowardices and cruelties, heroizing us to the top of our bent in a series of delightful vagabond lovers to whom the more serious or stable aspects of that relationship meant nothing in the world.

Nevertheless it was Bernard Shaw who first made us aware of our spiritual predicament with regard to that Future which in such odd ways we sought to serve. He showed us what the Future, which we sought to serve, would think of us. He made us realize that the Future, instead of putting up statues to us, would laugh at us. He made us laugh at ourselves.

Curiously enough, the older generation did not discover—has never discovered—what Shaw was making fun of. It supposed that Shaw was attacking the conventions. But Shaw was doing nothing of the sort—he was laughing at us for attacking the conventions so feebly and foolishly. He did not make fun of marriage. He made fun of those who thought they could easily invent something better than marriage. He did not heap his scorn upon capitalism, but rather upon those who thought they could destroy capitalism merely with fine words or fine emotions. He said: Jericho's walls are stronger than you think, and you will have to do more than march around it blowing your horn if you expect ever to take possession.

Because he spoke in our own dialect, he was regarded as a rebel; but he was rather our privileged satirist, permitted to tell us how foolish we are. In our own language he delivered to us the advice of a Methodist vestryman: High ideals are all very well, but it is necessary to learn to pay your debts; and when the real revolution comes, you will find your real leader telling you the same thing. You will have to work, and keep your account books straight, in the Future just as in the present; and if you don't do it in the Future the difference will be that instead of being admired for your "genius," you will be put in jail as a counterrevolutionary!

He seemed to say to us: Are you quite sure you want the Future, after all? You may not like it. And very possibly it may not like

you! You will probably be surprised to find how sober and industrious and respectable the Future will be. Revolutions have a way
of being highly moral, and real revolutionists are frequently people
of impeccably virtuous life. They haven't time to be anything else.
You may find the Future dull, you know!

To us, at this stage in our intellectual development, common
sense had the value of an epigram. And Bernard Shaw's common
sense brought us face to face with the question:

*Can you create a new civilization upon the ruins of the old?
Can you even get along in such a new civilization if someone else
creates it for you?*

Were we, in looking forward to a new world, indulging in the
same kind of illusions as our eighteenth-century great-grandfathers?
Would this new Revolution, like the last, bring realities different
from our dreams? And were we, by reason of our disillusionment
and chagrin, condemned to be unable to take part in the life of
the new age, but destined rather to turn back and seek refuge in
romantic dreams of the past? And, finally, how much blame for
that discrepancy might we lay upon that new world-order, and
how much upon ourselves?

The New Morality

MARGARET SANGER (1883–1966)   *A trained nurse and mother of
three, Mrs. Sanger was an inveterate activist who resisted "tame
domesticity" and set out to free womankind from the tyranny
of the unwanted baby. Not only had her own mother died after
having eleven children, but her work took her to New York's
East Side where she saw poor families overburdened with
children and treated horrifying cases of abortion. Resolved to
do something for these women, she launched her courageous
campaign for birth control. Through the dissemination of con-*

From *Woman and the New Race* (New York: Truth Publishing Co., 1920), pp.
167–70, 175, 177–79, 181, 184–85. Reprinted by permission of Coward-McCann,
Inc. Copyright 1920 by Brentano's; renewed 1948 by Margaret Sanger.

traceptual knowledge, she hoped to free woman from sexual
domination and to create a new sex morality.

Upon the shoulders of the woman conscious of her freedom rests
the responsibility of creating a new sex morality. The vital difference between a morality thus created by women and the so-called
morality of today, is that the new standard will be based upon
knowledge and freedom while the old is founded upon ignorance
and submission. . . .

We get most of our notions of sex morality from the Christian
church—more particularly from the oldest existing Christian
church, known as the Roman Catholic. The church has generally
defined the "immoral woman" as one who mates out of wedlock.
Virtually, it lets it go at that. In its practical workings, there is
nothing in the church code of morals to protect the woman, either
from unwilling submission to the wishes of her husband, from
undesired pregnancy, nor from any other of the outrages only too
familiar to many married women. Nothing is said about the crime
of bringing an unwanted child into the world, where often it cannot
be adequately cared for and is, therefore, condemned to a life of
misery. The church's one point of insistence is upon the right of
itself to legalize marriage and to compel the woman to submit
to whatever such marriage may bring. It is true that there are
remedies of divorce in the case of the state, but the church has
adhered strictly to the principle that marriage, once consummated,
is indissoluble. Thus, in its operation, the church's code of sex
morals has nothing to do with the basic sex rights of the woman,
but enforces, rather, the assumed property rights of the man to
the body and the services of his wife. They are man-made codes;
their vital factor, as they apply to woman, is submission to the
man.

Closely associated with and underlying the principle of submission, has been the doctrine that the sex life is in itself unclean.
It follows, therefore, that all knowledge of the sex physiology or
sex functions is also unclean and taboo. Upon this teaching has
been founded woman's subjection by the church and, largely
through the influence of the church, her subjection by the state
to the needs of the man.

Let us see how these principles have affected the development of the present moral codes and some of their shifting standards. When we have finished this analysis, we shall know why objectors to birth control raise the "morality" question.

The church has sought to keep women ignorant upon the plea of keeping them "pure." To this end it has used the state as its moral policeman. Men have largely broken the grip of the ecclesiastics upon masculine education. The ban upon geology and astronomy, because they refute the biblical version of the creation of the world, is no longer effective. Medicine, biology and the doctrine of evolution have won their way to recognition in spite of the united opposition of the clerics. So, too, has the right of woman to go unveiled, to be educated, and to speak from public platforms, been asserted in spite of the condemnations of the church, which denounced them as destructive of feminine purity. Only in sex matters has it succeeded in keeping the bugaboo alive. . . .

If Christianity turned the clock of general progress back a thousand years, it turned back the clock two thousand years for woman. Its greatest outrage upon her was to forbid her to control the function of motherhood under any circumstances, thus limiting her life's work to bringing forth and rearing children. Coincident with this, the churchmen deprived her of her place in and before the courts, in the schools, in literature, art and society. They shut from her heart and her mind the knowledge of her love life and her reproductive functions. They chained her to the position into which they had thrust her, so that it is only after centuries of effort that she is even beginning to regain what was wrested from her. . . .

Fear and shame have stood as grim guardians against the gate of knowledge and constructive idealism. The sex life of women has been clouded in darkness, restrictive, repressive and morbid. Women have not had the opportunity to know themselves, nor have they been permitted to give play to their inner natures, that they might create a morality practical, idealistic and high for their own needs.

On the other hand, church and state have forbidden women to leave their legal mates, or to refuse to submit to the marital embrace, no matter how filthy, drunken, diseased or otherwise repulsive the man might be—no matter how much of a crime it might be to bring to birth a child by him.

Woman was and is condemned to a system under which the lawful rapes exceed the unlawful ones a million to one. She has had nothing to say as to whether she shall have strength sufficient to give a child a fair physical and mental start in life; she has had as little to do with determining whether her own body shall be wrecked by excessive childbearing. She has been adjured not to complain of the burden of caring for children she has not wanted. Only the married woman who has been constantly loved by the most understanding and considerate of husbands has escaped these horrors. Besides the wrongs done to women in marriage, those involved in promiscuity, infidelities and rapes become inconsequential in nature and in number.

Out of woman's inner nature, in rebellion against these conditions, is rising the new morality. Let it be realized that this creation of new sex ideals is a challenge to the church. Being a challenge to the church, it is also, in less degree, a challenge to the state. The woman who takes a fearless stand for the incoming sex ideals must expect to be assailed by reactionaries of every kind. . . .

In spite of the age-long teaching that sex life in itself is unclean, the world has been moving to a realization that a great love between a man and woman is a holy thing, freighted with great possibilities for spiritual growth. The fear of unwanted children removed, the assurance that she will have a sufficient amount of time in which to develop her love life to its greatest beauty, with its comradeship in many fields—these will lift woman by the very soaring quality of her innermost self to spiritual heights that few have attained. Then the coming of eagerly desired children will but enrich life in all its avenues, rather than enslave and impoverish it as do unwanted ones today. . . .

Subversion of the sex urge to ulterior purposes has dragged it to the level of the gutter. Recognition of its true nature and purpose must lift the race to spiritual freedom. Out of our growing knowledge we are evolving new and saner ideas of life in general. Out of our increasing sex knowledge we shall evolve new ideals of sex. These ideals will spring from the innermost needs of women. They

will serve these needs and express them. They will be the foundation of a moral code that will tend to make fruitful the impulse
which is the source, the soul and the crowning glory of our sexual
natures.

The Repeal of Reticence

AGNES REPPLIER (1858–1950)   *A wise, witty and urbane essayist,*
Miss Repplier was no Victorian spinster. An insatiable interest
in life kept her involved in current affairs long after most of
her male contemporaries had retired to their pipes and armchairs.
Forthrightly disapproving of the modern tendency to force sex
education upon children, she was convinced a playground or
swimming pool would do more to keep them mentally and
morally sound than hours of fidgeting through lectures on
obstetrics.

There is nothing new about the Seven Deadly Sins. They are as
old as humanity. There is nothing mysterious about them. They
are easier to understand than the Cardinal Virtues. Nor have they
dwelt apart in secret places; but, on the contrary, have presented
themselves, undisguised and unabashed, in every corner of the
world, and in every epoch of recorded history. Why then do so
many men and women talk and write as if they had just discovered
these ancient associates of mankind? Why do they press upon our
reluctant notice the result of their researches? Why this fresh
enthusiasm in dealing with a foul subject? Why this relentless
determination to make us intimately acquainted with matters of
which a casual knowledge would suffice?

Above all, why should our self-appointed instructors assume that
because we do not chatter about a thing, we have never heard
of it? The well-ordered mind knows the value, no less than the
charm, of reticence. The fruit of the tree of knowledge, which is

From the *Atlantic Monthly*, CXIII (Feb., 1914), pp. 297–300. Reprinted by permission of the publisher.

now recommended as nourishing for childhood, strengthening for youth, and highly restorative for old age, falls ripe from its stem; but those who have eaten with sobriety find no need to discuss the processes of digestion. Human experience is very, very old. It is our surest monitor, our safest guide. To ignore it crudely is the error of those ardent but uninstructed missionaries who have lightly undertaken the rebuilding of the social world.

Therefore it is that the public is being daily instructed concerning matters which it was once assumed to know, and which, as a matter of fact, it has always known. When *The Lure* was being played at the Maxine Elliott Theatre in New York, the engaging Mrs. Pankhurst arose in Mrs. Belmont's box, and, unsolicited, informed the audience that it was the truth which was being nakedly presented to them, and that as truth it should be taken to heart. Now, it is probable that the audience—adult men and women—knew as much about the situations developed in *The Lure* as did Mrs. Pankhurst. It is possible that some of them knew more, and could have given her points. But whatever may be the standard of morality, the standard of taste (and taste is a guardian of morality) must be curiously lowered when a woman spectator at an indecent play commends its indecencies to the careful consideration of the audience. Even the absurdity of the proceeding fails to win pardon for its grossness. . . .

The "Conspiracy of Silence" is broken. Of that no one can doubt. The phrase may be suffered to lapse into oblivion. In its day it was a menace, and few of us would now advocate the deliberate ignoring of things not to be denied. Few of us would care to see the rising generation as uninstructed in natural laws as we were, as adrift amid the unintelligible, or partly intelligible things of life. But surely the breaking of silence need not imply the opening of the floodgates of speech. It was never meant by those who first cautiously advised a clearer understanding of sexual relations and hygienic rules that everybody should chatter freely respecting these grave issues; that teachers, lecturers, novelists, story-writers, militants, dramatists, social workers, and magazine editors should copiously impart all they know, or assume they know, to the world. The lack of restraint, the lack of balance, the lack of soberness and common sense, were never more apparent than in the obsession of sex which has set us all a-babbling about matters once excluded from the amenities of conversation.

Knowledge is the cry. Crude, undigested knowledge, without limit and without reserve. Give it to boys, give it to girls, give it to children. No other force is taken account of by the visionaries who—in defiance or in ignorance of history—believe that evil understood is evil conquered. "The menace of degradation and destruction can be checked *only* by the dissemination of knowledge on the subject of sex-physiology and hygiene," writes an enthusiast in the *Forum*, calling our attention to the methods employed by some public schools, noticeably the Polytechnic High School of Los Angeles, for the instruction of students, and urging that similar lectures be given to boys and girls in the grammar schools. . . .

The point of view of the older generation was not altogether the futile thing it seems to the progressive of today. It assumed that children brought up in honor and goodness, children disciplined into some measure of self-restraint, and taught very plainly the difference between right and wrong in matters childish and seasonable, were in no supreme danger from the gradual and somewhat haphazard expansion of knowledge. . . .

The justifiable reliance placed by our fathers upon religion and discipline has given place to a reliance upon understanding. It is assumed that youth will abstain from wrong-doing, if only the physical consequences of wrong-doing are made sufficiently clear. There are those who believe that a regard for future generations is a powerful deterrent from immorality, that boys and girls can be so interested in the quality of the baby to be born in 1990 that they will master their wayward impulses for its sake. What does not seem to occur to us is that this deep sense of obligation to ourselves and to our fellow creatures is the fruit of self-control. A course of lectures will not instill self-control into the human heart. It is born of childish virtues acquired in childhood, youthful virtues acquired in youth, and a wholesome preoccupation with the activities of life which gives young people something to think about besides the sexual relations which are pressed so relentlessly upon their attention.

The world is wide, and a great deal is happening in it. I do not plead for ignorance, but for the gradual and harmonious broadening of the field of knowledge, and for a more careful consideration of ways and means. There are subjects which may be taught in class, and subjects which commend themselves to individual teaching. There are topics which admit of *plein-air* handling, and topics which civilized man, as apart from his artless brother of the jungles, has veiled with reticence. There are truths which may be, and should be, privately imparted by a father, a mother, a family doctor, or an experienced teacher; but which young people cannot advantageously acquire from the platform, the stage, the moving-picture gallery, the novel, or the ubiquitous monthly magazine.

Democracy and Education

JOHN DEWEY (1859–1952)   *As an educator, Dewey viewed the traditional school as uselessly formal and symbolic. Since society had undergone a thorough and radical change, he believed that education, if it was to have any meaning for life, must pass through an equally complete transformation. His school was to be a miniature of capitalist society but socially oriented—imbued with democratic purpose—rather than profit oriented. In this way he hoped to introduce the humane and progressive aspects of modern industrial society while eliminating the pecuniary and class values which stemmed from business.*

The devotion of democracy to education is a familiar fact. The superficial explanation is that a government resting upon popular suffrage cannot be successful unless those who elect and who obey their governors are educated. Since a democratic society repudiates the principle of external authority, it must find a substitute in voluntary disposition and interest; these can be created only by education. But there is a deeper explanation. A democracy is more than a form of government; it is primarily a mode of associated living, of conjoint communicated experience. . . .

From *Democracy and Education* (New York: The Macmillan Co., 1916), pp. 101–2, 137–43. Reprinted by permission of The Macmillan Co.

The widening of the area of shared concerns, and the liberation of a greater diversity of personal capacities which characterize a democracy, are not of course the product of deliberation and conscious effort. On the contrary, they were caused by the development of modes of manufacture and commerce, travel, migration, and intercommunication which flowed from the command of science over natural energy. But after greater individualization on one hand, and a broader community of interest on the other have come into existence, it is a matter of deliberate effort to sustain and extend them. Obviously a society to which stratification into separate classes would be fatal, must see to it that intellectual opportunities are accessible to all on equable and easy terms. . . .

Before the time of Rousseau educational reformers had been inclined to urge the importance of education by ascribing practically unlimited power to it. All the differences between peoples and between classes and persons among the same people were said to be due to differences of training, of exercise, and practice. Originally, mind, reason, understanding is, for all practical purposes, the same in all. This essential identity of mind means the essential equality of all and the possibility of bringing them all to the same level. As a protest against this view, the doctrine of accord with nature meant a much less formal and abstract view of mind and its powers. It substituted specific instincts and impulses and physiological capacities, differing from individual to individual (just as they differ, as Rousseau pointed out, even in dogs of the same litter), for abstract faculties of discernment, memory, and generalization. Upon this side, the doctrine of educative accord with nature has been reënforced by the development of modern biology, physiology, and psychology. It means, in effect, that great as is the significance of nurture, of modification, and transformation through direct educational effort, nature, or unlearned capacities, affords the foundation and ultimate resources for such nurture. . . .

Nature not merely furnishes prime forces which initiate growth but also its plan and goal. That evil institutions and customs work almost automatically to give a wrong education which the most careful schooling cannot offset is true enough; but the conclusion is not to educate apart from the environment, but to provide an environment in which native powers will be put to better uses.

A conception which made nature supply the end of a true education and society the end of an evil one, could hardly fail to call out a protest. The opposing emphasis took the form of a doctrine that the business of education is to supply precisely what nature fails to secure; namely, habituation of an individual to social control; subordination of natural powers to social rules. It is not surprising to find that the value in the idea of social efficiency resides largely in its protest against the points at which the doctrine of natural development went astray; while its misuse comes when it is employed to slur over the truth in that conception. It is a fact that we must look to the activities and achievements of associated life to find what the development of power—that is to say, efficiency—means. The error is in implying that we must adopt measures of subordination rather than of utilization to secure efficiency. The doctrine is rendered adequate when we recognize that social efficiency is attained not by negative constraint but by positive use of native individual capacities in occupations having a social meaning.

Translated into specific aims, social efficiency indicates the importance of industrial competency. Persons cannot live without means of subsistence; the ways in which these means are employed and consumed have a profound influence upon all the relationships of persons to one another. If an individual is not able to earn his own living and that of the children dependent upon him, he is a drag or parasite upon the activities of others. He misses for himself one of the most educative experiences of life. If he is not trained in the right use of the products of industry, there is grave danger that he may deprave himself and injure others in his possession of wealth. No scheme of education can afford to neglect such basic considerations. Yet in the name of higher and more spiritual ideals, the arrangements for higher education have often not only neglected them, but looked at them with scorn as beneath the level of educative concern. With the change from an oligarchical to a democratic society, it is natural that the significance of an education which should have as a result ability to make one's way economically in the world, and to manage economic resources usefully instead of for mere display and luxury, should receive emphasis. . . .

Here again we have to be on guard against understanding the aim too narrowly. An over-definite interpretation would at certain periods have excluded scientific discoveries, in spite of the fact that in the last analysis security of social progress depends upon them. For scientific men would have been thought to be mere theoretical dreamers, totally lacking in social efficiency. It must be borne in mind that ultimately social efficiency means neither more nor less than capacity to share in a give and take of experience. It covers all that makes one's own experience more worthwhile to others, and all that enables one to participate more richly in the worthwhile experiences of others. Ability to produce and to enjoy art, capacity for recreation, the significant utilization of leisure, are more important elements in it than elements conventionally associated oftentimes with citizenship. . . .

Whether or not social efficiency is an aim which is consistent with culture turns upon these considerations. Culture means at least something cultivated, something ripened; it is opposed to the raw and crude. When the "natural" is identified with this rawness, culture is opposed to what is called natural development. Culture is also something personal; it is cultivation with respect to appreciation of ideas and art and broad human interests. When efficiency is identified with a narrow range of *acts,* instead of with the spirit and meaning of *activity,* culture is opposed to efficiency. Whether called culture or complete development of personality, the outcome is identical with the true meaning of social efficiency whenever attention is given to what is unique in an individual—and he would not be an individual if there were not something incommensurable about him. Its opposite is the mediocre, the average. Whenever distinctive quality is developed, distinction of personality results, and with it greater promise for a social service which goes beyond the supply in quantity of material commodities. For how can there be a society really worth serving unless it is constituted of individuals of significant personal qualities?

The fact is that the opposition of high worth of personality to social efficiency is a product of a feudally organized society with its rigid division of inferior and superior. The latter are supposed to have time and opportunity to develop themselves as human beings; the former are confined to providing external products.

When social efficiency as measured by product or output is urged as an ideal in a would-be democratic society, it means that the depreciatory estimate of the masses characteristic of an aristocratic community is accepted and carried over. But if democracy has a moral and ideal meaning, it is that a social return be demanded from all and that opportunity for development of distinctive capacities be afforded all. The separation of the two aims in education is fatal to democracy; the adoption of the narrower meaning of efficiency deprives it of its essential justification.

The Social Value of the College-Bred

WILLIAM JAMES (1842–1910)   *As a member of the Harvard faculty during the nineties, he favored President Eliot's attempt to liberalize the curriculum by introducing more modern subjects. He likewise defended the plan to shorten the college course from four to three years for those lacking scholarly incentive. Yet he would never have approved of today's large mass-education factories, for he was against all big organizations on the ground that "the bigger the unit you deal with, the hollower, the more brutal, the more mendacious is the life displayed."*

Of what use is a college training? We who have had it seldom hear the question raised; we might be a little nonplussed to answer it offhand. A certain amount of meditation has brought me to this as the pithiest reply which I myself can give: The best claim that a college education can possibly make on your respect, the best thing it can aspire to accomplish for you, is this: that it should *help you to know a good man when you see him.* This is as true of women's as of men's colleges; but that it is neither a joke nor a one-sided abstraction I shall now endeavor to show.

What talk do we commonly hear about the contrast between

From an address delivered at a meeting of the Association of American Alumnae at Radcliffe College, Nov. 7, 1907, and first published in *McClure's Magazine*, XXX (Feb., 1908), pp. 419–22.

college education and the education which business or technical or professional schools confer? The college education is called higher because it is supposed to be so general and so disinterested. At the "schools" you get a relatively narrow practical skill, you are told, whereas the "colleges" give you the more liberal culture, the broader outlook, the historical perspective, the philosophic atmosphere, or something which phrases of that sort try to express. . . .

Now, what is supposed to be the line of us who have the higher college training? Is there any broader line—since our education claims primarily not to be "narrow"—in which we also are made good judges between what is first-rate and what is second-rate only? What is especially taught in the colleges has long been known by the name of the "humanities," and these are often identified with Greek and Latin. But it is only as literatures, not as languages, that Greek and Latin have any general humanity-value; so that in a broad sense the humanities mean literature primarily, and in a still broader sense the study of masterpieces in almost any field of human endeavor. . . .

The sifting of human creations!—nothing less than this is what we ought to mean by the humanities. Essentially this means biography; what our colleges should teach is, therefore, biographical history, that not of politics merely, but of anything and everything so far as human efforts and conquest are factors that have played their part. Studying in this way, we learn what types of activity have stood the test of time; we acquire standards of the excellent and durable. All our arts and sciences and institutions are but so many quests of perfection on the part of men; and when we see how diverse the types of excellence may be, how various the tests, how flexible the adaptations, we gain a richer sense of what the terms "better" and "worse" may signify in general. Our critical sensibilities grow both more acute and less fanatical. We sympathize with men's mistakes even in the act of penetrating them; we feel the pathos of lost causes and misguided epochs even while we applaud what overcame them.

Such words are vague and such ideas are inadequate, but their meaning is unmistakable. What the colleges—teaching humanities by examples which may be special, but which must be typical and pregnant—should at least try to give us, is a general sense of what, under various disguises, *superiority* has always signified and may still signify. The feeling for a good human job anywhere, the admiration of the really admirable, the disesteem of what is cheap and trashy and impermanent—this is what we call the critical sense, the sense for ideal values. It is the better part of what men know as wisdom. Some of us are wise in this way naturally and by genius; some of us never become so. But to have spent one's youth at college, in contact with the choice and rare and precious, and yet still to be a blind prig or vulgarian, unable to scent out human excellence or to divine it amid its accidents, to know it only when ticketed and labelled and forced on us by others, this indeed should be accounted the very calamity and shipwreck of a higher education.

The sense for human superiority ought, then, to be considered our line, as boring subways is the engineer's line and the surgeon's is appendicitis. Our colleges ought to have lit up in us a lasting relish for the better kind of man, a loss of appetite for mediocrities, and a disgust for cheapjacks. We ought to smell, as it were, the difference of quality in men and their proposals when we enter the world of affairs about us. Expertness in this might well atone for some of our awkwardness at accounts, for some of our ignorance of dynamos. The best claim we can make for the higher education, the best single phrase in which we can tell what it ought to do for us, is, then, exactly what I said: It should enable us to *know a good man when we see him.*

That the phrase is anything but an empty epigram follows from the fact that if you ask in what line it is most important that a democracy like ours should have its sons and daughters skillful, you see that it is this line more than any other. "The people in their wisdom"—this is the kind of wisdom most needed by the people. Democracy is on its trial, and no one knows how it will stand the ordeal. Abounding about us are pessimistic prophets. Fickleness and violence used to be, but are no longer, the vices which they charge to democracy. What its critics now affirm is that its preferences are inveterately for the inferior. So it was in the beginning, they say, and so it will be world without end. Vulgarity enthroned and institutionalized, elbowing everything superior from the highway, this, they tell us, is our irremediable destiny; and the picture-papers of the European continent are already drawing Uncle Sam with the hog instead of the eagle for his heraldic emblem. The privileged aristocracies of the foretime, with all their iniquities, did at least preserve some taste for higher human quality, and honor certain forms of refinement by their enduring traditions. But when democracy is sovereign, its doubters say, nobility will form a sort of invisible church, and sincerity and refinement, stripped of honor, precedence, and favor, will have to vegetate on sufferance in private corners. They will have no general influence. They will be harmless eccentricities.

Now, who can be absolutely certain that this may not be the career of democracy? Nothing future is quite secure; states enough have inwardly rotted; and democracy as a whole may undergo self-poisoning. But, on the other hand, democracy is a kind of religion, and we are bound not to admit its failure. Faiths and utopias are the noblest exercise of human reason, and no one with a spark of reason in him will sit down fatalistically before the croaker's picture. The best of us are filled with the contrary vision of a democracy stumbling through every error till its institutions glow with justice and its customs shine with beauty. Our better men *shall* show the way and we *shall* follow them; so we are brought round again to the mission of the higher education in helping us to know the better kind of man whenever we see him.

The notion that a people can run itself and its affairs anonymously is now well known to be the silliest of absurdities. Mankind does nothing save through initiatives on the part of inventors, great or small, and imitation by the rest of us—these are the sole factors active in human progress. Individuals of genius show the way, and set the patterns, which common people then adopt and follow. . . .

In this very simple way does the value of our educated class define itself: We more than others should be able to divine the worthier and better leaders. The terms here are monstrously simplified, of course, but such a bird's-eye view lets us immediately take our bearings. In our democracy, where everything else is so shifting, we alumni and alumnæ of the colleges are the only permanent presence that corresponds to the aristocracy in older countries. We have continuous traditions, as they have; our motto, too, is *noblesse oblige;* and, unlike them, we stand for ideal interests solely, for we have no corporate selfishness and wield no powers of corruption. We ought to have our own class-consciousness. "*Les Intellectuels!*" What prouder club-name could there be than this one, used ironically by the party of "redblood," the party of every stupid prejudice and passion, during the anti-Dreyfus craze, to satirize the men in France who still retained some critical sense and judgment! . . .

Critical sense, it has to be confessed, is not an exciting term, hardly a banner to carry in processions. . . . [Yet] vague as the phrase of knowing a good man when you see him may be, diffuse and indefinite as one must leave its application, is there any other formula that describes so well the result at which our institutions *ought* to aim? If they do that, they do the best thing conceivable. If they fail to do it, they fail in very deed. It surely is a fine synthetic formula. If our faculties and graduates could once collectively come to realize it as the great underlying purpose toward which they have always been more or less obscurely groping, a great clearness would be shed over many of their problems; and, as for their influence in the midst of our social system, it would embark upon a new career of strength.

A Social Bill of Rights

SIMON N. PATTEN (1852–1922)   *Though not so young as some new radicals, Patten was one of the most provocative. An economist, he received his doctorate from the University of Halle in 1878, then taught at the University of Pennsylvania from 1889 until his retirement in 1917. Convinced the real source of exploitation lay not in political causes but in old traditions, habits and prejudices, he sought to persuade Americans that the mental habits of poverty were no longer valid in an affluent society. The unparalleled productivity of modern industry, he declared, had created a social surplus in which every person had a right*

From *The Theory of Prosperity* (New York: Macmillan, 1902), pp. 215–21, 224–28, 236–37.

to share. This right to share was not a right to equality but to
that income necessary to secure to every citizen the best physical
conditions.

Freedom consists not merely of political rights, but is dependent
upon the possession of economic [and social] rights, freely recognized and universally granted to each man by his fellow citizens.
These . . . rights measure freedom in proportion as there is a
mutual agreement concerning their desirability, and as complete
adjustment makes their realization possible. Only those rights that
American conditions permit and the impulses of unimpeded
activity may attain can be properly considered ideal. I shall enumerate a few, which, at the present time, seem to be in harmony
with the forces making for adjustment, and if so must be incor-
porated in the national thought and become as clearly defined as
are political rights. The rights here enumerated will doubtless be
added to as time goes on and conditions of adjustment to American
environment improve, or as that environment itself changes. For
the present they may be considered under the following heads:

THE RIGHT TO SECURITY

Security is [a] right . . . which must be fully preserved in modern
industry. The product of a man's industry must be left in his
possession, and all his industrial relations must be free from arbitrary changes. A bad monetary standard is no less harmful than
an unjust system of taxation. Speculation and other arbitrary
changes in prices also violate the right of security by forcing men
to sell at low prices and to buy back the final product at high rates.
Security, moreover, is not merely a question of property rights.
It also relates to utilities and activities. The consumer has a right
to stable prices and the workman to a steady position. An arbitrary
discharge of workmen disturbs industrial processes and should be
carefully guarded against. . . .

THE RIGHT TO A HOME

Marriage is a permanent coöperation between the sexes under

such conditions that its purity can be maintained, and children raised that will be a credit to parents and the community; and it involves everything needed to secure these ends. There should be no necessity of living in a social environment where either party is tempted to break marital vows, or where the lack of income to support a family prevents pure social relations. . . . A home is not merely a place in which to sleep and eat; these are merely animal needs. It is a secluded retreat with a standard of comfort above the mere physical wants; for without privacy and income there is no home. . . .

THE RIGHT TO DEVELOP

Education has become an essential feature of state activity. Each generation should reach a closer adjustment to its environment and be able to secure better conditions from it than its predecessors enjoyed. This means that sons should be better prepared for life, and their education should be extended through a longer period. The longer children are in school, the more complete can this preparation be, and the more efficient will they be when they enter the industrial world. . . . The right to develop means the right of contact with all the elevating forces in a civilization as long as life lasts. Whatever narrows the environment of individuals or limits their activities, stops their growth and checks social progress.

THE RIGHT TO WHOLESOME STANDARDS

An opportunity to develop depends on the social surroundings of a people as much as it does on the educational advantages. If a man must work and keep his family in contact with the degrading influences found in cities, it is impossible for him or them to maintain their moral purity. Wholesome social standards are a part of the conditions demanded for the steady improvement of each person and family. It is not enough that moral principles and elevating ideals be taught in the schools. These can have but little permanent influence unless embodied in practical rules of conduct which individuals observe throughout life. School knowledge should be converted into social standards to which all must con-

form. Any community will be contaminated if a minority is allowed
to violate social conventions and to introduce degrading practices.
Men tend to sink to the level of their community or class. A
progressive nation must therefore rigidly preserve its social standards and supplement them by higher and more complete expressions of national life. . . .

THE RIGHT TO COMFORT

In modern nations the productive power is more than sufficient
to produce the minimum of existence. There is a social surplus
above the costs of production in which every worker has a right
to share. All men cannot be made wealthy, but they can be made
comfortable by some of the social surplus going to each of them.
The right to comfort is a right to share in the social surplus; it
demands that the workman get on each increment of his production
some surplus above its cost. To be free is to be comfortable, to
have a home and the decencies that go with it. . . .

THE RIGHT TO LEISURE

The right to leisure is a corollary to the right to comfort. No
matter what income a person receives, he cannot be comfortable
without some time for enjoyment. Leisure means more than time
to eat and sleep. The full revival of mental and physical powers
demands a period of rest in which the loss of surplus energy can
be restored. A normal working day must end while work is still
pleasurable. Any drain on the system reduces the vitality of the
worker, and causes a reduction in future production greater than
the present gain from overwork. The right to leisure is in harmony
with the greatest efficiency, and cannot be lost by workmen without detriment to other classes besides themselves.

THE RIGHT TO RECREATION

The right to recreation may be regarded as an outcome of the
narrow division of labor demanded by production on a large scale;
for then work is a constant repetition of single acts, tiring some
parts of the body but leaving other parts without sufficient exercise.

The normal man must have all the parts of his body developed and all his mental powers kept alive. Recreation is the only process by which this is accomplished. Each one must have outside of his industrial occupation enough activity to revive and sustain the mental and physical powers of the normal man. . . .

Leisure is a demand for time; recreation is a demand for active occupation outside of labor hours, and involves conditions that can be secured only by large social expenditures. Walking, cycling, travelling, and other forms of exercise are made agreeable only by pleasant surroundings; hence, good roads, attractive streets, fine parks, and wholesome places of resort are necessary. Mental recreation also demands churches, concerts, lectures, libraries, public discussions, and other means of exciting spiritual life. Present expenditures for these purposes indicate that this right is partially recognized, but it must gain more complete recognition before industrial efficiency reaches its maximum.

THE RIGHT TO CLEANLINESS

The isolated worker in a primitive society had all the conditions upon which health, vigor, and physical well-being depended. The control of a quantity of land enabled him to avoid the evil consequences naturally arising from the pollution caused by himself, his family, and his stock. With a sparse population nature easily restores normal conditions by transforming refuse matter into useful products; but the close proximity of men in advanced societies destroys their power to keep clean and their surroundings pure without similar cleanliness and purity on the part of their neighbors. The filth of one house or region destroys the exemption from disease which isolated families enjoy. A whole city may suffer from an epidemic started among a few families or in some neglected street. Where no disease is communicated, the refuse of uncleanly places contaminates the air and depresses everyone. Even food is poisoned by the presence of noxious compounds and by microbes. The surplus energy of city people is reduced by these evils and no hope of improvement exists except in measures affecting all persons and places. Clear water, pure air, and clean streets are matters of public interest, and for these ends the social surplus should be freely used. Public control should be extended to everything that lowers the vitality of the working population.

THE RIGHT TO SCENERY

The close contact of men in modern societies also affects men unfavorably through their loss of touch with nature. The beautiful in nature is marred or destroyed by the processes through which wealth is created. The eye needs protection as well as other organs of the body, and the impressions that come through it are as important as those made by any other contact with the external world. Men should provide for their visual environment with the same care they exert in providing for other material conditions. Not only must natural scenery be preserved and restored, but the demands of city life for corresponding advantages in its architecture, museums, and parks must be met. The eye should never be needlessly wearied nor its sensitiveness to harmonious relations destroyed. Bad streets, incongruous buildings, and glaring advertisements depress men, reduce their productive power, and check the growth of social feelings.

THE RIGHT TO RELIEF

Besides the general rights belonging to every person in the industrial world, there are [those] which grow out of special conditions. Every one is liable to misfortunes, and the hazards of business are such that forethought cannot guard against them. The safest of investments become worthless, health breaks down, accidents happen, employment is uncertain, and sickness reduces families to a condition where aid is necessary. Against these and similar hardships no individual can adequately provide, and if he could, it would be more economical to have them guarded against by public measures. . . . The evil may lie in the environment, as in the case of a failure of crops; it may be due to accidents for which others are to blame; to the diseases and degradation of bad local conditions; or to social disorders over which single persons have no control. In such cases social evils should be met by social action. Make the individual responsible for the results of his own acts, but do not let him suffer from what he could not avoid. A system of relief is an essential to industrial freedom; economic activity will not reach its maximum until it is so effective that the energy of individuals can be applied to the satisfaction of their own wants. the social surplus is more than sufficient to provide for all the exigencies that persons cannot control.

The New Social Issue

WILLIAM GRAHAM SUMNER (1840–1910)   *As   professor   of political and social science at Yale from 1872 to his death, he was a hard-headed and outspoken foe of radical reform. An exponent of the evolutionary determinism of Herbert Spencer, he viewed society as a vast and complex organism far beyond man's comprehension. To allow the "social tinker" to meddle with nature's intricate mechanism was therefore, in his opinion, to court disaster. Hence he opposed government intervention and socialism, and advocated a limited liberty within an iron-clad absolutism.*

The effect of the great improvements in the arts during the last century is to produce a social and economic order which is controlled by tremendous forces, and which comprehends the whole human race; which is automatic in the mode of its activity; which is delicate and refined in its susceptibility to the influence of interferences. It is therefore at once too vast in its magnitude and scope for us to comprehend it, and too delicate in its operation for us to follow out and master its details.

Under such circumstances the conservative position in social discussion is the only sound position. We do not need to resist all change or discussion—that is not conservatism. We may, however, be sure that the only possible good for society must come of evolution, not of revolution. We have a right to condemn, and to refuse our attention to flippant and ignorant criticisms or propositions of reform; we can rule out at once all plans to reconstruct society, on anybody's system, from the bottom up. We may refuse

From *The Challenge of Facts and Other Essays*, Albert G. Keller, ed. (New Haven: Yale University Press, 1914), pp. 207–12.

to act today under the motive of redressing some wrong done, ignorantly perhaps, one or two more centuries ago; or under the motive of bringing in a golden age which we think men can attain to, one or two or more centuries in the future. We may refuse to listen to any propositions which are put forward with menaces and may demand that all who avail themselves of the right of free discussion shall remain upon the field of discussion and refrain from all acts until they have duly and fairly convinced the reason and conscience of the community. We may demand that no strain shall be put on any of our institutions, such as majority rule, by a rash determination to override dissent and remonstrance and to realize something for which there has been collected a hasty majority, animated by heterogeneous motives and purposes.

The institutions which we possess have cost something. Few people seem to know how much—it is one of the great defects in our education that we are not in a position to teach the history of civilization in such a way as to train even educated men to know the cost at which everything which today separates us from the brutes has been bought by the generations which have preceded us. As time goes on we can win more, but we shall win it only in the same way, that is, by slow and painful toil and sacrifice, not by adopting some prophet's scheme of the universe; therefore we have a right to ask that all social propositions which demand our attention shall be practical in the best sense, that is, that they shall aim to go forward in the limits and on the lines of sound development out of the past, and that none of our interests shall be put in jeopardy on the chance that Comte, or Spencer, or George, or anybody else has solved the world-problem aright. If anybody has a grievance against the social order, it is, on the simplest principles of common sense, the right of busy men whose attention he demands that he shall set forth in the sharpest and precisest manner what it is; any allegation of injustice which is vague is, by its own tenor, undeserving of attention.

Finally, we each have a right to have our liberty respected in such form as we have inherited it under the laws and institutions of our country. The fashion of the day is to sneer at this demand and to propose to make short work of it so soon as enough power shall have been collected to carry out the projects of certain social sects. Let us, however, give a moment's calm attention to it; the point is worth it, for here is where the tendencies now at work in society are to meet in collision. I do not mean by liberty any power of self-determination which all should allow to each or which each may demand of God, or nature, or society; I mean by it the aggregate of rights, privileges, and prerogatives which the laws and institutions of this country secure to each one of us today as conditions under which he may fight out the struggle for existence and the competition of life in this society. I call this liberty a thing which we have a "right" to demand, because, as a fact, the laws give us that right now; when I speak of rights and liberty, therefore, I wish to be understood as standing upon the law of the land and not on any platform of metaphysical or ethical deduction.

Such being the notion of liberty, it is plain that it stands on the line where right and might meet; where war passes over into peace, the guarantees of rights under law taking the place of the domination of might under lawlessness, and the limitation of rights by other rights taking the place of the limitation of powers by other powers. Many of the proposed changes in society aim to alter the demarcation of rights, and they aim to do this, not for a fuller realization of peace, order, liberty, and security, by a nicer adjustment of rights, but they avowedly aim to do it in the interest of certain groups and classes of persons. At this point, therefore, parties must be formed and issues must be joined. On one side is liberty under law, rights and interests being adjusted by the struggle of the parties under the natural laws of the social and industrial order and within barriers set by impersonal and "equal" legislation; on the other, state regulation, consisting of legislation planned to warp rights and interests in favor of selected groups under some *a priori* and arbitrary notion of justice, and administered by persons who, by the fundamental principle of the system, must assume to be competent to decide what ought to be done with us all and who must at the same time themselves be above the most fundamental weaknesses of human nature. There is room for a vast range and variety of opinion and sentiment on either side of this issue, but it is the issue which is upon us and on which every man must take sides.

One of the world-improvers said: "We must know how to do violence to mankind in general, in order to make them happy." He naïvely expressed the sentiment which animates the whole school of opinion to which he belonged, from its extremest right wing to its extremest left wing. They must of course know just what men need to render them happy and they must be fearless in doing violence, that is, in trampling on liberty and causing misery, in order to enforce happiness.

If now we look to see who are to be the victims of the proposed readjustment of society, it is plain that they are men who, at this moment, hold the world of trade, industry, finance, transportation, law, and politics in their hands; and they hold it, not because they inherited it or because they belong to any privileged class, but they have obtained control of it by natural selection and because they have made it. Is it likely that they will be intimidated? Are they men to be coerced by clamor, or terrorism, or denunciation, or threats? So far there has scarcely even been discussion except on one side, and the disputants on that side are beginning already to count the battle won. It takes a long time for men who are absorbed in practical life to find out what the literary men are, for the time being, interested in, and still longer for them to make up their minds that talk is to come to anything; that point has not yet been reached, even by the educated community, in regard to the issue which I have described. When it is reached we shall see whether the people of the United States have lost their political sense or not.

It is impossible to look with any complacency on the probability that this issue is to be raised and fought out. No doubt the new power of mankind in these last two or three centuries to reflect on the phenomena and experiences of life has been and is rich in advantage for the race; it has taken the place of an instinctive living under the traditional and simple acquiescence in it, and has developed the reason and conscience of all; but it is at present a sort of disease. A society which brings all its inheritance of thought and faith into question at once, and before it has prepared an adequate apparatus for dealing with the questions and problems which it raises, may fall into chaos. And it is that issue in particular—one which shows that the people are not firm in their conception of liberty and are not ready and hard-headed in their judgment of social fads and whims—which brings with it the greatest jeopardy for the essential welfare of society.

Constitutional liberty, so far as we have been able to realize it, stands just now as a happy phase of civil institutions which we have been able to realize for a moment in the interval between the downfall of aristocracy and the rise of democracy; for there can be no doubt that the epidemic of socialism is only the turning of all social powers in obeisance and flattery toward the new and rising power. We are passing through a transition over to a new illustration of the fact that the thing which forever rules the world is not what is true or what is right, even relatively, but only what is strong. The main question which remains to be solved is whether the elements of strength in the new order are distributed as many now believe; whether democracy is a stable order at all or whether it will at once fall a prey to plutocracy. So surely as democracy yields to socialism, socialism will prove a middle stage toward plutocracy.

The New Politics

WALTER LIPPMANN (1889–   )   *An intellectual prodigy, he raced through Harvard in three years, striking up an acquaintance with William James on the way, and emerged a pragmatist. Although a confirmed Socialist as an undergraduate, after three months as secretary to a Socialist mayor of Schenectady he became at the age of twenty-three disenchanted with all political dogma. What he sought in his first book, therefore, was not to present a definite political program, but to promote the revolution in men's minds he believed had to come before any revolution in their politics.*

Politics does not exist for the sake of demonstrating the superior righteousness of anybody. It is not a competition in deportment.

From *A Preface To Politics* (New York: Mitchell Kennerley, 1913), pp. 1–9, 83–84, 266–71. Reprinted by permission of the author.

In fact, before you can begin to think about politics at all you have to abandon the notion that there is a war between good men and bad men. That is one of the great American superstitions. More than any other fetish it has ruined our sense of political values by glorifying the pharisee with his vain cruelty to individuals and his unfounded approval of himself. You have only to look at the Senate of the United States, to see how that body is capable of turning itself into a court of preliminary hearings for the Last Judgment, wasting its time and our time and absorbing public enthusiasm and newspaper scareheads. . . .

But if the issue is not between honesty and dishonesty, where is it?

If you stare at a checkerboard you can see it as black on red, or red on black, as series of horizontal, vertical or diagonal steps which recede or protrude. The longer you look the more patterns you can trace, and the more certain it becomes that there is no single way of looking at the board. So with political issues. There is no obvious cleavage which everyone recognizes. Many patterns appear in the national life. The "progressives" say the issue is between "Privilege" and the "People"; the Socialists, that it is between the "working class" and the "master class." An apologist for dynamite told me once that society was divided into the weak and the strong, and there are people who draw a line between Philistia and Bohemia.

When you rise up and announce that the conflict is between this and that, you mean that this particular conflict interests you. The issue of good-and-bad-men interests this nation to the exclusion of almost all others. But experience shows, I believe, that it is a fruitless conflict and a wasting enthusiasm. Yet some distinction must be drawn if we are to act at all in politics. With nothing we are for and nothing to oppose, we are merely neutral. This cleavage in public affairs is the most important choice we are called upon to make. In large measure it determines the rest of our thinking. Now some issues are fertile; some are not. Some lead to spacious results; others are blind alleys. With this in mind I wish to suggest that the distinction most worth emphasizing today is between those who regard government as a routine to be administered and those who regard it as a problem to be solved.

The class of routineers is larger than the conservatives. The man who will follow precedent, but never create one, is merely an obvious example of the routineer. You find him desperately numerous in the civil service, in the official bureaus. To him government is something given as unconditionally, as absolutely as ocean or hill. He goes on winding the tape that he finds. His imagination has rarely extricated itself from under the administrative machine to gain any sense of what a human, temporary contraption the whole affair is. What he thinks is the heavens above him is nothing but the roof.

He is the slave of routine. He can boast of somewhat more spiritual cousins in the men who reverence their ancestors' independence, who feel, as it were, that a disreputable great-grandfather is necessary to a family's respectability. These are the routineers gifted with historical sense. They take their forefathers with enormous solemnity. But one mistake is rarely avoided: They imitate the old-fashioned thing their grandfather did, and ignore the originality which enabled him to do it.

If tradition were a reverent record of those crucial moments when men burst through their habits, a love of the past would not be the butt on which every sophomoric radical can practice his wit. But almost always tradition is nothing but a record and a machine-made imitation of the habits that our ancestors created. The average conservative is a slave to the most incidental and trivial part of his forefathers' glory—to the archaic formula which happened to express their genius or the eighteenth-century contrivance by which for a time it was served. To reverence Washington they wear a powdered wig; they do honor to Lincoln by cultivating awkward hands and ungainly feet. . . .

Often as not the very effort to make the existing machine run more perfectly merely makes matters worse. For the tinkering reformer is frequently one of the worst of the routineers. Even machines are not altogether inflexible, and sometimes what the reformer regards as a sad deviation from the original plans is a poor rickety attempt to adapt the machine to changing conditions. Think what would have happened had we actually remained stolidly faithful to every intention of the Fathers. Think what would happen if every statute were enforced. By the sheer force of circumstances we have twisted constitutions and laws to some approximation of our needs. A changing country has managed to live in spite of a static government machine. Perhaps Bernard Shaw was right when he said that "the famous Constitution survives only because whenever any corner of it gets into the way of the accumulating dollar it is pettishly knocked off and thrown away. Every social development, however beneficial and inevitable from the public point of view, is met, not by an intelligent adaptation of the social structure to its novelties but by a panic and a cry of Go Back."

I am tempted to go further and put into the same class all those radicals who wish simply to substitute some other kind of machine for the one we have. Though not all of them would accept the name, these reformers are simply utopia-makers in action. Their perceptions are more critical than the ordinary conservatives'. They do see that humanity is badly squeezed in the existing mould. They have enough imagination to conceive a different one. But they have an infinite faith in moulds. This routine they don't believe in, but they believe in their own: if you could put the country under a new "system," then human affairs would run automatically for the welfare of all. Some improvement there might be, but as almost all men are held in an iron devotion to their own creations, the routine reformers are simply working for another conservatism, and not for any continuing liberation.

The type of statesman we must oppose to the routineer is one who regards all social organization as an instrument. Systems, institutions and mechanical contrivances have for him no virtue of their own; they are valuable only when they serve the purposes of men. He uses them, of course, but with a constant sense that men have made them, that new ones can be devised, that only an effort of the will can keep machinery in its place. He has no faith whatever in automatic governments. While the routineers see machinery and precedents revolving with mankind as puppets, he puts the deliberate, conscious, willing individual at the center of his philosophy. This reversal is pregnant with a new outlook for statecraft. I hope to show that it alone can keep step with life; it alone is humanly relevant; and it alone achieves valuable results.

Call this man a political creator or a political inventor. The essential quality of him is that he makes that part of existence which has experience the master of it. He serves the ideals of human feelings, not the tendencies of mechanical things. . . .

This is the heart of a political revolution. When we recognize that the focus of politics is shifting from a mechanical to a human center we shall have reached what is, I believe, the most essential idea in modern politics. More than any other generalization it illuminates the currents of our national life and explains the altering tasks of statesmanship.

The old effort was to harness mankind to abstract principles—liberty, justice or equality—and to deduce institutions from these high-sounding words. It did not succeed because human nature was contrary and restive. The new effort proposes to fit creeds and institutions to the wants of men, to satisfy their impulses as fully and beneficially as possible. . . .

It is perfectly true that that government is best which governs least. It is equally true that that government is best which provides most. The first truth belongs to the eighteenth century: the second to the twentieth. Neither of them can be neglected in our attitude towards the state. Without the Jeffersonian distrust of the police we might easily grow into an impertinent and tyrannous collectivism; without a vivid sense of the possibilities of the state we abandon the supreme instrument of civilization. The two theories need to be held together, yet clearly distinguished.

Government has been an exalted policeman; it was there to guard property and to prevent us from quarreling too violently. That was about all it was good for. Yet society found problems on its hands—problems which Woodrow Wilson calls moral and social in their nature. Vice and crime, disease, and grinding poverty forced themselves on the attention of the community. A typical example is the way the social evil compelled the city of Chicago to begin an investigation [of prostitution]. Yet when government was asked to handle the question it had for wisdom an ancient conception of itself as a policeman. Its only method was to forbid, to prosecute, to jail—in short, to use the taboo. But experience has shown that the taboo will not solve "moral and social questions"—that nine times out of ten it aggravates the disease.

Political action becomes a petty, futile, mean little intrusion when its only method is prosecution.

No wonder then that conservatively-minded men pray that moral and social questions be kept out of politics; no wonder that more daring souls begin to hate the whole idea of government and take to anarchism. So long as the state is conceived merely as an agent of repression, the less it interferes with our lives, the better. Much of the horror of socialism comes from a belief that by increasing the functions of government its regulating power over our daily lives will grow into a tyranny. I share this horror when certain socialists begin to propound their schemes. There is a dreadful amount of forcible scrubbing and arranging and pocketing implied in some socialisms. There is a wish to have the state use its position as general employer to become a censor of morals and arbiter of elegance, like the benevolent employers of the day who take an impertinent interest in the private lives of their workers. Without any doubt socialism has within it the germs of that great bureaucratic tyranny which Chesterton and Belloc have named the Servile State.

So it is a wise instinct that makes men jealous of the policeman's power. Far better we may say that moral and social problems be left to private solution than that they be subjected to the clumsy method of the taboo. When Woodrow Wilson argues that social problems are not susceptible to treatment in a party program, he must mean only one thing: that they cannot be handled by the state as he conceives it. He is right. His attitude is far better than that of the Vice Commission: It too had only a policeman's view of government, but it proceeded to apply it to problems that are not susceptible to such treatment. Wilson, at least, knows the limitations of his philosophy.

But once you see the state as a provider of civilizing opportunities, his whole objection collapses. As soon as government begins to supply services, it is turning away from the sterile tyranny of the taboo. The provision of schools, streets, plumbing, highways, libraries, parks, universities, medical attention, post-offices, a Panama Canal, agricultural information, fire protection—is a use of government totally different from the ideal of Jefferson. To furnish these opportunities is to add to the resources of life, and

only a doctrinaire adherence to a misunderstood ideal will raise
any objection to them. . . .

Once you realize that moral and social problems must be treated
to fine opportunities, that the method of the future is to compete
with the devil rather than to curse him; that the furnishing of
civilized environments is the goal of statecraft, then there is no
longer any reason for keeping social and moral questions out of
politics. They are what politics must deal with essentially, now
that it has found a way. The policeman with his taboo did make
moral and social questions insusceptible to treatment in party
platforms. He kept the issues of politics narrow and irrelevant, and
just because these really interesting questions could not be handled,
politics was an over-advertised hubbub. But the vision of the new
statecraft in centering politics upon human interests becomes a
creator of opportunities instead of a censor of morals, and deserves
a fresh and heightened regard.

The party platform will grow ever more and more into a program of services. In the past it has been an armory of platitudes
or a forecast of punishments. It promised that it would stop this
evil practice, drive out corruption here, and prosecute this-and-that
offense. All that belongs to a moribund tradition. Abuse and disuse
characterize the older view of the state: guardian and censor it
has been, provider but grudgingly. The proclamations of so-called
progressives that they will jail financiers, or "wage relentless
warfare" upon social evils, are simply the reiterations of men who
do not understand the uses of the state.

A political revolution is in progress: The state as policeman is
giving place to the state as producer.

The Rock of Ages

PAUL ELMER MORE (1864–1937)   *A conservative critic and writer,*
        he was editor of the Nation *from 1909 until 1914 when he began*

From *Aristocracy and Justice*, Shelburne Essays, Ninth Series (Boston: Houghton
Mifflin Co., 1915), pp. 116–20, 135, 208–12. Reprinted by permission of Mrs.
Mary Darrah Fine, the copyright holder.

a twenty-year teaching career at Princeton University. Along with Irving Babbitt, he was a leader of the literary movement known as the New Humanism, which was aristocratic rather than democratic in its critical outlook. If his preoccupation with the Greek classics prevented him from appreciating what he called the "sentimentalisms" of the day, it did enable him to see that the problems of justice and discipline which had concerned men since antiquity could not be lightly thrust aside.

Man is a political animal. His life is closely knit with that of his fellows, and it is not enough to trace the meaning of justice to a state of the isolated soul; we must consider how this virtue bears on the conduct of a man among men, in society. . . .

Abstractly, no doubt, the definition of this social justice is simple and ready at hand. Society is composed of men who vary in the degree of individual justice to which they have attained, some being by disposition and training more self-governed, more rational, than others. By an inevitable analogy, therefore, we extend to society the idea of justice learned from our personal experience, precisely as we extended it to Nature. We cannot, in fact, do otherwise, since this is the only idea of justice possible to us. . . .

Here, first of all, we come into conflict with two opposite theories of social justice which are as old almost as history, and which will doubtless go on flourishing as long as the human mind retains its tendency to gravitate to the indolent simplicity of extremes. One of these theories passes now under the name of Nietzsche, who . . . converts the law of might into a criterion of social justice. . . . His theory is falsified by a double error: It supposes that mankind will be willing to base its conduct on an idea of justice derived from natural evolution, and in despite of that inner consciousness which demands the satisfaction of both the reason and the feelings; and it assumes that social progress guided by strength and reason alone, whether possible or not, would be towards the higher, because happier, life. . . .

The other theory springs from the same tendency of the mind to sink to extremes, suffering in this case the attraction of the feelings. It has various names—humanitarianism, socialism, equalitarianism—masquerading in as many a lovely *ism,* or *isme,* or *ismus*

as any other international mania, and sometimes arrogating to itself
the more plausible title of democracy. . . . It is false and one-sided,
being based on the exclusive appeal of the feelings, just as
Nietzscheism is, theoretically, based on the claim of the reason.
We think there is a higher and a lower in the scale of nature, we
are conscious of reason and feeling in our own souls, we observe
a similar distribution of characters in society. It would be pleasant,
no doubt, to feel that every man had all his desires gratified, but
reason, which is the faculty of seeing distinctions, binds us to
believe that the State cannot progress in the orderly manner of
evolution unless there, as in Nature, a certain advantage of honour
accrues to those individuals who are themselves governed by
reason, with the privilege of imposing their will upon those who,
from the rational point of view, are inferior to them.

Social justice, then, is neither Nietzschean nor equalitarian. It
is such a distribution of power and privilege, and of property as
the symbol and instrument of these, as at once will satisfy the
distinctions of reason among the superior, and will not outrage
the feelings of the inferior. . . .

Not even a Rousseau could cover up the fact of the initial
inequality of men by the decree of that great Ruler, or Law, call
it what you will, which makes one vessel for dishonour and another
for honour. That is the so-called injustice of Nature. And it is
equally a fact that property means the magnifying of that natural
injustice into that which you may deplore as unnatural injustice,
but which is a fatal necessity, nevertheless. This is the truth, hideous
if you choose to make it so to yourself, not without its benevolent
aspect to those, whether the favorites of fortune or not, who are
themselves true—ineluctable at least. Unless we are willing to
pronounce civilization a grand mistake, as, indeed, religious enthusiasts have ever been prone to do (and humanitarianism is more
a perverted religion than a false economics), unless our material
progress is all a grand mistake, we must admit, sadly or cheerfully,
that any attempt by government or institution to ignore that
inequality, may stop the wheels of progress or throw the world
back into temporary barbarism, but will surely not be the cause
of wider and greater happiness. . . .

What are the results of this glorification of humanity? . . . As for our own age, only a fool would dogmatize; we can only balance and surmise. And in the first place a certain good must almost certainly be placed to the credit of humanitarianism. It has softened us and made us quicker to respond to the sufferings of others; the direct and frightful cruelty that runs through the annals of history like a crimson line has been largely eliminated from civilization, and with it a good deal of the brutality of human nature. . . .

But in other directions the progress is not so clear. Statistics are always treacherous witnesses, but so far as we can believe them and interpret them we can draw no comfort from the prevalence of crime and prostitution and divorce and insanity and suicide. At least, whatever may be the cause of this inner canker of society, our social passion seems to be powerless to cure it. Some might even argue that the preaching of any doctrine which minimizes personal responsibility is likely to increase the evil. Certainly a teacher who, like Miss Jane Addams, virtually attributes the lawless and criminal acts of our city hoodlums to a wholesome desire of adventure which the laws unrighteously repress, would appear to be encouraging the destructive and sensual proclivities which are too common in human nature, young and old. Nor are the ways of honesty made clear by a well-known humanitarian judge of Denver, who refused to punish a boy for stealing a Sunday-School teacher's pocketbook, for the two good reasons, as his honour explained in a public address, "that the boy was not responsible, and, secondly, that there were bigger thieves in the pews upstairs." So, too, a respectable woman of New York who asks whether it may not be a greater wrong for a girl to submit to the slavery of low wages than to sell herself in the street, is manifestly not helping the tempted to resist. She is even doing what she can with her words to confuse the very bounds of moral and physical evil.

There is, in fact, a terrible confusion hidden in the New Morality, an ulcerous evil that is ever working inward. Sympathy, creating the desire for even-handed justice, is in itself an excellent motive of conduct, and the stronger it grows, the better the world shall be. But sympathy, spoken with the word "social" prefixed, as it commonly is on the platforms of the day, begins to take on a dangerous connotation. And "social sympathy" erected into a theory which leaves out of account the responsibility of the individual and seeks to throw the blame of evil on the laws and on society, though it may effect desirable reforms here and there in institutions, is bound to leave the individual weakened in his powers of resistance against the temptations which can never be eliminated from human life. The whole effect of calling sympathy justice and putting it in the place of judgment is to relax the fibre of character and nourish the passions at the expense of reason and the will. And undoubtedly the conviction is every day gaining ground among cool observers of our life that the manners and morals of the people·are beginning to suffer from this relaxation in many insidious ways apart from acts which come into the cognizance of the courts. The sensuality of the prevailing music and dancing, the plays that stir the country as organs of moral regeneration, the exaggeration of sex in the clothing seen in the street, are but symptoms more or less ominous to our mind as we do or do not connect them with the regnant theory of ethics. And in the end this form of social sympathy may itself quite conceivably bring back the brutality and cruelty from which it seems to have delivered us.

The Limits of Technique

The Sorcerer's Apprentices

The twentieth-century American took for granted that man through technique had mastered the forces of nature. As Bacon foretold, modern man had come to rely more and more on forces other than his own, and on instruments which superseded his senses. Man had detached immense forces from nature; yet, as Henry Adams grimly reminded his fellowmen: "Every day Nature violently revolted, causing so-called accidents with enormous destruction of property and life, while plainly laughing at man, who helplessly groaned and shrieked and shuddered, but never for a single instant could stop. The railways alone approached the carnage of war; automobiles and firearms ravaged society, until an earthquake became almost a nervous relaxation." At such times it seemed that man, like the sorcerer's apprentice, had summoned up forces he could not control, and these forces "grasped his wrists and flung him about as though he had hold of a live wire or a runaway automobile." [1]

It was a new century, said Adams, and "what used to be called electricity is its God." Wandering about the great gallery of machines at the Paris Exposition of 1900, he began to feel the forty-foot dynamo as a moral force, a symbol of infinity, much as early Christians had felt about the cross. "The planet itself seemed less impressive, in its old-fashioned, deliberate, annual or daily revolution, than this huge wheel, revolving within arm's length at some vertiginous speed, and barely murmuring." [2] Before long, he began to pray to it. "You are free to deride my sentimentality if you like," he wrote to a friend, "but I assure you that I . . . go down to the Champ de Mars and sit by the hour over the great dynamos, watching them run as noiselessly and as smoothly as the planets, and asking them—with infinite courtesy—where in Hell they are going." [3] Between the dynamo and the cross, he could find no rational connection. As far as he could see, man had translated himself into a new universe which had no common scale of values with the old.

The machine, as Adams was acutely aware, had altered both the relations of man to nature and the relations of men to each other. Through the extension of the use of machinery, man's control over nature had grown more effective, but it was less direct. Under the handicraft system, the tool had been an accessory to the workman's skill, but under machine industry the element of skill was largely transferred to the machine, and the workman became an accessory, attendant to wheels and levers. Also the centralization of industry and the enlargement of the physical unit of greatest economic efficiency beyond the capacity of the individual had made modern man far more dependent on technical aids—machines, furnaces, railways—and on industrial collectives—factories, corporations, labor unions—than on nature itself. The irony was, however, that to the extent he escaped nature, man discovered he was obliged to submit to the rule of technology.

Outwardly and inwardly, the age belonged to the machine. The Baconian idea of employing science in the satisfaction of material wants had given a wholly unforeseen extension to the mechanical arts, and had equipped man in less than fifty years with more tools than he had made during the thousands of years he had lived on earth. There appeared to be nothing that men could do, or have, or hope to have, that was not in some way bound up with machinery. The power and spirit of the modern age was organized around the machine process. Business, as it approached the industrial ideal, functioned with machinelike efficiency. Politics, in both the best and worst sense, was "machine politics." Schools and colleges were regarded, favorably and unfavorably, as factories; the modern state, at its most vigorous, became a war machine. And, as befitted a mechanistic culture, morals were inventions, and ideals were byproducts of technical progress.

Under the influence of the machine, Americans had become, as Lippmann said, literally an eccentric people. "There isn't a human relation, whether of parent and child, husband and wife, worker and employer, that doesn't move in a strange situation. . . . There are no precedents to guide us, no wisdom that wasn't made for a simpler age. We have changed our environment more quickly than we know how to change ourselves."[4] Faced by ceaseless technological change, nothing seemed real but the future. "When one gets light by pushing a button, heat by turning a screw, water by touching a faucet, and food by going down in an elevator"—a writer remarked in the *Atlantic*—"life is so detached from the healthy exercise and discipline which used to accompany the mere process of living, that one must scramble energetically to a higher plane or drop to a much lower one."[5] Since the miracles and marvels of technical progress justified themselves largely in terms of quantity production and cash results, the temptation was to substitute quantity for value as the supreme criterion of life. Thus, as Veblen suggested and Lewis Mumford said, for those whose thoughts were shaped by the technical processes, "the belief that values could be dispensed with constituted the new system of values."[6]

In their admiration for the new life thrust upon them by the machine, Americans failed to confront the fact that technique, like its brain-child the machine, was indifferent to the purposes to which it was put. The essential technique of gunpowder, for instance, was the same whether it was used to blast coal from a mine, to build dams and roads, or to inflict death upon men at war. Thus the consequences of technique, like its uses, were ambivalent. It was both an instrument of liberation and repression; it freed man from back-breaking labor, but imprisoned him in a factory. It made for greater material wealth by increasing efficiency, but impoverished the human spirit by routinizing life. Although the typewriter, the telephone and the automobile were remarkable technological achievements, Veblen wondered whether they "have not wasted more effort and substance than they have saved," because they had increased the pace and volume of correspondence, commerce and travel out of all proportion to the real need.[7] Similarly technique had nobly served human needs, yet at the same time enslaved its beneficiaries in a purposeless materialism by fostering the delusion that the world would be a better place when everybody had a bathtub and an automobile.

But while the achievements of technique stirred an unqualified admiration in modern man, it did not follow that the type of man and civilization that the machine culture was manufacturing were as good and beautiful as they were remarkable. Calling attention to the war between the automatism of matter and the *élan vital* of spirit, Adams speculated whether man might become merely a means whereby the machine perpetuated itself and extended its dominion. "Man has mounted science," he told his brother, "and is now run away with. I firmly believe that before many centuries more, science will be the master of man. The engines he will have invented will be beyond his strength to control. Some day science may have the existence of mankind in its power, and the human race commit suicide by blowing up the world." [8]

Business and Civilization

Just as machines were instruments of man's control over nature, corporations were social machines to which the modern American became almost as completely subordinate in his relations to men as he had become a mere adjunct of the machine in his relations to nature. Yet, despite its phenomenal economic success, the giant industrial corporation had proved to be a far from ideal instrument of social control.

The predominance of business was, as Dewey remarked, "the pragmatism of American life." [9] What Americans called civilization was virtually synonomous with the social consolidation brought about under the corporate auspices of business and technology. But along with the rise of great cities and great industrial complexes had come alarming symptoms of social disintegration which made men wonder if the splendid new empire of business was to be erected upon the grave of civilization. "Our bignesses—cities, factories, monopolies, fortunes," said Lloyd, are the obesities of an age gluttonous beyond its powers of digestion. Mankind are crowding upon each other in the centres, and struggling to keep each other out of the feast set by the new sciences. . . . Our size has got beyond our science and our conscience. The vision of the railroad stockholder is not far-sighted enough to see into the office of the General Manager; the people cannot reach across even a ward of a city to rule their rulers; Captains of Industry "do not know" whether the men in the ranks are dying from lack of food and shelter; we cannot clean our cities nor our politics. . . ." [10]

Such considerations led Brooks Adams, brother of Henry, to infer that the extreme complexity of the administrative problems presented by modern industrial civilization was beyond the compass of the capitalistic mind. Modern civilization was changing faster than any environment ever previously changed, and consequently had an unprecedented need for the administrative or generalizing type of mind. But it was precisely in this requisite that Adams suspected the new capitalist to be weak. The modern capitalist had evolved under the stress of an environment which demanded excessive specialization in the direction of moneymaking under highly complex industrial conditions. "To this money-making attribute all else has been sacrificed, and the modern capitalist not only thinks in terms of money, but . . . . looks upon life as a financial combat of a very specialized kind, regulated by a code which he understands and has indeed himself concocted, but which is recognized by no one else in the world." [11] The most distressing aspect of the situation to Adams was that the modern capitalist would not take responsibility for the new civilization he had created. He knew nothing, and cared less, about the wider problems facing society. To him, to paraphrase Lloyd, science was a never-ending inventory stored up by nature for his use, government a fountain of privilege, and the nation an army of customers. As civilizations had usually broken down because of administrative difficulties, Adams felt that unless the capitalist mind could rise to an appreciation of diverse social conditions, as well as to a level of political sagacity far higher than it had attained in recent years, American civilization must inevitably disintegrate.

The failure of America to develop the kind of administrative intelligence able to recognize and coordinate conflicting social interests was attributed by Adams largely to the capitalist attitude toward education. American business had long owned the leading universities by right of purchase and had in general used education to promote capitalistic ideas. But this was of lesser moment than the fact that business had commercialized education. Rather than encouraging a higher order of intelligence which could at best be produced only in small quantity and at high cost, business had insisted all education must be immediately and crassly useful. Special training was chiefly needful for technologists who were not masters but servants.

Highly indicative of this lopsided emphasis was the amazing drive for industrial education that hit this country at the beginning of the century. The motives behind this "mental epidemic" for vocational training were mixed, but were chiefly three: prejudice, opportunism, jingoism. Many native Americans, apprehensive about the upward climb of the "new immigrants," sought to restrict their education to the manual arts; secondly, industrialists and businessmen wanted to obtain, at public expense, a well trained labor force able to handle tools and machines, educated enough to read and understand directions but not to question the requirements of modern large-scale industry; thirdly, a number of patriotic citizens and businessmen, convinced that rivalry in trade and commerce was to be the warfare of the future, were determined that America should win industrial supremacy of the world. Since Germany, the most powerful rival of the United States and Britain in world trade, had evolved the most effective methods of attaining the highest industrial efficiency in the shortest time, it was argued that the German system of industrial education must be introduced in this country. The result was an astonishing campaign for the recruitment and training of a new-style army, an industrial army, which for many Americans now acquired the same urgency it had assumed a generation earlier in Germany.

Spurred on by the business community, educators set out to provide the services of an army of semi-skilled workers who would "adjust nicely to the industrial machine." Since officers for this new army were already provided by the colleges and professional schools, their task was to recruit and drill the rank and file in the public schools. Perversely borrowing from John Dewey, who had disparaged the American school system as undemocratic class education because it benefited only a minority preparing for college and the professions, the advocates of industrial education pushed toward a totalitarian solution. In their resolve that American education should be as "democratic" as that of Germany, they urged the establishment of an elitist system of "differentiated" education which would sort pupils according to "their evident or probable destinies." "It used to be thought," said a spokesman, "that it is contrary to the genius of American principles of social equality that any young person should select his own calling, or that he should have it selected for him at an early age. Every boy and girl is a possible occupant of the White House. Such teaching is far more weirdly Utopian than that of our present day social dreamers." Instead special education was recommended as frankly adapting the school to the needs of those classes who were destined to tend the machines and go down in the mines.[12]

Although the attempt to press lower-class Americans into the industrial service of the nation proved abortive, the "factoryizing" of higher education was easily accomplished. The American university was made to function like a large industrial corporation. The board of trustees or regents, composed largely of businessmen, was exactly comparable to a board of directors; the college president, whose duty was to maintain profits and raise funds, managed the educational factory with assistance from higher technicians or deans; the professors were the underpaid workers who manned the production lines, and the students were, of course, the raw material to be converted into vendible commodities. The underlying presumption behind this businesslike administration of scholastic routine, was, as Veblen perceived, that learning was a saleable commodity, "to be produced on a piece-rate plan, rated, bought and sold by standard units, measured, counted and reduced to staple equivalence by impersonal, mechanical tests." [13] By reducing learning to the acquisition of academic profits or credits, this mechanistic system encouraged perfunctory and mediocre work and deterred both students and teachers from a free pursuit of knowledge. Instead of improving educational performance, the introduction of business techniques in the universities tended not only to retard the acquisition of knowledge, but ultimately to defeat the ends of the university—the cultivation of exceptional minds.

The same techniques were at work in another, more far-reaching department of the educational system—the periodical press. Though educational media of the most influential kind, newspapers and magazines were commonly regarded as a field of business enterprise, and therefore business methods were applied more openly and consistently than in academic enterprise where these techniques were disguised by scholastic formalities. Only incidently a purveyor of news, opinion and information, the periodical press served primarily as a vehicle for advertisements. Since the profits of publication came from the sale of advertising space and not from the subscriptions of readers hungry for truth and eager for accurate information, the aim of the publishers was to make their product appeal to as many as possible, for the larger the circulation, the greater the market value of advertising space. As a consequence, the end product was pretty much along the lines of H. G. Wells description of the *New York Journal:*

. . . that enormous bale of paper is eloquent of a public void of moral ambitions, lost to any sense of comprehensive things, deaf to ideas, impervious to generalizations, a public which has carried the conception of freedom to its logical extreme of entire individual detachment. These telltale columns deal all with personality and the drama of personal life. They witness to no interest but the interest in intense individual experiences. The engagements, the love affairs, the scandals of conspicuous people are given in pitiless detail in articles adorned with vigorous portraits and sensational pictorial comments. . . . Murders and crimes are worked up to the keenest pitch of realization, and any new indelicacy in fashionable costume, any new medical device or cure, any new dance or athleticism, any new breach in the moral code, any novelty in sea-bathing or the woman's seat on horseback, or the like, is given copious and moving illustration, stirring headlines, and eloquent reprobation. There is a colored supplement of knock-about fun [comics], written chiefly in the quaint dialect of the New York slums . . . and it presents a world in which the kicking by a mule of an endless succession of victims is an inexhaustible joy to young and old. "Dat ole Maud!" There is a smaller bale dealing with sport. In the advertisement columns one finds nothing of books, nothing of art; but great choice of bust developers, hair restorers, nervous tonics, clothing sales, self-contained flats, and business opportunities.[14]

Such standards as survived were rendered harmless, not to say pointless, by the necessity for business reasons to avoid anything that might hamper the purposes of the advertiser. Nothing must be published that might discredit his claims or good faith, or cast a sinister shadow on the activities of American businessmen. Although the short-lived muckraking magazines successfully flouted this *obiter dictum,* theirs was a brief glory, for after a few controversial years of criticism and aspiration, virtually all succumbed either to an advertising boycott or other overt business pressures.[15] Typical of the survivors, *Collier's* and the *American Magazine* renounced muckraking for a policy of genial optimism calculated to please that large body of Americans who were in the habit of buying freely. The net cultural effect of this "systematic insincerity" on the part of the business-controlled press was to exalt the meretricious, to encourage what Veblen called "the crasser forms of patriotic, sportsmanlike, and spendthrift aspirations," and to discourage the exercise of that wide-ranging critical intelligence upon which historically the hopes of civilization have always rested.[16]

A More Efficient America

Nearly all men of pragmatic persuasion, whether conservative or liberal, regarded the state as the most desirable instrument of social control. From Theodore Roosevelt and Brooks Adams to Walter Lippmann and Edward Ross, their dream envisaged a kind of modified state capitalism, run along the lines of a big modern corporation, with a trained administrative elite firmly in control, a powerful but disciplined industry, and an orderly, informed, forward-looking public.

"Call it what you will: empire, dictatorship, republic, or anything else," Adams told Roosevelt. "We must have a power strong enough to make all the interests equal before the law, or we must dissolve into chaos."[17] Croly shared the same conviction. National politics must aim primarily at efficiency—"that is, at the successful use of the force resident in the state."[18] The new radicals likewise deplored the disorder of American society. If the younger critics were to meet the issues of their generation, asserted Lippmann, they must give their attention "not so much to the evils of authority, as to the weaknesses of democracy." His vision was the "state-making dream," as Wells called it. By revising the "old virtues of authority," Lippmann hoped for an end to the confusions that wasted human possibilities. "This is what mastery means: the substitution of conscious intention for unconscious striving."[19]

A clear statement of what the new radicals meant by "mastery" was Edward A. Ross's influential text, *Social Control*. Appearing in 1901, the book expressed confidence in the manageability of society and in the ability of intellectuals to manage it. Of all controls, Ross found the state the least sentimental because the state was "an organization that puts a wise minority in the saddle." This "wise minority" consisted of managers, technicians, planners, and other bureaucrats who would be compelled to take power from the politicians in order to meet the demand for specialized knowledge in a highly complex industrial society. "As the enlightenment of the public wanes relatively to the superior enlightenment of the learned castes and professions, the mandarinate [the intellectual elite] will infallibly draw to itself a greater and greater share of social power."

Since there was no absolute moral order imposed from above, no instinct for good conduct, it was up to man, asserted Ross, to establish his own social control. Although sympathy, sociability, the individual sense of justice, custom and belief all played important roles, successful social organization ultimately depended only upon one thing—obedience to the aims of society. Other than primitive physical punishment, there were two effective ways to enforce obedience: the first, and formerly the most formidable, engine of control was the law; the second, and most modern, was the planned development and manipulation of public opinion. The law had proved effective in the more primitive societies of the past, but it was his belief that superior methods of control were inward rather than outward. Ross therefore advocated "moral engineering," or the methods of propaganda as the technique best suited to control the great social organizations of the twentieth century. "We are come to a time when ordinary men are scarcely aware of the coercion of public opinion, so used are they to follow it. They cannot dream of aught but acquiescence in an unmistakable edict of the mass." By thus supplementing the sanctions of the law, society avoided putting itself into undisguised opposition to a man's wishes and was therefore not so likely to raise the spirit of rebellion.[20]

"Sin" was now defined as conduct harmful to the "sacred interests of society," and morals—instead of being ready-made formulas to be invoked by pastors, teachers, and parents—became mere temporary expressions of the social will.[21] Primitive public opinion, however, was instinctual and passionate, flooded with unconscious prejudices that made critical thinking difficult. It therefore had to be shaped and guided. Recognition of this fact was regarded as the first step in a businesslike understanding of the matter. Since men's actions in society were, more often than not, the result of irrational impulses, the empirical art of social control consisted largely, as Lippmann's mentor, Graham Wallas, put it, in "the creation of opinion by the deliberate exploitation of subconscious non-rational inference." [22] With open eyes, the "wise minority" were "to make reason serve the irrational, ' by using intellectualized propaganda to shape men's conduct and thus set in motion the dynamics for a "splendid human civilization." And as Lippmann correctly surmised, America seemed to be moving toward some such statecraft.[23]

After 1914 and the beginning of war in Europe, Americans became far more interested in the realization of positive political and social purposes than they had been ten years earlier. Along with a growing hostility toward Progressivism, there was much talk about "efficiency in public business." Staunch Progressives such as Richard T. Ely called for more and better management in government and, in an astonishing turnabout, now condemned popular participation through the initiative, referendum and recall as "suitable only to a primitive rural democracy." "We must in one way or another let others choose for us," said Ely. "Our aim must be to give [wider] scope to the wise administrator." [24] Among the new radicals, Croly had always pinned his hopes on an elite rather than the masses, and in 1916 he was joined by Lippmann, for whom the real question now was how "the minority which has some sense of the problem . . . [would] come to the top." [25]

In spite of the current unpopularity of Progressivism, Croly's *New Republic* assured liberal readers that American public opinion was still loyal to the idea of a continuing forward movement, explaining, "The existing reaction seeks to discipline progressivism rather than to destroy it." Not without condescension, the editors pronounced it "an honest, if confused and blundering, effort to adapt traditional impulses and ideals to the unprecedented contemporary social needs," and then went on to tell why the Progressives had not been equal to the job. In their zeal to eradicate abuses, they had been betrayed into the adoption of "inefficient and only semi-efficient remedies." They trusted "overmuch to the efficacy of political and legislative mechanism," and out of the desire for a conscious nationalism, had failed to serve a "higher conception of public interest." [26] What the editors meant by "efficient remedies" came out in an editorial by Lippmann who, under the spur of preparedness, demanded not only armaments, but a willingness "to unify and socialize the railroads and the means of communication, to regulate rigorously basic industries . . . to control the food supply and shipping and credit." [27] Even more definitive of the direction of radical thought and its "higher conception of public interest" was a *New Republic* article in which Bourne told Americans they had use for German ideals. After all, he asked, what was the new social politics of liberalism "but a German collectivism half-heartedly grafted on a raw stock of individualist 'liberty' ?" American ideals must be "just as daring, just as modern, just as realistic" as the German, but they must be "pragmatically truer and juster." In place of the sterile German will to conquer, Americans would use the "pulsating ideal of organized energy" to work out a "democratic socialized life." [28]

Once America prepared to fight, however, and started to muster the might of the state for military rather than social purposes, some young radicals began to have misgivings about the program of the new politics. While Croly, Lippmann, and Weyl were crying up militant nationalism in the pages of the *New Republic,* Bourne experienced a change of heart and joined with Van Wyck Brooks and *The Seven Arts,* a new "little magazine," in denouncing the war as the bankruptcy of political nationalism. Nor were Floyd Dell and John Reed able to accept the war and conscription as steps in the working out of a political theory "whereby brains would ultimately rule mankind." [29] The emerging superstate in Germany with its totalitarian manners and military trappings was a disturbing distortion of the "highly-organized and benevolently-administered State Trust" they had pictured. "State Capitalism now loomed as the final and worst intrenchment of the forces of the enemy," said Dell. "You could strike against a private employer—you couldn't do even that against the State. The private employer could send troops against you; but the state could put you into uniform, and send you to work under military orders. . . . We had thought to capture the State; would it not be better to destroy it?" [30]

Pragmatic Nationalism

With the coming of war, the new politics was put to the test. In this modern twentieth-century allegory, however, it was not the old issue of absolute good against absolute evil, but of critical intelligence pitted against willful barbarism—a novel confrontation between new techniques of social control and the old, faceless forces of determinism. The United States' entry into the war was supported by President Wilson on pragmatic grounds that more good than harm would come to America from fighting. We were in the war, the President calmly assured his countrymen, not to kill Germans but to win the peace. With ends so clear and certain— the destruction of German militarism, the spread of democracy and self-determination of peoples, the establishment of a just peace and of an international organization to preserve peace—there was little concern about the means.

Cheerfully, matter-of-factly, with scarcely a murmur of protest, American intellectuals obediently fell into line behind the President and conservative business interests. "The American nation needs the tonic of a serious moral adventure," Croly had written the year before;[31] and now he boasted, with more egoism than accuracy, that while the bankers and capitalists had favored war, "the effective and decisive work" on behalf of war had been accomplished by intellectuals.[32] Confident that the war was motivated by democratic ends, neither he nor the others saw anything incompatible in such a mixture of expediency and idealism. The world's problems, Ralph Barton Perry had contended, could be solved neither by absolute war nor absolute peace. What was needed was a "wise and balanced mind" that could accept war as a "deplorable present necessity" and pursue peace as a "glorious hope." [33]

The war program of the intellectuals was inspired by Dewey's popular philosophy of instrumentalism. A "high mood of confidence and self-righteousness" and a "keen sense of control over events" made them eligible to discipleship under Professor Dewey.[34] Like them, the philosopher was hostile to impossibilism, to apathy, to any attitude that suggested a slackening of determination to use the emergency to consolidate the gains of democracy. When it came to great questions of social morality, war and peace, Dewey had taken the stand that attachment to any particular principle or ideal, such as pacifism, was less important than a willingness to reexamine and, if necessary, to revise one's convictions in order to divert existing tendencies to new ends. To emphasize the relativist or social character of morality, he insisted, was not to make an ideal of adjustment to "things as they are" but rather to stress that the choice lay between a morality which was effective because related to what was and a "mushy belief in disembodied moral forces," which was futile and empty because it disregarded actual conditions. On this existential basis, Dewey rationalized the war.[35]

To Dewey and his sanguine disciples, war was simply a means for "getting things done." Accordingly their immediate concern was for administrative efficiency. If the war was feebly and wastefully conducted, not only would the human cost of war be vastly increased, but chaos was bound to result. The intellectuals could control the situation only by showing a mastery of it. To act swiftly and methodically would not only shorten the war, but keep the conduct of the war out of the hands of the jingoes. Therefore, if the will to conquer were to be put to work for a "scientific peace," there was no pausing until trends were certain. As Lippmann said, "We have to act on what we believe, on half-knowledge, illusion and error. Experience itself will reveal our mistakes; research and criticism may convert them into wisdom."[36] They had no fear of losing control of the means because it was generally assumed that Americans were educated to a higher level of political intelligence than most peoples and were not to be moved by mock heroics, the hip-hurrah and herd psychology of war. With pride Dewey pointed to their earnest sense of a "nasty job to be done" as a "novel psychosis for war."[37]

Although Dewey at least was aware that even in the most successful enterprises aims and results never wholly coincided and

that the forces let loose by war might have unexpected consequences, he chose deliberately to look on the bright side. War,
he assured readers of the *Independent* in 1918, offered "unin-
tended" social possibilities, especially in technological innovation
and in the development of new techniques of social organization
and control. Out of the fiery ordeal of war, he prophesied, there
should emerge not only a scientifically more efficient America but
a new, humanly improved democracy.[38]

He was right, certainly, about war forcing the pace of technological activity. Under the pressure of military demand, steel
production kept step with bloodshed, and afterward, war-swollen
plants did find an outlet in steel-framed skyscrapers. The submarine
and the airplane—which Dewey regarded as the greatest mechanical achievements of the war—were, on the other hand, not so
successfully converted from malevolence to social service. Although the airplane found peacetime uses, the combined effect of
the two did not, as Dewey hoped, "do more to displace war than
all the moralizing in existence." [39] Rather the devilishness of the
new machinery of death—the insidious terror of craft that struck
inhumanly under cover of the water and dropped destruction from
the clouds—served to widen the scale of war and to intensify its
deadliness. The airplane, instead of bringing international cooperation by obliterating nationalistic frontiers, was made use of in
coming decades to obliterate civilian populations within those
boundaries. From the technical standpoint, improvement of the
mechanism of war did not make war impossible but, as William
Jennings Bryan argued, only more efficient:

> If we measure the war by the destructiveness of the implements
> employed, nothing so horrible has ever been known before. They used
> to be content to use the earth's surface for the maneuvers of war, but
> now they have taken possession of the air, and thunder bolts more
> deadly than the thunder-bolts of Jove fall as if from the clouds on
> unsuspecting people. And they have taken possession of the ocean's
> depths as well, and death-dealing torpedoes rise from out the darkness
> to multiply the perils of the sea. They have substituted a long-range
> rifle for a short-range rifle, a big-mouthed gun for a little-mouthed
> gun, a dreadnought for a battle ship, and a super-dreadnought for a
> dreadnought, to which they have added the submarine. And they now
> pour liquid fire on battle lines and suffocate soldiers in the trenches

with poisonous gases. Inventive genius has been exhausted to find new ways by which man can kill his fellowman! [40]

Though Hiram Maxim might proclaim the machinegun "the greatest life-saving instrument ever invented," [41] in view of its end products—the dead and mutilated, physical and cultural devastation, moral corruption—modern warfare justified Bryan's condemnation as the most efficient technique of social suicide ever devised by man.

What Dewey and the pragmatic proponents of war failed to perceive was that war was the supreme tragedy of a modern mechanized society for, as Mumford has pointed out, war sanctioned savagery and deified the machine. By placing in the hands of armies instruments of ruthlessness of which only the most savage conquerors of the past would have taken advantage, technique had changed war from an exhibition of skill and courage into a manufactory of death. "The difference between the Athenians with their swords and shields fighting on the fields of Marathon, and the soldiers who faced each other with tanks, guns, flame-throwers, poison gases, and hand-grenades on the Western Front, is the difference between the ritual of the dance and the routine of the slaughter house." [42] Dismayed by the spectacle of huge war engines that dwarfed their makers and controlled the strategy of armies, "seeming to possess a kind of independent and maleficent will of their own," thoughtful men like Paul Elmer More speculated whether modern man was in the position of a "too cunning Frankenstein," having set loose the demon of his own ruin.[43] For it appeared, as Dewey had inadvertently conceded, that the forces called into being had "acquired an independent being" and were effecting "consequences more significant than those consciously desired." [44]

As Dewey also anticipated, the mobilization of America's industrial forces and their conversion from peaceful uses to war and destruction led to tighter political control over the economy and to the systematic utilization of experts by government. In the fierce heat of war, competition—the heart of Wilson's cherished "new freedom"—was abandoned, and there ensued, as Tugwell said, "an era of combination such as put the pale efforts of the nineties to shame." [45] Industries which did not readily respond to the invitation to combine were actually called together in Washington and lectured by government officials for not doing what they would have been punished for a few months earlier. This new intimacy

"We smash 'em HARD"

One of the Yank Veterans

"Did I bayonet my first Hun? Sure! How did it feel? It *doesn't* feel! There *he* is. There *you* are. One of you has got to go. I preferred to stay.

"So when sergeant says, 'Smash 'em, boys'—we do. And we go them one better like good old Yankee Doodle Yanks. For bullets and bayonets are the only kind of lingo

that a Hun can *understand!*"

＊ ＊ ＊ ＊

The *dependable* Yank, whose photograph appears above, first met the *dependable* Owl Cigar while boosting that *dependable* investment—the Liberty Loan.

We didn't tell him about the $2,000,000 stock of leaf that is always aging for Owl and White Owl. Nor the over 100,000,000 Owls and White Owls sold last year. We just swapped him a White Owl for a smile. And it doesn't look like the smile came hard, does it?

Why don't you, too, try an Owl or White Owl—*today?*

DEALERS:
If your distributor does not sell these dependable cigars, write us.
GENERAL CIGAR CO., INC., 119 West 40th Street, New York City

TWO   DEPENDABLE   CIGARS

WHITE OWL * Invincible Shape 7c

OWL * Square-end 6c

WHITE OWL

OWL 6c **white OWL 7c**

Branded for your

Banded protection

This bloodthirsty doughboy echoed the official propaganda of World War I. Through advertisements in newspapers and magazines, motion pictures, and billboards, the U.S. Committee of Public Information sold hate like cigars and made the manufacture of patriotism chief among the war industries.   From *The Saturday Evening Post*, Aug. 31, 1918.

between government and business was presided over by Wall Street financier Bernard Baruch, who, as head of the War Industries Board, imposed dictatorial controls to ensure that the economy would run like a well-oiled machine. Here, as Wiebe has said, "was the America of Herbert Croly's dreams, a corporate society led by the federal government, only Bernard Baruch had replaced Theodore Roosevelt."[46] The key administrators, "dollar-a-year men," were drawn from big business, but offices and laboratories swarmed with "men of special knowledge" drafted from colleges and factories who found the war an industrial engineer's Utopia. The efficiency of this combined military and economic machine amazed not only the enemy but our allies. As the war assumed more and more the character of a struggle between national economic systems, the captain of industry became in effect a military officer of his country, and the ordinary citizen became a private enlisted for the national service.[47]

Contrary to Dewey's expectations, however, the war did not afford an object lesson in the supremacy of public need over private profit. As far as American business was concerned, the German invasion of France not only cured the depression of 1914, but inspired a big gamble in war-order stocks which increased in price by $866 million during a single year, paying in one case a dividend of 2,900 per cent.[48] The enthusiastic response of American businessmen tended to support Maxim's contention, "War is an industry. As a matter of stern fact, war is, and has always been, the biggest and most vital industry of mankind."[49] Welcoming the orders which poured into the United States, *The Banker* told its readers that "hay should be made while the sun shines, for after the war is over we will not continue to have the trade monopoly . . . which we now enjoy." While trade papers generally endorsed the traffic in munitions, the *Wall Street Journal* justified loans to the Allies on the grounds that we were not lending money for war, but "financing American trade."[50] By 1917, the war boom had boosted earnings of manufacturing corporations 330 per cent above those of 1913. Even after the United States joined the Allies, American businessmen continued to treat the war as a business problem—just as Brooks Adams had predicted they would. Rather than government control stamping out profiteering, it soon became apparent that American industry under coordinated guidance and with its new cooperative efficiency possessed not only an enhanced productive power but a valuable advantage in the markets. "During the war there was virtually no competition for orders . . . for the problem then was not who would get patronage, but who must accept it. Every large plant engaged in an essential industry was compelled to enlarge, work overtime, and drive in order to attain the production that was allocated to it. . . . Competition in price was practically done away with by Government action."[51] When businessmen discovered that the strength developed for military purposes could be used to exploit buyers, they had no patriotic qualms in putting it to profitable use both during and after the war.

War, as a prominent official conceded, had "literally brought business into the business of Government,"[52] and afterwards corporate leaders were able to retain their informal hegemony over the political economy. Although disdaining to extend the elaborate system of controls into peacetime, big businessmen nevertheless displayed an addiction in the 1920's to the efficient combination war had sanctioned and an habituation to a kind of friendly cooperation between government and business somewhat removed from Dewey's postwar vision of democratic collectivism.

The pragmatic nationalism Dewey had called for, inspired by the "sense of a job to be accomplished" and based upon a "businesslike psychology," was never given fair trial. It was quickly sacked for a win-the-war psychosis deliberately stirred up by tried and true techniques of public manipulation. Trading on the old war cries of hate and fear, honor and profit, patriotism and power, the U.S. Committee of Public Information, the official propaganda machine, soon made the manufacture of patriotism chief among the war industries. Through pamphlets, speakers, newspapers and magazines, motion pictures, posters and billboards, the state mobilized public opinion as it had conscripted men, money and materials.[53] The eagerness of the nation's foremost writers, scholars and reformers to enlist in the hysterical endeavor to "sell" the war made clear that, in practice, the social control which Ross had hoped would lead the masses to higher ends meant, not the triumph of reason over irrationality, but the systematic cultivation of the irrational, turning emotion from a means into an end.

The effectiveness of Uncle Sam's salesmanship was attested to by new sense of solidarity among the American people. As with the soldier, so with civilians, there was now a "demand for closed ranks, for mass formations, for lining up with eyes right, and forward by platoons." For the first time the political offender became a conspicuous figure in American life. In New York, a Columbia professor who had opposed United States entrance into the war was summarily dismissed; in California, a San Franciscan was sent to jail for laughing at rookies drilling on the Presidio. Public reaction to dissent and criticism began to exhibit what the *Nation* called a "spirit of ruthless brutality." A teacher in Iowa, suspected of being "disloyal," was painted yellow by a mob; in Montana a lynching party murdered an official of the I.W.W.; Ohio vigilantes kidnapped and flogged a prominent liberal who opposed such "war-madness." Pacifists were harassed and imprisoned; conscientious objectors were subjected to humiliation, and some were actually tortured. At one barracks, "conschies" reportedly were made to stand during the first week with their hands crossed on their chests and during the second week hanged by their wrists. Bursting with love of country, angry mobs descended on public schools, tore up German books, and demanded the German language be abolished.[54]

Along with conscription of thought, there was a government-imposed censorship that became more oppressive every day. Under hastily passed espionage and sedition laws, civil liberties were virtually abolished, wartime legislation making almost any criticism of governmental policy illegal. The antiwar radical journal, *The Masses,* was denied mailing privileges for allegedly printing treasonable materials; its editor, Max Eastman, narrowly escaped a lynch mob of soldiers. *The Seven Arts* was pushed out of business, many thought, because of Bourne's savage articles against the war. America had not been in the war ten weeks before "Peace without victory" changed officially into "Conquer or submit." Early in 1917, the Committee on Public Information cautioned that "speculation about possible peace" was a dangerous topic. A few weeks later, the President himself decried German "peace intrigue" and vowed war to the limit, warning "Woe be to the man or group of men that seeks to stand in our way."[55]

Through all the turmoil Dewey steadfastly refused to worry. He was not at first "specially concerned" that liberty of thought and speech might seriously suffer, though he did think conscientious objectors deserved "something better than accusations." While he tried to explain away persecution as due to Americans' unfamiliarity with the ways and usages of war, he was visibly shaken by the increase of intolerance to the point where treason was "every opinion and belief which irritates the majority of loyal citizens." Finally, however, by November 1918, Dewey was forced to admit that the "cult of irrationality" had got out of hand. Americans had reached an emotional pitch where there was something suspicious about any manifestation of reason or balanced judgment. In such an atmosphere of "moral mob rule and psychological lynch law," there was real danger that suppression of the free discussion of war aims and peace policies would hamper effective American participation in the war. Dewey had always believed the ultimate American participation should not consist in men nor guns, but in the final determination of peace which was made possible by the contribution of men and guns. A few months before, he reflected ruefully, to win the war had meant to bring about a state of affairs which would make any similar war impossible in the future. Now, under persuasion of the cult of the irrational, Americans were coming to accept the military defeat of Germany as a complete enough victory in itself, irrespective of any further consequences.[56]

It was a chastened Pragmatist who at last conceded, "The appeal is no longer to reason; it is to the event." Even if the President was prepared to come forward at the right time with the wisest of all peace measures, if these measures came before "a people intellectually unprepared and apathetic," said Dewey, the world would have the physical fact of peace, but not its meaning. Already he foresaw the time when conservative critics of democracy would come forward with frank disparagement of the League of Nations and would propose as a substitute for the prevention of future wars "a more assiduous devotion to those principles of exclusive and militant nationalism of which Prussia has been the efficient exemplar."[57]

Force and Ideas

The war was to have been "the first real test of . . . our whole American pragmatic philosophy." In a *New Republic* editorial of 1915 portentously entitled "Mental Unpreparedness," Bourne proclaimed America had reached a parting of intellectual ways. "We can put our ideals behind us and turn and worship them, or we can put them ahead of us and struggle toward them." It was "an issue between an old immutable idealism and a new experimentalism."[58]

Since then Pragmatism had been put to the test and found wanting. With the arrogance of the young, it had assumed the right to formulate the aims of life and the values by which those aims were tested, aims and values which, as it turned out, were helpless to prevent the degradation of democratic ideals or to check the social neuroses of war. Had the Pragmatists not issued a special claim upon reality, said Van Wyck Brooks, no one would have held them responsible.[59] But the Pragmatists had claimed they alone apprehended reality and were able to do something about it. For more than twenty years their philosophy had been the rationalization of the whole spirit of American life, and the observable result seemed to be that Americans, in living out this philosophy, had confused means with ends, sacrificing vital human values to the sterile demands of social efficiency. Pragmatism, which as a philosophy of experimentalism had prided itself upon intelligently breaking away from the morality of routine and habit, had slipped with distressing ease into the brutal service of war—the most routine and immoral habit of man.

The war, Bourne now observed bitterly, had revealed "a younger intelligentsia, trained up in the pragmatic dispensation, immensely ready for the executive ordering of events, pitifully unprepared for the . . . idealistic focussing of ends." Like Lippmann, the young men being sucked into the war organization were "liberal, enlightened, aware . . . . a wholly new force in American life, product of the swing in the colleges from a training that emphasized classical studies to one that emphasized political and economic values." Practically all of them were "lined up in service of the war-technique." There seemed, in fact, a peculiar congeniality between the war and them. It was "as if the war and they had been waiting for each other." While Dewey, it was true, had called for "a more attentive formulation of war-purposes and ideas," he called to deaf ears. For his disciples had learned all too literally the instrumental attitude toward life, and being immensely intelligent and energetic, they made themselves "efficient instruments of the war-technique, accepting with little question the ends as announced from above." [60]

It had never occurred to those who, like Bourne, had taken Dewey's philosophy almost as an American religion, that values could be subordinated to technique. Yet such a debacle had been foreseen by Henry Adams as the unavoidable product of a one-sided consciousness that exaggerated the mechanics of life at the expense of the quality of living. Shuddering at the bloody consequences of this "amputated Intelligence," he perceived the weakness of such a philosophy of adjustment to be that there was no possibility of thought getting beyond itself. Unable to rise above the existent situation, it could only yield to action for action's sake.[61]

So American intellectuals, in embracing war, had confused the event with the ideal, war with peace. In their eagerness to get somewhere, they had neglected to ask whether it was a desirable place to get. They discovered too late that war was a special form of conflict in which the aim was not resolution of ideas but annihilation of the enemy. The forces of history had not favored intelligence as much as they thought. "I assumed," Croly afterwards confessed, "that the American people would take as much interest in the declared political objects of the war as they would in their exertions on behalf of military victory. These suppositions proved to be wrong." [62] Once war was on, moral issues became afterthoughts, and the intellectuals had no choice but to ride the tiger.

Ironically, the post-mortem had already been written in the first issue of the *New Republic*. "If our thought has been ineffective," the magazine editorialized at the beginning of war in 1914, "we shall not save ourselves by not thinking at all, for . . . . the fact remains that the final argument against cannon is ideas. The thoughts of men which seem so feeble are the only weapons they have against overwhelming force. It was a brain that conceived the gun, it was brains that organized the armies, it was the triumph of physics and chemistry that made possible the dreadnought. Men organized this superb destruction; they created this force, thought it, dreamed it, planned it. It has got beyond their control. It has got into the service of hidden forces they do not understand. Men can master it only by clarifying their own will to end it, and making a civilization so thoroughly under their control that no machine can turn traitor to it." [63]

Notes

Introduction

1. Henry Adams, *The Education of Henry Adams* (New York: Modern Library, 1931), pp. 499, 496, 494. First printed privately in 1907.
2. *Ibid.*, pp. 500, 240, 330.
3. *Ibid.*, p. 239.
4. Thorstein Veblen, "The Place of Science in Modern Civilization." *American Journal of Sociology*, II (March, 1906), 585–609.

Prologue: The Pragmatist and the Progressive

1. George Santayana, "The Genteel Tradition in American Philosophy," address delivered before the Philosophical Union of the University of California in 1911, reprinted in *Winds of Doctrine* (New York: Harper, 1957), pp. 187–88.
2. Van Wyck Brooks, "America's Coming-of-Age" (1915), reprinted in *Three Essays on America* (New York: Dutton, 1934), pp. 17–18, 30.
3. William James, *Pragmatism* (New York: Longmans, Green, 1907), pp. 218, 222.
4. *Ibid.*, p. 12.
5. Quoted in James Weinstein, *The Corporate Ideal in the Liberal State 1900–1918* (Boston: Beacon, 1968), p. 34.
6. Henry Steele Commager, *Documents of American History* (New York: Appleton-Century-Crofts, 1949), II, 143–46, 178–80.
7. James Weinstein, *The Decline of Socialism in America 1912–1925* (New York: Monthly Review Press, 1967), pp. 93–118.
8. Weinstein, *Corporate Ideal*, p. ix and *passim*.
9. George W. Perkins, "Business: The Moral Question," *World's Work*, XXII (June, 1911), 14469–71.
10. Quoted in Weinstein, *op. cit.*, p. 33.
11. Quoted in D. Wilhelm, "The 'Big Business' Man As a Social Worker," *Outlook*, Aug. 22, 1914, p. 1009.
12. Weinstein, *op. cit.*, p. 153.

355

13. Robert H. Wiebe, *Businessmen and Reform: A Study of the Progressive Movement* (Cambridge: Harvard University, 1962), p. 216.

14. Quoted *ibid.*, p. 196.

15. Quoted from a statement of the Philadelphia Board of Trade, *ibid.*, p. 188.

16. *Ibid.*, p. 180.

17. "Pragmatism in Business and Politics," *Commercial & Financial Chronicle*, Oct. 19, 1912, p. 1009.

18. William Allen White, *The Autobiography of William Allen White* (New York: Macmillan, 1946), p. 367.

19. David W. Noble, "The Paradox of Progressive Thought," *American Quarterly*, V (Fall, 1953), 201–03.

20. Woodrow Wilson, *The New Freedom* (New York: Doubleday, Page, 1913), p. 44.

21. Theodore Roosevelt, *Progressive Principles* (New York: Progressive National Service, 1913), p. 195.

22. Wilson in speech at Richmond, Va., 1912, *Congressional Record*, 62d Cong., 2d sess., XLVIII, 3921.

23. Herbert Croly, *The Promise of American Life* (New York: Macmillan, 1909; Capricorn, 1964), p. 147.

24. Roosevelt, *op. cit.*, p. 300.

25. Wilson, *op. cit.*, p. 3.

26. Woodrow Wilson, "The Lawyer and the Community," *North American Review*, CXCII (Nov., 1910), 605.

27. Roosevelt, *op. cit.*, p. 11.

28. *Ibid.*, pp. 206–07.

29. Wilson, *op. cit.*, p. 284.

30. Wilson, *New Freedom*, p. 111.

31. White, *op. cit.*, p. 428.

32. *Ibid.*, pp. 428–29.

33. Vernon Louis Parrington, *Main Currents in American Thought* (New York: Harcourt, Brace, 1927, 1930), III, 408, 410.

34. White, *op. cit.*, p. 516.

35. Ray Stannard Baker, *Woodrow Wilson, Life and Letters* (Garden City: Doubleday, Page, 1927–39), VI, 506.

Chapter I: The Capitalist Revolution

1. In this connection see Joseph A. Schumpeter, "The Creative Response in Economic History," *Journal of Economic History*, VII (Nov., 1947), 150–53.

2. Alfred D. Chandler, Jr., "The Beginnings of 'Big Business' in American Industry," *Business History Review*, XXXIII (Spring, 1959), 1–31.

3. U.S. Commission on Industrial Relations, *Final Report*, 64th Cong., 1st sess., Sen. Doc. No. 415, I, 80 ff.

4. *Abstract of the Census of Manufactures, 1919* (Washington, 1920), Table 195, p. 340.

5. Ray Stannard Baker, "What the United States Steel Corporation Really Is and How It Works," *McClure's*, XVIII (1901), 6.

6. John Moody, *The Truth About the Trusts* (New York: Moody, 1904), pp. 485–93.

7. *Ibid.*, pp. 492–93.

8. *Congressional Record*, 60th Cong., 1st sess., p. 3450.

9. *House Report*, No. 1593, 62d Cong., 3d sess., pp. 86–97.

10. Louis D. Brandeis, *Other People's Money* (New York: Stokes, 1914), pp. 30–33.

11. Jack London, *The Iron Heel* (New

York: Macmillan, 1907; 1958), p. 89.

12. David A. Wells, *Recent Economic Changes* (New York: Appleton, 1898), pp. 27–29, 50–59, 327–37, 465–66.

13. Edwin G. Nourse, "The Place of Agriculture in Modern Industrial Society," *Journal of Political Economy*, XXVII (July, 1919), 565–70.

14. Quoted in Norman Pollack, *The Populist Response to Industrial America* (New York: Norton, 1966), p. 30.

15. Norman Pollack, *The Populist Mind* (Indianapolis: Bobbs-Merrill, 1967), p. 43.

16. William Jennings Bryan, *The First Battle* (Chicago: Conkey, 1897), pp. 199–205.

17. William Graham Sumner, "The Concentration of Wealth: Its Economic Justification," *Independent* (1902), reprinted in *The Challenge of Facts and Other Essays*, A. G. Keller, ed. (New Haven: Yale, 1916), p. 84.

18. Charles R. Flint, "Combinations and Critics," *The Trust: Its Book*, James H. Bridge, ed. (New York: Doubleday, Page, 1902), pp. 1–38.

19. James J. Hill, "Combinations and the Public," *loc. cit.*, p. 106.

20. Quoted in "The Passing of a Business-man Type," *Independent*, Aug. 3, 1911, pp. 270–71.

21. Quoted in Weinstein, *Corporate Ideal*, p. 128.

22. Walter Lippmann, *Drift and Mastery* (New York: Kennerley, 1914; Prentice-Hall, 1961), p. 39.

23. Marshall M. Kirkman, *The Science of Railways* (Chicago: World Railway, 1898), II, 13, 120.

24. Lippmann, *op. cit.*, p. 43.

25. *Ibid.*, p. 31.

26. Thorstein Veblen, *The Theory of Business Enterprise* (New York:

Scribner's, 1904; Mentor, 1958), pp. 16–36.

27. O. K. Fraenkel, ed., *The Curse of Bigness, Miscellaneous Papers of Louis D. Brandeis* (New York: Viking, 1934), pp. 109–10.

28. Henry Demarest Lloyd, *Lords of Industry* (New York: Putnam's, 1910), p. 168.

29. Louis D. Brandeis, *Business—A Profession* (Boston: Small, Maynard, 1914), pp. 319–20.

30. Moody, *op. cit.*, pp. 494.

31. S. C. T. Dodd, "The Present Legal Status of Trusts," *Harvard Law Review*, VI (Nov., 1893), quoted *ibid.*, p. xv.

32. Perkins, *loc. cit.*, p. 14470.

33. Quoted by the *Literary Digest*, Dec. 28, 1912, p. 1213.

34. Gabriel Kolko, *The Triumph of Conservatism* (Glencoe: Free Press, 1963), pp. 37, 40.

35. Henry Demarest Lloyd, *Wealth Against Commonwealth* (New York: Harper, 1894), pp. 494, 501.

36. William Jennings Bryan, speech of Sept. 16, 1899, *Chicago Conference on Trusts* (Chicago: Chicago Civic Federation, 1900), p. 511.

37. W. Scott Morgan, *History of the Wheel and Alliance, and The Impending Revolution* (Fort Scott, Kansas: Rice, 1889), quoted in Pollack, *Populist Mind*, p. 259.

38. Henry R. Hatfield, "The Chicago Conference on Trusts," *Journal of Political Economy*, VIII (Dec., 1899), 5–6.

39. Theodore Roosevelt, "Seventh Annual Message," Dec. 3, 1907, Jas. D. Richardson, ed., *A Compilation of the Messages and Papers of the Presidents* (New York: Bureau of National Literature, 1917), XIV, 7070 *et seq.*

40. Theodore Roosevelt, *An Autobiography* (New York: Macmillan, 1913), pp. 463–64.

41. Wilson, *New Freedom*, p. 197.

42. *Ibid.*, p. 194.

43. *Ibid.*, pp. 190, 284.

44. *Ibid.*, p. 257.

45. Arthur S. Link, *Woodrow Wilson and the Progressive Era* (New York: Harper & Row, 1954), p. 66.

46. Thurman W. Arnold, *The Folklore of Capitalism* (New Haven: Yale University, 1937), p. 211.

47. Lippmann, *Drift and Mastery*, pp. 82–85.

48. Theodore Roosevelt, *New Nationalism* (New York: Outlook, 1910), pp. 42, 54–9.

49. Bridge, *op. cit.*, p. xxxiii; *Harper's Weekly*, July 21, 1894, p. 675.

50. Veblen, *op. cit.*, p. 157.

51. Samuel Gompers, *Labor and the Employer* (New York: Dutton, 1920), pp. 32–33, 41, 43–44.

52. Samuel Gompers, "Organized Labor and the Trusts," *Independent*, June 20, 1901, pp. 1487–88; "The Control of Trusts," *Chicago Conference*, pp. 329–30; also quoted in Bridge, *op. cit.*, pp. 177–78.

53. U.S. Commission on Industrial Relations, *Final Report*, 64th Cong., 1st sess., Sen. Doc. No. 415, pp. 718–24.

54. Wiebe, *op. cit.*, p. 31.

55. Clarence E. Bonnett, *Employers' Associations in the United States* (New York: Macmillan, 1922), pp. 3–34, 291–385, 456.

56. Vincent St. John, *The I.W.W., Its History, Structure, and Methods* (Chicago: I.W.W., 1919), p. 9.

57. Basil M. Manly, *Report of the Director of Research and Investigation*, U.S. Commission on Industrial Relations (Washington, 1916), pp. 21–68; John

R. Commons, *et al.*, *History of Labor in the United States* (New York: Macmillan, 1918–35), III, 331. Differing views on real wages are offered by Paul H. Douglas, *Real Wages in the United States, 1890–1926* (Boston: Houghton Mifflin, 1930) and Albert Rees, *Real Wages in Manufacturing, 1890–1914* (Princeton: Princeton University, 1961).

58. *Twenty-First Annual Report*, Commissioner of Labor (Washington, 1907), pp. 12–15.

59. *Report of the Secretary of War* (Washington, 1894), I, 57.

60. Eugene Debs, "Revolutionary Unionism," in *Debs: His Life, Writings, and Speeches* (Girard, Kan.: Appeal to Reason, 1908), p. 217.

61. *Ibid.*, p. 208; St. John, *op. cit.*, p. 37.

62. Harry McClintock, "Hymn of Hate," reprinted in *Rebel Voices, An I.W.W. Anthology*, J. L. Kornbluh, ed. (Ann Arbor: Michigan, 1964), pp. 29–30.

63. Manly, *op. cit.*, p. 92.

64. Samuel Yellen, *American Labor Struggles* (New York: Harcourt, Brace, 1936), pp. 205–50; Graham Adams, Jr., *The Age of Violence, 1910–15* (New York: Columbia, 1966), pp. 146–203; Walter Lippmann, "Rockefeller on the Stand," *New Republic*, Jan. 30, 1915, pp. 12–13.

65. Manly, *op. cit.*, p. 66.

66. Frederic C. Howe, *The City, The Hope of Democracy* (New York: Scribner's, 1905), pp. 11–12.

67. Richard T. Ely, *The Coming City* (New York: Crowell, 1902), pp. 23–25.

68. Brooks Adams, *The Theory of Social Revolutions* (New York: Macmillan, 1914), p. 203.

69. Frank Norris, *The Pit* (1902), quoted in Charles N. Glaab and A. Theodore Brown, *A History of Urban America* (New York: Macmillan, 1967), p. 267.

70. F. J. Kingsbury, "The Tendency of Men to Live in Cities," *Journal of Social Science*, XXXIII (Nov., 1895), 5–18.

71. Stephen Crane, "New York's Bicycle Speedway," New York *Sun*, July 5, 1896.

72. Ward McAllister, *Society As I Have Found It* (New York: Cassell, 1890), p. 157.

73. Henry James, *The American Scene* (New York: Harper, 1907; Scribner's, 1946), pp. 76–77, 92.

74. Theodore Dreiser, *Newspaper Days* (New York: Liveright, 1922), p. 487; *A Traveler at Forty* (New York: Century, 1913), p. 512.

75. Rudyard Kipling, *From Sea to Sea* (New York: Doubleday, McClure, 1899), pp. 139–44.

76. Quoted in Lewis Mumford, *The City in History* (New York: Harcourt, Brace & World, 1961), p. 464.

77. *First Report,* Tenement House Department of the City of New York, 1902–03, I, 5.

78. Jane Addams, *Democracy and Social Ethics* (New York: Macmillan, 1902), pp. 2–7.

79. *Ibid.*

Chapter II: The Capitalist Ethic

1. Croly, *op. cit.,* p. 10.

2. Adams, *op. cit.,* p. 344.

3. Elbert Hubbard, *The Romance of Business* (East Aurora, N.Y.: Roycrofters, 1916), pp. 9–10.

4. Quoted in James P. Wood, *The Story of Advertising* (New York: Ronald, 1958), p. 314.

5. Frederick Winslow Taylor, "The Principles of Scientific Management," *American*, LXXI (1911), 570–78, 785–93, LXXII (1912), 101–13.

6. Frederick W. Taylor, *Scientific Management* (New York: Harper, 1947), p. 59.

7. William James, "The Power of Men," *American*, LXV (1907), 56–65.

8. Walter Lippmann, "More Brains, Less Sweat," *Everybody's*, XXV (1911), 827–28.

9. Henry Davis Bushnell, "Educational Efficiency," *Atlantic*, CVII (1911), 498–99; Frederic Winslow Taylor, "Comparison of University and Industrial Discipline and Methods," *Science*, XXIV (1906), 577–83.

10. Edward A. Ross, *Changing America* (New York: Century, 1912), pp. 84, 92–93.

11. Manly, *op. cit.,* pp. 127–39.

12. Gompers, *op. cit.,* pp. 295–97.

13. Arthur B. Reeve, "Our Industrial Juggernaut," *Everybody's*, XVI (Feb., 1907), 148.

14. Walter E. Weyl, *The New Democracy* (New York: Macmillan, 1912), p. 161.

15. *Ibid.,* p. 162.

16. "A Contract with the People," Progressive Party Platform of 1912, reprinted in Roosevelt, *Progressive Principles,* pp. 314–30.

17. Quoted in Robert Hunter, *Poverty* (New York: Macmillan, 1904), pp. 11, 98.

18. "Newport Society," *Harper's Weekly,* Sept. 30, 1893, pp. 929–30; Emily Harrington, "Housekeeping on Half-a-Million a Year," *Everybody's,*

XIV (1906), 497–504.

19. Quoted in the *Nation*, Jan. 23, 1902, p. 64.

20. John A. Fitch, *The Steel Workers* (New York: Charities Publ. Com., 1910), pp. 150–65.

21. W. H. Mallock, "The Significance of Modern Poverty," *North American Review*, CLIX (Sept., 1894), 288–99.

22. E. L. Godkin, "Social Classes in the Republic," *Atlantic*, LXXVIII (December, 1896), 721–28.

23. Andrew Carnegie, "The Advantages of Poverty," *Nineteenth Century*, XXIX (March, 1891), 367–85.

24. Francis A. Walker, "Causes of Poverty," *Century*, LV (Dec., 1892), 245–56.

25. Manly, *op. cit.*, p. 22.

26. Quoted in Cleveland Amory, *The Last Resorts* (New York: Harper, 1948), p. 16.

27. Weyl, *op. cit.*, p. 198.

28. *Ibid.*

29. Jacob H. Hollander, *The Abolition of Poverty* (Boston: Houghton Mifflin, 1914), p. 6.

30. William Dean Howells, "The Worst of Being Poor," *Harper's Weekly*, XLV (1902), 261.

31. Lippmann, *op. cit.*, pp. 36–37.

32. Weyl, *op. cit.*, p. 197.

33. *Ibid.*, p. 180. See especially Dewey W. Grantham, Jr., "The Progressive Movement and the Negro," *South Atlantic Quarterly*, LIV (Oct., 1955), 461–77.

34. Ray Stannard Baker, *Following the Color Line* (New York: Doubleday, Page, 1908; Harper & Row, 1964), pp. 270, 304.

35. Booker T. Washington, *Up from Slavery* (Garden City, N.Y.: Doubleday, Page, 1901), pp. 230–37.

36. Thomas E. Watson, "The Negro Question in the South," *Arena*, VI (Oct., 1892), 548.

37. *Ibid.*, pp. 544–47.

38. Quoted in C. Vann Woodward, "Tom Watson and the Negro in Agrarian Politics," *Journal of Southern History*, IV (Feb., 1938), pp. 32–33.

39. E. L. Godkin, "Negro Problem," *Nation*, Jan. 23, 1890, p. 64.

40. Thomas Nelson Page, "The Lynching of Negroes," *North American Review*, CLXXVIII (Jan., 1904), 33–48.

41. Baker, *op. cit.*, pp. 176, 269, 294, 134.

42. William English Walling, "The Race War in the North," *Independent*, Sept. 3, 1908, pp. 529–34.

43. Baker, *op. cit.*, pp. 10–11, 14–15.

44. Quoted *ibid.*, p. 223.

45. Quoted in Francis L. Broderick and August Meier, *Negro Protest Thought in the Twentieth Century* (Indianapolis: Bobbs-Merrill, 1965), p. 50.

46. W. E. B. DuBois, "The Immediate Program of the American Negro," *The Crisis*, IX (April, 1915), 310–12.

47. John Bates Clark, "The Society of the Future," *Independent*, July 18, 1901, pp. 1649–51.

48. William Lawrence, "The Relation of Wealth to Morals," *World's Work*, I (Jan., 1901), 290.

49. Gerald Stanley Lee, *Inspired Millionaires* (Northampton, Mass.: Mt. Tom Press, 1908), pp. 288–89.

50. Wiebe, *op. cit.*, pp. 218, 88–89, 186–87.

51. Weinstein, *Corporate Ideal*, p. 129.

52. Alvin S. Johnson, "The Soul of Capitalism," *Unpopular Review*, I (April–June, 1914), 277–44; "Unsocial Investments," *ibid.*, II (July–Sept., 1914), 1.

53. E. D. H. Klyce, "Scientific Manage-

ment and the Moral Law," *Outlook*, Nov. 18, 1911, pp. 659–63; Harrington Emerson, *Efficiency As a Basis for Operation and Wages* (New York: Engineering Magazine, 1909), p. 157; William H. Allen, "The 'Goodness' Fallacy," *World's Work*, XIII (1906), 8186–89.

54. Veblen, *op. cit.*, p. 170.

55. *Ibid.*, pp. 170–71. See also Thorstein Veblen, *The Instinct of Workmanship* (New York: Macmillan, 1914; Huebsch, 1918), pp. 304, 340–43.

56. Gerald Stanley Lee, *Crowds* (Garden City, N.Y.: Doubleday, Page, 1914), p. 72.

57. Carroll D. Wright, *The Industrial Evolution of the United States* (New York: Flood & Vincent, 1895), p. 345.

58. Carroll D. Wright, *Some Ethical Phases of the Labor Question* (Boston: American Unitarian Assn., 1903), pp. 131, 151–53, 155.

59. Gerald Stanley Lee, *The Voice of the Machines* (Northampton, Mass.: Mt. Tom Press, 1906), p. 36.

60. Lee, *Crowds*, p. 103.

61. *Ibid.*, p. 139.

62. Lippmann, *op. cit.*, p. 53.

63. "The Advertiser As a Public Benefactor," *Independent*, Nov. 8, 1915, p. 212.

64. "The Moral Value of Advertising," *ibid.*, Dec. 15, 1917, p. 500; "Social Value of Advertising," *Current Opinion*, Nov. 2, 1914, p. 361.

65. Ross, *op. cit.*, pp. 100–01.

66. William James, "The Medical Advertisement Abomination," *Nation*, Feb. 1, 1894, pp. 84–85.

67. Lippmann, *op. cit.*, p. 52.

68. Henry F. May, *Protestant Churches and Industrial America* (New York: Harper, 1949), pp. 119–24.

69. Washington Gladden, "The Church and the Reward of Iniquity," *Independent*, April 20, 1905, pp. 867–70.

70. Ida M. Tarbell, "Testing the Tariff by Moral Effects," *American*, LXXII (June, 1911), 186.

Chapter III: The Modern Leviathan

1. Thomas Hobbes, *Leviathan* (Oxford: Oxford University, 1943), pp. 132, 137–38.

2. Mary E. Lease quoted in Ida M. Tarbell, *The Nationalizing of Business* (New York: Harper, 1936), p. 141.

3. Thomas E. Watson, editorial, *People's Party Paper*, 1893, quoted in Pollack, *Populist Mind*, p. 26.

4. Ignatius Donnelly, *Caesar's Column* (Chicago: Shulte, 1890).

5. Veblen, *Theory of Business Enterprise*, p. 128.

6. London, *Iron Heel*, pp. 129–39; William Dean Howells, *Traveler from Altruria* (New York: Harper, 1894; Sagamore, 1957), pp. 171–82.

7. Adams, *Education*, pp. 345–55; Lloyd, *Wealth Against Commonwealth*, pp. 1–2.

8. William Allen White, *The Old Order Changeth* (New York: Macmillan, 1910), pp. 11–12.

9. Wilson, "Lawyer and the Community," pp. 611–13.

10. John P. Davis, *Corporations* (New York: Capricorn, 1961), II, 280. First published in 1904.

11. Parrington, *Main Currents*, III, 406–07.

12. Lincoln Steffens, *The Shame of the Cities* (New York: McClure, Phillips, 1904), and "IT: An Exposition of the Sovereign Political Power of Orga-

nized Business," *Everybody's*, XXIII (Sept., 1910), p. 296.

13. John Graham Brooks, *The Social Unrest* (New York: Macmillan, 1903), p. 47.

14. David Graham Phillips, *The Treason of the Senate* (Chicago: Quadrangle, 1964), p. 98.

15. *Banker's Magazine*, LXII (1901), 498.

16. William Graham Sumner, "The Conflict of Plutocracy and Democracy," *Earth Hunger and Other Essays* (New Haven: Yale, 1913), p. 299.

17. Link, *op. cit.*, pp. 70–72.

18. Quoted in William Appleman Williams, *The Contours of American History* (Chicago: Quadrangle, 1966), p. 390. See also Link, *op. cit.*, pp. 75–80.

19. Editorial, *International Socialist Review*, XIII, 6 (Dec., 1912), 495. Quoted in Weinstein, *Corporate Ideal*, p. 132.

20. Woodrow Wilson, *Division and Reunion* (New York: Longmans, Green, 1902), p. 12.

21. Croly, *Promise of American Life*, pp. 32–38; Lippmann, *Drift and Mastery*, pp. 101–02, 164; Charles A. Beard, *An Economic Interpretation of the United States Constitution* (New York: Macmillan, 1913)

22. J. Allen Smith, *The Spirit of American Government* (New York: Macmillan, 1907), pp. 29–31, 297–303.

23. Croly, *op. cit.*, p. 32.

24. *Ibid.*, p. 35.

25. *Ibid.*, p. 50.

26. *Ibid.*, pp. 44–45.

27. *Ibid.*, p. 23.

28. Woodrow Wilson, "Living Principles of Democracy," *Harper's Weekly*, April 9, 1910, pp. 9–10.

29. Bonnett, *op. cit.*, pp. 317–18.

30. Quoted in *American Federationist*, XXI (June, 1914), 483.

31. William J. Ghent, "The Next Step: A Benevolent Feudalism," *Independent*, April 3, 1902, pp. 781–88; "Feudalism or Individualism?" *ibid.*, July 10, 1902, pp. 1647–50.

32. Sereno S. Pratt, "Our Financial Oligarchy," *World's Work*, X (1905), 6704–14.

33. Quoted in Weinstein, *op. cit.*, p. 56.

34. Quoted in Wiebe, *op. cit.*, p. 166.

35. Steffens, "IT," p. 292.

36. Lloyd, *op. cit.*, p. 511.

37. Manly, *op. cit.*, pp. 17.

38. *Final Report*, C.I.R., p. 96.

39. Adams, *op. cit.*, pp. 148–49.

40. *Ibid.*

41. Manly, *op. cit.*, p. 7809.

42. "At the Parting of the Ways," *Outlook*, April 16, 1910, pp. 830–31.

43. Franklin H. Giddings, "Imperialism?" *Political Science Quarterly*, XIII (Dec., 1898), 593.

44. William Appleman Williams, *The Great Evasion* (Chicago: Quadrangle, 1964), p. 38.

45. Thomas A. Bailey, "America's Emergence As a World Power: The Myth and the Verity," *Pacific Historical Review*, XXX (1961), 11.

46. *Ibid.*, p. 15.

47. Strong, *Our Country*, p. 214.

48. Quoted in W. T. Stead, *The Americanization of the World* (New York: Markly, 1901), pp. 354–55, 359.

49. Quoted in Julius Pratt, *Expansionists of 1898* (Baltimore: Johns Hopkins, 1936), pp. 252–53, 268–78, 279–315.

50. John A. Hobson, *Imperialism* (London: Allen & Unwin, 1938), pp. v–vi.

51. Charles A. Conant, *The United*

States in the Orient (Boston: Houghton Mifflin, 1901), pp. 226, 61–62, 91–92.

52. Woodrow Wilson, "The Ideals of America," *Atlantic*, XC (1902), 726.

53. Quoted in Pratt, *op. cit.*, pp. 279–316. See also Richard Hofstadter, "Manifest Destiny and the Philippines," *America in Crisis*, Daniel Aaron, ed. (New York: Knopf, 1952), pp. 173–200; Alfred K. Weinberg, *Manifest Destiny* (Baltimore: Johns Hopkins, 1935), pp. 252–323.

54. Croly, *op. cit.*, p. 289. See William E. Leuchtenburg, "Progressivism and Imperialism," *Mississippi Valley Historical Review*, XXXIX (Dec., 1952), 483–504.

55. Reprinted in Commager, *Documents*, II, 192–93. See also Fred H. Harrington, "The Anti-Imperialist Movement in the United States, 1898–1900," *Mississippi Valley Historical Review*, XXII (1935), 211–30.

56. William Jennings Bryan, *et al.*, *Republic or Empire* (Chicago: Independence, 1899), pp. 17, 32, 85.

57. Earnest Crosby, *Plain Talk in Psalm and Parable* (Boston: Small, Maynard, 1899), p. 58.

58. Rufus S. Tucker, "A Balance Sheet of the Philippines," *Harvard Business Review*, VIII (Oct., 1929), 10–23.

59. Brooks Adams, "War As the Ultimate Form of Economic Competition," *Proceedings*, U.S. Naval Institute, XXIV (1903), 829–81.

60. Brooks Adams, *The New Empire* (New York: Macmillan, 1902), pp. xxxiv, 2–3.

61. Brooks Adams, *America's Economic Supremacy* (New York: Macmillan, 1900), pp. 21, 85.

62. *Ibid.*, pp. 47–48.

63. *Ibid.*, pp. 52–53.

64. Franklin H. Giddings, *The Responsible State* (Boston: Houghton Mifflin, 1918), pp. 49 *et seq.*

65. Friedrich von Bernhardi, *Germany and the Next War* (New York: Longmans, Green, 1914), pp. 25–28.

66. *Ibid.*; see Heinrich von Treitschke, *Politics* (London: Constable, 1916).

67. Burgess, *Political Science*, I, 42–43, 52–57.

68. Theodore Roosevelt, *Fear God and Take Your Own Part* (New York: Doran, 1916), pp. 59 *et seq.*, 18; "The Law of Civilization and Decay" (book review), *Forum*, XXII (1896–97), 579, 589; *The Works of Theodore Roosevelt* (New York: Scribner's, 1926), XIII, 322–23, 331. Phrase "hairy-chested Darwinian virtues" from Hofstadter, *Age of Reform*, p. 276.

69. Croly, *op. cit.*, pp. 255, 264; Alfred Thayer Mahan, *The Interest of America in Sea Power* (Boston: Little, Brown, 1897), p. 18; Hudson Maxim, *Defenseless America* (New York: Hearst, 1915), pp. vi–vii.

70. Homer Lea, *The Valor of Ignorance* (New York: Harper, 1909), pp. 42, 45, 82, 84, 170, 176–77; *The Day of the Saxon* (New York: Harper, 1912), pp. 6–7.

71. Theodore Roosevelt, *America and the World War* (New York: Scribner's, 1915), p. xii.

72. Merle Curti, *Peace or War* (Boston: Canner, 1959), pp. 196–227.

73. Reprinted in Hudson Maxim, *Leading Opinions Both For and Against National Defense* (New York: Maxim, 1916), pp. 44–45.

74. Quoted in *Congressional Record*, 64th Cong., 1st sess., Appendix, p. 861.

75. *Seven Seas*, I (Sept., 1915), 13.

76. *Ibid.*, I (Nov., 1915), 28.

77. Armin Rappaport, *The Navy League of the United States* (Detroit: Wayne State, 1962), pp. 20–21, 26, 43–52, 205–10.

78. Walter G. Fuller, "The Battle Cry of Peace," *Masses*, VII (Dec., 1915), quoted in William L. O'Neill, ed., *Echoes of Revolt: The Masses 1911–1917* (Chicago: Quadrangle. 1966), p. 275.

79. John Reed, "At the Throat of the Republic," *Masses*, VIII (July, 1916), 7–8, 10–12.

80. *Ibid.*

81. *LaFollette's Magazine*, VII (Nov., 1915), 1; *Congressional Record*, 64th Cong., 1st sess., pp. 276–90. For text of Ford's advertisement see Maxim, *Leading Opinions*, pp. 73–77.

82. "Can War Be Prevented?" *Independent*, Jan. 3, 1916, p. 5.

83. James Bissett Pratt, "The Idealism of War," *Forum*, LIV (Oct., 1915), 396.

84. *Ibid.*, p. 397.

85. *Ibid.*, p. 402.

86. "Force and Ideas," *New Republic*, Nov. 7, 1914, p. 7.

87. Alfred J. Nock, "Peace the Aristocrat," *Atlantic*, CXV (May, 1915), 593–99.

88. Randolph Bourne, "A Moral Equivalent for Universal Military Service," *New Republic*, July 1, 1916, pp. 217–19.

89. "The Sum of All Villainies," *New Republic*, Feb. 13, 1915, pp. 36–37.

90. Reinhold Niebuhr, "The Nation's Crime Against the Individual," *Atlantic*, CXVII (Nov., 1916), 611.

91. Grosvenor B. Clarkson, *Industrial America in the World War* (Boston: Houghton Mifflin, 1923), p. 9.

92. "Are We to Have a Benevolent Despotism?" *North American Review*, CCVII (Jan., 1918), 17–21.

93. Clarkson, *op. cit.*, p. 154.

94. *Ibid.*, p. 344.

Chapter IV: The Breakdown of Absolutes

1. Adams, *Education*, pp. 455–56.

2. *Ibid.*, pp. 452, 458.

3. John Dewey, *Reconstruction in Philosophy* (New York: Holt, 1920), Mentor, 1952), pp. 46–52.

4. Francis Bacon, *Magna instauratio* (1620), *De Dignitate et augmentis scientiarium* (1623), R. F. Jones, ed. (New York: Odyssey, 1937), pp. 267–71.

5. James, *Pragmatism*, p. 45.

6. Bacon, *op. cit.*, p. 413.

7. *Ibid.*, p. 441.

8. Dewey, *op. cit.*, pp. 104–05.

9. Ralph Barton Perry, *The Present Conflict of Ideals* (New York; Longmans, Green, 1918), p. 58.

10. Jacques Loeb, "Mechanistic Science and Metaphysical Romance," *Yale Review*, IV (1915), 785.

11. Bacon, *op. cit.*, p. 264.

12. John B. Watson, "Psychology As the Behaviorist Views It," *Psychological Review*, XX (1913), 176.

13. Veblen, "Place of Science," pp. 585–86.

14. William M. Salter, "Pragmatism: A New Philosophy," *Atlantic*, CI (May, 1908), 657; E. E. Slosson, "What Is Pragmatism?" *Independent*, Feb. 21, 1907, pp. 422–25; P. G. Agnew, "What is Pragmatism?" *Forum*, XLI (Jan., 1909), 70–7; "Fascinations of the Pragmatic Method," *Current Literature*, XLIII (Aug., 1907), 183–86. "Newest Philosophy," *ibid.*, XLII (June, 1907), 652–53.

15. Quoted in Ralph Barton Perry, *The*

Thought and Character of William James (New York: Braziller, 1954), pp. 299–300.

16. James, *op. cit.*, pp. 43–81.

17. William James, *The Will to Believe* (New York: Longmans, Green, 1897), pp. 1–31, 145–83; Perry, *op. cit.*, pp. 264–71.

18. J. B. Burke, "Fashionable Philosophy at Oxford and Harvard," *Living Age*, May 30, 1908, pp. 559–61; Josiah Royce, "The Eternal and the Practical," *Philosophical Review*, XIII (1904), 113–42; Vernon Lee, "What Is Truth?" *Yale Review*, I (1912), 600–19; A. O. Lovejoy, "Pragmatism and Realism," *Journal of Philosophy*, VI (1909), 575–80; J. E. Russell, "Objective Idealism and Revised Empiricism—Discussion," *Philosophical Review*, XV (1906), 633.

19. George Santayana, *The Middle Span* (New York: Scribner's, 1935), p. 7.

20. George Santayana, *Character and Opinion in the United States* (New York: Scribner's, 1936), p. 43; John J. Fisher, "Santayana on James," *American Philosophical Quarterly*, II (1965), 71.

21. Josiah Royce, *William James and Other Essays on the Philosophy of Life* (New York: Macmillan, 1911), p. 24; Paul Elmer More, "New Stage of Pragmatism," *Nation*, May 6, 1909, pp. 456–59.

22. Vernon Lee, "Two Pragmatisms," *North American Review*, CLXLII (Oct., 1910), 449–63; Arthur O. Lovejoy, "The Thirteen Pragmatisms," *Journal of Philosophy*, V (1908), 5–12, 29–39.

23. Letter to James Ward, Florence, Nov. 1, 1892, in Philip P. Wiener, *Evolution and the Founders of Pragmatism* (Cambridge: Harvard, 1949), p. 108.

24. Santayana, *Character and Opinion*, pp. 40–41.

25. *Ibid.*

26. Wiener, *op. cit.*, p. 99.

27. James Bissett Pratt, *What Is Pragmatism?* (New York: Macmillan, 1909), pp. 248–49.

28. John Dewey, "Science as Subject-Matter and as Method," *Science* (1910), reprinted in *John Dewey on Education*, R. D. Archambault, ed. (New York: Modern Library, 1964), pp. 182–92.

29. John Dewey, "From Absolutism to Experimentalism," *Contemporary American Philosophy*, G. P. Adams and W. P. Montague, eds. (New York: Russell, 1962), II, 13–27; "William James," *Characters and Events* (New York: Holt, 1927), I, 113.

30. Dewey, *Reconstruction in Philosophy*, pp. 96–112.

31. John Dewey, *The Influence of Darwin on Philosophy* (New York: Holt, 1910; Smith, 1951), p. 74. Also "The Supremacy of Method," reprinted in *Classic American Philosophers*, Max H. Fisch, ed. (New York: Appleton-Century-Crofts, 1951), pp. 344–60; *Essays in Experimental Logic* (Chicago: University of Chicago, 1916; Dover, 1956), pp. 303–34, 415.

32. *Ibid.*, pp. 46–76. See also *Logical Conditions of a Scientific Treatment of Morality* (Chicago: University of Chicago, 1903), pp. 10–14. Among his later works see *Human Nature and Conduct* (New York: Holt, 1922), especially the Introduction and the chapter on "The Nature of Aims"; *The Quest for Certainty* (New York: Minton, Balch, 1929), Chapter X, "The Construction of Good"; *Philosophy and Civilization* (New York: Putnam's, 1931), essay "Science and Society."

33. Pratt, *op. cit.*, pp. 231–35, 253.

34. James H. Leuba, "The Psycho-physiology of the Moral Imperative," *American Journal of Psychology*, VIII (1896–97), 530.

35. Perry, *Conflict of Ideals*, pp. 66–67, 331–47.

36. Dewey, *On Education*, pp. 74–75.

Chapter V: The New Radicalism

1. Floyd Dell, *Intellectual Vaga-bondage* (New York: Doran, 1926), p. 111.

2. Randolph Bourne, *Youth and Life* (Boston: Houghton Mifflin, 1913), pp. 14–15.

3. Brooks, *Three Essays*, pp. 101–02, 24.

4. Dell, *op. cit.*, p. 109.

5. Martin, *Passing of the Idle Rich*, pp. 14–16.

6. Brooks, *op. cit.*, pp. 129–30, 149.

7. James Harvey Robinson, "A Journal of Opinion," *New Republic*, May 8, 1915, pp. 9–11.

8. Bourne, *op. cit.*, p. 47.

9. *Ibid.*, pp. 227–46.

10. *Ibid.*, pp. 16–17.

11. Dell, *op. cit.*, pp. 223–24.

12. F. Dwight, "Two Kinds of Radicalism," *Independent*, Oct. 25, 1906, pp. 985–89; John T. Graves, Jr., "Radicalism," *Forum*, XLIX (May, 1913), 561–62.

13. Brooks, *op. cit.*, p. 153.

14. Bourne, *op. cit.*, pp. 16–17.

15. Carl Sandburg, "To Billy Sunday," *Masses*, VI (Sept., 1915), 11.

16. Max Eastman, "The Tanenbaum Crime," *ibid.*, V (May, 1914), 6–8; "The Church and the Unemployed," *ibid.*, V (April, 1914), 10–11.

17. Sarah N. Cleghorn, "Comrade Jesus," *ibid.*, p. 10.

18. Quoted in Charles Howard Hopkins, *The Rise of the Social Gospel in American Protestantism 1865–1915* (New Haven: Yale, 1940), pp. 316–17.

19. Dell, *op. cit.*, p. 148.

20. H. L. Mencken, *The Vintage Mencken* (New York: Vintage, 1959), p. 232.

21. Christopher Lasch, *The New Radicalism in America* (New York: Knopf, 1965), p. 90.

22. "Sex O'Clock in America," *Current Opinion*, LV (Aug., 1913), 113.

23. Quoted in "Havoc of Prudery," *Current Literature*, L (Feb., 1911), 174–75.

24. "Bernard Shaw and Morals," *Living Age*, Dec. 27, 1913, pp. 818–21.

25. Charlotte Gilman, "Is Cupid a Convention?" *Independent*, Aug. 15, 1907, p. 373.

26. Edmund L. Pearson, "The One Subject," *Nation*, July 16, 1914, pp. 68–69.

27. Theodore Roosevelt, "Achievement for Humanity," *Outlook*, Jan. 18, 1913, p. 116.

28. Pearson, *loc. cit.;* "New Game of Playing with Fire," *Century*, LXXXV (March, 1913), 795–96.

29. *Current Opinion*, LV (Aug., 1913), 114.

30. *Ibid.*, pp. 113–14.

31. Dell, *op. cit.*, p. 132.

32. H. L. Mencken, "The Flapper," *Smart Set*, XLV (1915), 1–2.

33. Floyd Dell, *Homecoming* (New York: Farrar & Rinehart, 1933), p. 272.

34. Edward Carpenter, *Love's Coming of Age* (Chicago: Kerr, n.d.), pp. 59, 94.

35. Floyd Dell, *Love in Greenwich Village* (New York: Doran, 1926), p. 35.

36. W. O. Inglis, "Is Modern Dancing Indecent?" *Harper's Weekly*, May 17, 1913, pp. 11–12; L. Crozer, "New Cult of Dancing," *Good Housekeeping*, LV (Nov., 1912), 620–28; "New Reflections on the Dancing Mania," *Current Opinion*, LV (Oct., 1913), 262–64; "Problems That the Tango Has Inflicted on the Church," *ibid.*, LVI (March, 1914), 206; "Recrudescence of Paganism," *Current Literature*, L (April, 1911), 415–16.

37. "Glory of Being Wicked," *Atlantic*, CVII (May, 1911), 715–16.

38. *Nation*, May 21, 1914, p. 599.

39. "Old Morality," *Dial*, Aug. 16, 1911, pp. 91–92.

40. Arthur Pollock, "Are We Immoral?" *Forum*, LI (Jan., 1914), 52–56.

41. Dell, *Vagabondage*, p. 129.

42. "How Psycho-Analysis Has Obsessed the World with Sex," *Current Opinion*, LVI (June, 1914), 441. See John C. Burnham, "Psychoanalysis in American Civilization Before 1918" (unpublished doctoral dissertation, Standford University, 1958), p. 348.

43. Lippmann, *Drift and Mastery*, p. 123 *ff*.

44. Dell, *op. cit.*, p. 135.

45. Abigail Adams, quoted in Alice Felt Tyler, *Freedom's Ferment* (New York: Harper, 1962), pp. 425–26.

46. C. P. Gilman, "Are Women Human Beings?" *Harper's Weekly*, May 25, 1912, p. 11.

47. E. J. Ward, "Women Should Mind Their Own Business," *Independent*, June 22, 1911, pp. 1370–71.

48. Ida M. Tarbell, "Democratization of Women," *Ladies' Home Journal*, XXX (Jan., 1913), 24.

49. L. Housman, "Petticoat Government," *Contemporary Review*, CIV (Nov., 1913), 663–72.

50. Ida M. Tarbell, "Making a Man of Herself," *American*, LXXIII (Feb., 1912), 427–30.

51. C. D. Groth, "Man—the Timid Sex," *Harper's Weekly*, March 19, 1910, p. 7.

52. Susanne Wilcox, "Wider Morality for American Women," *Independent*, June 20, 1912, pp. 1362–64.

53. Emma Goldman, "Marriage and Love," *Anarchism and Other Essays* (New York: Mother Earth, 1911), pp. 236–37.

54. *Ibid.*

55. "Ellen Key's Startling Views on Love and Marriage," *Current Literature*, L (April, 1911), 403–05; H. A. Larsen, "Ellen Key: An Apostle of Life," *Forum*, XLVI (Oct., 1911), 385–99.

56. Margaret Deland, "The Change in the Feminine Ideal," *Atlantic*, CV (March, 1910), 290–302.

57. Goldman, *op. cit.*, p. 243.

58. Margaret Sanger, *Women and the New Race* (New York: Truth, 1920), pp. 2–3, 5.

59. Max Eastman, "Is the Truth Obscene?" *Masses*, VI (March, 1915), 5–6.

60. Margaret Sanger, *An Autobiography* (New York: Norton, 1938), pp. 108–10.

61. Quoted in *Survey*, Feb. 11, 1911, p. 803.

62. Quoted in *Current Opinion*, LV (Aug., 1913), 114.

63. *Ibid.*

64. Anne W. Allen, "Victorian Hypocrisy," *Atlantic*, CXIV (Aug., 1914), 174–88.

65. Agnes Repplier, "The Repeal of Reticence," *Atlantic*, CXIII (Feb., 1914), 297–304.

66. Lasch, *op. cit.*, p. 65.

67. Lippmann, *op. cit.*, p. 123.

68. Weyl, *op. cit.*, p. 225.

69. Lippmann, *op. cit.*, p. 118.

70. *Ibid.*, p. 151.

71. Croly, *op. cit.*, p. 401.

72. *Ibid.*, pp. 402–03.

73. Quoted in Merle Curti, *The Social Ideas of American Educators* (Paterson, N.J.: Littlefield & Adams, 1959), p. 310.

74. *Ibid.*, p. 251.

75. *Ibid.*, pp. 230–31.

76. *Ibid.*, p. 231.

77. Randolph Bourne, *Education and Living* (New York: Century, 1917), pp. 3, 6, 10, 215, 219, 231–36.

78. B. O. Flower, "Twentieth-Century Education," *Arena*, XXIX (Jan., 1903), 84–89; "Full-Orbed Education," *ibid.*, XL (Sept., 1908), 222–23.

79. Abraham Flexner, "Aristocratic and Democratic Education," *Atlantic*, CVIII (Sept., 1911), 386–95; "Bulwarking Democracy Through Practical Education," *Arena*, XXXIII (May, 1905), 537–41.

80. Weyl, *op. cit.*, p. 329.

81. John Dewey, "American Education and Culture," *New Republic*, July 1, 1916, p. 215.

82. John Dewey, "Current Tendencies in Education," *Dial*, April 5, 1917, p. 287.

83. John Dewey, *Democracy and Education* (New York: Macmillan, 1916), pp. 100–16, 386.

84. *Ibid.*, p. 110; "The School as Social Center," N.E.A. *Proceedings*, 1902, pp. 373–83; "Ethical Principles Underlying Education," National Hebart Society, *Third Yearbook*, 1897, reprinted in *John Dewey on Education*, R. D. Archambault, ed. (New York: Modern Library, 1964), p. 109.

85. Dewey, *Democracy and Education*, pp. 357, 24.

86. *Ibid.*, p. 111.

87. L. B. R. Briggs, "Old-Fashioned Doubts About New-Fashioned Education," *Atlantic*, LXXXVI (Oct., 1900), 463–70; Alfred E. Stearns, "Some Fallacies in the Modern Educational Scheme," *ibid.*, CXVIII (Nov., 1916), 641–42.

88. Cornelia A. P. Comer, "A Letter to the Rising Generation," *ibid.*, CVII (Feb., 1911), 145.

89. Agnes Repplier, "Popular Education," first appeared in the *Atlantic* then was reprinted in *Counter-Currents* (Boston: Houghton Mifflin, 1916), pp. 190, 165, 169–70, 175.

90. "Useless Learning," *Independent*, April 2, 1908, p. 764; Paul Elmer More, "Old Education and the New," *Nation*, June 29, 1916, pp. 694–96; Paul Shorey, "The Bigotry of the New Education," *ibid.*, Sept. 6, 1917, pp. 253–56.

91. Paul Elmer More, "Rousseau and Education," *Nation*, April 30, 1908, pp. 393–96.

92. Quoted in John A. Reed, "The Present-Day College," *Forum*, L (Dec., 1913), 804.

93. G. Boas, "Some Blank Misgivings," *Atlantic*, CXX (Dec., 1917), 789–91.

94. Quoted in Reed, *loc. cit.*, p. 790–91.

95. *Ibid.*

96. Quoted in "Are College Students As Wicked As They Are Represented?" *Current Literature*, LI (Nov., 1911), 540–42.

97. E. Bok, "Is the College Making Good?" *Outlook*, Aug. 16, 1913, pp. 851–57; Aug. 30, 1913, pp. 991–95.

98. Lincoln Steffens, "How to Get an Education Even in College," *Harper's*

Weekly, April 11, 1914, pp. 9–11.

99. Randolph Bourne, "College Life Today," *North American Review,* CLXLVI (Sept., 1912), 365; *Youth and Life,* pp. 323–24.

100. Bourne, *loc. cit.,* pp. 370–71.

101. Reed, *loc. cit.,* pp. 801, 793.

102. Thorstein Veblen, *The Higher Learning in America* (New York: Huebsch, 1918; Sagamore, 1957), pp. 50–51.

103. Charles A. Beard, "University and Democracy," *Dial,* April 11, 1918, p. 336.

104. Veblen, *op. cit.,* p. 118.

105. *Ibid.,* p. 116.

106. "Mediaevalism in the Colleges," *New Republic,* Aug. 28, 1915, pp. 87–88.

107. Bourne, *loc. cit.,* p. 371.

108. Veblen, *op. cit.,* p. 5.

109. Bourne, *loc. cit.,* p. 371.

110. William James, "The Ph.D. Octopus," *Harvard Monthly* (1903), reprinted in *Memories and Studies* (New York: Longmans, Green, 1911), pp. 333–34, 336, 338.

111. "Stanford's Ideal Destiny," address, 1906, *ibid.,* p. 362; Curti, *op. cit.,* pp. 443, 447, 412; William James, *Talks to Teachers on Psychology* (New York: Holt, 1907), pp. 9–10.

112. William James, "The Social Value of the College-Bred," *McClure's,* XXX (Feb., 1908), 418–22.

113. Ralph Barton Perry, "A Defence of Liberal Education," *Forum,* LIII (Feb., 1915), 214–19.

114. Paul Elmer More, *Aristocracy and Justice* (Boston: Houghton Mifflin, 1915), pp. 36–37; Shorey, *loc. cit.,* 255.

115. Perry, *loc. cit.,* p. 219.

116. Quoted in Charles P. Howland, "Education for the Future," *New Republic,* Nov. 10, 1917, pp. 46–47.

117. Simon Patten, *The New Basis of Civilization* (New York: Macmillan, 1907), pp. 197–98.

118. Veblen, *Place of Science,* pp. 73–74.

119. Simon Patten, "The Present Problems in the Economic Interpretation of History," *Annals of the American Academy of Political and Social Science,* XXIV (Nov., 1904), 540–55; "The Theory of Social Forces," *ibid.,* VII (Jan., 1896), *sup.,* pp. 48, 16–17; *New Basis of Civilization,* pp. 186–87; "The Theory of Dynamic Economics," reprinted in *Essays in Economic Theory* (New York: Knopf, 1924), pp. 33–34; 38, 52–54, 43, 74, 276–77, 322–23, 325–29, 339–40; *The Theory of Prosperity* (New York: Macmillan, 1902), p. 215; "Extravagance As a Virtue," *Current Opinion,* LIV (Jan., 1913), 51–52.

120. Sumner, *Challenge of Facts,* pp. 31–32, 127–28, 17, 37–38, 25, 33.

121. Herbert W. Schneider, "Political Implications of Recent Philosophical Movements," *A History of Political Theories, Recent Times,* C. E. Merriam and H. E. Barnes, eds. (New York: Macmillan, 1924), pp. 313, 332–37, 343.

122. Herbert W. Schneider, *A History of American Philosophy* (New York: Columbia, 1963), p. 488.

123. Herbert Croly, "A School of Social Research," *New Republic,* June 8, 1918, pp. 167–71.

124. Albion W. Small, "The Meaning of the Social Movement," *American Journal of Sociology,* III (Sept., 1897), 341–45.

125. Randolph Bourne, review of Paul Elmer More's *Aristocracy and Justice, New Republic,* April 1, 1916, pp. 245–47.

126. Edward A. Ross, *Sin and Society* (Boston: Houghton Mifflin, 1907; Peter Smith, 1965), pp. viii–xi.

127. Walter Lippmann, *A Preface to Politics*, (New York: Kennerley, 1913), p. 193; *Drift and Mastery*, pp. 113–19.

128. Lippmann, *A Preface to Politics*, pp. 51, 80, 38–39, 49, 31–32, 13–15, 21–22, 307, 200–02.

129. *Nation*, Sept. 11, 1913, pp. 241–42; *North American Review*, CXCIX (April, 1914), 617–22.

130. "A Sociological Nightmare," *Unpopular Review*, I (1914), 248–51.

131. *Ibid.*; "The New Irrepressible Conflict," *ibid.*, 1; Fabian Franklin, "The Democrat Reflects," *ibid.*, 44.

132. More, *Aristocracy and Justice*, pp.

211, 3, 34–35, 37, 58–59, 197, 203, 23, 31–33, 110, 122, 133, 26, 29, 135.

133. Quoted in Paul Elmer More, *The Demon of the Absolute* (Princeton: Princeton University, 1928), pp. v–vii; Bourne, review, *loc. cit.*, p. 245.

134. Brooks, *Three Essays*, p. 127.

135. F. M. Colby, review of Walter Lippmann's *A Preface to Politics*, *North American Review*, CXCIX (April, 1914), 617–22.

136. *Ibid.*

137. Bourne, *Youth and Life*, pp. 168, 231.

138. Lippmann, *Drift and Mastery*, p. 116.

139. Dewey, *Reconstruction in Philosophy*, pp. 94–112.

Epilogue: The Limits of Technique

1. Adams, *Education*, pp. 485, 494–95.

2. *Ibid.*, p. 380.

3. W. C. Ford, ed., *Letters of Henry Adams, 1892–1918* (Boston: Houghton Mifflin, 1938), p. 301.

4. Lippmann, *Drift and Mastery*, pp. 92–93.

5. Comer, *loc. cit.*, p. 147.

6. Lewis Mumford, *Technics and Civilization* (New York: Harcourt, Brace & World, 1963), pp. 268–83.

7. Veblen, *Instinct of Workmanship*, pp. 315–20.

8. W. C. Ford, ed., *A Cycle of Adams Letters 1861–65* (Boston: Houghton Mifflin, 1920), I, 135.

9. Dewey, *Characters and Events*, I, 121.

10. Lloyd, *Wealth Against Commonwealth*, pp. 2, 510.

11. Adams, *Theory of Social Revolutions*, pp. 203–29.

12. Sol Cohen, "The Industrial Education Movement, 1906–17," *American Quarterly*, XX (Spring, 1968), 95–110.

13. Veblen, *Higher Learning*, p. 163.

14. Quoted in Van Wyck Brooks, *The World of H. G. Wells* (New York: Dutton, 1915), pp. 180–81.

15. Louis Filler, *Crusaders for American Liberalism* (New York: Collier, 1961), pp. 330–41.

16. Veblen, *Theory of Business Enterprise*, pp. 181–85.

17. Quoted in Daniel Aaron, *Men of Good Hope* (New York: Oxford, 1951), pp. 274–75.

18. Croly, *op. cit.*, p. 255.

19. Lippmann, *Drift and Mastery*, pp. 17, 145–48, 156.

20. Edward A. Ross, *Social Control, A Survey of the Foundations of Order* (New York: Macmillan, 1901), pp. 88, 93–95, 98–105. See also Lasch, *op. cit.*,

pp. 168–80.

21. Ross, *Sin and Society*, pp. vii–viii.

22. Graham Wallas, *Human Nature in Politics* (London: Constable, 1908), pp. xi, 98–113.

23. Lippmann, *Preface to Politics*, pp. 228–30, 235–37, 250, 317.

24. Richard T. Ely, "Progressivism, True and False—An Outline," *Review of Reviews*, LI (Feb., 1915), 209–11.

25. Quoted in Charles Forcey, *The Crossroads of Liberalism* (New York: Oxford University, 1961), p. 247.

26. "The Tide of Reaction," *New Republic*, Jan 16, 1915, pp. 6–8.

27. Quoted in Forcey, *op. cit.*, p. 247.

28. Randolph Bourne, "American Use for German Ideals," *New Republic*, Sept. 4, 1915, pp. 117–18.

29. John Reed, "This Unpopular War," *Seven Arts*, Aug., 1917, reprinted in *The Education of John Reed* (New York: International, 1955), pp. 166–75.

30. Dell, *Vagabondage*, pp. 152–53.

31. Herbert Croly, "The Effect on American Institutions of a Powerful Military and Naval Establishment," *Annals of the American Academy of Political and Social Science*, LXVI (July, 1916), 157–72.

32. "Who Willed American Participation?" *New Republic*, April 14, 1917, pp. 308–09.

33. Ralph Barton Perry, "Fact of War and Hope of Peace," *New Republic*, June 19, 1915, pp. 166–68.

34. "A War Program for Liberals," *ibid.*, March 31, 1917, pp. 249–50.

35. John Dewey, "What Are We Fighting For?" *Independent*, June 22, 1918, pp. 474, 480–83.

36. Lippmann, *Preface to Politics*, p. 106.

37. John Dewey, "What America Will Fight For," *New Republic*, April 18,

1917, reprinted in *Characters and Events*, II, 564.

38. Dewey, "What Are We Fighting For?" pp. 481, 484.

39. *Ibid.*, p. 474.

40. William Jennings Bryan, speech at Johnstown, Pa., Nov. 1, 1915, reprinted in Maxim, *Leading Opinions*, p. 48.

41. Maxim, *Defenseless America*, p. 83; *Leading Opinions*, p. 150.

42. Mumford, *op. cit.*, pp. 307–11.

43. More, *Aristocracy and Justice*, pp. 223–24.

44. Dewey, *loc. cit.*, p. 474.

45. Rexford G. Tugwell, "America's War-Time Socialism," *Nation*, Aug. 6, 1927, pp. 264–69.

46. Wiebe, *op. cit.*, p. 221.

47. Bernard Baruch, *American Industry in the War* (New York: Prentice-Hall, 1941), pp. 15–107, 377–408; William Hard, "Alcohol to Zinc," *New Republic*, June 2, 1917, pp. 127–29; J. M. Clark, "The Basis of War-Time Collectivism," *American Economic Review*, VII (1917), 772–90.

48. "The Big Gamble in War Order Stocks," *Current Opinion*, CIX (Dec., 1915), 433–34; "The War Orders," *Nation*, April 8, 1915, pp. 398–99; Charles M. Schwab, "After All, It's Peace Orders That Count Most," *System*, XXX (Oct., 1916), 335–41; A. Ireland, "War As a Business Problem," *North American Review*, CLVII (May, 1918), 720–28.

49. Maxim, *Defenseless America*, p. 83.

50. Quoted in Harold C. Syrett, "The Business Press and American Neutrality, 1914–1917," *Mississippi Valley Historical Review*, XXXII (Sept., 1945), 217–19, 230.

51. Clarkson, *op. cit.*, p. 313.

52. *Ibid.*, p. 312.

53. George Creel, *How We Advertised America* (New York: Harper, 1920).

54. H. C. Peterson and Gilbert C. Fite, *Opponents of War, 1917–1918* (Madison: University of Wisconsin, 1957), pp. 194–207; *Nation, 100th Anniversary Issue* (New York: *Nation*, 1965), p. 286.

55. Quoted in Lasch, *op. cit.*, pp. 203–04.

56. John Dewey, "Conscription of Thought," *New Republic*, Sept. 1, 1917, *op. cit.*, II, 569; "Conscience and Compulsion," *ibid.*, July 14, 1917, pp. 576–80; "In Explanation of Our Lapse," *ibid.*, Nov. 3, 1917, p. 571; "The Cult of Irrationality," Nov. 9, 1918, *ibid.*, pp. 587–91.

57. Dewey, *ibid.*, pp. 571, 590.

58. "Mental Unpreparedness," *New Republic*, Sept. 11, 1915, pp. 143–44.

59. Van Wyck Brooks, "Our Awakeners," *Seven Arts*, II (June, 1917), 235–48.

60. Randolph Bourne, "Twilight of Idols," *ibid.*, II (Oct., 1917), 688–702.

61. Henry Adams, "A Letter to American Teachers of History," (1910), *The Degradation of Democratic Dogma* (New York: Macmillan, 1920), p. 205.

62. Herbert Croly, "Liberalism vs. War," *New Republic*, Dec. 8, 1920, pp. 36–37.

63. "Force and Ideas," *ibid.*, Nov. 7, 1914, p. 7.